RENAISSANCE FIG

The Renaissance saw a renewed and energetic engagement with classical rhetoric; recent years have seen a similar revival of interest in Renaissance rhetoric. As Renaissance critics recognised, figurative language is
the key area of intersection between rhetoric and literature. This book
is the first modern account of Renaissance rhetoric to focus solely
on the figures of speech. It reflects a belief that the figures exemplify
the larger concerns of rhetoric, and connect, directly or by analogy,
to broader cultural and philosophical concerns within early-modern
society. Thirteen authoritative contributors have selected a rhetorical
figure with a special currency in Renaissance writing and have used
it as a key to one of the period's characteristic modes of perception,
forms of argument, states of feeling or styles of reading.

SYLVIA ADAMSON is Professor of English Language and Literature
at the University of Sheffield, and Chair of Renaissance Studies in the
School of English.

GAVIN ALEXANDER is a University Senior Lecturer in the Faculty
of English, University of Cambridge and Fellow of Christ's College,
Cambridge.

KATRIN ETTENHUBER is Fellow and Lecturer in English at
Pembroke College, Cambridge, and a Newton Trust Lecturer in the
Faculty of English, University of Cambridge.

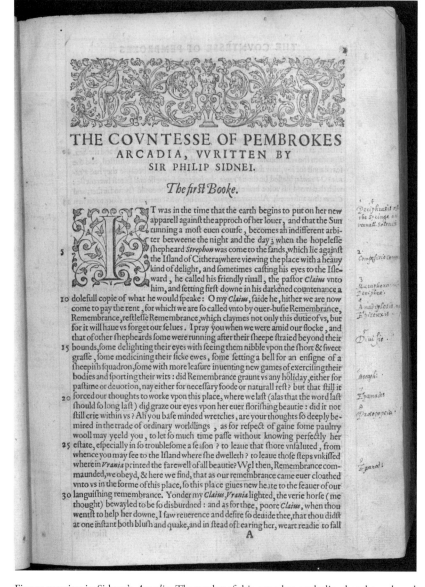

THE COVNTESSE OF PEMBROKES
ARCADIA, VVRITTEN BY
SIR PHILIP SIDNEI.

The firſt Booke.

IT was in the time that the earth begins to put on her new apparell againſt the approch of her louer, and that the Sun running a moſt euen courſe, becomes an indifferent arbiter betweene the night and the day ; when the hopeleſſe ſhepheard *Strephon* was come to the ſands, which lie againſt the Iſland of Cithera; where viewing the place with a heauy kind of delight, and ſometime caſting his eyes to the Iſleward, he called his friendly riuall, the paſtor *Claius* vnto him, and ſetting firſt downe in his darkened countenance a
10 dolefull copie of what he would ſpeake : O my *Claius*, ſaide he, hither we are now come to pay the rent, for which we are ſo called vnto by ouer-buſie Remembrance, Remembrance, reſtleſſe Remembrance, which claymes not only this dutie of vs, but for it will haue vs forget our ſelues . I pray you when we were amid our flocke, and that of other ſhepheards ſome were running after their ſheepe ſtraied beyond their
15 bounds, ſome delighting their eyes with ſeeing them nibble vpon the ſhort & ſweet graſſe, ſome medicining their ſicke ewes, ſome ſetting a bell for an enſigne of a ſheepiſh ſquadron, ſome with more leaſure inuenting new games of exerciſing their bodies and ſporting their wits : did Remembrance graunt vs any holiday, either for paſtime or deuotion, nay either for neceſſary foode or naturall reſt ? but that ſtill it
20 forced our thoughts to worke vpon this place, where we laſt (alas that the word laſt ſhould ſo long laſt) did graze our eyes vpon her euer floriſhing beautie : did it not ſtill crie within vs ? Ah you baſe minded wretches, are your thoughts ſo deeply bemired in the trade of ordinary worldlings , as for reſpect of gaine ſome paultry wooll may yeeld you , to let ſo much time paſſe without knowing perfectly her
25 eſtate, eſpecially in ſo troubleſome a ſeaſon ? to leaue that ſhore vnſaluted, from whence you may ſee to the Iſland where ſhe dwelleth ? to leaue thoſe ſteps vnkiſſed where in *Vrania* printed the farewell of all beautie? Wel then, Remembrance commaunded, we obeyd, & here we find, that as our remembrance came euer cloathed vnto vs in the forme of this place, ſo this place giues new heate to the feauer of our
30 languiſhing remembrance. Yonder my *Claius, Vrania* lighted, the verie horſe (me thought) bewayled to be ſo disburdned : and as for thee, poore *Claius*, when thou wentſt to help her downe, I ſaw reuerence and deſire ſo deuide thee, that thou didſt at one inſtant both bluſh and quake, and in ſtead oft earing her, weart readie to fall

A

Figure-spotting in Sidney's *Arcadia*. The reader of this copy has underlined and numbered the rhetorical figures in the text and named them in the margin, noting, on this page, 1. A Periphrasis of the Springe or vernall Solstice, 2. Compositio Contr: (i.e. oxymoron), 3. Metaphora with Periphra: 4. Anadiplosis, as Epizeuxis, 5. Divisio, 6. Metaph: 7. Epanados, 8. Prosopopeia, 9. Epanod: The *Arcadia* proved a rich source of illustrative examples for Abraham Fraunce (in *The Arcadian Rhetorike*, 1588) and John Hoskyns (in *Direccions for Speech and Style*, c. 1599).

RENAISSANCE FIGURES OF SPEECH

EDITED BY

SYLVIA ADAMSON, GAVIN ALEXANDER
AND KATRIN ETTENHUBER

CAMBRIDGE
UNIVERSITY PRESS

CAMBRIDGE UNIVERSITY PRESS
Cambridge, New York, Melbourne, Madrid, Cape Town, Singapore,
São Paulo, Delhi, Tokyo, Mexico City

Cambridge University Press
The Edinburgh Building, Cambridge CB2 8RU, UK

Published in the United States of America by Cambridge University Press, New York

www.cambridge.org
Information on this title: www.cambridge.org/9780521187053

© Cambridge University Press 2007

First published 2007
First paperback edition published 2011

Printed in the United Kingdom at the University Press, Cambridge

A catalogue record for this publication is available from the British Library

ISBN 978-0-521-86640-8 Hardback
ISBN 978-0-521-18705-3 Paperback

in memory of Jeremy Maule
1952–1998

Contents

Illustrations

ix

Contributors

SYLVIA ADAMSON is Professor of English Language and Literature at the University of Sheffield and Chair of Renaissance Studies in the School of English. Her publications range across the fields of literature and (historical) linguistics and include 'The Literary Language 1476–1776', in volume 3 of *The Cambridge History of the English Language* (1999) and (as co-editor) *Reading Shakespeare's Dramatic Language* (2001). She is currently completing *A History of Literary English since 1476*.

GAVIN ALEXANDER is a University Senior Lecturer in the Faculty of English, University of Cambridge and a Fellow of Christ's College. His publications include *Writing After Sidney: The Literary Response to Sir Philip Sidney, 1586–1640* (2006) and *Sidney's 'The Defence of Poesy' and Selected Renaissance Literary Criticism* for Penguin Classics (2004) as well as numerous articles on literary and musical topics.

BRIAN CUMMINGS is Professor of English at the University of Sussex and Leverhulme Trust Major Research Fellow, 2009–2012 and Director of the Centre for Early Modern Studies, University of Sussex. His publications include *The Literary Culture of the Reformation: Grammar and Grace* (2002).

IAN DONALDSON is Honorary Professorial Fellow at the University of Melbourne. He has published studies of Jonson and Shakespeare and of Renaissance comedy. With David Bevington and Martin Butler, he is a General Editor of *The Cambridge Edition of the Works of Ben Jonson*. *A life of Ben Jonson* will be published in 2011.

KATRIN ETTENHUBER is a Fellow and Lecturer in English at Pembroke College, Cambridge and a Newton Trust Lecturer in the Faculty of English, University of Cambridge. The author of various articles on early-modern topics, she is currently completing a book entitled *John Donne and Renaissance Cultures of Interpretation*.

RUSS MCDONALD is Professor of English Literature at Goldsmiths College, University of London. Previously Professor of English at the University of North Carolina at Greensboro, he is the author of numerous books on and editions of Shakespeare, including most recently *Shakespeare and the Arts of Language* (2001), *Shakespeare: An Anthology of Criticism and Theory 1945–2000* (2003) and *Shakespeare's Late Style* (2006).

JANEL MUELLER is Professor Emerita of English and of the Humanities and William Rainey Harper Professor in the University of Chicago. Her books include *The Native Tongue and the Word: Developments in English Prose Style, 1380–1580* (1984), a two-volume edition of the works of Queen Elizabeth I with Leah Marcus and Mary Beth Rose (2000, 2003), the completion of Josephine Roberts's edition of Lady Mary Wroth's *Urania* with Suzanne Gossett (1999) and *The Cambridge History of Early Modern English Literature* with David Loewenstein (2003).

PATRICIA PARKER is Margery Bailey Professor of English and Dramatic Literature and Professor of Comparative Literature, Stanford University. Her many books include *Literary Fat Ladies: Rhetoric, Language, Culture* (1987), *Shakespeare from the Margins* (1996), and (as co-editor) *Shakespeare and the Question of Theory* (1985) with Geoffrey Hartman and *Women, 'Race', and Writing in the Early Modern Period* (1994) with Margo Hendricks.

WILLIAM POOLE is a Fellow and Tutor in English at New College, Oxford. His publications include *Milton and the Idea of the Fall* (2005). He co-directs the AHRC-funded project 'Language-planning and free-thinking in late seventeenth-century England'.

CLAIRE PRESTON is a Fellow and Lecturer in English at Sidney Sussex College, Cambridge. Her books include *Edith Wharton's Social Register* (2000), *Thomas Browne and the Writing of Early Modern Science* (2005) and *Bee* (2006).

SOPHIE READ is Lecturer in English and Fellow of Christ's College, Cambridge. She is currently working on a book on 'The Rhetoric of Real Presence in the Seventeenth Century'.

R. W. SERJEANTSON is a Fellow and Director of Studies in History at Trinity College, Cambridge. He is the author of the chapter on 'Proof and Persuasian', in *The Cambridge History of Early Modern Science*, ed. Katharine Park and Lorraine Daston (2006), and the editor of *Generall Learning: A Seventeenth-Century Treatise on the Formation of the General Schola*, by Meric Casaubon (1999). He is currently editing vol. III of the new Oxford Francis Bacon.

QUENTIN SKINNER is the Barber Beaumont Professor of the Humanities at Queen Mary, University of London. His previous books include *The Foundations of Modern Political Thought* (1978), *Reason and Rhetoric in the Philosophy of Hobbes* (1996), *Visions of Politics* (2002) and *Hobbes and Republican Liberty* (2008), all published by Cambridge University Press.

Preface

The idea for this volume came out of two series of lectures on Renaissance figures of speech organised in the Faculty of English at Cambridge in 1995 and 1996 by Sylvia Adamson and the late Jeremy Maule. The dedication of this volume to Jeremy is a small tribute to his role in fostering the properly historicised study of early-modern rhetoric by scholars and students over the past two decades. Many of his ideas are reflected in chapters presented here, and in some cases they are direct responses to the thoughtful and thought-provoking suggestions, offered in passing, that many of us remember receiving from him. The editors hope that this volume represents a new approach to the subject of the kind that he wished to see.

We would like to thank Sarah Stanton at Cambridge University Press for her encouragement and astute advice. In the later stages of production we benefited from the skills of our copy-editor, Susan Beer, and our indexer, David Parry, who also disentangled some knotty points of referencing.

We are grateful to the Judith E. Wilson Fund of the Faculty of English, University of Cambridge and to the Master and Fellows of Christ's College, Cambridge for funding a symposium in September 2005 at which the contributors met, exchanged views, and offered preliminary versions of their chapters. The dialogue begun then continues in this volume and, we hope, will not end here.

Note on spelling and references

In quotations, use of i/j and u/v has been brought into line with modern practice, and any contractions and abbreviations have been silently expanded. For books printed before 1700, place of publication is London unless otherwise stated. References to classical texts are to the editions in the Loeb Classical Library series unless otherwise stated. Bibliographical details for a number of these are included in the 'Suggestions for further reading', pp. 291–4 below.

Introduction: the figures in Renaissance theory and practice

The common scholemasters be wont in readynge, to saye unto their scholers: Hic est figura: and sometimes to ask them, Per quam figuram? But what profit is herein if they go no further?

Richard Sherry (1550)

A figure is ever used to a purpose, either of beautie or of efficacie . . .

George Puttenham (1589)

Critical sophistication in this period comes in the form of rhetorical analysis, but while we may be impressed by the technical acumen which can applaud a 'pretty epanorthosis', it is more difficult for us to feel the same kind of enthusiasm for such verbal effects.

Neil Rhodes (1992)

The central concern of this volume is to provide a more complete account of the value and appeal of the figures of rhetoric to literary studies than has previously been available. Our method of enquiry takes the form of a set of case studies of specific figures, which, taken together, aim to elucidate the opinion of Puttenham and answer the scepticism represented by Rhodes.[1] The role of this introduction is to provide a context for the case studies by setting the figures in their place in the larger rhetorical system and setting rhetoric in its place in Renaissance literate culture.

To ask questions about the role of the rhetorical figures in English Renaissance literature is to engage with a theoretical system that at first glance might not seem to fit at all. The system of classical rhetoric inherited by the Renaissance had theorised public speaking, rather than private writing, and was an expression of the political and legal cultures of ancient Greece and Rome, a world away from those of early-modern Europe. To understand the relevance of rhetoric to Renaissance literature, we need to appreciate both how central to many areas of Renaissance society rhetoric became, and how complex were the longstanding relations between literature and rhetoric.

Central to the rebirth of classical learning that gives the Renaissance its name was the reappraisal of classical rhetoric and the rediscovery of key texts by Quintilian, Cicero and others.[2] The northern humanists who influenced and led the overhaul of England's educational system in the early sixteenth century put rhetoric at the heart of the school and university curriculum, with a new sense of the vital continuity between this training and civic life. Courtiers, civil servants, politicians, churchmen, lawyers – ideally all were expected to apply their rhetorical education for the good of society. Editions of key classical texts – such as Aristotle's *Rhetoric*; Cicero's various orations and treatises; the anonymous *Rhetorica ad Herennium* ['Rhetoric to Herennius']; and Quintilian's *Institutio oratoria* ['Education of an Orator'] – were supplemented by editions of less well-known Greek and Latin rhetoricians, and complemented by a host of new treatises, almost all in Latin and with schoolroom use in mind, by scholars such as Erasmus (1512), Susenbrotus (1540) and Talaeus (1544).

A humanist education emphasised practice as well as theory. In addition to learning the terminology and techniques of rhetorical composition – including long lists of the rhetorical figures – sixteenth- and seventeenth-century students would practise what they had learned, first with the traditional *progymnasmata* (literally 'pre-exercises') and then with larger-scale declamations or debates, including arguments *in utramque partem* ['on both sides of the question'] which developed an ability to see things from more than one point of view. The school exercises or *progymnasmata* were based on those developed by such pedagogues as Aphthonius (4th c. AD); extended editions of Aphthonius were reprinted many times in the sixteenth century, and Rainolde's English version was printed in 1563.[3] A student might be required to write a speech in the person of a figure from myth, or a description of a scene, to praise a subject, or to undertake a comparison between two historical figures. These exercises were seen as developing some of the building blocks of larger-scale orations, but we can recognise their affinity to literary techniques too.

All writers of the period had been trained to understand their use of language in traditional rhetorical terms: how they selected a subject and its key points (*inventio*), how they organised their argument (*dispositio*), how they clothed it in language (*elocutio*), and how they memorised the oration (*memoria*) and then performed it (*pronuntiatio* or *actio*). A particularly important distinction was that involved in the interplay between *res* or matter – what was said – and *verba* or words – how it was said. Renaissance rhetoric, both as a practice of education and as an object of theory, followed the lines of classical rhetoric closely, but not uncritically. Each theorist offered his own version of the traditional accounts and taxonomies, and in some cases the departures were radical, as when the influential French scholar Petrus Ramus assigned *inventio* (invention) and *dispositio* (arrangement) to logic and left rhetoric proper with only *elocutio* (style) and *pronuntiatio* (performance). The rhetorical treatise of Ramus's collaborator Audomarus Talaeus thus focused almost entirely on the rhetorical figures, as other treatises did for more practical than philosophical reasons: the result was that the figures dominated the rhetorical education and for many were synonymous with rhetoric itself. Lee Sonnino talks of 'that consistently disintegrating attention to ornament alone which was the chief Renaissance abuse of the classical tradition',[4] but it might equally be argued that it was in the area of *elocutio* – and specifically the theory and description of the figures – that Renaissance rhetoric managed actually to take classical theory forwards instead of merely summarising it. Simple statistics provide an index of the period's special interest in the subject: one of the most popular of the inherited handbooks, the *Ad Herennium*, gave its students sixty-five figures to learn; the second edition of Peacham's *Garden of Eloquence* (1593) raised the number to two hundred. There is plenty of evidence that the knowledge was absorbed and applied. Milton, as T. O. Mabbott reports, left marginal jottings in his copy of Harington's English translation of Ariosto: 'He even numbered the similes (over 130 of them) . . . and treats the "sentences" in the same way. Besides pithy sayings and proverbs he often wrote the word "proverbe".'[5] One of the aims of this volume is to show that Renaissance writers were not just obsessed with spotting the figures, like schoolboys collecting stamps, but that they did something new with them. In Milton's case, the time spent studying similes in Harington's Ariosto arguably changed the relation between metaphor and simile in the English poetic tradition.

RHETORIC AND LITERATURE

Aristotle had given quite separate treatments of poetics and rhetoric, but this was an approach that was not to be repeated until the later Renaissance. Rhetoricians believed that many of their techniques were based on those of the poets, and made frequent use of quotations from literary authors in illustrating rhetorical devices. Of course, any writer in prose who had learned the art of rhetoric would tend to employ rhetorical techniques of arrangement and style just as much when writing an essay or a romance as when composing an oration. But poets found that the rhetorical figures worked in verse too. So, as Cicero famously observes: 'The truth is that the poet is a very near kinsman of the orator, rather more heavily fettered as regards rhythm, but with ampler freedom in his choice of words, while in the use of many sorts of ornament he is his ally and almost his counterpart.'[6] It can be hard to draw the line between literary and rhetorical theory in the classical and Renaissance periods. The author of *On the Sublime*, a text that came to have a major influence on imaginative literature, believes he is writing about oratory, whereas Demetrius, in the important *On Style*, shows no such bias. Horace's *Art of Poetry* makes the important and inevitable step of writing about poetry as if it is oratory, with an aim of teaching (*docere*) and delighting (*delectare*); a point Sidney develops in *The Defence of Poesy* when he completes the transfer of the so-called 'affective triad' from rhetoric to poetry by explicitly adding the need to move (*movere*). Quintilian had borrowed examples from Ovid and Virgil to illustrate his guide to public speaking. Ben Jonson returned the compliment when he advised William Drummond to read Quintilian, on the grounds, Drummond recalls, that he 'would tell me the faults of my Verses as if he lived with me'.[7]

Rhetoric could describe literary writing on several levels. Like oratory, literary writing could usefully be analysed in terms of the fundamental Ciceronian distinction between *res* (subject matter) and *verba* (words). It also made sense to think of the author of a sonnet or play as working on parallel lines to an orator, in coming up with a conceit or plot (*inventio*), organising his materials (*dispositio*), and employing stylistic devices (*elocutio*). An actor, too, was seen as like an orator, in needing to remember his lines (*memoria*) and then perform them convincingly (*pronuntiatio*). Within a work, recognisably rhetorical situations could be represented, from debates or speeches of praise through to political argument or courtroom drama. But what about a scene between two lovers – does that count as rhetoric? It may well do so, once we remind ourselves that rhetoric is able to describe any situation in which a speaker tries to persuade a particular auditor or audience to believe something, and does so using argument (*logos*) as well as appeals to emotion (*pathos*) and his or her own self-presentation (*ethos*). We can take just one example, the scene in which Shakespeare's Troilus and Cressida meet together as lovers for the first time. Left alone for a moment by Pandarus, they talk:

CRESSIDA   Will you walk in, my lord?
TROILUS   O Cressid, how often have I wished me thus!
CRESSIDA   Wish'd, my lord? The gods grant – O my lord!
TROILUS   What should they grant? What makes this pretty abruption?[8]

The *Oxford English Dictionary* records this as the first occurrence of the word 'abruption', a Latinate English term for what Shakespeare's readers (and many of his audience) would have recognised as an aposiopesis, 'a forme of speech by which the Orator through some affection, as either of feare, anger, sorrow, bashfulnesse or such like, breaketh off his speech before it be all ended'.[9] The use of that word 'abruption' nicely blurs the question of whether Troilus himself is spotting the figure, and so of whether we should view any rhetorical artifice here – any simulation of bashfulness, say – as Shakespeare's or Cressida's. The author of *On the Sublime* justifies many rhetorical figures on the grounds that they simulate the behaviour of people in real life;[10] or, as Quintilian puts it: 'It was . . . nature that created speech, and observation that originated the art of speaking.'[11] So we might make Shakespeare the rhetorician here, and say that he is using the figure to signify that Cressida really experiences the emotion that the figure simulates. Or we might infer rhetorical self-consciousness in Cressida herself, and think that she is using the figure as one of Mary Wroth's artful women does, 'desiring to bee thought bashfull, but more longing to bee intreated for the rest'.[12] Much of the difficulty of Shakespeare's play hinges on just this question of how artful Cressida is.

In reading this scene from the perspective of rhetorical theory we have been following an important Renaissance development, whereby rhetoric becomes as much a set of tools for reading as an art of composition. A rhetorically educated reader was in a position both to appreciate and to disarm a text; rhetorical reading may have begun as a preparation for com-position – with schoolboys marking rhetorical figures in the margins of their Ovids to help them internalise the rules – but it did not have to stop there, and complemented increasingly complex practices of interpretation developed in the period's biblical and legal exegeses.

At the same time as the theory of rhetoric conditioned the reading and writing of literature, some scholars turned again to the task of developing theories of poetics, but these were far from being insulated from rhetoric, in either the overview or the details. Of the five parts of rhetorical theory and the five stages of rhetorical composition, however, *elocutio* was the one most readily transplanted from oratorical to literary theory. Though Puttenham's *Arte of English Poesie* (1589) offers comment on many aspects of poetic composition, its early editors, Willcock and Walker, are correct in saying that 'the Figures constitute the *pièce de resistance* of this book'. For Puttenham, as for most of his contemporaries, literary rhetoric meant *elocutio* and *elocutio* meant figures of speech.

THE FIGURES IN RHETORICAL THEORY

Elocutio deals with certain larger categories, such as the various styles (the simplest division is that of the plain, middle, and grand styles), but its building blocks are the figures. Perhaps the most important thing to grasp, in a spirit of liberation rather than frustration, is that the theory of the figures is built on shifting sands. Definitions mutate over time, as indeed do the sets and subsets of the kinds of figures that contain those definitions. We might begin with one classification of the kinds of figures, and then see how that maps on to other classical and Renaissance accounts. A figure is a shape or form, the meaning of the Latin word *figura* as of the Greek term it translates, *schēma*. That shape may be imposed on the patterns of ordinary speech. So, for example, the catchphrase of a popular British entertainer, 'Nice to see you, to see you nice', inverts ordinary word order in its second clause for effect, thereby bringing its words into the shape or form of the figure antimetabole (or chiasmus). But the shape may also be imposed at the level of thought, as when, in making an argument, we decide to anticipate the objections of our opponent, dealing with things (rather than words) out of order, a figure known as prolepsis. We can call these two kinds of figure the figure of speech and the figure of thought. There is a third kind of operation, which in some treatises is not classified as a figure at all – the trope. A trope (the Greek word means 'turn') is what we have when the thought itself is changed, and not only the pattern of its delivery. So if I talk about my mind as an unweeded garden, for example, I am using the trope of metaphor, discussing one thing as if it were another, and thereby adding something quite new to the concept of a mind, for instance that things in it grow at varying rates, that those with the shallowest roots may die if not nourished, and that a mind might benefit from some process of regulation akin to gardening.[13]

That division of things – tropes on the one hand, figures of speech and thought on the other – is offered by Quintilian, the author of the most comprehensive classical treatise we have. But other categorisations were also offered. One problem in tracing the theory of figures through classical and Renaissance discussions is that of translation. The system comes from Greek via Latin to the modern European vernaculars, but terms from each language coexist. Peacham, in the first edition of *The Garden of Eloquence* (1577), offers a treatment of the figures, which he divides into tropes and schemes, with the schemes either grammatical (equivalent to figures of speech) or rhetorical (figures of thought), and with further subdivisions in each case. This structure is similar to Quintilian's, but differentiates the synonymous terms figure and scheme by making the latter a subset of the former. A classical philologist might find this muddled, but it has remained popular to view a scheme as a *kind* of figure. A competing system is offered by the *Rhetorica ad Herennium*, and has been taken up by Richard Lanham. Here, the first division is into figures of speech and figures of thought, and it is the figures of speech that contain the further subsets of schemes and tropes. The present volume's title – like most of its contributors – follows modern practice in using the term 'figures of speech' to mean the rhetorical figures generally, and not just certain schemes.

The scope of these various categories was never clear. Demetrius, writing in the late second or early first century BC, was the first to distinguish between figures of thought (*schēmata dianoias*) and figures of speech (*schēmata lexeos*).[14] In the early Latin rhetoricians we have instead of *figure* the terms *ornamentum* or *exornatio*, both meaning ornament, with the former carrying with it meanings also of military equipment; and these ornaments are of thought (*sententiarum*, the genitive plural of *sententia*) or speech (*verborum*). A sententia can be a thought or a sentence, either matter or words, so whether such a thing is to be imagined as already formed into words before it is shaped by the figure really depends on how one chooses to translate. When Quintilian seeks to clarify things, he gives us a host of terms most of which are hard to translate, opposing figures of thought (*dianoia*), 'that is of the mind, feeling or conceptions' ['mentis vel sensus vel sententiarum'], to figures of speech (*lexis*), 'that is of words, diction, expression, language or style' ['verborum vel dictionis vel elocutionis vel sermonis vel orationis'].[15]

Things are no clearer when we come to individual figures. As we shall see in this volume, some figures have enjoyed relative stability from one theoretical account to the next, while others have mutated over time or oscillated sharply between divergent definitions. Unsurprisingly, theorists also disagree over where to place particular figures within the broader categories of trope, figure of thought and figure of speech. Aposiopesis, the figure we saw Cressida (or Shakespeare) using, is an interesting example. Quintilian was insistent that simply to omit words was not what this figure was about – there had to be some work required of the auditor, some uncertainty about what had not been said – and so he classified it as a figure of thought. Puttenham, on the other hand, lists it as an auricular figure (the simplest kind, equivalent to a figure of speech). In the 1577 edition of *The Garden of Eloquence*, Peacham had it both ways, classifying the figure both as a syntactical scheme (equivalent to a figure of speech) and as a rhetorical scheme (or figure of thought). But by the 1593 edition, he has decided that the figure belongs at the more complex end of his classification, where it is listed with those rhetorical schemes (or figures of thought) 'as do after a sort commit the cause in hand . . . to the consideration and judgements of others'.[16] Similar variation is found in the classification of a number of the figures included in this volume; though it may frustrate our desires for some sort of systemic stability, often it actually helps us to think about what is at stake when the figure is put into use.

Quintilian makes the sensible point, in discussing cases like these, that what matters is not the name or *genus* of a figure, but what it does: we should concentrate on 'the thing itself, by whatever name it is known'. Something can be a trope as well as a figure, and 'a Figure of Thought can contain several Figures of Speech'.[17] Richard Lanham acutely draws attention to the fact 'that the confusion has been a *creative* one . . . The vast pool of terms for verbal ornamentation has acted like a gene pool for the rhetorical imagination, stimulating us to look at language in another way.'[18]

One cause of the taxonomic confusion may be a recurrently felt need to discriminate between figurative operations that *represent* thought and those that actively *provoke* it. The way particular figures migrate between different categories suggests that the distinction is hard to sustain in particular cases, but that it remains useful as a general principle of approach and in some cases it can reveal a great deal. When Brutus speaks to the Roman people in justification of the assassination of Caesar, Shakespeare gives him a rhetoric based in figures of speech, most especially compar or isocolon, which, as McDonald's chapter points out, was the speech-pattern associated with a measured man: 'As Caesar lov'd me, I weep for him; as he was fortunate, I rejoice at it; as he was valiant, I honor him; but, as he was ambitious, I slew him. There is tears for his love; joy for his fortune; honor for his valor; and death for his ambition.'[19] Antony's rhetoric, on the other hand, is based in tropes and figures of thought, particularly those that directly elicit an audience's participation, such as the figure of paralepsis, by which we raise and then disappoint expectation, emphasising something by saying that we will not say it ('Let but the commons hear this testament – | Which, pardon me, I do not mean to read'; ''Tis good you know not that you are his heirs', 130–1, 145). This is accompanied by the directly affective figures of apostrophe, by which we turn to address another ('O judgment! thou art fled to brutish beasts, | And men have lost their reason', 104–5); and the vivid description (enargeia) of the moment of assassination (174–89). The different approaches of the two orators go beyond their selection of figures, however, because the figures are just a part of a larger system. What

Brutus gives us is *logos*, plain argument, where Antony gives us *pathos*, strong emotions. What both therefore offer is a contrast in *ethos*, the moral character the orator projects in order to persuade the audience to believe what he says; in this, Antony is far more successful, at least with his on-stage audience. But again we might be prompted to ask where does Shakespeare stand? In Skinner's chapter, we see how Brutus can be read as an exponent of the rhetoric of self-exculpation, a murderer seeking justification for his crime (in this case, the measured tread of his prose helps him convey that killing Caesar was an unavoidable necessity). But it's worth noting that Antony's speech turns him into a murderer too, when the mob, inflamed by his rhetoric, kill the harmless poet Cinna, mistaking him for one of the conspirators. Is Antony (and by implication *pathos*) then equated with the dangers of demagoguery? As we judge between the two styles and the two men, we find that, on the larger scale, *Julius Caesar* can be understood as an instance of Shakespeare turning into dramatic form the schoolroom exercise of arguing on both sides of a question [*in utramque partem*].

THE FIGURES IN PRACTICE

In *Troilus and Cressida* and *Julius Caesar*, we have seen two brief examples of the complexity of the figures in literary use. This volume makes the further contention that when Renaissance writers use a figure they are simultaneously thinking with the figure and about the figure. Practice engages with theory, and develops it. Two further examples may clarify this contention. In his poem 'No Platonic Love' (1651), William Cartwright offers us what is almost a textbook instance of the figure climax or gradatio, by which the end of one phrase is repeated as the beginning of the next, successively:

> I was that silly thing that once was wrought
> > To practise this thin love:
> I climbed from sex to soul, from soul to thought,
> > But thinking there to move,
> Headlong I rolled from thought to soul, and then
> From soul I lighted at the sex again.[20]

The figure is sometimes classified as a figure of speech, because it may appear to be a simple trick of repeating words. But in constructing a chain of consequences the figure does more than this, as many treatises recognise in classifying it as a figure of thought. The key is in the Greek and Latin terms, which refer to a ladder (Greek *climax*) or staircase (Latin *gradatio*).[21] The figure should describe an ascent and not merely a sequence, so that a sentence 'seems to be climbing higher and higher at each step'.[22] Cartwright uses this ladder to think about another, the Platonic ladder of love. According to the Renaissance Platonists, love takes us up a ladder or set of stairs, 'which at the lowermost stepp have the shadowe of sensuall beawty, to the high mansion place where the heavenlye, amiable and right beawtye dwelleth, which lyeth hid in the innermost secretes of God'.[23] But when Cartwright tries to take that last step, from thought to God, he loses his footing and tumbles down: the Platonic search for enlightenment has become a game of snakes and ladders. The figure is brilliantly appropriate to the conceit, with rhetorical failure matching the persona's moral and spiritual failure. And the pairing serves to criticise both the Platonic model and the rhetorical figure – both can be accused of imposing patterns on human realities which seem easy but may prove impossible.

Another meta-rhetorical moment occurs in *1 Henry IV*, where Shakespeare again uses the figure of aposiopesis:

HOTSPUR   O, I could prophesy,
                    But that the earthy and cold hand of death
                    Lies on my tongue. No, Percy, thou art dust,
                    And food for –
PRINCE   For worms, brave Percy.[24]

Here there is no suggestion that Hotspur is using the figure, either ingenuously or artfully. He is not intending to die to make a rhetorical point. Rather, his death in mid-speech represents Shakespeare's reflection on the abruption of a promising life by untimely death. Events are being read like texts. A figure is being interpreted figuratively and applied to the world beyond language.[25] This process, as many of the chapters in the volume attest, is widespread in Renaissance thinking.

What we have seen exemplified in practice in these two examples is given theoretical grounding in a rather surprising source, a school textbook on rhetoric, published in 1678, when early Renaissance optimism about the benign power of rhetoric had largely given way to scepticism or hostility. In the sixteenth century, Puttenham had figuratively testified to his belief in the power of the figures by personifying many of them, giving them agent names, for instance, the 'overreacher' and the 'loud liar' for hyperbole, 'the interpreter' for synonymia. Samuel Shaw's book, *Words Made Visible*, takes the prosopopoeia a stage further by bringing figures of speech on stage (like Vices and Virtues in old morality plays). His Prologue justifies this by positing a thorough-going homology between language and life:

there is a certain Vein of Rhetorick running through the Humane Nature . . . which infects all their Sentiments, and modifies all their Actions . . . That the most illiterate people, in their most ordinary communication, do Rhetoricate by *Instinct*, as well as others do by Art, is very obvious . . . But that's not all; for men live *Tropes* and *Figures* as well as speak them: and this is the thing that is principally design'd to be represented to you.[26]

Hence the figures are naturally and inevitably formative influences in morals, politics, and religion, as they explain:

DIGRESSION: . . . I am that *Figure* by whom men digress from the matter in hand to something else that seems alien to it . . . I am a Master in Morals also . . . By me the *Popes Holiness* gets into England, the *French King* into *Flanders*, the *Turk* into *Poland*; and indeed generally all *Conquerours* are what they are . . . I cannot indeed speak it without vanity, but it is true, tho I were no Figure, that the whole life of man, is a meer *digression* from the business that he came into the World to perform.

METONYMY: . . . I have Metonimiz'd the World indeed. It is by a real Metonimy that men of devout and refin'd minds discern the *Creator*, where others see nothing but the *Creature*; that *Idolatrous*, and covetous, and proud men, put the *Creature* in room of the *Creator*; that all *Hypocrites* present us with the *sign* instead of the *thing signifi'd*; that all *Lawyers* seek themselves instead of their Client; and indeed in all ill-order'd Common-wealths, that true *Subjects* are respected as *Adjuncts*, and meer *Adjuncts* are embrac'd as the best *Subjects*.[27]

The figures, then, refuse to be contained within textbooks and school exercises, but permeate Renaissance literature and culture as dynamic and evolving nuclei of thought and expression. One of the sources of the energy of the rhetorical system is the way the smallest matrices can function, by analogy, as metaphors for the largest, but are also intimately (and metonymically) connected to them. The very technique of likening one thing to another is, indeed, an example of this: comparison is a school exercise, analogy is a topic, simile is a figure of thought, and compar (the figure of parallel syntax) is a figure of speech. Smaller structures will be found employed within larger ones, like a set of Russian dolls. A sentence, a line of argument, or a life may proceed by degrees (gradatio), or be broken off short (aposiopesis), or complete a perfect circuit (periodos).

THE SCOPE AND ORGANISATION OF THIS VOLUME

Each of the thirteen chapters in this collection selects a rhetorical figure with a special currency in early-modern writing and uses it as a key to one of the period's characteristic modes of perception, forms of argument, states of feeling or styles of reading. Though different contributors have different emphases, our overall aim has been to provide a synthesis of formalist and historicist approaches, attending equally to the linguistic specificity of the figures as forms of words and to the historical specificity of their functions in Renaissance writing and their power as formative influences on Renaissance thought and culture.

The organisation of the volume echoes that of the Renaissance rhetorical handbook. Each figure has its own entry and each entry begins with a definition and illustration of the figure in terms of local linguistic practice before moving on to the larger concerns that it exemplifies, whether within the history of rhetoric or in the other cultural fields in which it manifests itself, such as architecture, music, moral philosophy and theology. Like entries in a rhetorical handbook, the chapters can be read in any order, but they have been arranged in groups to indicate affinities in the form or function of their chosen figures.

Sylvia Adamson, Russ McDonald, Janel Mueller and Sophie Read deal with forms that, while central to Renaissance writing styles, pose particular challenges for modern reading practices. Adamson's chapter on synonymia observes that the multiplication of synonyms is the first method of cultivating eloquence that Erasmus recommends in his seminal textbook, *De copia*. Adamson offers a brief history of the Renaissance theory and practice of synonymia with the aim of rehabilitating the aesthetic of formal variation that it epitomises. McDonald argues that the figure of speech known as compar represents not merely a tactic for arranging clauses but a design principle of wide artistic and cultural significance, which asserts itself in the ethical and political thought of the period as well as in its architecture and landscape gardening. In her chapter on periodos, Mueller explores some of the varied meanings ascribed to the figure – aesthetic, theological, biological – and some of the varied forms it took during the course of its evolution into the modern sentence or paragraph. She argues that the shift from rhetorical to syntactic definitions, largely completed by the end of the seventeenth century, marks a major watershed in the history both of style and of thought. Read defends the various punning figures from the attacks they have suffered from the time the term *pun* was invented in the late seventeenth century. By examining their use in the sermons of Lancelot Andrewes and the tragedies of Shakespeare, she recovers some of the serious purposes Renaissance writers pursued through playing with words.

Gavin Alexander and Claire Preston take figures that make some of the Renaissance's strongest claims for the creative power of rhetoric, its ability to make the dead speak and to make the verbal visual. Alexander connects the literary creation of character to prosopopoeia, the figure by which the orator constructs a speaking voice, and ponders rhetorical theory's worrying tendency to ignore interiority and elide performance with identity. He argues that personhood in Renaissance fictions is built on the rhetorical idea that a self is the words it speaks. Ekphrasis, the figure that paints pictures in words, is at its most focused in the set-piece verbal description of a work of art, as Preston shows in her chapter on this device. Ekphrastic description presents writers with the opportunity to write self-consciously about their own art even as they show it off, because they are representing an act of representation.

The chapters by Patricia Parker and Quentin Skinner select two particularly complex and controversial figures which more overtly operate as cultural agents. Parker's chapter on hysteron proteron explores the ways in which the figure of setting the cart before the horse underwrites the connections between debates about language and rhetoric and questions of order and governance in the cultural and political spheres. Parker attends particularly to the ways in which 'the Preposterous' was used to figure religious and racial others in the period. Skinner's study of paradiastole uncovers the rhetorical implications of a fundamental principle of Aristotelian moral theory, that each virtue constitutes a mean between two vices (courage, for instance, stands between temerity and timorousness). The virtues and the vices accordingly display a tendency to shade into each other which can be rhetorically exploited. Paradiastole, the figure of re-description, can be used both to excuse apparent vice and to disparage seeming virtue. After a survey of its history and theory, Skinner considers its centrality to Shakespeare's *Julius Caesar*.

The chapters by Ian Donaldson and R. W. Serjeantson establish the links between figures of speech and the larger structures of discourse, which Renaissance rhetoric covered under the heads of *inventio* and *dispositio*. Donaldson examines syncrisis, the rhetorical exercise in which the respective qualities of two things were compared in order to arrive at an adjudication between them with the aim finally of persuading the hearer or reader to prefer one to the other. Transplanted from the Renaissance schoolroom, it shaped the form of the emergent art of literary criticism. In his chapter on testimony, Serjeantson reminds us that at the preliminary stage of rhetorical composition, the writer or orator had to seek out plausible arguments from among the 'topics'. After a brief introduction to the theory of the topics, drawing attention to their relation to the figures of speech, Serjeantson's chapter examines the topic of testimony, the appeal to authoritative witness, in Renaissance literary practice.

Finally, in the chapters by Katrin Ettenhuber, Brian Cummings and William Poole, we look at the limits of rhetorical decorum and of rhetorical figuration itself. Ettenhuber examines hyperbole, the figure of gross exaggeration. Renaissance theorists identified hyperbole as a powerful component of the grand style, but they also worried about the hermeneutic, epistemological and ethical problems implied by its conscious rhetorical excesses. Ettenhuber shows how Christian theology and classical theories of the sublime together serve to redeem a figure that Puttenham had personified as an 'overreacher' or a 'loud liar'. Metalepsis is a mysterious figure which, Cummings argues, can be seen as an extravagant or far-fetched metaphor, or a metaphor which has gone wrong or gone too far. His chapter uses the figure to reconsider some of the boundaries in Renaissance theory of metaphor and metonymy and to offer a revision to the traditional account of Erasmus's *De copia*.

Our collection of figures ends, like Puttenham's, with a review of the 'vices of style'. Poole considers the fine boundary line between legitimate and illicit deviations from 'the ordinary limits of common utterance', which makes a figure an ornament in one taxonomy and 'intollerable' in another. From a survey of the use of 'the vices' in a range of genres, he concludes that a new tolerance of the dark and the difficult accompanied the Renaissance adaptation of rhetoric from oratorical to literary ends.

The number of figures covered in this collection is relatively small. It would hardly fill a flower-bed in Peacham's garden of eloquence. But comprehensive coverage has not been our aim. Rather, we offer these case studies as exemplars of a new method for approaching the figures of speech, a set of transferable tools and procedures that we hope others might wish to adopt.

CHAPTER I

Synonimia, when by a variation and change of words, that be of lyke sygnifycation, we iterate one thing divers tymes.

> Virgill. *How doth the child, Ascanius, and is he yet alive? doth he eate etherial foode? and lyeth he not yet below among the cruell shades?*

here he demaundeth nothing else but whether Ascanius be alive or not, yet through affection, he expresseth one thing thrise[. S]ometime with wordes, thus.

> *Alas many woes, cares, sorrowes, troubles, calamities, vexations, and miseries doe besiege me round about . . .*

Lykewyse, whole sentences are repeated by this figure, & that eloquently. This example of Ecclesiasticus is very pretty:

> *The highest, sayeth he, doth not allowe the gifts of the wicked, and God hath no delight in the offrings of the ungodly: . . .*

This fygure delighteth the hearer verye much, for that the worthinesse of the former sentence, is repeated of the latter, with an interpretation of new words.

Henry Peacham, The Garden Of Eloquence (1577)

The rolling wheele that runneth often round,
The hardest steele in tract of time doth teare:
and drizling drops that often doe redound,
the firmest flint doth in continuance weare.

Edmund Spenser, Amoretti, Sonnet 18 (1595)

Synonymia: or, in other words

SYLVIA ADAMSON

WHAT IS SYNONYMIA?

As Peacham puts it, in the passage prefaced to this chapter, synonymia occurs 'when . . . we iterate one thing divers tymes' in different words.[1] At its simplest (sometimes called synonymia simplex), it takes the form of synonymous words arranged in doublets, such as Peacham's own *variation and change*, or in longer sequences, such as *woes, cares, sorrows, troubles, calamities, vexations, and miseries*. At its most complex, it aligns lexical synonyms with the syntactic parallelisms of the figure of parison (described in Russ McDonald's chapter below) to produce the densely echoic patterns typical of Hebrew poetry, as in the 'very pretty' example from Ecclesiasticus: *the highest doth not allow the gifts of the wicked and God hath no pleasure in the offerings of the ungodly*. But Peacham's first illustration (from Virgil) reveals a different, more attenuated, form of the figure, in which synonymia occurs without any synonyms as such. The semantic repetition takes place at the level of the thought rather than the word:[2]

How doth the child, Ascanius, and is he yet alive: doth he eate etherial foode? and lyeth he not yet below among the cruell shades: here he demaundeth nothing else but whether Ascanius be alive or not.

This example makes clear what has been only implicit in previous cases: that synonymia is ultimately a figure of reading as much as a figure of speech or thought. It occurs when a reader decides to interpret a sequence of words or phrases as a self-iteration. One of my aims in this chapter is to examine some of the factors affecting these interpretive decisions; another is to explain, if not recover, the Renaissance taste by which synonymia was enjoyed. The chapter as a whole is an exercise in historical reading.

S Y N O N Y M I A   A N D   T H E   M O D E R N   R E A D E R

In Spenser . . . and the other Elizabethan poets, the tautological structure is inextricable from the tautological diction. The formula in either case is a series of variations upon a single idea . . . (F. W. Bateson, *English Poetry and the English Language*)

Synonymia is a figure that has come down in the world. Among the figures in this volume, it is arguably the one that has suffered the most drastic loss of status between 1500 and the present day. The foundation-stone of Erasmus's theory of eloquence and of sixteenth-century literary practice, it had begun to fall out of fashion by 1600 and soon became associated with acknowledged 'vices of style' such as repetitiousness (tautology), redundancy (pleonasm), and general long-windedness (macrology).[3] It has not benefited from the late twentieth-century revival of rhetorical studies, apparently failing to interest either historians of rhetoric or the post-structuralist neo-rhetoricians, who have so notably revived (or re-invented) figures such as apostrophe, prosopopoeia, metonymy and metalepsis.[4] In literary criticism, it is either ignored or introduced apologetically as a stumbling-block to modern readers' enjoyment of Tudor writing. And in contemporary literary practice, it is typically deployed – where used at all – as a figure of failure or a figure of fun.

At one end of its modern spectrum is its 'realistic' use, illustrated below from a recent Ruth Rendell novel, where synonymia is a character indicator in the speech-style of a minor character, George Troy.

'I'm retired, you see,' he went on. 'Yes, I've given up gainful employment, a bit of an old has-been, that's me. No longer the breadwinner . . .;
But she – well, she has such grasp, she has such ability to *manage* things, organise, you know, get everything straight – well, shipshape and Bristol fashion . . .[5]

To judge by the comments of other characters, Rendell expects her readers to find Troy's verbal variations either irritating or pathetic, irritating as a form of futile verbosity, pathetic as a symptom of encroaching senility. A similar character designed to evoke a similar mixed response in an early-modern audience is Justice Shallow; but it's one index of the difference between the stylistic values of the two periods that the figure Shakespeare selects to dramatise Shallow's witless state is not synonymia but tautologia, where self-repetition pervades the words as well as the thought:[6]

Where's the roll? Where's the roll? Where's the roll? Let me see, let me see, let me see. So, so, so, so, so – so, so . . .;

I will not excuse you; you shall not be excus'd; excuses shall not be admitted; there is no excuse shall serve; you shall not be excus'd.[7]

For something completely different (apparently), we can turn to the famous 'dead parrot' sketch from *Monty Python*, where an extended synonymia provided the script for a bravura performance of Cleese-ian comic excess:

It's not pining, it's passed on. This parrot is no more. It has ceased to be. It's expired and gone to meet its maker. This is a late parrot. It's a stiff. Bereft of life, it rests in peace. If you hadn't nailed it to the perch, it would be pushing up the daisies. It's rung down the curtain and joined the choir invisible. This is an ex-parrot.[8]

The dead parrot sketch hinges on a discrepancy between audience-reaction (hilarity) and speaker-intention. The speaker (the Dissatisfied Customer) is using synonymia in something very close to its original function in the repertoire of classical court-room rhetoric, where it was primarily a device of vehement emphasis, intended to demolish the opposing party by reiterating the key point of the case against them while attracting the auditors' sympathy or admiration to the speaker himself.[9] Its forensic purpose misfires here, partly because the variant expressions for 'dead' are excessive in number – and often inappropriate in register – for the subject (a parrot), but also because the ill-assorted sequence irresistibly summons up the image of the text-type with which synonymia is now most closely associated. The Customer talks like an animated entry in *Roget's Thesaurus*.

For modern readers, the thesaurus (now installed in most word-processing programmes) is the text-type that both legitimates and institutionalises synonymia as a form. But, arguably, by institutionalising our expectations of the form, it disables the figure's expressive function. What makes the dead parrot sketch funny and George Troy pathetic is that both violate a norm by which those who consult a thesaurus (mental or physical) expect – and are expected – to extract the *single* instance that best suits their purpose.

This expectation has a more specific force in the case of literary texts. Modern academic reading practice is deeply imbued with Coleridge's definition of poetry as 'the best words in the best order' and with the Coleridgean ideal of organic form, which encourages us to interpret that definition as implying that there is a unique and non-substitutable expression for any given thought. In literary criticism, this mind-set has proved inimical to rhetoric in general (because, in Coleridgean terms, it appears to accept a 'mechanical' rather than 'organic' relation between form and meaning) and synonymia, with its rehearsal of overtly equivalent forms, is a particularly challenging case. It has posed problems even for those critics who have acknowledged the pervasive presence of the figure in Renaissance writing.

In the early Oxford school, for example, Bateson, attempting a stylistic history of English literature, recognised synonymia as the 'representative mode' that distinguished Elizabethan from Metaphysical poetry.[10] He does not use the term synonymia (the Oxford philological tradition was curiously blind to rhetoric) but instead characterises the difference as a shift from 'tautological' to 'organic' modes. By *organic*, he refers particularly to the proliferation of meanings in a single form, by *tautological* to the proliferation of forms for a single meaning. Though ostensibly descriptive, both terms are heavily freighted with evaluation and it is no surprise to find Bateson endorsing Bacon's famous dismissal of the sixteenth century as a period that preferred 'copie' to 'weight' and interpreting 'copie' as verbosity, facile fluency, diffuseness.[11] These are the very qualities that Bateson and his consciously 'modern' contemporaries were rejecting in their Victorian predecessors and his account of the shift from Elizabethan to Metaphysical poetics can be seen, in part, as a backward projection of the battle lines Victorians v. Moderns. Hence his culminating illustration of the 'tautological mode' seems designed simply to debunk; it is 'an amusing example' from Spenser, as glossed by Sir Walter Raleigh (the first Merton Professor of Literature at Oxford):

> Beside his head there sate a faire young man,
>   *(This announces the theme, as in music.)*
> Of wondrous beautie, and of freshest yeares,
>   *(The fair young man was fair and young.)*
> Whose tender bud to blossome new began,
>   *(The fair young man was young.)*
> And flourish faire above his equal peares.
>   *(The fair young man was fair, fairer even than his equals, who were also his peers)*[12]

At first sight, Bateson's contemporary, C. S. Lewis, appears more sympathetic to this form of verbal variation, recognising in it not only the stylistic hallmark of Renaissance style (in this case drama rather than poetry), but also 'one of the principal conditions of [Shakespeare's] peculiar greatness'.[13] What he means by this, however, is that Shakespeare succeeds by transmuting the tradition he inherited, developing variation from a 'purely ornamental' device to become the means by which he triumphantly solved the problem of combining poetic and realistic utterance. The two phases are illustrated below:

GAUNT   His rash fierce blaze of riot cannot last,
                For violent fires soon burn out themselves;
                Small show'rs last long, but sudden storms are short;
                He tires betimes that spurs too fast betimes;
                With eager feeding food doth choke the feeder . . .

HAMLET   How weary, stale, flat, and unprofitable
                Seem to me all the uses of this world.
                Fie on't! ah fie! 'tis an unweeded garden,
                That grows to seed; things rank and gross in nature
                Possess it merely.[14]

In formal terms, the first passage (John of Gaunt's prophecy of Richard II's fate) could be given much the same analysis as Raleigh gives Spenser. The theme (as in music) is announced in the first line and varied in the following four, not (as in Spenser's case) by successive modifying phrases but by alternative metaphors or instances. All the lines encode the same proverbial wisdom (most familiar to us now in the 'more haste less speed' formula) and they are linked together by the lexical synonyms *rash fierce / violent / sudden / too fast / eager*. The excerpt from *Hamlet* is notably more asymmetrical in construction: the lexical variants are bunched in the first line (*weary, stale, flat, and unprofitable*) and the metaphoric variants of the last two lines cut across, instead of coinciding with, the blank verse line-unit. I will return later to the significance of these formal differences. More relevant here is the striking difference in the way Lewis reads the two passages. He reads the first – somewhat athwart its speaker's intentions – as 'written for the mere fun of the thing'. In his reading of the second, the ornamental has become the organic. He psychologises the variations, interpreting them as the sign of a mind groping for meaning, so that 'the best words in the best order' are something visibly arrived at rather than presented in pre-fabricated form. As Lewis puts it: the 'poetical metaphors' appear natural because Hamlet 'seems to stumble upon them by accident . . . amid a chaos of other grumbles as he chews over and over again the cud of the same bitter experience'. It's worth noting that Lewis's notion of 'real life' synonymia here is very like Rendell's. 'The man fumbles and returns again and again to his theme, and hardly knows which of his words has really hit the mark' applies equally well to both George Troy and Hamlet, the difference being that Troy remains trapped in cliché, whereas Hamlet does find the 'inevitable phrase'.

On closer inspection, then, Lewis's position is not so far from Bateson's. He retains the Coleridgean value for the 'one predestined and elected phrase' and is unable to extend the organic reading of Shakespeare's later practice of synonymia to his contemporaries. In unguarded moments, Lewis's own metaphors for this aspect of Renaissance style are apt to be derogatory (it turns 'round and round on the same spot like a dog that cannot make up its mind to lie down') and, like Bateson, he cannot resist reductive paraphrase, translating Cleopatra's eulogy of Antony, 'His legs bestrid the ocean; his rear'd arm | Crested the world; his voice was prop- ertied | As all the tuned spheres', as 'He was great. He was great. He was great.'[15]

I have chosen Bateson and Lewis as representative voices quite delib- erately, because, writing in the 1930s, they stand on the cusp of a divide in modern reading practice. Working within the organicist premises of post-Richards criticism, they find it difficult to read synonymic styles as valuable; on the other hand, unlike some later commentators, they find no difficulty in reading them as synonymic. The more deeply embedded organicism becomes as a model of reading within modern literary culture, the harder it becomes for critics to acknowledge or perceive synonymia at all. Readers of the Bateson–Lewis generation were formed by a school system in which English literature was a subsidiary subject to classics and in which much classroom time was devoted to translation activities (to and from at least two languages, classical and modern). No one who has spent this amount of time in translation, paraphrase and précis can dispute the separability – in some sense – of form and meaning. They might agree that all translation is betrayal but they will not claim that translation is impos- sible. And to concede the possibility of translation is to concede the basic premise of synonymia as a figure: that the 'same' meaning (with whatever depth of inverted commas) can be rendered in different linguistic forms. Bateson and Lewis were reading simultaneously in the vanguard of modern academic criticism and in the rearguard of Renaissance reading practices and pedagogy. And it is to Renaissance pedagogy that we must turn for the first answer to the questions I shall be addressing throughout this chapter: why was synonymia regarded as a virtue by Renaissance writers? What conditions could have secured its literary pre-eminence?

THE PEDAGOGICS OF SYNONYMIA

We should frequently take a group of sentences and deliberately set out to express each of them in as many versions as possible . . . (Erasmus, *De copia*)

This remorseless process of repetition and memorization testifies to the determi- nation of the Renaissance educator to leave nothing to chance . . . (Brian Vickers, *In Defence of Rhetoric*)[16]

The centrality of rhetoric to Renaissance education and the rigour with which the subject was inculcated have been richly documented.[17] Modern commentators have concluded (somewhat wistfully?) that 'the Renaissance educator' stood a better chance than most of moulding the minds of his students and influencing the forms of their independent literary production – when independent production was finally allowed them. The most immediate sign of the pedagogues' success was the widespread appearance in the 1530s of texts in consistent neo-Latin, written by English writers educated in the grammar schools founded to teach it at the start of the century.[18] But the influence of the educational revolution soon pervaded vernacular literature too, going well beyond the obvious classicisation of themes and genres to affect its rhetorical and linguistic structure. Though too little work has yet been done in establishing links between specific teaching methods and specific stylistic practices, persuasive parallels can be detected. The exercise of arguing on both sides of a given question (*in utramque partem*) may have sown the seeds not only of the mood of scepticism in moral philosophy (which is widely attributed to it) but of the characteristic forms of Tudor drama;[19] the exercise of syncrisis provided a methodology of contestatory antithesis for the emergent genre of literary criticism;[20] the exercise of testimony (citing witnesses to support an argument) is echoed in the massively quotative styles of Bacon and Burton and in the emergence of one of the Renaissance's innovatory genres, the cento.[21] In the case of synonymia, the pedagogic connection was noted at the time. In Shakespeare's great compendium of rhetorical excess, *Love's Labour's Lost*, synonymising is represented as the trademark vice of the schoolmaster. Holofernes, whose name recalls Gargantua's tutor in Rabelais, enters the play in the very act:

The deer was (as you know) *sanguis, in blood, ripe* as the pomewater, who now hangeth like a jewel in the ear of *caelo, the sky, the welkin, the heaven*, and anon falleth like a crab on the face of *terra, the soil, the land, the earth*.[22]

The historical origins of this stereotype – which Hoskins labels the 'schoolmaster foaming out synonimies'[23] – can be traced to the pre-eminence of one textbook, *De copia*, which Erasmus presented to Colet in 1512 for use in his newly founded grammar school, St Paul's. Adopted by countless other schools and schoolmasters, it became, for the next century at least, the standard schoolboys' introduction to Latin eloquence. And synonymia was, in the words of one of its admirers, the 'fons et origo' of the model of eloquence it inculcated.[24]

De copia is generally classed as a manual of rhetoric, but – remarkably in an age of imitation – Erasmus did not construct it on the pattern of the most popular manuals inherited from the classical period, the *Ad Herennium* and Quintilian's *Institutio*. Where he departs from their design is in devoting the whole of Book 1 of *De copia* to the art of verbal variation, culminating in the famous (or notorious) chapter 33, which offers (in the 1512 edition) 146 ways of saying 'your letter pleased me mightily' ['tuae litterae me magnopere delectarunt' and 195 variations on 'always, as long as I live, I shall remember you' 'semper dum vivam tui meminer']. The immediately preceding chapters (11–32) catalogue the techniques by which this virtuoso performance is achieved and Erasmus (again departing from classical precedent) gives the first place in the catalogue to synonymia, as being the most basic figure of varying and the prototype and foundation for more complex and large-scale forms. Erasmus's own view of the importance of the principle of synonymy can be gauged from the fact that the chapters following 33 are predominantly lists of synonymous words and phrases; he expanded these in successive editions, so that by 1534 the first book of *De copia* had become as much a thesaurus (in our modern sense of the term) as a textbook.[25]

In part, Erasmus's divergence in design from Quintilian (to whose material he is everywhere indebted) can be put down to a crucial difference in their target audience. Unlike Quintilian, Erasmus is writing his Latin rhetoric exclusively for those whose first language is *not* Latin. This fact has received curiously little mention from modern commentators, but it has rather profound consequences, not least the prominence given to synonymy, for the mastery of synonyms has always been seen as the key to advanced fluency in a second language, stocking the learner's memory with alternative forms and fostering the capacity to summon them up at need. As Erasmus puts it: 'in truth this training will contribute greatly to skill in extemporaneous speaking or writing; it will ensure that we will not frequently hesitate in bewilderment or keep shamefully silent'.[26] It will also ensure that we do not speak shamefully either. For *De copia* is part of the wider programme of Renaissance humanists to inculcate *good* Latin usage (revived from the 'golden age' between Terence and Virgil) and to extirpate the 'barbaric' Latin perpetrated by their medieval predecessors. By 1512, it must have been apparent that the programme was handicapped by the lack of a beginners' synonym book, especially as printers were meeting the growing demand by publishing new editions of such works as the *Synonyma* of John of Garland, a thirteenth-century compilation, which Pynson and de Worde between them printed at least ten times between 1496 and 1518.[27] Erasmus, with his usual combination of humanist principles and market pragmatism, aimed *De copia* at the gap. In the letter to Colet which prefaces the first edition, it is with previous authors of *synonyma* that he principally compares himself, notably those, including the much-revered Isidore of Seville, who are 'at so many removes from copia that they are unable to express their thoughts in good Latin even once'.[28] In this light, the thesaurus that Erasmus builds up in successive editions appears as much a labour of exclusion as inclusion. These (and these only) are the attested words and phrases of pure Latin (and in later editions he testifies to the purity of their genealogy by adding author attributions).

Chapter 11, which focuses on the lexical resources for synonymia, was the chapter that underwent most expansion. It demonstrates how the mental thesaurus is to be constructed. The student needs to make a collection of synonyms precisely because synonymy is never exact; there are always nuances of difference in denotation or connotation, in dialect or register, or simply in conventions of use (the foreign learner of English may well wonder, for instance, why *late* collocates naturally with *king* but absurdly with *parrot*). Modern language teachers would recognise chapter 11 as being essentially a discussion of the semantic, stylistic and sociolinguistic differentiae of synonyms, its aim being to ensure that a student's mental thesaurus is not only comprehensive but well annotated, so that he can distinguish alternatives which are 'polished', 'humorous', 'emphatic' or 'unusual, poetic, archaic, new, obsolete, harsh, barbarous and exotic'. The student who assiduously absorbs its lesson will find that the most appropriate word will come readily to mind for any given context 'for there is no word that is not the best in some place'.[29]

At this point, Erasmus seems to come close to the modern ideal of selectivity outlined above (pp. 19–22). He seems, that is, to imply that the cultivation of the mental thesaurus provides a repertoire which the speaker/writer then scans for the *mot juste* for a given context. Synonymia, the rehearsing of synonymic sequences, would be merely a means to this end. Indeed, in chapter 12, he says explicitly: 'I think it should be used as an exercise rather than in a speech.'[30]

Arguably, then, if *De copia* is responsible for the subsequent pervasiveness of synonymia in Renaissance writing, it is by the law of the unintended consequence. The synonymic style, that is, could have developed as an accidental by-product of the remorseless repetition which was such a feature of Renaissance schoolroom practice. The scenario is not improbable: an exercise practised daily for years becomes a habit of mind and thence of style; an exercise designed to create facility in a foreign language affects students' practice of their native vernacular. Moreover, whatever Erasmus's own intentions may have been, there is ample evidence that his

contemporaries and immediate successors, those who interpreted his textbook for the classroom, took synonymy as his primary motif. Veltkirchius,
perhaps his most influential mediator, whose annotated edition of 1536
was standard issue in English schools, argued that all the methods of varying in Book 1 could be 'referred wholly to three-fold synonymy, that is,
of words, construction, and figures . . . which three yet repeat the same
sentiment in first one set of words and then in another'. He rests his
interpretation on what Erasmus 'says specifically' at the end of chapter 32
about the aims of Book 1 as a whole:[31] 'In this first book we have briefly
pointed out nearly all forms by which speech is altered without changing the
thought.'[32]

There is no space here to trace the steps by which practices developed
for the teaching of Latin shaped the methods adopted for teaching the
vernacular when English became established as a separate subject in the
grammar-school curriculum in the later sixteenth century. One exemplary
schoolmaster will have to do duty for all. Joshua Poole's *Practical Rhetorick*,
published posthumously in 1663, declares its Erasmian origins in its subtitle:
*Certain little Sentences varied according to the Rules prescribed by Erasmus, in
his most Excellent Book De copia Verborum & Rerum*. The book is intended
'for young Beginners' and is designed to give them facility in English before
they embark on Latin. It is a direct transfer of foreign-language teaching
methods to the teaching of the native tongue and the method it makes central is what became known as 'varying an English'. Modelled on the famous
chapter 33 of *De copia*, it consists entirely of ways of rephrasing six maxims:
*Love overcometh all things; self love is blind; honour nourisheth arts; fortune is
unconstant; labour bringeth forth glory; the loss of time is most miserable*. The
technical instruction is imparted by means of marginal annotations, which
identify the rhetorical type of each variant. And in all cases – again following Erasmus's schema for teaching Latin – the first method of varying is by
'synonymia simplex'. So, for example, the section on *the loss of time is most
miserable* begins by listing synonyms for *miserable*: *lamentable, sad, heavy,
mournful, calamitous, to be bewayled, deplorable*.[33] Poole's earlier work, *The
English Parnassus* of 1657, was addressed more specifically to the would-be
writer of English verse. It too follows Erasmian precedents, providing an
anthology of semantically equivalent phrases culled from vernacular 'classics' and arranged under various thematic headings. By this means, Poole's
students could learn 'to call the birds, *The Summer's waits, the air's feathered parishioners, the wood's wild burgesses, the living ships with feathered
sails*'.[34]

THE AESTHETICS OF SYNONYMIA

Nature herself especially rejoices in variety; in such a great throng of things she
has left nothing anywhere not painted with some wonderful artifice of variety:
(Erasmus)[35]

The faculty which enabled a man to practice such variation . . . was for the
Elizabethans the essential faculty of the poet. They called it Wit. (C. S. Lewis)[36]

It might be a mistake, though, to press the law of unintended consequences
too hard in this instance, especially when it involves disregarding the judgment of Erasmus's near contemporaries about the centrality of synonymia
to *De copia*'s vision of eloquence. Their opinion is supported, I believe,
by the first ten chapters of the book, where Erasmus provides aesthetic
rather than pedagogic reasons for practising verbal variation. His primary
analogy with the variety of nature (above) might at first seem to point to
an aesthetic of radical *difference* (cabbages and kings, for instance) but his
glosses reveal that what he has in mind is rather the principle of *sameness
in difference*. We see this in the analogy, borrowed from Quintilian, of
the sculptor making different figures from the same piece of wax, and in
the allusion to Proteus, the shape-shifter god.[37] In both instances, though
the visible form changes, the underlying essence or identity remains the
same – just as the *res* of a synonymic series persists through its diverse
verbalisations.

Eloquence, as envisaged in these early chapters of *De copia*, has clearly
taken the evolutionary step from forensic courtroom skill to literary art;
its mode is celebratory and what it celebrates is *unity in difference* and
the virtuosity of the artificer in creating formal difference while giving his
audience the pleasure of perceiving conceptual unity. Lewis (above) is surely
correct in equating this kind of virtuosity with the Elizabethan definition
of 'wit' and seeing it as 'the essential faculty of the poet' in the period.
But it's important to add that this aesthetic is not confined to poetry. It
dominates contemporaneous developments in music, where the variation
form also rose to prominence, either influenced by literary rhetoric or as a
parallel manifestation of a more general stylistic zeitgeist.[38]

In both music and literature, the theme-variation relation was often
imaged in terms of the body and its clothing. Peacham, in the 1593 edition
of his rhetoric, makes this central to his definition of synonymia: 'This
figure adorneth and garnisheth speech, as a rich and plentiful wardrop,
wherein are many and sundry changes of garmentes, to bewtifie one and the
same person.'[39] There is no suggestion here of an organic relation between

thought and expression or of an expressive relation between style and self. Synonymia is a form of public display art, just as a well-stocked wardrobe is primarily a sign of opulence and a source of glamour (we are in the world of Imelda Marcos's shoes and Princess Diana's evening-dresses). The Tudor wardrobe, however, has social resonances beyond that of ostentatious wealth, since some aspects of clothing were (by law) the insignia of rank, making it possible to infer social standing from style of dress. Peacham makes a moral metaphor of this: 'This figure delighteth much both for the plenty of wordes and varietie of sentences, but most of all for that it signifieth the worthinesse of a word or sentence, deserving repetition in a changed habite.' Just as a sign of the nobility of a human individual is their prescriptive and exclusive right to wear gorgeous clothes, so a sign of the nobility of a 'word or sentence' is its adornment in 'a changed habite'. One implication is that synonymia should be reserved for foregrounding the most important parts of a discourse, as it is in Donne's fine periodic sentence, quoted in full in Mueller's chapter,[40] where the pivotal moment, expressing the nadir of the soul's darkness before dawn is marked by a synonymic sequence, itself composed of synonymic doublets:

though . . . thou have been *benighted* till now, *wintred* and frozen, *clouded and eclypsed, damped and benummed, smothered and stupified* till now, now God comes to thee . . .

With hindsight, Peacham's 1593 entry on synonymia marks at once the high-point and the turning-point of the fortunes of the figure. It is the high-point because it demonstrates how pervasive synonymia had become in the styles of the period. Peacham, a representative rather than an exceptional writer, finds it necessary (or instinctive?) to 'bewtifie' his own style with the device as he had not when writing the corresponding entry in his 1577 edition. His description of synonymia's 'rich wardrop' (above) simultaneously exemplifies it, with synonymic doublets adorning every clause: *adorneth and garnisheth, rich and plentiful, many and sundry, one and the same*. But are all these items 'deserving repetition in a changed habite'? Or has he overshot his own injunction, using the figure as a form of adornment rather than an index of 'worthinesse'? In 'the caution' which he appends, he certainly detects this fault in other writers: 'In the use of Synonimies it is not good to make too great a heape of words considering the encrease no matter, for by too great a multitude, long time is spent, litle matter exprest, and although the eares of simple hearers be satisfied, yet their minds are smally instructed.' While it's true that the Peacham of 1593 takes a more 'cautious' attitude to rhetoric in general than the Peacham of 1577, in the case of synonymia, the specific form of the caution was to prove remarkably prophetic of later developments, particularly in its antithesis of 'eares' and 'minds'.

Puttenham's *Arte of English Poesie* had divided figures into three classes: the 'auricular' figures, which appeal to the ear (by forms of phonetic and syntactic patterning), the 'sensable' figures which 'affect the minde' (by 'alteration of sense') and the 'sententious' figures 'which may execute both offices, and all at once to beautifie and geve sense and sententiousness'.[41] It is in this third class that Puttenham placed synonymia. Peacham's 1593 'caution' casts doubt on that judgment, suggesting specifically that synonymia is an auricular figure and more generally that the appeal of the purely auricular – or musical – figures was on the wane.[42]

Hoskins, writing around 1600 and a generation younger than Peacham, shows caution developing into scepticism. His rhetorical handbook is constructed on the Erasmian design, being divided on functional principles, into figures of varying, amplifying and illustrating. But in marked contrast to Erasmus, his first figure of varying is not synonymia but metaphor. Synonymia itself is shifted from the function of varying to the function of amplifying and denied an independent entry of its own.

Like Erasmus, Hoskins is writing partly in a pedagogic mode, giving 'directions for speech and style' to 'one of my young masters of the Temple' and he accepts the pedagogical value of synonymia in building up his student's mental thesaurus: 'you will be well stored . . . when you have made up your synonyma book after my direction'; 'the practice of it will bring you to abundance of phrases, without which you shall never have choice, the mother of perfection'. But for synonymia as a figure (as distinct from an exercise) he shows markedly less enthusiasm. He grants it the forensic function of emphasis: it 'hath his due season after some argument or proof' where 'I take the use of this amplification to be in anger, detestation, commiseration, and such passions as you, seeming throughly possessed with, would willingly stir in others.' But as a habitual feature of style, it is more suspect: 'it . . . will sooner yield a conjecture of superfluity of words than of sufficiency of matter'.[43] Words and matter, like the ear and the mind, so firmly allied in Erasmus's and Puttenham's categorisation of the figure, have come apart.

Hoskins is conscious of a recent change in aesthetic:

The taste of former times hath termed it sweet to bring in three clauses together, of the same sense, as,

Your beauty, sweet lady, hath conquered my reason, subdued my wit and mastered my judgment.

How this will hold amongst our curious successors, in their time, I know not. He that looks on the wearing of it will find it bare, how full of stuff soever it appeareth; for it passeth for parts of a division when indeed it is but variation of an English.

The style = clothing metaphor reappears here, but for Hoskins at least, Peacham's 'rich wardrop' contains only the emperor's new clothes. He gives his reason in the last clause, which downgrades 'variation' in favour of 'division'. Division is one of those complex rhetorical terms which (like syncrisis and testimony in this volume) can be applied either to the construction of argument or to a feature of style. In either case, it is concerned with dividing a whole into parts or a generalisation into specifics. The basis of the division can be logical or empirical, the latter illustrated by Hoskins's example of a tree, which 'you may divide . . . into the roots, body, branches and fruit'.[44] As a figure of speech, the function of division is to give a description 'more credibility and instruction, for it makes instances of that which, being generally spoken, would seem but a flourish' (or as Pooh Bah puts it, it 'lends verisimilitude to an otherwise bald and unconvincing narrative'). To many modern readers, division and synonymia might appear to be simply subspecies of variation; C. S. Lewis, for example, uses them indiscriminately to illustrate the dominant Renaissance style. But for Hoskins's generation, the distinction had become, in theory if not in practice, a crucial one: variation is to division as the ear to the mind as words to matter. In division, objects or topics are analysed, in variation they are only renamed; and the rehearsal of equivalent names has the merely auricular pleasure of music.

Hoskins associates the figure of division with Bacon and specifically with Bacon's interest in 'method and order';[45] and Hoskins's own disparagement of variation relative to division has obvious affinities with Bacon's rejection of sixteenth-century 'copie' in favour of 'weight'.[46] Later in the century, the shift of aesthetic to which both testify was to crystallise into Locke's enormously influential antithesis of 'wit' and 'judgment':

Wit lying most in the Assemblage of *Ideas*, and putting those together with quickness and variety, wherein can be found any resemblance or congruity . . . *Judgment*, on the contrary, lies quite on the other side, in separating carefully *Ideas* one from another, wherein can be found the least difference, thereby to avoid being misled by Similitude, and by affinity to take one thing for another.

Locke denigrates and rejects Wit in the same terms Hoskins and Peacham had applied to its local representative, synonymia: it is an art of public display, designed to impress unsophisticated 'simple hearers': 'that entertainment and pleasantry of Wit . . . strikes so lively on the Fancy; and [is] therefore so acceptable to all People, because its Beauty appears at first sight, and there is required no labour of thought, to examine what Truth or Reason there is in it.'[47]

But is 'wit' and its instantiation in synonymia so axiomatically labour-free? The Latin name for the figure, *interpretatio*, reminds us that its central motif is not so much sameness as the *discovery* of sameness, and, on one reading of the *Ad Herennium*, the author attributes its distinctive forensic force to the fact that (unlike simple repetition) it engages the audience proactively in the process of interpretation.[48] Modern linguistic studies have equally recognised that synonymic relations are often culture-specific or text-specific or even speaker-specific, so that identifying expressions as synonymous is always a collaborative act between reader and writer, requiring almost as much wit in the former as in the latter.[49] A failure of reading that proves the point has been preserved for us in one of the notorious oddities of St Matthew's Gospel, which describes Jesus preparing to ride into Jerusalem mounted, implausibly, on two animals at once:

> Then sent Jesus two Disciples, saying unto them, Goe into the village over against you, and straightway yee shall find an asse tied and a colt with her: loose them, and bring them unto mee . . . And the Disciples . . . brought the Asse, and the colt, and put on them their clothes, and they set him thereon.[50]

The absurdity has several sources, one of these being Matthew's determination to align New Testament narrative with Old Testament prophecy: 'All this was done, that it might be fulfilled which was spoken by the Prophet, saying . . . Behold, thy king commeth unto thee, meeke, and sitting upon an Asse, and a colt, the foale of an Asse.'[51] Another is his failure to realise that his chosen prophet, Zechariah, was using the figure of synonymia (presumably to emphasise the lowliness of the king's chosen steed). Some scholars have used the misreading to support the hypothesis that Matthew was a Gentile rather than a Jew and hence unfamiliar with the conventions of Hebrew literary language. Interestingly, Peacham seems to take particular care to ensure that his English Gentile readers, working with the new widely available vernacular versions of the Bible, will not make similar mistakes. He laboriously construes his example from Ecclesiasticus, in the text of the recently published Bishops' Bible of 1568:

> *the highest doth not allowe the gifts of the wicked, and God hath no delight in the offerings of the ungodly*: here the fyrst sentence is repeated by the latter, but yet with other wordes of the same signifycation, for in the former is *the highest*, in the latter

GOD: in the former *doth not alow*, in the latter *hath no delight*: in the one *giftes*, in the other *offringes*: in the fyrst *wicked*, in the last *ungodly* . . .[52]

Linguistically, the potential pitfall for readers of both Zechariah and Ecclesiasticus lies in their use of the connective *and*, which can signal either paraphrase or addition. *Or* is similarly ambiguous, denoting either an alternative option or a synonymic equivalent (as in 'do you believe in God, or a superior being?'). In present-day English, one of the commonest markers of paraphrase is the unambiguous *in other words*; but this phrase seems to have come into use only in the seventeenth century and in sixteenth-century texts *and* and *or* were by far the commonest connectives, where connectives were used at all.[53] In many, and perhaps the majority of cases, items in a Renaissance synonymic series have no explicit links (the rhetorical figure of asyndeton) and so are syntactically indistinguishable from items in a division or a simple list. Part of the aesthetic pleasure of synonymia, I want to suggest, was the delight in overcoming these difficulties to make the discovery of equivalence.

If, by 1600, the difficulties were not even perceived, it is because synonymia had *become* easy to read. This is partly because of its pedagogical prominence and partly because in the early vernacular examples the semantic equivalence of synonymy was supported by structural parallelism of syntax in prose, replaced, or reinforced, in poetry by the symmetries of line or stanza and the phonetic correspondences of alliteration and rhyme (as in the examples discussed earlier from Spenser and early Shakespeare). In Hoskins's example of a threadbare 'three clause' variation, a synonymic reading is by no means inevitable. There is no reason why 'hath conquered my reason, subdued my wit and mastered my judgment' can't be read as (in his terms) a division, where *conquered, mastered*, and *subdued* are interpreted as a narrative sequence of events and *wit, judgment*, and *reason* refer to different mental faculties (as we have already seen, Locke at least, regarded *wit* and *judgment* as antonyms rather than synonyms). But the structural repetition of the 'hath *Verb*ed my *Noun*' formula means that the line of least resistance is to interpret it as a synonymic variation – at least for readers who have been trained to read in this way.

In later variation sets, the structural guide-ropes are sometimes missing. Before synonymia was abandoned as a figure, one way in which the gathering dissatisfaction with it found expression was by complicating the process of interpretation. Something of the same sort happened in music, too. Where sixteenth-century variation sets took as their starting-point a well-known tune (such as the ballad-tune 'Walsingham'), seventeenth-century sets begin to use an original theme, thus requiring more, and more complex, work on the part of the audience.[54] In literary variation, the theme may be unstated or surprising, the semantic relations between the variants may be obscured, or their syntactic relations asymmetrical. The two examples below, for instance, both juxtapose a straightforward use of synonymia with a more difficult kind:

This same *Truth*, is a Naked, and Open day light, that doth not shew, the Masques, and Mummeries, and Triumphs of the world, halfe so Stately, and daintily, as Candlelights. *Truth* may perhaps come to the price of a Pearle, that sheweth best by day: But it will not rise, to the price of a Diamond, or Carbuncle, that sheweth best in varied lights. A mixture of a *Lie* doth ever adde Pleasure.[55]

Bacon here combines small-scale and large-scale synonymia: locally, there are the lexical sequences *naked-open, masques-mummeries-triumphs, stately-daintily, diamond-carbuncle* and the three sentences together offer metaphorical variations on a maxim in the same spirit as John of Gaunt. But not in the same style. Bacon places the simple (or 'naked') statement of his theme *a mixture of a lie doth ever add pleasure* after, instead of before, its more elaborated variants, requiring the reader to decode 'Candlelights' and 'a Diamond, or Carbuncle' into their non-metaphorical equivalent 'a Lie', while undergoing, during the suspense of interpretation, the process of feeling attracted by masques or triumphs and the 'varied lights' in which they are displayed. The final sentence administers a revisionary jolt and by collateral effect seems to discountenance the very 'enrichment' of the basic term which synonymia affords, turning its use into a self-consuming and ironically positioned manoeuvre.

Perplexities also beset the reading of this verse example:

> Then comes my fit again. I had else been perfect,
> Whole as the marble, founded as the rock,
> As broad and general as the casing air;
> But now I am cabin'd, cribb'd, confin'd, bound in
> To saucy doubts and fears.[56]

Synonymia is as richly represented in Macbeth's speech as it was in John of Gaunt's, but its resources are asymmetrically deployed. In the last two lines, where Macbeth describes his present state, lexical synonymia predominates, in a self-embedded form of the figure, with the doublet of the last line (*doubts and fears*) itself contained in the fourth item of a variation set, whose first three members are close-linked by alliteration: *cabin'd, cribbed, confin'd, bound in . . .* The contrasting desired but unattainable state (of being 'perfect') is expressed through three comparisons, which, though easily read as synonymous with 'perfect', are not such obvious variants on one another, the similarity of 'marble' and 'rock' being subverted by the radical dissimilarity of 'air'. As in Gaunt's speech, there are simple proverbial equivalents to hand, but here they complicate rather than assist understanding – how can one be simultaneously 'firm as a rock' and 'free as the air'? Even the auricular patterns of alliteration prove uncertain. Are we to read 'casing' as a premonitory echo of the 'cabin'd, cribb'd, confin'd' state with which it overtly contrasts?

As seen in Lewis's reading of Hamlet's speech above, the temptation for a modern reader is to psychologise these difficulties and interpret them as the index of the protagonist's state of mind. Simon Palfrey (to take one of the play's most recent commentators) comes very close to Lewis's account of Hamlet when he describes Macbeth's speech here as 'flailing, claustro-phobic, overlong listmaking' that 'marks his apprehension of inescapable unfreedom' and expresses 'anguished meta-poetic paralysis'.[57]

What are we to make of this similarity in reading? Does it reflect simi-larities in the characterisation of the two protagonists? or simply in the way synonymia is practised in Shakespeare's later style? Does it reflect mod-ern readers' difficulties with synonymia as a figure (whose repetitions are always seen as an excess that requires extenuation)? or would these mod-ern responses in fact tally with the reactions of the plays' early-modern audience? Clearly more extensive analysis of more numerous examples is required before these questions can be answered with any certainty. But even the material presented within the limits of this chapter offers some indications of the relative values that Renaissance writers and read-ers associated with the different types of synonymia. It's worth noting, for instance, that the formal symmetries of John of Gaunt's speech belong to a piece of (represented) public oratory, while my examples of asymmet-ric or occluded synonymia come from the period's new 'inward' genres of soliloquy (Macbeth and Hamlet) and essay (Bacon). This aligns sug-gestively with the different readings that Peacham gives to the differently constructed examples of the figure in the epigraph to this chapter. In Eccle-siasticus, where synonymia coincides point by point with compar to make a triumph of symmetry, he construes it as an example of praise poetry, in which repetition indexes the worthiness of the referent. By contrast, in Virgil, where the repetition is carried by inference rather than structure, he interprets the synonymia psychologically, as the spontaneous overflow of

Virgil's protagonist's emotion: 'through affection, he expresseth one thing thrise'.

In other words, Peacham, like Bacon and the later Shakespeare, may bear witness to the emergence of the modern propensity to interpret schematic figures of speech as impersonal verbal artefacts and to read disrupted patterns or elliptical forms as the index of an intervenient subjectivity.

CHAPTER 2

Compar, of the Grecians called *Isocolon* and *Parison*, is a figure or forme of speech which maketh the members of an oration to be almost of a just number of sillables, yet the equalitie of those members or parts, are not to be measured upon our fingers, as if they were verses, but to bee tried by a secret sence of the eare.

Henry Peacham, *The Garden of Eloquence* (1593)

But when I pleade, she bids me play my part.
and when I weepe, she sayes teares are but water:
and when I sigh, she sayes I know the art,
and when I waile she turnes hir selfe to laughter.

Edmund Spenser, *Amoretti*, sonnet 18 (1595)

. . . then might you see shippes sayle where sheepe fedde, ankers cast where ploughes goe, fishermen throw theyr nets, where husbandmen sowe theyr Corne, and fishes throw their scales where fowles doe breede theyr quils: then might you gather froth where nowe is dewe, rotten weedes for sweete roses, and take viewe of monstrous Maremaides, insteed of passing faire Maydes.

John Lyly, *Gallathea* (1592)

Compar or parison: measure for measure

RUSS McDONALD

> The world is made by Simmetry and proportion, and is in that respect
> compared to Musick, and Musick to Poetry.
>> Thomas Campion, *Observations in the Art of English Poesy*

> We live, I regret to say, in an age of surfaces.
>> Lady Bracknell in *The Importance of Being Earnest*

Assessing attitudes towards artifice is one of the most reliable ways of distinguishing between modern and early-modern culture. The triumph of modernism in the twentieth century brought with it a suspicion of anything ornamental or highly wrought, an aesthetic typified in Mies van der Rohe's famous phrase 'less is more' and Adolf Loos's essay 'Ornament as Crime'. Such a notion would have been incomprehensible to European artists of the Renaissance: in writing, in visual design, in the arts and crafts generally, English people of the sixteenth century favoured objects that were ornamental, 'curious', and unabashedly arranged. Artisans and audiences were devoted, in the words of Richard Lanham, to 'the style which shows'; they did not share Lady Bracknell's regrets.[1]

A taste for equivalence underwrites the highly structured Elizabethan style, and in literary composition the balanced distribution of constituent parts is achieved by means of the rhetorical figure known as compar or parison. Put simply, these terms designate the use of similarly structured phrases or clauses. Henry Peacham defines the figure as a 'forme of speech which maketh the members of an oration to be almost of a just number of sillables, yet the equalitie of those members or parts, are not to be measured upon our fingers, as if they were verses, but to bee tried by a secret sence of the eare'.[2] The writer most frequently associated with parison is John Lyly, whose taste for it shapes these two sentences from the first paragraph of *Euphues*:

This younge gallant, of more wit then wealth, and yet of more wealth then wisdom, seeing himselfe inferiour to none in pleasant conceipts, thought himselfe superiour

39

to all in honest conditions, insomuch that he deemed himselfe so apt to all things, that he gave himselfe almost to nothing, but practicing of those things commonly which are incident to these sharp wits, fine phrases, smooth quipping, merry taunting, using jesting without meane, and abusing mirth without measure. As therefore the sweetest rose hath his prickel, the finest velvet his brack, the fairest flowre his bran, so the sharpest witte hath his wanton will, and the holiest heade his wicked waye.[3]

All the features of parisonic construction are easily perceived: similarly structured phrases and clauses, frequent antitheses, matching words united by alliteration, and other supporting parallelisms. A less ostentatious example occurs in Brutus's forum speech in *Julius Caesar*: 'As Caesar lov'd me, I weep for him; as he was fortunate, I rejoice in it; as he was valiant, I honour him; but as he was ambitious, I slew him' (3.2.24–5).[4] The initial appeal of such carefully arranged words is musical, and in the theoretical and descriptive commentaries from Cicero, Quintilian and the *Rhetorica ad Herennium* down to Puttenham, Hoskins and Blount, compar is treated among the 'kinds of Similarities of Sound',[5] as an instrument of oratorical or literary composition calculated to ensure surface balance and aural smoothness. In *The Arte of English Poesie*, Puttenham translates parison as 'the figure of even'.[6]

This essay seeks to attribute greater significance to compar or parison than has hitherto been customary, elevating it from the subaltern position of a tactic for arranging clauses to an influential principle of artistic and philosophical significance. Although abundant attention was paid in the first half of the twentieth century to the syntactical structures of English prose, Brian Vickers argued in the 1960s that much of the scholarship on the topic had been 'purely factual, statistical, non-imaginative'.[7] Vickers sought, in a lengthy chapter entitled 'Syntactical symmetry', to modify the relatively crude narrative established by Morris Croll and George Williamson. But while others have joined in this effort to complicate our understanding of Tudor style, few critics have been willing to read imaginatively and contextually, to look beyond the central texts of the prose masters towards other realms which the taste for symmetry manifestly governs.

Without depreciating the insights that recent studies of political and social contexts have afforded, I would propose that familiar literary texts be examined not only in light of what people thought – the ideas and social practices of the age – but also in light of what they saw. Ultimately, parison belongs to the larger category of repetition, and repetition to the more general category of rhythm – a structural effect with musical, visual, and even tactile manifestations. Thus the figure of balance may be seen to assert itself in a variety of disciplines and sub-disciplines, notably Elizabethan prose and verse, the geometries of landscape gardening, the sartorial designs favoured by Elizabethan aristocrats, religious and secular music by the likes of Gibbons and Byrd, and other media as well. I shall limit my investigation to a single major context from visual culture: English architecture in the sixteenth century, specifically the new style by which builders and their patrons began to transform the appearance of the English country house. Reading the figure of balance in both the emerging Tudor prose style and in contemporary architectural projects helps, in the first place, to cleanse a major rhetorical scheme of the stigma of frivolity and affectation; it also illuminates aspects of early-modern English culture that literary scholars rarely think about. This interdisciplinary treatment of writing and building offers more than mere analogy. Rather, it reveals a governing principle of Elizabethan design, the commitment to order and consonance in a realm where those values were becoming hard to maintain. And it attests to a cultural coherence that modern disciplinary discreteness tends to obscure.

POETS AND CARPENTERS

A prompt for developing such a resemblance is found in the vocabulary of the period, particularly in the etymological identification of 'poet' and 'maker'.[8] From the fourteenth to the seventeenth centuries the term 'maker' ('makar' in Scots) is used with surprising frequency as an alternative designation for poet. The slightly broader sense of 'maker' allows room for the metaphor of writer as builder, a characterisation implicit in all the rhetorical pamphlets intended to teach the foundations of literary composition. Peacham's preamble to *The Garden of Eloquence*, for example, employs various architectural metaphors: 'by [eloquence] the true felicitie of man is found out and held up, without her it falleth by a sudden, and woefull ruine';[9] and Puttenham insists that the poet, because 'he useth his metricall proportions by appointed and harmonicall measures and distaunces . . . is like the Carpenter and Joyner'.[10] According to one modern authority, 'classical architecture proved to be a useful metaphor for language, connected as they both were to the common heritage of ancient Rome and its related forms of construction and composition'.[11] Another unexplored link between the disciplines of rhetoric and architecture arises from the innocent and potentially sinister connotations of the word 'design' ('craft' and 'scheme' invite a similarly dual interpretation). The rhetorician teaches the writer to carry out 'designs' on the reader; words used seductively compel assent by producing delight in the ear and mind of the perceiver. Similarly,

the architect distributes his materials so as to woo and enchant the beholder
of a building.

The impulse to arrange words into equivalent syntactical units and to
organise spatial volumes into similar shapes derives from a cultural conception of the natural world as the basis for design, what Sir Henry Wotton in
The Elements of Architecture (1624) refers to as 'the great Paterne of Nature'.
For him, as for many of his predecessors and contemporaries, the organisation of the human body validates the effect of equivalence in patterned
construction:

> For surely there can be no *Structure*, more uniforme, then our *Bodies* in the whole
> *Figuration*: Each side, agreeing with the other, both in the number, in the qualitie,
> and in the measure of the Parts: And yet some are round, as the *Armes*, some flat, as
> the *Hands*, some prominent, and some more retired: So . . . wee see that *Diversitie*
> doth not destroy *Uniformitie*, and that the Limmes of a noble *Fabrique*, may bee
> correspondent enough, though they be various.[12]

In developing his argument, Wotton articulates the complementary principles of uniformity and diversity, a relationship to which I shall return
below. For now, the vital point is his identification of the structure of an
impressive building, what he calls 'a noble Fabrique', with that of the human
frame. The corporal origins of the laws of writing and of architecture are
detectable even in the vocabulary of our own critical discourse, notably in
our tendency to speak of 'the textual body' or the 'bones' of a house. These
terms derive from the diction of the Renaissance rhetoricians and architectural writers, who took their cue from the analogy between the body
and proper structure that informs the writings of Cicero and Quintilian,
the ancient masters of oratory, and Vitruvius, their architectural counterpart. In thinking about the length and arrangement of clauses and other
units of sentences, it is useful to remember that the Greek *colon* becomes in
Latin *membrum*, and according to Heinrich Lausberg, 'this usage has been
transferred from the fundamental meaning "part of the body, *membrum*"'.[13]

Parisonic structure is a form of symmetry, and the noun 'symmetry'
makes its earliest appearances in English in medical writing, specifically in
Robert Copeland's 1542 translation of Galen. Visually, such organic notions
pervade Sir John Shute's *The First and Chief Groundes of Architecture* (1563).
In setting forth the orders of columns available to the builder, Shute praises
their contribution to similitude and employs an earlier version of Wotton's corporal analogy, beginning with 'this piller Tuscana, as it is figured,
invented and made by the Ionians, upon the Simetrie of a strong man'
(figure 1).[14] His dedication to the Queen, which begins with a reference

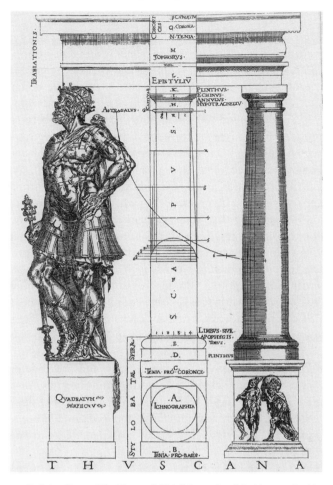

1. Sir John Shute, *The First and Chief Groundes of Architecture* (1563).

to Cicero, also asserts the analogy that would become ideologically central
to the Elizabethan state, a symmetrical relation between the harmoniously
composed human body and the healthy body politic: 'as the members of
the body doing without impedimentes their naturall dueties, the whole
body is in an helthful hermonye, able to performe all that belongeth to the
same. So is it in a publike weal when all men in their calling, doe labour
not onely for their owne gayne, but also for the profit and commoditie of
their Countrye.'[15]

PARISONIC SOUNDS

Like most rhetorical schemes, parison is called by different names, depending on who is doing the calling. Compar and parison are normally used interchangeably, but the balance they denote may also be designated by the term isocolon, the figure with which most literary scholars are familiar. Although it is idle to spend too much time differentiating between terms, I would propose that parison be considered the broader category, since the equivalence of sound implicit in its name can be achieved by a variety of means, one of them being isocolon, or parallel 'members' (*cola*). Quintilian, for example, illustrates the 'kinds of Similarities of Sound' with 'quantum possis, in eo semper experire ut prosis' ['In whatever you *can* do, try always to do good'], suggesting that 'most scholars call this *parison*; though the Stoic Theon thinks that in *parison* the cola must be similar'.[16] Often writers will seek parity in both arrangement and duration. In Latin prose, as in the example from Quintilian just cited, such similarity is often reinforced by words with similar endings (homoeoteleuton), or by the more specific resemblance of words with similar case endings (homoeoptoton, sometimes called similiter cadens). English writers occasionally attempt such parallelism, as in the following example from Peacham: 'He is esteemed eloquent which can invent wittily, remember perfectly, dispose orderly, figure diversly, pronounce aptly, confirme strongly, and conclude directly.'[17] However, since such terminal possibilities are diminished in a non-inflected language, English writers often pursue a similar effect with less obvious forms of matching, particularly alliterative and assonantal echo.

In *Directions for Speech and Style*, John Hoskins offers the most ample definition of parison:

For comparison [COMPAR, or PARISON]: comparison is an even gait of sentences answering each other in measures interchangeably . . . . It is a smooth and memorable style for utterance, but in penning it must be used moderately and modestly. A touch of agnom[ination] of the letter is tolerable with a *compar*, as in the first words of Philanax his speech,

If ever I could wish my faith untried and my counsel untrusted,
and where there is a *similiter cadens*; but a more eminent falling alike in this:

My years are not as many but that one death may conclude them, nor my faults
so many but that one death may satisfy them.
Without consonancy or fall or harping upon letter or syllable, and yet a *compar* because they say the words match each other in rank:

Save his gray hairs from rebuke and his aged mind from despair,
answer each other. Again:

> *Rather seek to obtain that constantly by courtesy which you cannot assuredly enjoy by violence,*

verb to verb, adverb to adverb, and substantive to substantive.

> *Loneliness can neither warranty you from suspicion in others nor defend you from melancholy in yourself.*[18]

The keynote in Hoskins's description is correspondence – of length, of structure, of sounds, of parts of speech, of syllables.

Based as it is on identity of sound, parison is usually classified with figures of similitude and sometimes associated with methods of amplification, techniques for expanding and comparing. It is frequently related to other means of expansion such as synonymia, the use of several words (usually in parallel form) to explain a term or idea;[19] naturally it may be employed along with antitheton, a figure of thought built on contrary ideas; and occasionally it may even be linked to other tropes involving semantic resemblance, such as the simile. Parison is, of course, an instrument of delight, 'causing', in Peacham's words, 'delectation by the vertue of proportion and number'.[20] At the same time, however, it serves a heuristic function, enlarging and dividing a topic for purposes of analysis, comparison, and discrimination. By arranging ideas into parallel forms, whether phrases or clauses, the prose writer calls the reader's attention to an especially significant idea; at the same time, however, such an arrangement focuses the reader's mind on the semantic similarities, differences, or oppositions exposed in parallel structures. Sixteenth-century writers and readers were aware that figures such as parison were liable to seem meretricious and could be easily abused, but the power of such structures to organise information and direct the mind was a primary source of their appeal to the humanist writer.

SIMILITUDE IN POETRY AND PROSE

Parison – along with its rhetorical cognates – is one of the cornerstones of early-modern English writing. Puttenham, in explaining the function of 'the figure of even', indicates that parison can be used in verse as well as prose, citing a short poem of his own composition to illustrate the figure. An instructive instance of such poetic parallelism animates the stanza describing the character of Avarice as he passes in procession at the House of Pride in Book I of *The Faerie Queene*:

> Most wretched wight, whom nothing might suffise,
>   Whose greedy lust did lacke in greatest store,
>   Whose need had end, but no end covetise,

> Whose wealth was want, whose plenty made him pore,
> Who had enough, yet wished ever more;
> A vile disease, and eke in foote and hand
> A grievous gout tormented him full sore,
> That well he could not touch, nor go, nor stand:
> Such one was *Avarice*, the fourth of this faire band.[21]

The parallel clauses are not precisely identical, but they fulfil Peacham's 'secret sense of the ear'. The third and fourth lines are similarly divided in half, expressing contraries of different kinds. In the third line, 'Whose need had end, but no end covetise', the opposition of 'end' and 'no end' is typical of the way that parallel structure serves to underscore antithesis. A more complex arrangement characterises line four, 'Whose wealth was want, whose plenty made him pore': the paradoxes inherent in each clause are magnified by the alliteration, making the identity between opposites even more insistent. And the obvious parallelisms are supported by minor ones, as in the penultimate line of the stanza, the relatively simple but nonetheless effective 'he could not touch, nor go, nor stand'.

The Faerie Queene is an especially fertile source because any examples of parison are surrounded and supported by a host of other similitudes, most notably rhyme, alliteration, and assonance. In the stanza devoted to Avarice, the figure known as anaphora, the repetition of the same word at the beginning of lines or clauses, also reinforces the harmonics of the description. One of Shakespeare's most memorable passages, from the deposition scene of *Richard II*, depends upon this combination of anaphora and parison:

> I give this heavy weight from off my head
> And this unwieldy sceptre from my hand,
> The pride of kingly sway from out my heart.
> With mine own tears I wash away my balm;
> With mine own hands I give away my crown;
> With mine own tongue deny my sacred state;
> With mine own breath release all duteous oaths.
> All pomp and majesty I do forswear;
> My manors, rents, revenues I forgo;
> My acts, decrees, and statutes I deny.
> God pardon all oaths that are broke to me;
> God keep all vows unbroke are made to thee.[22]

These lines invite far more detailed analysis than is possible here, but a cursory reading would observe some of the following. To begin with, the grammatical units in the first seven lines are identical with the length of the line; in other words, each phrase or clause is ten syllables long and without internal punctuation. In a figure known as epistrophe, the first three lines end with similar phrases, 'my head . . . my hand . . . my heart', and each of the nouns begins with the same letter. The showily anaphoric 'With mine own' helps to emphasise the identical length of the four prepositional phrases. The ninth and tenth lines are structured identically, with their syntax inverted (object, subject, verb), their list of objects equivalent, and rhythmically equivalent verb phrases at the end of each line. At the end of the excerpt, the rhyming of the last two lines creates a couplet pattern that continues in the remainder of Richard's speech. Most of the passage is in blank verse, of course, and it might be said that all blank verse represents a form of parisonic patterning, in that every line of iambic pentameter is similar in form and duration to every other line. Often dramatic poets take advantage of this succession of aurally equivalent ten-syllable units to underscore similarities and differences in the content of the lines.

Aural and visual geometries are layered in the garden scene of *The Spanish Tragedy*, where Kyd's sporting with poetic balances reinforces his narrative and theatrical complements. Bel-Imperia and Horatio, on the main stage, exchange patterned sentences, which receive an antiphonal, ironic response from Balthazar and Lorenzo, presumably spoken from the gallery above:

BEL-IMPERIA	Why stands Horatio speechless all this while?
HORATIO	The less I speak, the more I meditate.
BEL-IMPERIA	But whereon dost thou chiefly meditate?
HORATIO	On dangers past, and pleasure to ensue.
BALTHAZAR	On pleasures past, and dangers to ensue.
BEL-IMPERIA	What dangers and what pleasures dost thou mean?
HORATIO	Dangers of war, and pleasures of our love.
LORENZO	Dangers of death, but pleasures not at all.[23]

The aural gratifications of parisonic structure are heightened by reiterated words and phrases, what we might call a native appropriation of such Latin devices as epistrophe and antimetabole (the criss-cross figure illustrated in the fourth and fifth lines). Kyd takes these repetitive schemes almost to absurdity, a barrier crossed, at least to modern ears, in some of the rhymed verse-comedies and poetic plays descended from the English moralities.[24] Many other examples of poetic parison might be mentioned. To take only one example, shaped poems are exceedingly popular in the period: speaking of verses that offer 'ocular representation', Puttenham shows how to make 'your meeters being by good symmetrie reduced into certaine Geometricall figures'.[25]

I turn instead to the vital role of syntactical equivalence in sixteenth-century prose. The centrality of parisonic construction in the works of Roger Ascham, John Lyly and other Elizabethan prose writers has long been acknowledged, although its effects and influence have not been – nor were they at the time – universally applauded. Suspicion that an inordinate attraction to figures of sound was likely to tyrannise a writer's style, that the claims of the ear threatened to dominate those of the mind, has always dogged analysis of Tudor prose, especially in the case of Lyly. Francis Bacon indicted Ascham and his followers for precisely this failing: 'for men began to hunt more after words than matter; more after the choiceness of the phrase, and the round and clean composition of the sentence, and the sweet falling of the clauses, and the varying and illustration of their works with tropes and figures, than after the weight of matter, worth of subject, soundness of argument, life of invention, or depth of judgement'.[26] Although this is the most famous complaint, an earlier example is Gabriel Harvey's lament that parallelism had been 'somewhat overmuch affected of M. Ascham in our vulgar Tongue';[27] more recent versions are Albert Feuillerat's condescension to the 'tic-tac métronomique et méchanique de la phrase de Lyly'[28] and T. W. Baldwin's reference to 'empty and inflated Ciceronianism'.[29] Metronomic and empty or not, English Ciceronianism has always been defined partly by syntactical balance, and even though scholars such as Jonas Barish and Janel Mueller have challenged the crudity and ease with which that term has been applied, the attraction of Ciceronian sound patterns helped to generate a taste for equivalence in several generations of English humanist writers. It is worth reiterating that the properties we consider 'Ciceronian' were in fact employed by many of the writers who defined themselves as what we would call 'Anti-Ciceronian', most notably Bacon himself.[30]

Devotion to the figure of parison might be demonstrated by quotation from any number of well- and lesser-known works. Having initially cited the passage from *Euphues*, I here offer one earlier example, from Roger Ascham's *Toxophilus*:

> Princes beinge children oughte to be brought up in shoting:
>   both bycause it is an exercise moost holsom,
>   and also   a pastyme moost honest:
>   wherein labour prepareth the body to hardnesse,
>   the mind to couragiousnesse,
>   sufferyng neither the one to be marde with tendernesse,
>   nor yet the other to be hurte with ydleness:

as we reade how Sardanapulus and suche other were
   bycause they were
      not brought up
         with outwarde honest payneful pastymes to be men,
      but cockerde up
         with inwarde noughtie ydle wantonnesse to be women.[31]

My breaking of the sentence into its schematic units helps to point the principle of structural similitude with which Ascham divides and thus organises his subject. In the first pair of lines following the opening, the noun phrases are parallel: 'exercise moost holsom' and 'pastyme moost honest'. A series of four identically ending nouns follows 'labour prepareth', and these four are interlaced, with 'the one' referring back to 'body' and 'the other' referring back to 'mind'. The last complete clause, beginning 'they were not brought up', offers one of the clearest illustrations of the heuristic function of parallel arrangement, calculated as it is to make the moral oppositions unmistakable.

For serious humanist educators such as Ascham, and to a lesser extent perhaps for their less high-minded colleagues, such an appropriation of stylistic devices from Latin was more than a way of indulging their admiration for impressive sounds and shapes. Rather, it was a conscious effort to adapt the methods of a revered medium for the purposes of reaching a new audience and setting forth ideas in a proven and appealing form. Alvin Vos's concise judgment is helpful here: for Ascham, 'rhetoric is designed not primarily to adorn the truth, but to organise it efficiently'.[32] The pedagogic virtues of coordinate structures and binary oppositions are immediately apparent: the writer is able to invite comparison and contrast, to showcase opposites and encourage discrimination between apparently similar arguments and ideas. A related proof of this comparative impulse is Ascham's dependence on the simile, his 'characteristic trope'.[33] As he himself insists, in defending one of those similes, 'comparisons, sayth learned men, make playne matters'.[34] Ascham's self-consciousness about his writing is rooted in moral gravity, and thus the style of *Toxophilus* and *The Schoolemaster* is calculated to separate, elucidate, and promote understanding. The ostentatious figures about which Bacon and his modern progeny have carped, and of which parisonic structure most certainly is one, do indeed seem designed for display, but not merely self-display: they are instrumental in exhibiting, at least in Ascham's prose, the moral equivalents and antitheses that motivated the writer in the first place. Thus the delights of parison are part of a much greater set of cultural values. It is not too much to say, especially in light of Ascham's moral idealism and pedagogical fervor, that the rewards of parisonic structure represent an aural form of nothing less than justice.

For the mid sixteenth-century humanist, the identity of words and things was part of a larger system of meaning, indeed one of the proofs of the coherence of divine creation. According to Thomas Greene, 'the battle to maintain this unity was assumed in the North by Erasmus and Vives, among others, and in England particularly by Ascham. When he pleads against the divorce of words and matter, he is pleading really for a single coherent culture.'[35] This desire for unity is central to the thinking of the English humanists, characteristic of their deep commitment to the values of order and harmony. A related example of such thinking is Thomas Elyot's analysis of dance in *The Boke Named the Gouernour*, where the stars and planets maintain a 'fourme of imitation of a semblable mocion which [the Platonic commentators] called dauncing'.[36] Human dancers, according to Elyot, create patterns that represent cosmic harmonies. David Norbrook has usefully reminded us that the devotion to order was to some degree a convenient fiction of the Elizabethan state; in other words, he illustrates that the sixteenth century saw various challenges, purposeful and implicit, to the ideology of the harmonious monarchy.[37] Aware of this gap, Ascham and others were attempting to sustain the ideal of order: as Janel Mueller and others have shown, 'his new heights of moral concern for England raise to new power his attraction to varieties of sententious formulation'.[38] Ascham hoped not only to articulate a sense of cultural harmony but also – literally – to create it. So did many of the Elizabethan builders.

SYMPHONIE TO SYMMETRIE

Mies van der Rohe believed that 'architecture is the will of an epoch trans-lated into space',[39] and it is pertinent that the sixteenth-century will to order was enforced politically by some of the principal builders of the epoch, notably William Cecil. That will is expressed in the commitment to geometric design visible in the major construction projects. John Dee, in his 'Preface' to Billingsley's 1570 translation of Euclid, justifies the art of architecture in terms that will help to clarify my comparison of writing and building: 'The whole Feate of Architecture in buildyng, consisteth in Lineamentes, and in Framyng. And the whole power and skill of Linea-mentes, tendeth to this: that the right and absolute way may be had, of Coaptyng and ioyning Lines and angles: by which, the face of the buil-dyng or frame, may be comprehended and concluded.'[40] Dee's emphasis on geometric proportion, particularly as expressed in numerical ratios, is a common theme in sixteenth-century analysis. Wotton, for example, speaks of doors and windows in such terms:

These *inlets* of *Men* and of *Light*, I couple together, because I find their due Dimensions, brought under one Rule, by *Leone Alberti* (a learned Searcher) who from the Schoole of *Pythagoras* (where it was a fundamental *Maxime*, that the *Images* of all things are latent in *Numbers*) doth determine the comeliest Proportion, between breadths and heights, Reducing *Symmetrie* to *Symphonie*, and the *harmonie* of *Sounde*, to a kind of *harmonie* in *Sight* . . .[41]

Not only is good writing sometimes evoked as a model for sound building, and vice versa, but rhetoricians and writers on architecture often refer to other crafts and disciplines as well. Shute maintains, for example, that the architect 'ought first to be a very good Grammarian . . . must also have a good sighte in Musycke, and . . . must also besides all thise be in Philosophie, very experte'.[42] Modern scholarship has neglected this consciousness of interrelation among the arts in sixteenth-century culture.

Architecture is unusually hospitable to the study of such principles because its ratios are visible. Excepting Gresham's Royal Exchange, all the important building executed during Elizabeth's reign was domestic, specif- ically the country houses conceived by her courtiers as appropriate spaces for entertaining their sovereign and honouring themselves. Historically speaking, the definitive trend in Tudor architecture was the reorientation of the medieval great house away from the inner court and towards the exterior landscape. Feudal defensiveness was a thing of the past: prosperity and relative peace ensured that the castle had become not a stronghold but a showplace. With visual interest now focused on the exterior, 'the general design . . . progresses from an asymmetrical elevation, with the main emphasis on the entrance, to a symmetrical elevation with the main entrance-piece and the ends in a coherent design'.[43] Beginning around 1530, virtually every existing great house in England was reconfigured along these lines, the most common change being the addition of an elaborate façade based upon principles of bilateral symmetry. And new construction, from the middle to the end of the century, was even more rigorously balanced. David Evett, writing of Hatfield House and Audley End, two very late examples of the shift I am describing, points out that 'the disposition of spaces seems to assert a level of authority, a degree of conscious ordering'.[44] His perception clarifies the parallel between architectural authority and authorship.

2. Longleat House, Wiltshire; the east façade.

A persuasive way of identifying the structure of sentences and buildings is to examine the symmetrical façade that dominates such monumental buildings as Longleat (1570s) (figure 2), Wollaton Hall (1580s), and Hardwick Hall (1590s). According to John Summerson, the most significant properties of Longleat are 'its complete extraversion' and 'its absolute symmetry on both axes'.[45] Positioned at a moderate distance from the north front, the viewer immediately perceives the controlled complexity of the surface. The dominance of the symmetry is achieved by the equal distribution of its masses, both horizontally and vertically, and strengthened by the placement and connection of the pilasters. Illustrating Wotton's principle of uniformity and diversity, the three storeys are simultaneously united and distinguished by the pilastered columns: Doric, Ionic, and Corinthian in ascending order. Glass having become widely available, the fenestration also enhances the impression of similitude, the divided glass planes offering an additional field for pleasing correspondences, similar in structure yet different in material, unified and diverse. Native bay windows are modified into rectangles and integrated rigorously into the symmetrical whole. Especially from the middle distance, the structure also impresses the perceiver with its insistent horizontality, an effect enhanced by the stringcourse, or horizontal moulding, that joins the bases of the pilasters on each of the three storeys. Its command is palpable: as one critic describes the effect of Longleat, 'it stares at us'.[46]

This shift from the vertical to the horizontal axis is discernible throughout English architecture from about 1550 on. Sometimes the emphasis on regularity seems to have become extreme: on the plan for Dowsby in Lincolnshire, John Thorpe has written in his own hand 'nothing out of square'.[47] Mark Girouard observes that at Longleat particularly, and in Elizabethan style generally, the bay window, along with the tower, the grid of glass, and occasionally the gable, was 'modified by being stripped of Gothic detail . . . and arranged with a strict symmetry . . . and a feeling for dramatic massing and recession'.[48] This scheme of absolute correspondence is the salient feature of most of the great domestic projects of the day, the attribute that made these houses 'modern', and the patrons and builders were attentive to these harmonic relationships. Cecil, in building the palace at Theobalds later taken over by James I, began by renovating an older structure according to the 'new principles of axiality and uniformity'.[49] He was influenced, at least in part, by his visit in 1579 to Holdenby, the great house that Christopher Hatton had constructed in Northamptonshire. In a surviving letter, Cecil wrote to Hatton full of praise for the sense of correspondence that overcame him on arrival: 'approaching to the house, being led by a large, long, straight fairway, I found a great magnificence in the front or front pieces of the house, and so every part answerable to other, to allure liking'.[50] The crucial phrase, 'every part answerable to other', is the architectural equivalent of Hoskins's definition of parison as 'an even gait of sentences answering each other in measures interchangeably'.

The 'feeling for dramatic massing and recession' mentioned by Girouard at Longleat is acknowledged, along with symmetrical order, to be a cardinal property of sixteenth-century architectural design.[51] A stepping or receding effect that seems to give depth or texture to a plane, recession may be observed not only in the symmetrical façade of the Elizabethan house but also in the arrangement of surrounding structures. The most recent authority on Tudor domestic architecture emphasises the innovative, holistic approach that began to influence construction projects in the latter half of the sixteenth century, demonstrating that owners and their craftsmen began to consider more consciously than before the harmonious relation of

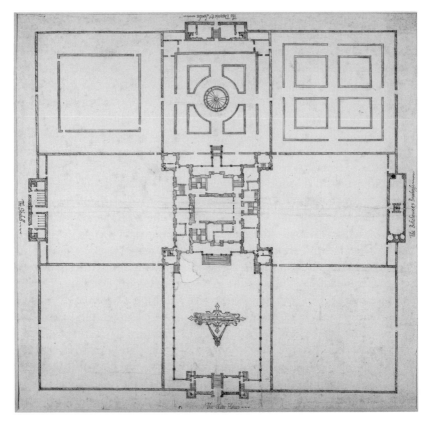

3. Robert Smythson, Plan of Wollaton Hall, *c.* 1580.

house, surrounding structures, and the setting into which these buildings were placed.[52] The Henrician doctor Andrew Boorde, offering instruction on the healthy siting of 'a house or mansion' in *A Compendyous Regyment or a Dyetary of Helth*, suggests that 'the gatehowse be opposyte or agaynste the halldore standynge a base, and the gatehowse in the mydle of the front entrynge into the place'.[53] Walls, gardens, gatehouses, banqueting houses, stables and other outbuildings were integrated visually into a design determined by the topographical situation and especially by the visual character of the great house, a scheme Henderson refers to as an 'ideal plan'. The drawing executed by Robert Smythson for Sir Francis Willoughby at Wollaton illustrates this concord between primary edifice and complementary structures (figure 3): for example, 'The Gatte House', 'The Stabell', 'The

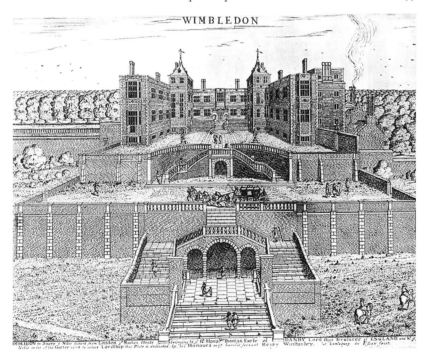

WIMBLEDON

4. John Thorpe, Plan of Wimbledon House, *c.* 1588.

Dayrie & Landre', and 'The Bakehouse & Bruehouse' not only coexist in harmony with the house they surround, but each of these buildings is itself symmetrically imagined. More and more frequently this grand plot exhibits the impact of symmetrical recession. John Thorpe's plan for Wimbledon House, begun in 1588 (and demolished in the eighteenth century), illustrates this characteristic layout (figure 4), with its several sets of stairs, terraced levels, balustrades, statues in the forecourt and symmetrically arranged main building.

It is this combination of horizontality and recession that provides the most instructive comparison with the characteristic structure of contemporary English prose. Consider the contribution of similar rhetorical effects to the following sentence from Ascham's *The Schoolemaster*:

But as for all the bloody beasts as that fat boar of the wood or those brawling bulls of Bashan, or any lurking dormouse blind, not by nature but by malice and, as may be gathered of their own testimony, given over to blindness for giving over God and his word, or such as be so lusty runagates as, first, run from God and his true doctrine, then, from their lords, masters, and all duty, next, from themselves and out of their wits, lastly, from their prince, country, and all due allegiance – whether they ought to be pitied of good men for their misery or contemned of wise men for their malicious folly let good and wise men determine.[54]

This passage is useful because it is not extravagant but illustrates moderately the principles of uniformity and correspondence typical of mid-century writing. Notable first is the length of the single sentence, a linearity of which the reader becomes increasingly conscious while moving through the chain of introductory phrases. The construction is controlled by what could be called a Ciceronian suspension, the delayed resolution magnifying the parisonic balance of the constituent units. The accumulation of parallel clauses and phrases, matched words and letters, establishes its impressive effects in much the same way that the carefully grouped main structure, walls, and front buildings co-operate in one of Thorpe's architectural schemes. We experience a kind of semantic recession as we move further and further through the series of antithetical pairs ('not by nature but by malice'; 'pitied of good men for their misery or contemned of wise men for their malicious folly') and serially organised prepositional phrases ('from God . . . from their lords . . . from their prince . . .'). In other words, as we read we seem to recede from, to step farther and farther away from, the grammatical security of the normative sentence, until finally we are returned from those depths by the semantic fulfilment of the final clause. The pleasure of this recessive effect is determined by the whole, a delight shaped and guaranteed by the expectation of comprehension and closure.

WORDS AND THINGS

Jonas Barish, in his seminal study of Jonson, offhandedly refers to Cicero as 'the Vitruvius of Renaissance prose',[55] a remark that offers a convenient passageway from literary to visual culture. Keeping in mind that Barish describes the early-modern perception of the two Romans and their work, the justice of the comment is, in a general sense, self-evident: as the English rhetoricians and pedagogues looked to Cicero and Quintilian for models on which to build an appropriate vernacular style, so writers on architecture and the learned aristocrats who undertook to build relied on Vitruvius for a vocabulary and syntax suitable to a 'modern' style of construction. But the comparison is more particularly apt in light of their common commitment, despite the different fields of creation, to isocolonic structure and ornamental correspondence. English writers apprehended Ciceronian principles more or less directly, with the help of Quintilian, thanks mainly to the humanist educational program. Although Vitruvius was known in the original (the physician Andrew Boorde read him, for example), his architectonic principles were also filtered through his Continental disciples, Sebastiano Serlio and Philibert de l'Orme. Cecil, for example, ordered de l'Orme's book, *Nouvelles Inventions* (1561), from Paris, and the Duke of Northumberland sent Shute to Italy to study Vitruvius and his influence. Both disciplines are characterised by an effort to meld Roman and English ideas and practices: David Evett speaks of the difficulty with which English writers attempted 'to wrench their recalcitrant native syntax into consonance with the Ciceronian patterns (a struggle that has attractive similarities to the contemporaneous push-and-pull between native and imported architectural devices)'.[56]

Humanist writers consciously sought to fashion a vernacular prose style worthy of ancient models and appropriate to their lofty cultural aims; their devotion to the figure of parison is one proof of the deliberate effort to appropriate the elegance of Latin construction for the emerging national literature. As Brian Vickers puts it, 'the use of structural symmetry in English is the direct continuity (subject to the language's limitations) of the traditional practices of Greece and Rome'.[57] At the risk of excessive simplification, we can say that the structures of Latin prose provided the larger frame, while the Anglo-Saxon tradition supplied instruments for ornamenting that frame with detail, in particular repetitive devices such as alliteration and repeated words. This mix of sources might be construed as a literary example of Wotton's complementary values of uniformity and diversity. The evolution of Elizabethan building can be similarly described, the gradual conversion of traditional features – windows, gatehouse, gardens – into what we loosely call a 'classical' design. Such appropriation of ancient ideas into the English landscape represents a spatial version of Ascham's classically derived devotion to authority and harmony.

In the sentence from *Julius Caesar* with which I began, Shakespeare invites the listener to reflect on the delights and the dangers of parisonic construction. Marcus Brutus's tragic experience is a product of his idealism: although admittedly Caesar has not yet demonstrated sinister ambition, Brutus elects to act as if he had done so. Thus the assassination represents an effort to remake the world according to his noble conception of how it ought to be. The aural symmetries of Brutus's *apologia* at Caesar's funeral imply both the attractiveness and the delusion of such an ideal, with the sting in the tail of the sentence: 'As Caesar lov'd me . . . I slew him.' Shakespeare admits the appeal and comfort of the humanist commitment to structural balance, but he also exposes the peril of allowing *verba* to bully *res*.

CHAPTER 3

The shortest pause or intermission they called *comma* as who would say a peece of a speach cut of. The second they called *colon*, not a peece but as it were a member for his larger length, because it occupied twise as much time as the *comma*. The third they called *periodus*, for a complement or full pause, and as a resting place and perfection of so much former speach as had bene uttered, and from whence they needed not to passe any further unles it were to renew more matter to enlarge the tale.

Puttenham, *The Arte of English Poesie* (1589), Book II

For as much helpe whereof as may be in this case, I have endevoured throughout the bodie of this whole discourse, that every former part might give strength unto all that followe, and every later bring some light unto all before: So that if the judgements of men doe but holde themselves in suspence as touching these first more generall meditations, till in order they have perused the rest that ensue, what may seeme darke at the first will afterwardes be founde more plaine, even as the later particular decisions will appeare, I doubt not, more strong, when the other have beene read before.

Richard Hooker, *Of the Lawes of Ecclesiastical Politie* (1594)

Periodos: squaring the circle

JANEL MUELLER

What is periodos, and what does it mean to write in periods? The literal sense of the Greek word is 'a going around'. It acquired technical senses from the Peripatetics, Aristotle and his followers, who used it to denote certain modes of rhythmically rounding out units of composition in music, in poetry, and in prose. In music, rhythm determines the values of tones and groupings with reference to any of a number of available measures. In poetry, rhythm arises from the interplay of words, phrases and sentences with and against an abstract metrical design. Prose, however, has no superordinate, sustained patterning comparable to the measures of music and verse. In prose, the compositional unit is the sentence; its rhythms result from particular dispositions of grammatically inflected words in phrases and clauses of varying length and complexity. Thus, when periodos was taken over into rhetorical theory and exposition, its domain could not be restricted to considerations of sound and rhythm, but necessarily had to include the effects of grammar and word choice, the forms of phrases and clauses, and the resulting conveyance of 'thought' or meaning. A basic notion of a rounding or a rounding-out did persist in the metaphorical extension of periodos as a technical term: one or more tactics for composing sentences that are at once comprehensive, goal-directed, and integrally complete, that is, 'periodic'.

In his *Rhetoric*, Aristotle offers a foundational definition of periodos in which the foregrounding of cognitive and semantic features is as characteristic of his mind as of the construct: 'By period', he says, 'I mean a sentence that has a beginning and an end in itself, and a magnitude that can be easily grasped' because its reader or hearer 'at every moment thinks he is securing something for himself and that some conclusion is being reached'.[1] A periodic sentence is also 'easy to understand' and can be 'easily retained in the memory'[2] – features which Aristotle connects with elements of linguistic form. He ascribes ease of retention to the rhythmic patterns that, while never as extensive or formative as poetic metre, were obligatory for the Greek period in helping it to approach the memorability of verse. He ascribes ease of understanding to the overall sense of syntactic form – 'a beginning and an end in itself' – produced by the periodic sentence; and this, for him, is correspondingly binary, two halves of sub-sentential components that perceptibly comprise a whole.[3] He then reaffirms the importance of the semantics of syntax in his general cautions against excessive brevity or excessive length of clauses and the periods of which they are members:

If too short, they often make the hearer stumble; for when he is hurrying on towards the measure of which he already has a definite idea, if he is checked by the speaker stopping, a sort of stumble is bound to occur in consequence of the sudden stop. If too long, they leave the hearer behind, as those who do not turn till past the ordinary limit leave behind those who are walking with them.[4]

To these authoritative formulations, Aristotle's successor, Demetrius, adds a few finishing touches in his treatise *On Style*. Demetrius picks up on an analogy used negatively by Aristotle to contrast with the effect of *periodos* – runners who lose breath and strength when they lose sight of their goal in a race. In one influential touch, he converts the racecourse analogy to a positive metaphor, adding a further metaphor drawn from etymology, the circle, to figure the dynamics of the periodic style:

The very use of the word 'period' implies that it has had a beginning at one point, will end at another, and is speeding towards a definite goal, like runners sprinting from the starting-place. For at the very beginning of their race the end of the course is already before their eyes. Hence the name 'period', an image drawn from paths which go round and are in a circle. In general terms, a period is nothing more nor less than a particular arrangement of words. If its circular form should be destroyed and the arrangement changed, the subject matter remains the same, but there will be no period.[5]

As subsequent discussion will show, both metaphors – the circuit of a racecourse and the circle – play a part in later developments in theory and practice, particularly in England.

QUINTILIAN AND THE CLASSICAL PERIOD

For the Renaissance inheritors of this paradigm, it was Quintilian who, in *Institutio oratoria* 9.4, provided the most acutely reasoned and developed account of the interworkings of syntax and semantics in periodic sentence composition, repeatedly illustrating with examples from the orations of Cicero. The account opens with a nested taxonomy of syntactic units. The smallest is *commata* or 'cuts' ['incisa'], consisting of short, simple phrases or even, at times, single words; the *comma* is a unit of simple thought. The next largest units are *cola* or 'limbs', single or multiple clauses comprised of *commata* and interconnected grammatically with each other, which express more complex thoughts but do not stand independently on their own. The largest unit is the main sentence structure, the period, which incorporates instances of the other two in an overall design governed by two syntactic criteria, sequencing ['ordo'] and linkage ['iunctura'], together with one auditory criterion, rhythm ['pedes' – metrical feet]. The period is the vehicle for complex, completed thought; it is also the culminating example of the art he calls 'composition'.[6]

Quintilian's determination to work through for himself the interplay of sense, style and sound in periodic composition yields some notable advances in conceptualisation. Regarding a *comma* or 'cut', he says, 'most people define it as part of a colon. A comma, in my view, is a complete thought without completed rhythm.' As one example he gives Latin *diximus* – 'we have said' in English – which may be considered a thought but, because the verb 'say' is transitive, is incomplete as an utterance and, it can be added, as a unit of meaning as well. Quintilian continues his line of analysis: 'A colon, however, is a thought which is rhythmically complete, but separated from its parent body and ineffective on its own. "O callidos homines!" ['O prudent men!' – an interjection from a periodic sentence of Cicero's] is complete, but it has no force without the rest; it is like a hand or a foot or a head on its own . . . So when does it' – the period – 'begin to be a complete body? When the conclusion appears', says Quintilian, illustrating with the ending of the same periodic sentence in Cicero: '"Quem quaeso nostrum fefellit id vos ita esse facturos?"' ['I ask, which of us failed to see that this is what you were going to do?'].[7] In Quintilian's organic figuration, each unit of the period is a unit of sense – 'a hand or a foot or a head on its own' – and, as such, 'commata and cola are truncated fragments, and inevitably require a conclusion' – which is to say, incorporation within a period.[8] Quintilian's alternative representation of *commata* and *cola* as species of complete thoughts that nevertheless cannot qualify as free-standing sentences leads him to define the period as follows: 'There are two types, one simple, when a single thought is deployed in a period of some length, and one made up of cola and commata, which contains several thoughts . . . A period contains at least two cola. An average number seems to be four but it often allows more . . . It must comprise a complete thought; it must be open and intelligible, and not too long to be retained in the memory.'[9] Here Quintilian demonstrates his independence of mind in amending Aristotle's normative notion of the overall binary structure of a period. With an eye, repeatedly, to Cicero's practice, he allows for more elaborated, multi-membered periodic constructs as long as intelligibility and memorability – with the added help of rhythm – are sustained.

Quintilian concludes his account by considering what objectives and themes lend themselves best to periodic composition – all within the presumed context of an orator's pleading of lawsuits. His reflections on the use of the period trade heavily on a sense of the power it exerts through a purposive dynamic of expansiveness kept under steady and perceptible formal control, especially when it is used to set up a subject or to draw conclusions, in the form of judgements, about it: 'The period is well suited to the introduction of important causes, where the subject calls for concern, recommendation of the client, or pity. It also suits commonplaces and every kind of amplification . . . The period is also very important in the epilogue.' Quintilian further connects the directive impact on a hearer's thoughts and emotions with the pleasurable excitement of being taken along the artful, intricate circuit of a period: 'All this more ample type of composition is to be used when the judge not only understands the facts but has also been won over by the speech, trusts himself to the pleader, and begins to be guided by his own pleasure.' Beyond the usefulness of periodic composition in 'demonstrative oratory' – the genre devoted to praising or blaming – the other genre for which it is particularly suited, in Quintilian's view, is historiography: 'History requires . . . a certain cyclical structure, for its cola are all connected with one another . . . in the way that men who join hands to steady their steps lend mutual support to one another.'[10]

VIVES AND THE HUMANIST PERIOD

In English Renaissance manuals of rhetoric and in continental ones circulating in England during the sixteenth century, there is almost no treatment of periodos as a term or of its identifying principles of sentence composition. A notable exception is the Quintilian-like figure of Juan Luis Vives, the Christian humanist who taught Mary Tudor as a princess, and authored both the educational plan of *De tradendis disciplinis* ['On transmitting the disciplines'] and the rhetorical philosophy of *De ratione dicendi* ['On the guiding principle for speaking']. The first book of the latter work recalls Quintilian's gradation from ornament to composition in its culminating discussion of periodos. Vives' subject is *sermo*, the resources of spoken language, which he considers the unique means for realising our natural human capacities and for coping purposively with our historical situation.

Analysis and discussion of *sermo* – its constituent elements (words, sounds, syllables, basic phrases and order in regard to these) and its powers of expression ('magnitudo in verbis' – verbal extension to encompass greatness of things or ideas; 'dilatatio sermonis' – amplification of words and to narrate, describe, discuss, or respond to a prior argument) – come to a head in discussion late in Book 1, on the types and uses of periodic sentences, and in the subsequent remarks on 'ordinatio verborum', or natural and artificial arrangements of words and their respective effects. Vives is concerned above all with the inventive and communicative workings of speech, the linguistic 'actions' of minds perceiving, thinking, knowing and engaging with one another.

What Vives has to say about the architecture of the periodic sentence is strongly reminiscent of Cicero's practice and Quintilian's theory. At points, however, he goes beyond both in his reflections on the psychodynamics of the relation between speaker and hearer that is contracted in *sermo*. Periods, remarks Vives, round themselves out either by connection or by subordination, registering this force at their beginning, middle, or ending – even, at times, in a deduced conclusion. Examples can be found everywhere. Periods acquire strength from being cut ['incisa'] into fours and joined internally, like a foursquare structure of stones held together without plaster or mortar. The most beautiful periods are made either from antithetical members or from a process of reasoning ['argumentum'] ingeniously turned. There are periods of one member only, which have cuts instead of connection – again, the passing acknowledgement of the linguistic fact of simple sentences – and periods of two, of three and even of four members. When periods have many members or are excessively long, their force is weakened, as when a very long javelin is thrown.[11]

But, continues Vives, there are speakers who consider the guiding principle ['ratio'] of language and the nature and minds of their hearers. Instead of heaping the sentence members together, they present them in turns governed by similarity or difference of meaning: either the one and then the other, or two together; or in a period of four members they place two at the front, then two later, the one pair agreeably, the other crosswise. In periods where the members are of like length, these turns are called *isocoli*, or they are called symmetrical, and proportional, if also like in form; they are judged too by their duration in time, or by a certain expectation and noting by the ear, of equality in the number and measure of their syllables.[12] Members that have been separated can be conjoined, and those that have been conjoined can be separated and divided, as is shown when elements are transposed in the contemplation of nature. The guiding principle of accounts of meanings is intermediate between external and internal, for it arises in the mind but is directed from the mind to the words and what they signify. In their arrangements words should be very common ones, first of all, so that fellow humans can understand them, and they are to be spoken clearly, as is the manner customary with those who speak well and correctly about things. Obscurity that arises from these same things – words and their arrangements – is not a part of this work if it is the fault of the hearers, declares Vives, for this indeed is not a fault of the speech. If, for example, the hearer does not understand the language we use, if he does not understand a proper word in current use, and, not least if he is slow-witted or does not pay attention, the speaker's words will have certain shadows for him. Nevertheless, words in ordinary use will have clarity in themselves, and will sustain clarity in what precedes and what follows them, if they are set in order. As disordered things are confused and engender obscurity, so, however many things there are, if you set them in order, they will be perspicuous. Order – here Vives gestures back at the periodic composition of clauses and phrases which he has just discussed – is most instrumental to human understanding.[13]

PERIODOS AS A FIGURE OF ORDER IN SIXTEENTH-CENTURY PROSE

Though Vives' account of periodos is unique among sixteenth-century rhetorical handbooks circulating in England, his conception of the form and its significance does find echoes in the vernacular practice of his English contemporaries (see, for instance, Russ McDonald's account of Ascham's sentence-design in his chapter on compar). As mentioned earlier, Quintilian had suggested that the writing of history was an appropriate genre for the use of periodic sentence composition, and had suggested an analogy between its articulated interconnections and the social cohesion so prized by those who recorded the disruptions of a given body politic. Sixteenth-century English historiography is, in fact, a productive site for this resource of style. An early instance from Edward Hall's *Union of the Two Noble and Illustre Famelies of Lancastre and Yorke* (1548) pointedly sustains the associations of the period with order and purposive design that have already been noted:

But the olde devided controversie betwene the fornamed families of Lancastre and Yorke by the union of Matrimony celebrate and consummate betwene the high and mighty Prince kyng Henry the seventh, and the lady Elizabeth his moste worthy quene, the one beeyng indubitate heire of the hous of Lancastre, and the other of Yorke was suspended and appalled in the person of their moste noble, puissant and mighty heire Kyng Henry the eight, and by hym clerely buried and perpetually extinct.[14]

Hall's period instals a suspension-completion dynamic in the main clause as the principal determinant of form. The subject–verb–verbal complement nucleus of the main clause – 'controversy', 'was suspended and appalled [quelled]', 'Henry VIII' – spreads out along almost the whole length of this single grand sentence. Grandeur here consists of a heavy cladding of modifiers, redoubled lexical primaries – nouns, verbs, adjectives and adverbs – added at virtually every available node of phrase structure: thus, 'old divided', 'Lancaster and York', 'celebrate and consummate', 'high and mighty', 'Henry VII and lady Elizabeth', 'most noble, puissant and mighty', 'clearly buried and perpetually extinct'. Although the underlying momentum is one of expectant attending while the dependent modifiers play out their intricacies and make way for the declared cessation of the Wars of the Roses and the emphatic naming of Henry VIII at sentence end, the overall meaning is enriched by a subtler syntactic movement that reveals why Henry VIII, in particular, could be credited with this momentous historical effect. This syntactic movement proceeds by way of three binary constructions – first, the noun phrase 'union of matrimony', then the preposition 'between' with its object phrase (Henry VII and Elizabeth), and finally, a correlative construction (the one, heir of the house of Lancaster, and the other, of York). Taken together, the suspended thought – what would end the Wars of the Roses? – and the linked binary phrases that uniquely identify 'the person of their . . . heir' produce a complex perception of Henry VIII as the agent and the beneficiary of the emergent English nation centralised in the Tudor state.

By the closing decades of the sixteenth century, periodic sentence structure appears sufficiently naturalised within history-writing to serve quite different expressive purposes – not the external manifestations of social and political order, but the internal disorder of an individual psychology and its contorted logic. Thus, in 'The History of Scotland' section of his *Chronicles*, Raphael Holinshed evokes Macbeth's perturbation when, after the witches have uttered their prophecies, King Duncan suddenly and openly appoints his eldest son, Malcolm, still a minor, as his successor to the Scottish throne:

Mackbeth sore troubled herewith, for that he saw by this means his hope sore hindered, where by the old lawes of the realme the ordinance was that if he that should succeed were not of able age to take the charge upon himselfe, he that was next of bloud unto him should be admitted, he began to take counsell how he might usurpe the kingdome by force, having a just quarrell so to doo, as he took the matter, for that Duncane did what in him lay to defraud him of all maner of title and claime which he might in time to come pretend unto the crowne.[15]

Holinshed's first structural motive is to suspend meaning by spreading apart the subject and the verb phrase of his main clause, putting enough distance between them to warrant a resumptive subject pronoun just before the verb phrase: 'Macbeth . . . he began to take counsel.' But suspension produced by clausal spread in the main construction is abruptly superseded by a pivotal turn at a subordinate level, as the clausal complement to the verb phrase follows directly – 'take counsel how he might usurp the kingdom by force'. This usurpation of one compositional motive by another expressively patterns the larger form of the period after its thematic subject: Macbeth's obsessive brooding on why and how he could become king in place of Duncan. Further expressive effects include the enchaining of subordinate clauses with their articulated connectives after the initial naming of Macbeth, to detail and trace his state of mind: 'for that he saw . . . where the ordinance was that if . . . he that was next . . . should be'. Expressiveness persists in a second enchaining of subordinate constructions with articulated connectives, beginning with the delusive formulation 'having a just quarrel' and now tracing Macbeth's fully paranoid thoughts, which bring the period to its troubled and inconclusive conclusion: 'which he might in time to come pretend unto the crown'.

BACON AND THE COMPOSITION OF THE SENTENCE

Given what even such a selective sampling has shown about the possibilities for developing a complex thought process and guiding or testing it in the writing of a periodic sentence in English, Francis Bacon's singling out of this mode of composition and its conceptual underpinnings for attack in *The Advancement of Learning* (1605) is as puzzling as it is unlooked for. Initially, in the first book, it appears that Bacon's target is a general one – the misguided study of eloquence and style among certain Renaissance rhetoricians, which has led to misplaced priorities:

Men began to hunt more after words than matter; more after the choiceness of the phrase, and the round and clean composition of the sentence, and the sweet falling of the clauses, and the varying and illustration of their works with tropes and figures, than after the weight of matter, worth of subject, soundness of argument, life of invention, or depth of judgment.[16]

The faulting of 'round and clean composition of the sentence' may leave the reader momentarily wondering why this is a bad thing, but otherwise

Bacon's criticisms seem justified in the context. In the second book of the *Advancement*, however, the negative connotations of 'round and clean composition of the sentence' begin to be developed and emphasised. Starting from agreement with those theorists who insist that logical rigor must rule every operation of proving or demonstrating, Bacon acknowledges that analogy or proportionality – 'that which Aristotle calleth demonstration in orb or circle' – has its place as one among 'the four kinds of demonstrations', the other three being 'the immediate consent of the mind or sense', 'induction', and 'syllogism'. Yet all four kinds are limited enough in one way or another to make Bacon regard them warily:

Every of these hath certain subjects in the matter of sciences, in which respectively they have chiefest use; and certain others, from which respectively they ought to be excluded; and the rigour and curiosity in requiring the more severe proofs in some things, and chiefly the facility in contenting ourselves with the more remiss proofs in others, hath been amongst the greatest causes of detriment and hindrance to knowledge. The distributions and assignations of demonstrations, according to the analogy of sciences, I note as deficient.[17]

Bacon correctly observes that analogy (A is like B) or proportionality (A is to B as C is to D) – Aristotle's 'demonstration in orb or circle' – can never yield a proof of some fact or result in the natural sciences. Nonetheless he holds firm to his conception of the structure of human knowledge as having its basis in correlation and correspondence, 'the analogy of sciences'. Bacon returns to this conception three chapters later where he addresses 'Transmission of knowledge: Methods magistral and of probation' and again invokes 'demonstration in orb or circle'.

Here Bacon's context is the invention, disposition or arrangement, and delivery of subject matter, which Aristotle, Quintilian and Vives regard as conjoint operations in logic and rhetoric. In this context, however, Bacon takes a momentous step which follows his boldly reformist elder contemporary, Petrus Ramus (Pierre de la Ramée, d. 1572), whose influence was proliferating in England at the time.[18] Ramus rejected any overlap between logic and rhetoric, categorically assigning invention and arrangement to logic, reserving only style and delivery to rhetoric. 'Method' – the branch of logic or rhetoric which teaches how to arrange thoughts and topics for investigation or for literary composition – 'hath been placed, and that not amiss', declares Bacon, 'in logic, as a part of judgement'. He then pursues the implications, as he sees them, of this stringent division of labour between logic and rhetoric. In the process, however, Bacon bears involuntary witness to the traditional closeness of the two arts by using the term 'method' for them both – 'method referred to use' of knowledge (rhetoric), 'method referred to progression' of knowledge (logic):

> The doctrine of method containeth the rules of judgement upon that which is to be delivered; for judgement precedeth delivery, as it followeth invention. Neither is the method or the nature of the tradition material only to the use of knowledge, but likewise to the progression of knowledge . . . And therefore the most real diversity of method is of method referred to use, and method referred to progression: whereof the one may be termed magistral, and the other of probation.[19]

According to Bacon, the chief 'use' of knowledge is to transmit it in such a manner that it will be put to further use; this is the proper business of rhetoric. But he purports to find only impropriety in the rhetorical transmission of knowledge in his day. He launches an attack on the method he terms 'magistral' – recognisably aiming at the workings and effects of periodic sentence composition as he represents them:

> As knowledges are now delivered, there is a kind of contract of error between the deliverer and the receiver. For he that delivereth knowledge, desireth to deliver it in such form as may be best believed, and not as may be best examined; and he that receiveth knowledge, desireth rather present satisfaction, than expectant inquiry; and so rather not to doubt, than not to err: glory making the author not to lay open his weakness, and sloth making the disciple not to know his strength . . . [Such] methods are more fit to win consent to belief, but less fit to point to action; for they carry a kind of demonstration in orb or circle, one part illuminating another, and therefore satisfy.[20]

Bacon could be singling out the most artful and most demanding sentence form of his day to stand for rhetoric at its best, and then dismissing rhetoric, even at its best, where the transmission of knowledge is at stake, because rhetoric is, by definition, the art of persuasion. This definition is presupposed in the philosophical seriousness brought to the subject by Aristotle, as well as the psycholinguistic observations of Quintilian and the sociolinguistic concerns of Vives; it also deeply informs the history of rhetorical practice. Bacon's remarks on the receiver of knowledge desiring present satisfaction, on the author's glorying and the disciple's slothfulness, could even be a malicious twist on Quintilian's commendation of perio-dos, quoted in discussion above: 'All this more ample type of composition is to be used when the judge not only understands the facts but has also been won over by the speech, trusts himself to the pleader, and begins to be guided by his own pleasure.' But persuasion does not appear to be the sticking-point for Bacon in launching this attack because he declares that being 'fit to point to action' is one of his own criteria for rhetoric. At issue, then, in Bacon's attack on periodos is which rhetorical method, not whether rhetorical method, is to be used.[21]

What Bacon sees here through the lens of Ramist dichotomising is at best one function of periodic sentence composition, which could be termed 'magistral' if this can mean 'magisterial' – setting out a complex subject in intricate order and interconnection – and at most one type of period, the grandly 'spread' main clause. In this era clausal spread does recurrently function as an authoritative mode, as if purporting to say everything that a particular subject demands, as in the example of Hall on Henry VIII.[22] Bacon, however, does not see – or does not see fit to acknowledge – the significant capacities of periodic sentences to track an errant train of thought and expose it as such, as in the example of Holinshed on Macbeth. Bacon's attack on periodos is programmatic and, to that extent, predetermined by *a priori* commitments. To further his innovative and ultimately influential call for direct observation of nature and for an experimental approach to the discovery of knowledge, he posits the need for a closely correspondent mode of transmitting such knowledge. This, which Bacon calls the method 'of probation', gives 'the analogy of sciences' a new rhetorical direction, turning it away from the correlatives and connections of the periodic circuit and towards the 'threading' or 'transplanting' of simple sentence-units:

> But knowledge that is delivered as a thread to be spun on, ought to be delivered and intimated, if it were possible, in the same method wherein it was invented: and so is it possible of knowledge induced . . . A man may descend unto the foundations of his knowledge and consent; and so transplant it into another, as it grew in his own mind . . . The writing in aphorisms hath many virtues, whereto the writing in [magistral] method doth not approach . . . For first, it trieth the writer, whether he be superficial or solid: for aphorisms, except they should be ridiculous, cannot be made but of the pith and heart of sciences; for discourse of illustration is cut off; recitals of examples are cut off; discourse of connexion and order is cut off; descriptions of practice are cut off. So there remaineth nothing to fill the aphorisms but some good quantity of observation: and therefore no man can suffice, nor in reason will attempt, to write aphorisms, but he that is sound and grounded.[23]

The premium placed on the probational method of writing in aphorisms can be accounted for in the context of Bacon's larger objectives, but from other perspectives its reliance on dubious and arbitrarily stated assumptions remains puzzling. Is the simple sentence the unit in which humans register new perceptions and new knowledge in their minds? Even if this is so, is the simple sentence-unit the obligatory vehicle for transmitting new perceptions and new knowledge to others? It is a truism in modern science that the method of making a discovery – the trials and errors, the dead ends of investigative research – sets no necessary precedent for communicating the discovery. Communication proceeds instead through orderly, detailed accounts of procedures and results which are tested by undertaking to replicate them. If anything, the character of a complex thought experiment, which the periodic sentence regularly assumes, seems to offer appreciably more promise as an instrument for transmitting or eliciting knowledge than does the rudimentary concision of an aphorism. It must be conceded that aphorisms of a universalising kind have been widely valued as contributions to the store of received human wisdom. But any such ascription of value would better suit the context of Vives' reflections on *sermo* and *ordo*; it sorts oddly with the calls for new modes and methods of knowledge production in the *Advancement of Learning*.

CIRCUIT AND APHORISM IN DONNE

Bacon's disparagement of the periodic sentence and his advocacy of the aphorism acquire significance not as causes but as symptoms of a broader shift of sensibility in prose composition that begins to manifest itself in the earlier seventeenth century in England. While the pivot or turn and the rounding-out of complexly suspended members to an integral closure retain their formal and thematic appeal, these features are found operating less consistently within a single, capacious sentence-unit. Binary conjunctions – especially correlatives and antitheses – also continue to figure prominently in the texture of discourse. But more openness of weave is observable in the relaxation of formal correspondences at clausal and phrasal levels and in the sudden, striking prominence accorded to simple sentence-units, with or without articulated conjunctions, within larger sentence wholes. The shift of sensibility consists in certain strategic departures from periodic sentence-form that temporarily fix attention on compact units without sacrificing an overall dynamic of suspension and completion. A recurring 'aphoristic effect' is created, all the while that a 'periodic effect' is sustained and often intensified by rhythmical patterning in the prose.

Religious writing of a meditative cast is a particularly conspicuous site of the newer tendencies to pursue periodic composition while introducing aphoristic high points in units of discourse that extend beyond the compass of a single sentence. Since one of the most notable practitioners in this vein, John Donne, is insistent regarding his personal loyalties and what he characterises as his providential placement within the Church of England, his prose style may bear witness to the resonances of periodic structure in the collects of the *Book of Common Prayer*, which would have left memory traces through regular recitation in public worship.[24] Whatever the origins of his distinctive style, Donne adapts the dynamic of the expanded, internally accentuated period to the discovery and communication of God's ways in this world and beyond – this being the knowledge, and these the mental trajectories, now to be accommodated by this complexly capacious form.

In his Christmas sermon at St Paul's Cathedral in 1624 Donne proposes to correlate syntactic and semantic circuitry with widening and deepening connotations of the sun as the image of sovereign divinity. He embarks on a round of reflections on seasonal and diurnal variations of the sun and its light, phenomena which would have been in abeyance on a late December evening in London:

If some King of the earth have so large an extent of Dominion, in North, and South, as that he hath Winter and Summer together in his Dominions, so large an extent East and West, as that he hath day and night together in his Dominions, much more hath God mercy and judgement together: He brought light out of darknesse, not out of a lesser light; he can bring thy Summer out of Winter, though thou have no Spring; though in the wayes of fortune, or understanding, or conscience, thou have been benighted till now, wintred and frozen, clouded and eclypsed, damped and benummed, smothered and stupified till now, now God comes to thee, not as in the bud of the spring, but as the Sun at noon to illustrate all shadowes, as the sheaves in harvest, to fill all penuries, all occasions invite his mercies, and all times are his seasons.[25]

Expanding towards the compass points, 'North, and South', 'East and West', periodicity begins to take shape in the recognisable forms of interlaced binary constructions, 'If some king have . . . much more hath God', and the reiterated and reinforcing sequence, 'so large . . . as that . . . so large . . . as that', itself intensified by a heavy quotient of verbatim repetition: 'so large an extent', 'together in his Dominions'. The pivot, 'much more hath God mercy and judgment together', qualifies syntactically as a sentence ending as well, which could provide an appropriate periodic close. But the colon punctuation forecloses any such closure, introducing instead a new syntactic initiative, not hinged on any conjunction, but sustained by redoubled, closely synonymous phrases and clauses whose insistent rhythmic patterning derives its force from repetition within variation: 'He brought . . . he can bring . . . though thou have . . . thou have been', 'wintred and frozen . . . smothered and stupified', 'till now . . . till now'. The urgent rhythms of this new syntactic initiative ostensibly propel the thought on a course of development beyond the earlier pivot on the conjunction of

God's mercy and judgement. But the sequence – 'he can bring thy Summer out of Winter, though . . . thou have been benighted till now, . . . wintred . . . till now' – is, for the most part, a drum-roll at a standstill. Rhythm has advanced, but thought has not, for the new syntactic initiative is a close semantic equivalent of the preceding pivotal clause. Significantly, however, the locutions have become personal with the sudden introduction and reiteration of direct address – 'thou', 'thou'. While periodic effect is temporarily suspended, and no movement occurs along a larger trajectory, the meaning first phrased impersonally – God hath mercy and judgment together – attains aphoristic effect in a memorably personal encapsulation: 'He can bring thy Summer out of Winter, though thou have no Spring.'

While intact and self-sufficient from one perspective, this encapsulation now devolves through engagement in the series of 'though' constructions, modulating into another new syntactic initiative which, this time, also comprises a new semantic initiative. The pivot is on 'now, now', not another verbatim repetition, but two distinctly different adverbs: the 'now' of 'till now' the object of an adverbial phrase expressing sequential time; the 'now' of 'now God comes to thee' an adverbial conjunction introducing a new clause and a new, paradoxically atemporal sense of the present. No longer is Donne discoursing about the diurnal and seasonal round of the sun as an image of God's workings in the soul. He is speaking, rather, of supernatural suddenness and immediacy, of a decisive breaking-in of the divine upon the human, to make a transformative impact. But the attendant syntactic expression is not ruptural; it sustains the further development of thought. The interlinkages of periodic sentence-form resume with an antithetical binary correlation, 'not as . . . but as', whose latter member becomes the first of a pair of parallel constructions: 'as the sun at noon to illustrate all shadows, as the sheaves in harvest to fill all penuries'. At this point, again, periodicity pivots to apparent completeness with another syntactically possible sentence-ending, replete with phrasal and clausal correspondences. Yet, again, Donne refuses closure after 'penuries', instead appending with the minimal hinge of comma punctuation a pair of simple sentence-units, parallel in form, closely synonymous in meaning, and rhythmically joined to what precedes them by their reiteration of 'all': 'all occasions invite his mercies, and all times are his seasons'. Contrapuntally positioned to follow three successive circuits of periodicity, the paired simple sentence-units conclude this complexly sustained discursive construction with a striking example of aphoristic effect.[26] Yet the aphorisms and the periodicity conduce to one and the same recognition, the encompassing thought of God's goodness to humankind – also the central meaning of the occasion, Christmas.

As the seventeenth century continued its course, the dual sensibility displayed in combining aphoristic effect with an enlarged, relaxed periodicity found a mode of consolidation. This typically took the form of the four-membered period that Quintilian had favoured, with the further specifications, from Vives, of a four-square structure holding together without plaster or mortar – evidently, clauses integrated without explicit connectives.[27] Despite the retention of the name 'period' by rhetorical theorists, it is obvious that any such four-membered sentence, if paratactically assembled, will be markedly different. It will not develop as a traceable circuit of one or more turns proceeding to its anticipated close, and confirmed in its ending. Instead, cohesion will rely on semantic intuition, keyed by phrasing and by theme, to group the four members as a set or to make pairings based on likeness or difference. Alternatively, if conjunctions are supplied, the demands on intuition will be lessened, but compactness will eliminate the sense of a circuit.[28] The eventual mode of consolidation finds realisation in English neoclassical style – particularly in the elegant antitheses and correlatives of Alexander Pope's rhymed couplets. Nonetheless, as early as the 1630s, Ben Jonson both anticipates the new mode of the incised, squared period and suggests how his own conception of it took shape as he selectively appropriates and silently recasts borrowings from Vives and Bacon on prose composition in *Timber, or Discoveries*.

In the discussion that draws on Vives' *De ratione dicendi*, Jonson registers more acutely than any of his English predecessors Vives' profoundly social conception of language and the conditions of its use. In Jonson's distillation, 'Speech is the only benefit man hath to express his excellencie of mind above other creatures. It is the Instrument of Society.' But as he proceeds to take up a subject which Vives elaborates, the necessity of ordering words and sentences so that they will be open and understandable to one's hearers, Jonson waxes short. He imposes sharp limits on authorial responsibility. He emphasises the failings of hearers or readers – as the presupposed medium slides from speech to writing – and he drives a qualitative distinction, not found in Vives, between the writer's self-understanding and the readers' lack of understanding:

As wee must take the care that our words and sense bee cleare; so, if the obscurity happen through the Hearers, or Readers want of understanding, I am not to answer for them; no more then for their not listening or marking; I must neither find them eares, nor mind; But a man cannot put a word so in sense, but some thing about it will illustrate it, if the Writer understand himselfe. For Order helpes much to Perspicuity, as Confusion hurts.[29]

As a consequence of Jonson's sharp distinction between writer and readers, Vives' conception of order as the fundamental means by which language becomes broadly intelligible and communicative contracts into Jonson's conception: order as the manifestation of the writer's self-understanding, a property of his mind. His own curt, declarative style intermittently pre-figures the thought movements that will find congenial expression in the incised, squared period: 'I am not to answer for them'; 'I must neither find them ears, nor mind.' Unsurprisingly, moreover, Jonson distils into one compact sentence Vives' more discursive commendation of the four-membered period, and in a following sentence revises Vives' warning about excessive length into his own further commendation of brevity: 'The con-gruent, and harmonious fitting of parts in a sentence, hath almost the fastening, and force of knitting, and connexion: as in stones well squar'd, which will rise strong a great way without mortar. Periods are beautifull when they are not too long; for so they have their strength too, as in a Pike or Javelin.'[30] Significant divergences between Vives' image and Jonson's own additions, including 'harmonious fitting of parts' and 'rise strong a great way' climax in the final addition, 'beautiful when they are not too long, for so they have their strength too'. Vives had written: 'When the members are many or too long, the strength of the period is weakened, as with a very long spear when it is thrown.'[31] Jonson declares for the emergent new mode – the incised, squared period – on the weight of his authorial judgment, itself grounded in his assertion and demonstration of self-knowledge.

Jonson begins to wind down his treatment of prose composition by reflecting on what he and the majority of his English predecessors clas-sify under 'figura', 'the figure and feature in Language'. In the matter of sentence-form, he offers his readers and the would-be authors among them an either-or choice between the circle and the square: 'whether it be round, and streight, which consists of short and succinct Periods, numerous and polish'd; or square and firme, which is to have equall and strong parts, every where answerable, and weighed'. His confidence in the intrinsic superior-ity of the squared sentence reaches a revealing height in his wording of a subsequent task that he puts to his readers. Jonson recasts a passage from Bacon's *Advancement of Learning*: 'Make exact animadversion where style hath degenerated, where flourish'd, and thriv'd in choisenesse of Phrase, round and cleane composition of sentence, sweet falling of the clause, varying an illustration by tropes and figures, weight of Matter, worth of Subject, soundnesse of Argument, life of Invention, and depth of Judgement.'[32] What Bacon had presorted, prejudged, and denounced as a negative turn in the history of Renaissance prose style – a pursuit 'more after the choiceness of the phrase, and the round and clean composition of the sentence . . . than after the weight of matter, worth of subject, soundness of argument, life of invention, or depth of judgment' – Jonson conflates into a spectrum of stylistic possibility in prose, relying on those readers who share his self-knowledge, his confidence, and his values to make the repeated choice for weight, worth, soundness, life of invention, and depth of judgement. Doing so will require them to hone their sentence forms deliberately and laboriously to the incised, square period. Jonson is emphatic about that.

Thus while, at mid-century and thereafter, Milton would marshal the resources of the rounded, multi-membered, intricately elaborated period at appropriate junctures in his English prose tracts, and Edward Hyde, Earl of Clarendon, would rely at key junctures on authoritatively spread main clauses in composing his post-Civil War *History of the Rebellion*,[33] the literary future would confirm Jonson's predilection for the succinct, incised, squared sentence, behind which stands Bacon's praise of the aphorism. This future would bring a more normative, less exploratory, and less experimental approach to the writing of prose than that afforded in the expansive, intricate, purpose-driven circuitry that is the glory but, ultimately, also the liability of the English Renaissance periodic sentence. Except in its aphoristic and rhythmically highlighted moments, it proves finally too demanding by the measures of human attention and memory. Since these same measures were the bases on which Aristotle first distinguished and commended this mode of sentence composition, a longer perspective on early-modern developments enables us to recognise the so-called 'neoclassical' period and its attendant formal features not as definitive or final, but as one among several in a series of historically specific uses to which the prodigious linguistic capacities of periodos have been productively subjected in English.

CHAPTER 4

Paronomasia is a figure which declineth into a contrarie by a likelihood of letters, either added, changed, or taken away . . .

Antanaclasis is a figure which repeateth a word that hath two significa-tions, and the one of them contrary, or at least, unlike to the other.
Henry Peacham, The Garden of Eloquence (1593)

Syllepsis, when . . . one word serveth to many sences . . .
Angel Day, A Declaration of . . . Tropes, Figures or Schemes (1592)

Hap'ly that name of chast, unhap'ly set
This batelesse edge on his keene appetite . . .
William Shakespeare, The Rape of Lucrece (1594)

That led me to the wilde of Passion, which
          Some call the wold;
   A wasted place, but sometimes rich.
   Here I was robb'd of all my gold,
Save one good Angell, which a friend had ti'd
          Close to my side.
George Herbert, The Pilgrimage (1633)

Puns: serious wordplay

SOPHIE READ

In rhetorical terms, the pun is something of an anomaly. It is not a category the ancient authorities recognised, nor is it to be found in any sixteenth-century handbook of rhetoric. Aristotle and Quintilian are silent on the subject; Puttenham doesn't mention it, nor does Peacham, or Hoskins, or Day. One might conjecture, considering its marked absence from their treatises, that Renaissance writers had no use for the word – that they didn't know what punning was. And one would be half right. The Elizabethans and the Jacobeans *did* pun, of course: they were notorious for the practice. But that isn't what they called it. This detail did not, however, discourage subsequent commentators. 'The Age in which the punn chiefly flourished,' writes the early eighteenth-century critic Joseph Addison in the *Spectator*, 'was the Reign of King *James* the First.' His incredulity at the insidiousness of the device, which he considers a very low form of wit indeed, is barely concealed; that it should be found in the most serious works of the greatest writers of the time is, for him, particularly bewildering: 'The sermons of Bishop *Andrews*, and the Tragedies of *Shakespear*, are full of them. The Sinner was Punned into Repentance by the former, as in the Latter nothing is more usual than to see a Hero weeping and quibbling for a dozen lines together.'[1] The sort of wordplay now comprehended by the catch-all term 'pun' was described instead in the sixteenth and early seventeenth centuries with a panoply of rhetorical figures, their names taken, as was customary, from classical sources. This chapter will consider the chief among them – syllepsis, antanaclasis and paronomasia – as they appear in Andrewes' sermons and Shakespeare's tragedies. It will attempt to confront the astonishment of an Addison, and to separate and characterise the very different punning strategies of bishop and playwright here lumped together as indistinguishable occasion for contempt. Ultimately, the aim is to recover a sense of what these men and their immediate contemporaries thought they were doing when they were playing with their words: to understand not only how the rhetorical turns work in their literary context, but also why their deployment was so absolutely natural in the early seventeenth century and so unthinkably strange a bare century later.

The problem is partly one of terminology. It was not until a generation after this period of most inventive and determined wordplay that the term by which it is now most commonly known appeared, and this presents significant problems of definition and interpretation.[2] The *OED* has the word witnessed first in this sense in 1662, citing as the earliest instance of its use Dryden's play *The Wild Gallant*, where it occurs as part of an anatomy of dubious wit: 'A bare Clinch will serve the turn; a Carwichet, a Quarterquibble, or a Punn.' It has, however, been antedated twenty or so years to a royalist pamphlet published in Oxford during the civil war; even here, though, the pun is found shuffling into a line-up of the usual frivolous forms, those suspect devices of degenerate humour avoided by the discerning intelligence: 'Quibbles, Crops, Clinches, Puns, Halfe-jests, jests, fine sentences, witty sayings'.[3] Ever since its introduction into the language, 'pun' has been a disdainful term for what was by Addison's time regarded quite unequivocally as a vice, and never an ornament, of style; a word no Elizabethan would have recognised is used to accuse the authors of the age of a flawed and defective literary sensibility – a misplaced levity that expresses itself in this clownish verbal sporting.

The process of recovery is far from straightforward. There is, to begin with, no very exact correspondence between the nomenclature of the rhetoricians and the slang terms – 'quibble', 'clench', 'catch', and above all 'pun' itself – that coexisted with and then supplanted it. The difference is one of precision, and of prestige. While to deploy the figure of antana-clasis and to quibble on a word are, in effect, more or less the same thing, it is clear that if what a writer conceives of and intends as the former is thought of by a reader as the latter, an interpretative fissure has opened: the flowers of rhetoric evidently do not smell as sweet by any other names. The situation is complicated further by a lack of consensus among the rhetoricians themselves as to what constitutes which device: to distinguish and provide working definitions for the three main rhetorical figures which constitute the pun is a necessary, but necessarily inexact, act of restitution.[4] Syllepsis is a case in point; though the term is only arguably understood to mean a particular kind of wordplay in the Renaissance, no alternative designation exists. This chapter, following Sister Miriam Joseph's influen-tial example, will take it to refer to the type of pun where a single word or sound has two meanings, both of which are operated by the context either to complementary or ironic effect.[5] When Othello cries 'O perjur'd woman, thou do'st stone my heart', for example, he intends a lament about the injuries Desdemona's supposed infidelity inflicts on him: his heart is battered, stoned, the fate marked out for the woman taken in adultery in the Gospel of St John.[6] He also, however, describes the consequence of this perception on his resolve: his heart is become stone, hardened to its murderous purpose. The pun, 'stone', is subtle. It doesn't draw attention to itself: the intelligibility of the line is not compromised if only one of the senses is taken, its meaning rather enriched if both are understood. The grammatical construction releases a fruitful ambiguity latent in the word, and it does so without strain, either phonological or conceptual: that the two senses are clearly related etymologically lends the connection a kind of legitimacy, and it is this that Othello exploits as sanction for his terrible determination. 'You stone my heart, which inevitably turns my heart to stone against you': the neatness of the syllepsis, based though it is on a misconstruction, acts as a fleeting confirmation of his decision to kill what has hurt him. Desdemona's death is justified by the semantic accident of the pun.

The modern sensibility prefers the mechanics of a rhetorical effect to be hidden from view; anything which smacks of contrivance or artifice, any construction which leaves the scaffolding in place, is regarded with some suspicion. Syllepsis can display virtuosity, and this has won for it a measure of acceptance; the single word that conceals multiple meanings offers the intellectual satisfaction of their discovery. 'There is great joy to be had from puns', as Stephen Booth recognises, 'but all of it ordinarily belongs to the person who senses opportunity in a linguistic situation.'[7] In other words, the more obvious the pun to the reader (regardless of what feats of ingenuity went into its fabrication), the less pleasure there is to be derived from it. This is perhaps why antanaclasis, the figure in which a word occurs and is then repeated in a different sense, has never been rehabilitated even to the extent that syllepsis has; the repetition flags the effect, and it shades from being clever into being clever-clever. This hasn't always been the case. In the Renaissance, obviousness was no impediment to joy: quite the opposite, in fact. The elusiveness of an adequate contemporary term, or indeed a clear definition, for the wordplay that exploits the multiple meanings of a single word, gestures at a certain caution: the very obscurity that recommends syllepsis to a modern reader may well have seemed to a contemporary one mere accidental ambiguity. In *The Garden of Eloquence*, Peacham describes the enjoyment to be found in a well-turned antanaclasis, but makes clear the importance of its distinction: two senses demand two words. 'This figure as it uniteth two words of one sounde', he writes, 'so it distinguisheth them asunder by the diversitie of their sence, wherby it moveth many times a most pleasant kind of civile mirth.'[8] When Andrewes employs the device in his sermon for Ash Wednesday 1619, if it isn't mirth to which he wishes to move his congregation, an antanaclasis is undoubtedly occasion for reverent delight. His intention is to point out to his auditors the happy coincidence of a word's meanings, and to use the accident to underwrite a devotional imperative: 'the *first day of Lent*; it fitts well, as a welcome into this time, a time *lent* us (as it were) by GOD'.[9] The modern ear assigns to such repetition a squib-like ring of redundancy: the perception is overwhelmingly one of similarity, and the interest of difference has to be worked for.

The last of these punning figures, paronomasia, is perhaps the most contrived of all; it depends not on the diversity of meanings to be mined from one word, as syllepsis and antanaclasis do, but on finding a likeness of sound between two different words: the connection thus forged can pretend to no validity except that of phonetic coincidence. Peacham warns that it ought to be 'sparingly used, and especially in grave and weightie causes': that it is a 'light and illuding forme', which 'seemeth not to be found without meditation and affected labor'.[10] Contemporary awareness of its hazards, however, prevented neither Shakespeare nor Andrewes from employing paronomasia in the most serious of contexts. Desdemona, for example, catches her husband's habit of wordplay in trying to determine the reasons for his sudden coldness towards her; 'I cannot say Whore', she asserts, immediately before saying its sound again: 'It do's abhorre me now I speake the word' (4.2). Andrewes' associative imagination takes a slightly different turn: he uses a phonetic similarity to emphasise an opposition, wondering at the reverence of the splendid magi for the humble Christ-child in the stable at Bethlehem: was He not, Andrewes questions, 'More like to be *abhorred* than *adored* of such Persons?'[11]

Over and over, the force of the gathering objection to punning in general and to paronomasia in particular seems to have been that the fortuitousness of the connections it insists on makes it fundamentally a comic device; its appearance on the lips of a dying hero or, perhaps even more shockingly, at the climax of a sermon, came increasingly to be regarded as wilfully and absurdly inappropriate. Robert South, in his 1660 sermon 'The Scribe Instructed', makes it clear that his objection to the presence of puns in the pulpit is on religious as well as stylistic grounds; he sees a dangerous influence in those preachers who strive for elegance of expression, with 'their sermons so garnished with quibbles and trifles, as if they played with truth and immortality; and neither believed these things themselves, nor were willing that others should'.[12] For South, himself a witty and careful sermon-writer, wordplay in such a context betrays an irreligious levity bordering on the blasphemous: that it should stem from a sincere theological conviction is clearly inconceivable.

Andrewes' particular brand of high-church Anglicanism and his predilection for the jingling sound-effect left him to languish unread and unthought-about until T. S. Eliot's attempted rehabilitation at the start of the last century; the case of the man with whom he shares Addison's censure is, however, rather different.[13] Critical engagement with Shakespeare's puns has been long-standing and profound, from an Augustan distaste which culminated in the strident condemnation of Samuel Johnson, through Coleridge's spirited but impressionistic defence, to the modern and more positive reassessment initiated by Empson and followed by the studies of Sister Miriam Joseph and Molly Mahood in the 1940s and 1950s. Johnson first. His judgement is decided, expressed with customary vigour, and worth quoting almost in full:

A quibble is to *Shakespeare*, what luminous vapours are to the traveller; he follows it at all adventures, it is sure to lead him out of his way, and sure to engulf him in the mire. It has some malignant power over his mind, and its fascinations are irresistible . . . A quibble is the golden apple for which he will always turn aside from his career, or stoop from his elevation. A quibble poor and barren as it is, gave him such delight, that he was content to purchase it, by the sacrifice of reason, propriety and truth. A quibble was to him the fatal *Cleopatra* for which he lost the world, and was content to lose it.[14]

To this eighteenth-century sensibility, the pun was anathema, and to suggest that Johnson has a sneaking fondness or at least a subconscious weakness for it (as Mahood does in pointing out his own play on 'fatal' as both 'deadly' and 'destined') clearly goes against the spirit of this fulmination.[15] It is, however, more nuanced a criticism than is sometimes recognised. Johnson's chief objection is not necessarily to puns in general, though he certainly doesn't have much time for them, but once again to puns in tragedy, where they disturb, distract, divert: immediately before the passage just quoted, he complains that 'terrour and pity' – emotions which it is of course, according to Aristotle, the function of tragedy to provoke – 'as they are rising in the mind, are checked and blasted by sudden frigidity', and it is in this context that the attack is made.[16] The indecorousness of the inevitably comic quibble interrupting at a moment of high seriousness, in other words, ruins Johnson's mood.

It is evident, then, that what the early critics of Andrewes and Shakespeare fasten on is the improper positioning of their puns; but why should there have been such a reductive shift in the perception of the pun's range? Word-play was, of course, to be found in humorous contexts in the Renaissance, but it was not confined to them. It is unlikely, for example, that Siward's comment on the death of his son, at the bloody climax of *Macbeth*, was ever intended either to prompt a moment of relaxing laughter or to compromise the seriousness of the scene: 'Had I as many Sonnes, as I have haires, | I would not wish them to a fairer death' (5.7). The play on the homophone 'hairs' / 'heirs' does not diminish the old man's pride or his grief; though even white hairs far outnumber children, he had exactly as many sons as heirs, and the intrusion of this sense points up the loss as it underscores the anxieties of inheritance and succession that colour the play. Kenneth Muir, in his consideration of the Shakespearean pun in general and the punning in *Macbeth* in particular, describes the significance of the change: 'The banishing of the pun except for comic purposes was the symbol of a radical defeat: it was a turning away from the genius of the language.'[17] Given what is lost by an attitude as rigid as Addison's or Johnson's, an explanation for this revolution in feeling must be sought. It is not simply that the weight of paronomasia in the blanket term 'pun' drags syllepsis and antanaclasis with it to the bottom, though that is undoubtedly a factor; at work, too, are the forces of historical linguistics and philosophical advance. The first obstacle for an eighteenth-century reader of Shakespeare's plays or Andrewes' sermons is precisely that he *is* a reader: as Sylvia Adamson points out, 'sermons and drama, dominant genres in the . . . period, are both performance arts and their oral/aural mode of operation provides the most favouring conditions for the pun'.[18] The coincidence of sound that reaches an elegant and momentary consummation in the ear of an auditor can, however, have rather a different aspect on the page, where the necessity of transcription fixes it in one form only ('hairs'), leaving the other ('heirs') to ghost the word as an illegitimate, if insistent, alternative. The difficulty is exacerbated by the move towards a standardisation of spelling that made such decisions more pressing than they had been up to that point; many words that an Elizabethan could, if he liked, spell a number of ways – 'hart'/'heart' is a frequent example from the courtly lyrics of the period, or 'deer'/'dear' – lose the easy intrinsic ambiguity they had previously enjoyed. The eye perceives an arrangement of letters which designate a particular thing, regardless of what the sound associated with that arrangement might also signify; attempts to operate a subsidiary meaning begin to seem forced or contrived.

The impulse to standardise spelling that hobbled so many puns in par-ticular was prompted by an alteration in attitude towards the language that condemned their use in general. From the second half of the seventeenth century, the sense that there was some power immanent in words which could allow even their accidental correspondences to suggest meaningful, almost magical, links, started to fade; in its place grew a belief that plainness and transparency were the qualities most to be admired, and consequently that the rhetorical embellishments which encouraged ambiguity were an irritating defect. This dictum found its most notorious expression in Thomas Sprat's opinion that an achievable ideal would be to return the language to some sort of (entirely imaginary) 'primitive' state, 'when men deliver'd so many *things*, almost in an equal number of *words*'.[19] Such a system could clearly have no place for punning. That neither Andrewes nor Shakespeare would have sympathised with Sprat's rationalising semantics is evident from their habit of routinely shoe-horning two things into one word; but though the two writers appear together in the *Spectator*'s stocks because of this bare and embarrassing fact, a more measured consideration reveals a distinction not just in how they pun, but in the beliefs about language that inspired them to do it.

Take, for example, a fairly obvious instance of antanaclasis, found in both authors and previously offered by Puttenham, in two lines of rather lumpen verse, as an illustration of the figure: 'To pray for you ever I cannot refuse, | To pray upon you I should you much abuse.'[20] When Shakespeare exploits the opportunity offered by words of such contrasting senses sharing a sound, it is as a throwaway line in the mouth of one of Falstaff's rascally companions in *I Henry IV*: 'they pray continually unto their Saint the Common-wealth; or rather, not to pray to her, but prey on her' (2.1). As might be expected from a man of his calling and habits of composition, Andrewes approaches the same correspondence in a spirit of serious enquiry which nonetheless works itself out in an intricate pattern of wordplay. He doesn't believe in coincidence: accidents of language are made to witness the fundamental truths of his religion, and a similarity in sound, even one so apparently unpromising as that between 'pray' and 'prey', can always be turned to spiritual account. No pun is too contrived, no connection thus arrived at too far-fetched; all are evidence of a divinely instituted linguistic order that can be intuited or reconstituted by the loving intensity of his exegetical intelligence.

It is Ash-Wednesday in 1622, and Andrewes is discussing hypocrisy. The terms in which he introduces his meditation demonstrate quite conclusively that he did not consider himself to be 'playing with truth and immortality', whatever South's opinion; they should also caution against too ready a conflation of Andrewes' practice with Shakespeare's. 'There want not,' he begins, 'that make His *Church* a very *Stage*; and *play with Religion*, and *play Religion* and every part of it: so carrying themselves in things pertaining to GOD, as if they had some *Play* or *Pageant* in hand.'[21] For Andrewes, there is no contradiction in playing with the word 'play' – as he does by engineering the antanaclasis that divides and distinguishes its three senses – in the cause of condemning those who don't take their worship sufficiently seriously; it is as if faith is proof enough against the possibility of this kind of conflict.[22] And from playing, he moves, through the logic of paronomasia, to praying: 'Will you see *Prayer* playd? Looke upon the *Players* . . . that under colour of *a long prayer*, now and then *prey upon the houses* and goods of a sort of *seduced widowes*: and make as good gaine of their Prayers, as *Judas* would have done of his *Almes*.'[23] In Andrewes' hands, the pun that provided Puttenham and Shakespeare with occasion for a smart but glancing witticism takes on a more profound resonance: it contrives to insist with graceful economy on the treacherous rapacity of the religious hypocrite. That 'prey' and 'pray' share a sound is construed as a warning against the dangers of letting the appearance of devotion be taken for its reality, a warning that it is Andrewes' duty to amplify through expository punning. The word must be held down and unmasked, its two senses separated and searched so that one cannot be concealed by the other.

Punning for Andrewes is a positive articulation of faith, because he believes that his scrutiny will turn up shards of revelatory meaning: the dispersed and fragmentary evidence of a perfect linguistic order, distorted by disobedience – Babel, and before that the Fall – and lost beneath the accretions of time and use. Those who attack punning in the pulpit for its irreligiosity fail to realise that it might be motivated not by an unseemly sportive humour, but by this bent for devotional archaeology. Puns are *objets trouvés*, and the meaning they generate cannot be manufactured, only ever discovered. Andrewes displays an unshakeable belief in the significance and the authenticity of the connections he unearths – all puns must be of divine institution, and both share in the power and follow the precedent of the pun on which the Church itself was founded: 'thou art Peter [*Petrus*], and upon this rock [*petram*] I will build my church' (Mat. 16:18). Indeed, as a formidable linguist (he was one of the translators of the King James Bible), Andrewes is ever alive to the possibility of Scriptural punning; consider his explanation of a happy Hebraic coincidence:

It will not be amisse to tell you; The *word*, that is *Hebrew* for *flesh*, the same is also *Hebrew*, for *good tydings*, (as we call it, *the Gospell*:) Sure, not without the *Holy Ghost* so dispensing it. There could be no other meaning; but that, some *Incarnation*, or *Making flesh*, should be generally *good newes* for the whole world.[24]

His evident delight in uncovering a pun which can be seen to confirm the mystical union of the word and the flesh is underpinned by his sense of its rightness in theological terms: 'There could', he asserts, 'be no other meaning.' Nor is Andrewes in any doubt as to how such an apt correspondence might have been instituted in the language; it is there because the Holy Ghost willed it so, and to dust it off and interpret the implications is both a proof of faith and a devotional act.

There is another theological dimension to Andrewes' incessant wordplay. As Peter McCullough astutely observes, 'It is not an exaggeration to say that Andrewes has a sacramental understanding of language', and this understanding expresses itself through the rhetorical structures of his sermons.[25] Part of the point of punning is to insist that a word can be two things at once: that it can comprehend two meanings simultaneously, and that the relationship thus established between them has an objective validity. As an ordained priest, Andrewes was empowered to administer the Holy Communion. The mysterious transformation by which bread and wine become body and blood, where a substance can signify twice in the same space, exerts a powerful creative pull; this deep interest is reflected not just in the subject of the sermons, but in their style. Andrewes' punning animates his prose with greatest intensity when form and substance coincide: when his rhetoric reaches for a way to articulate the incarnation of the Word in Christ and its permanent reiteration on earth, the sacrament of the Eucharist. The pun which lodged most rewardingly in his imagination exemplifies this dynamic: over the course of a dozen years, Andrewes returns four times to the pun immanent in the Word being silenced into flesh as it becomes speechless (in Latin, *infans*) in the infant Jesus. In 1606, when it occurs to him first, he pauses only briefly to notice the humility of Christ's coming wordless into the world: 'Great, *ut Verbum*, *infans* . . . that the *word*, not be hable to *speake a word*; He, that *thundereth* in heaven *cry* in a *cradle*.'[26] The bilingual paronomasia that finds 'infant' in *infans* is reinforced by an antanaclasis at once so commonplace and so profound that it seems strange to classify it as a rhetorical device; it is the conceptual correspondence at the centre of the Christian religion, between words as the currency of human communication and the Word made flesh: Christ.

Five years later, in a sermon ringing with triumphantly revelatory wordplay, it is the question of corporeality that arrests Andrewes. He lights again on the moment of the incarnation: 'I adde yet further: what *flesh*? The flesh of an *Infant*. What, *Verbum Infans*, the *Word* an *Infant*? The *Word*, and not be able to speake a word?'[27] The etymological connections between *infans* and 'infant' allow Andrewes to claim an unassailable authority in his argument; as the Word is made speechless in being bodied forth as a child, so Andrewes tries the analogous trick of making his own words solidify into tangible proof of the incarnation, pulling the two terms together and waiting to see what will issue. Here, he performs a Eucharistic transformation on a linguistic level: an imitative devotional act. Why puns are at once so dear to Andrewes and so abhorrent to his critics is because they are unearned: puns must either be accepted as a gift or rejected as cheating. Andrewes' fourth and final articulation of the *infans* pun, in the sermon delivered on Christmas Day 1618, expresses above all his reverent delight at the providential coincidence of meaning. This time, he invites his congregation to marvel not just at what the pun might signify, but at the fact that it should exist at all: '*Signes* are taken for wonders: (*Master we would faine see a Signe*, that is, a *miracle*.) And, in this sense, it is a *Signe*, to wonder at. Indeed, every word (heer) is a wonder . . . *an infant*; *Verbum infans*, the *Word* without a *word*; the æternall *Word* not hable to speake a *word*; A wonder sure.'[28] Every word is a sign, a wonder. Andrewes accepts the pun as a mark of grace, undeserved and unfathomable but freely given nevertheless, just as he accepts the miracle of the incarnation and the mystery of the Eucharist. Punning is a natural form of discourse for a man of such sacrament-centred piety; the Eucharist is, after all, a mystery which transcends human reason and can be apprehended only by faith. It is also the most perfect pun of all: divine and human take place in the same Word, distinct but indistinguishable.

Andrewes' wordplay, then, has a specifically devotional intent, and to criticise it, as Addison does, for representing an inappropriate and frivolous intrusion into the serious business of sermon-making is to miss the point. But such a defence clearly cannot extend to Shakespeare's puns: though the implacable enmity of pulpit and stage in the sixteenth and seventeenth centuries is often overstated, not least by the preachers and playwrights themselves, the ends of each are very different, however similar-sounding the means. The active theological engagement that underpins Andrewes' prose doesn't shore up Shakespeare's verse in the same way; his inspiration and authority have a different foundation. And there is a distinction at the level of practice as well as of theory: to restore to the pun the diversity of its Renaissance nomenclature is, among other things, to reveal a subtle difference in the rhetorical strategies of the two writers. Though the works of both are scattered with antanaclasis and paronomasia, Andrewes hardly ever uses syllepsis, the figure which is the vehicle for some of Shakespeare's most searching and profound wordplay. This could, in part, be due to the figure's uncertain status in the period: its conflation with the grammatical turn, its potential to shade over into the vice of ambiguity.[29] Mahood, in describing the attitude of an Elizabethan preacher to his text, gestures at another reason: 'A simple piece of poetic parallelism is developed into two topics on the assumption that where there are two words there are two things.'[30] Andrewes, in other words, dismantles the word to show how it works. He is more concerned to resolve than to generate (or risk) ambiguity, to exfoliate and explicate layers of existent meaning rather than to leave, as Shakespeare does, a pregnant word in an audience's ear. Andrewes' habit is patiently to unearth the scattered constituent senses or resonances of a word; Shakespeare's swift syllepses mark the spot where such meanings lie buried, but the listener is left to labour the pun himself.

Consider, for example, the peculiarly loaded quality of Lady Macbeth's grim punning as she frames the servants at the scene of her husband's crime. 'If he doe bleed, | Ile guild the Faces of the Groomes withall, | For it must seeme their Guilt' (2.2). The verb, 'guild', activates the secondary sense of 'Guilt' – its homophone 'gilt', the thin layer of gold, or a substance that looks like it, used to decorate or disguise a surface. What might seem like antanaclasis, if 'guild' and 'Guilt' sound close enough, or paronomasia if they don't, resolves itself as syllepsis. The two senses of 'Guilt' are operated in the instant that word is heard to generate a macabre joke: the royal blood with which the innocent grooms are gilded will mark them out as guilty of the crime. Perhaps, as Muir speculates, this wordplay is 'to suggest the overwrought condition of Lady Macbeth's nerves and her contempt for her husband's lack of self-control',[31] or perhaps, as Johnson would no doubt rather have concluded, it is there because Shakespeare never could resist the *ignis fatuus* of that particular pun, especially in the context of kingship. He uses it in *2 Henry IV* ('England, shall double gill'd, his trebble guilt' (4.2)), *Henry V* ('for the Gilt of France (O guilt indeed)' (1.1)), and in *Richard II* ('Wipe off the dust that hides our Scepters gilt' (2.1)). E. E. Kellett's judgement seems just: 'It is certain that Shakspere would not have resisted the quibble even if its effect had been to spoil the force of the scene.'[32] It is not only this scene whose force is intensified by the pun, however. When Macbeth comes to excuse himself for the expedient execution of the gilded grooms, his wife's gory witticism has stuck in his throat: he blames the affecting sight of Duncan's 'Silver skinne, lac'd with his Golden Blood' (2.3) for their too-hasty dispatch. Her conflation of 'guilt' with 'gilt' suggests his adjective 'golden', whose resonance as a description of royal blood is deepened by the history of interchangeability between the colours of red and gold.[33] 'Golden', in turn, calls forth 'silver': aged, and ashen in death, as well as precious. The hypocrisy of the whole is sharpened by the

unspoken presence of the originary pun, with its further associations of
the fraudulent, the ersatz; Lady Macbeth's feigned faint ('Helpe me hence,
hoa' (2.3)) is an apt termination to her husband's performance.

This type of syllepsis – at once dense and fleeting – is evidently very
different from the leisurely declensions through which Andrewes puts his
antanaclases. In a sermon, transparency is paramount; this is not to say that
there can be no place for rhetorical sophistication or intellectual acrobat-
ics, but what is clear to the preacher he must attempt to make clear to his
congregation. In a play, the characters betray themselves, either deliberately
or unwittingly, through their speech: to themselves, to those they share a
stage with, and to the audience. Sometimes the playwright betrays himself
through his characters. The punning rhetoric of Shakespeare's tragedies, in
its varying degrees of complexity, is one way of negotiating these unstable economies of concealment and revelation. King Richard, for example,
knows exactly what he says when he bends Bullingbrooke's command to a
bitter joke:

BULLINGBROKE   Goe some of you, convey him to the Tower.
RICHARD   Oh good: convey: Conveyers are you all
               That rise thus nimbly by a true Kings fall.

(4.1)

The two principal meanings of 'convey' ('to escort' and 'to steal; to manage
with secrecy, privacy or craft') are here exploited to allow an open statement
of grievance; the quibble is Richard's, and its force is meant to be felt by all
who hear it. Othello, in contrast, can have no notion of how double-edged
is the word with which he commits Desdemona to Iago's care: 'A man he
is of honesty and trust: | To his conveyance I assigne my wife' (1.3). This
time, the pun must be the verbal equivalent of the playwright winking at
the audience, should any member of it be sufficiently alert to notice: no
one on stage can yet register the sinister subsidiary meaning.

Johnson's objection to Shakespeare's rhetorical practice in this respect is
predicated on the assumption that all puns are alien in the mouths of the
characters that speak them: that a pun can never be the authentic expression of a mind labouring under strong emotion, and so must always be the
tricksy interpolation of a playwright led 'out of his way' by the deceptive
charms of a piece of verbal ingenuity. This criticism, and the observation
on which it is founded, are refuted forcefully by Coleridge: 'No one can
have heard quarrels among the vulgar but must have noticed the close connexion of punning with angry contempt.' Elsewhere, on the same subject,
he writes: 'I have no hesitation in saying that a pun, if it be congruous with

the feeling of a scene, is not only allowable in the dramatic dialogue, but oftentimes one of the most effectual intensives of passion.'[34] Coleridge is, here, defending a particular instance of a marked pattern in Shakespeare's wordplay: old Gaunt on his death-bed, sporting with the senses of his name. 'Gaunt I am for the grave', he tells Richard, 'gaunt as a grave.' The king's response is echoed with growing incredulity by the critics of subsequent generations: 'Can sicke men play so nicely with their names?' (2.1). At this moment, above all others, propriety demanded solemnity, composure, a reverent acceptance of Fate; and it is at this moment, time and again, that a Shakespearean character spends his dying breath on a pun. Mercutio, cursing and quibbling as his rapier-wound kills him: 'aske for me tomorrow, and you shall find me a grave man' ([3.1]); Hamlet, poisoned, the pressure of his story weighing on his tongue, unable to speak it because 'this fell Sergeant death | Is strick'd in his Arrest' ([5.2]); Antony, heralding his resolution to self-slaughter with a distracted paronomasia: 'All length is Torture: since the Torch is out' ([4.14]). Even, perhaps, the fatal Cleopatra herself, concealing the name of the instrument of her suicide, the asp, in a last triumphant insult to Caesar: 'Oh could'st thou speake, | That I might heare thee call great *Caesar* Asse, unpolicied' ([5.2]). The assassination-scene of this play's *Carry On* spoof begins, in such company, to look rather acute: 'Infamy, Infamy!', cries a beleaguered Kenneth Williams: 'They've all got it in for me!'[35] That Shakespeare so often allows his characters to expire upon a pun suggests that there is something in the nature of this rhetorical genus he considers particularly fitting to the last moment of speech. It is not, or not simply, the potential for serio-comic posturing it affords the dying hero with an inclination for gallows-humour; nor is it just, though it is, as Russ Mcdonald perceives, 'a form of imaginative exercise, an artistic stroke, a defence against death'.[36] What the death-bed pun achieves is an urgent economy of expression; the final breath searches for coherence, and the connections made by punning exhibit, ultimately, a faith in meaning and in the power of the mind to discover or to create it. Playing with words at this juncture is a way of exerting control over a hostile fate; even at the approach of death, *homo rhetoricus* does not lose his eloquence, and it is through these insouciant double-speaking figures that he exercises it. At the absolute point of emotional crisis, it seems natural to Shakespeare that there should be an instinctive attempt to master the situation, and to imbue the few words that are left with the greatest possible significance – not, historically, a contentious view. 'Don't let it end like this', were, reportedly, the dying words of the Mexican revolutionary Pancho Villa: 'Tell them I said something.'

What Addison took in Andrewes and Shakespeare for a homogeneous technique, a regrettably common stylistic defect of Renaissance writing, was in fact the distinctive expression of a serious belief: in Andrewes' case, it is a belief that faith can find the buried fragments of a prelapsarian linguistic order; in Shakespeare's, a conviction that the human mind transported can forge a new one. They are men of their age, and this divergence reflects the bifurcation of contemporary rhetorical interest; when Peacham writes that the successful orator is 'next to the omnipotent God in the power of perswasion', he doesn't specify whether that place is to be taken by bishop or king, preacher or politician.[37] Both Andrewes and Shakespeare use puns, or more accurately the rhetorical figures of syllepsis, antanaclasis and paronomasia, as, in Adamson's words 'a source of knowledge – or at least a legitimate form of argument'.[38] That one word has two meanings, or that it sounds a bit like another, might prove the occasion for broad humour; it might inspire an intellectual connection, or reinforce an acknowledged theological truth. The quibble could clinch an argument, express a mentality divided against itself or resigned, at last, to an inevitable fate: its range and subtlety was a source of constant delight for both preacher and playwright. 'To the Elizabethan mind', Kellett remarks of the possibility of the pun, 'it seems to have come with the force of a new revelation as to the capacities of language, or like the discovery of Columbus on the Western World.'[39] The later seventeenth century lost this sense of rhetorical adventure; with its traditional designations forgotten, the pun became a comic turn, stranded by the standardisation of spelling and changes in theories about language. Addison's inability to understand how a sinner could be 'Punned into Repentance', or why a tragic character might be found 'weeping and quibbling for a dozen lines together', is symptomatic of an age which had lost sympathy for the idea of language as somehow magical, sacramental. To shake off this legacy of scepticism is to rediscover what Andrewes and Shakespeare thought their puns accomplished, and to realise just how seriously they were playing with their words.

CHAPTER 5

Prosopopoeia, when to thinges without life wee frame an action, speach, or person fitting a man . . .

Angel Day, *A Declaration of . . . Tropes, Figures or Schemes* (1592)

Foole, said my Muse to me, looke in thy heart and write.

Sir Philip Sidney, *Astrophil and Stella* (1591)

SNOUT	Thus have I, Wall, my part discharged so;
	And being done, thus Wall away doth go.
THESEUS	Now is the wall down between the two neighbours.
DEMETRIUS	No remedy, my lord, when walls are so wilful to hear
	without warning.
HIPPOLYTA	This is the silliest stuff that ever I heard.
THESEUS	The best in this kind are but shadows, and the worst
	are no worse if imagination amend them.

William Shakespeare, *A Midsummer Night's Dream*, 5.1.202–9

Prosopopoeia: the speaking figure

GAVIN ALEXANDER

Literature is full of voices. This is clearest in those kinds of writing – plays, monologues, and the like – that present nothing but the speaking voice. But even a narrator can be thought of as speaking in a voice; indeed, everything we read can be attributed to some sort of person, can be thought of as spoken by a character. When we pick up a love sonnet we wonder about the character who speaks its words. We have no way of telling if the voice is that of a real or an imaginary lover; and knowing that the sonnet is by a particular author will only help if we are happy to identify the person presented by the poem with the person of the author. A familiarity with rhetoric will teach us to be cautious, to think about the poem as an exercise in creating a lifelike speaking voice. We may still choose to think that this voice is that of the author, but rhetorical theory will remind us that such self-representation is no different from the representation of another, real or imagined, that even when we speak for ourselves we are wearing a mask, though of our own making.

There is something intrinsically literary – fictive – about the creation of speaking voices. In *The Defence of Poesy*, Philip Sidney argues that poetry is better at teaching moral lessons than either philosophy or history. In developing his point, he creates a debate between the philosopher and the historian, and allows the latter to speak for himself: 'The historian scarcely giveth leisure to the moralist to say so much, but that he . . . denieth in a great chafe that any man for teaching of virtue and virtuous actions is comparable to him. "I am *testis temporum, lux veritatis, vita memoriae, magistra vitae, nuntia vetustatis*. The philosopher," saith he, "teacheth a disputative virtue, but I do an active."'[1] In giving the historian a voice, Sidney writes with calculated irony. He has been arguing that philosophers cannot teach as effectively as can poets (by which Sidney means writers of fiction, in prose or verse), because all they can give you is principles. Historians can give you the life, but it is the flawed life of fact and not the ideal life of fiction. When they report those stirring battlefield speeches that inspire courage and patriotism in readers, Sidney argues, they are doing something poetical – they cannot claim to be reporting what was actually said. The speaking voice of Sidney's historian reminds us that the creation of character is the province of poets like Sidney. It may seem paradoxical, then, that the classical and Renaissance theory of literature has little to say about character. But the job was done by rhetorical theory, in its discussion of the figure of (to give it its strict etymological sense) person-making – prosopopoeia. In what follows, I will first of all examine this figure's origins, before looking at its development in Renaissance literature and theory, and then at the implications of its relationship with neighbouring figures, notably apostrophe. My aim is to show that the concern in literature of the English Renaissance with questions of character, persona, and identity appears in a new light when we remember the rhetorical basis of those questions.

PROSOPOPOEIA IN RHETORICAL THEORY

Prosopopoeia was one of the school exercises used to train future orators in essential skills. It is easy to see the connection between the speech in character as practised at school (Richard Rainolde gives as his example 'what lamentable Oracion Hecuba Quene of Troie might make, Troie being destroied')[2] and such literary works as Ovid's *Heroides* or its early-modern equivalent, Michael Drayton's *Englands Heroicall Epistles* (1597), which present speeches or letters in the voices of characters from myth or history. The rhetoric books defined prosopopoeia more or less broadly. The word could be applied to an entire speech ghost-written for an untrained speaker,[3] as well as to the more properly figurative operation whereby an orator would imagine what an ancestor, or victim, or city – or even the defendant – might have to say about the case in question.[4] It could also be used quite explicitly to describe the speech of characters in literary works, as when Quintilian discusses the study and recitation of poetry.[5] Some authorities, Quintilian reports, restrict the meaning of prosopopoeia 'to cases where both persons and words are fictitious', and indeed there was a variety of terms which were used to indicate such distinctions as that between the imaginary speech of the historical person and that of the invented character. But as Quintilian shrewdly observes, 'we cannot imagine a speech without we also imagine a person to utter it': unless the person or thing we are giving voice to is actually doing the speaking, it is prosopopoeia.[6]

One of the terms with which prosopopoeia overlapped and competed, however, proves crucial to an understanding of the broad implications of the figure: that term is ethopoeia.[7] That the two terms were to an extent interchangeable makes it clear that prosopopoeia is closely related to the concept of *ēthos*, one of very large, and rather different, significance within rhetorical theory. The Greek word *prosōpon* means a face or mask and from those core meanings derive subsidiary meanings of a dramatic part or character, a character in a philosophical dialogue or other book, even the character of an author.[8] It comes, especially in New Testament Greek, to mean a person. Through synecdoche (the figure which represents a whole by one of its parts, or vice versa), the face or mask stands for the rest of the human body, and in due course the whole person is denoted by the word *prosōpon*. The Greek word *ēthos* is equally complex and flexible. It means custom or usage, and thence disposition or character, especially – in Aristotelian usage – *moral* character. It too gravitates towards the literary, and can be used to mean a character in a play.[9] One word, then, describes appearance, the other behaviour. But they come together as synonyms describing dramatic character. They stand at either end of a chain whose components are linked by metonymy (the figure through which qualities or causes of things stand for the things themselves, or vice versa). That metonymic chain runs from face to person to moral character; to an extent it also runs from outer person (*prosōpon*) to inner person (*ēthos*).

Ēthos is a central term for Aristotle. In the *Poetics* Aristotle treats dramatic character under the separate categories of *ēthos* (moral character, such as a tragic hero displays in his actions and choices) and *dianoia* (intellect), which is the capacity of rational thought represented when the protagonist argues.[10] Aristotle sees a similar distinction operating in rhetoric. The orator makes arguments, but he also strives to give an impression of *ēthos*, moral character, to make those arguments more believable.[11] Aristotle sets the pattern for subsequent rhetorical theory with the moral neutrality of his account of the orator's *ēthos*. In order to inspire belief it is important that the speaker 'should show himself to be possessed of certain qualities and that his hearers should think that he is disposed in a certain way towards them'.[12] An 'impression that the speaker is speaking the truth'[13] is what is important in this account; orators who lie and pretend do not seem to be excluded. *Ēthos*, in this tradition, is something fictive, something made by the tragic poet or simulated by the orator.

A great deal of effort is expended on *ēthos* in subsequent rhetorical theory, but that theory never escapes from the problem blithely created by

Aristotle. The orator's moral character is clearly an important part of what will persuade an audience: if the audience think him a fool or a phoney, they are unlikely to believe what he tells them, whereas if they think he is a good and honest man, he will get his way. But as soon as the theory examines ways of presenting *ēthos*, it will struggle to draw a line between enhancing what is already there for good reasons, and simulating what is not there for bad reasons, especially since Aristotle showed no interest in such a line in the first place. Theorists like Cicero and Quintilian struggle to argue that the orator must be good and must believe what he says, and they are repeatedly betrayed in their efforts by the very dramatic metaphors that the word *ēthos* brought with it.

Orators were, after all, actors of a sort. Throughout Cicero's treatises, the benchmark of effective oratorical performance is the famous actor Roscius. Thomas Wright, in his treatise on *The Passions of the Minde in Generall* (1604), reminds us that 'Cicero expresly teacheth that it is almost impossible for an oratour to stirre up a passion in his audience, except he be first affected with the same passion himselfe' and after quoting the key passage from *De oratore* (2.45.189) cuts straight to Horace on the craft of the actor: 'And therefore *Horace* well observed, that he which will make me weepe must first weepe himself' (the famous *si vis me flere* passage of the *Ars poetica*).[14] Quintilian's own advice is also close to Cicero and Horace, and is worth quoting at length:

> The heart of the matter as regards arousing emotions, so far as I can see, lies in being moved by them oneself. The mere imitation of grief or anger or indignation may in fact sometimes be ridiculous, if we fail to adapt our feelings to the emotion as well as our words and our face . . . Consequently, where we wish to give an impression of reality, let us assimilate ourselves to the emotions of those who really suffer; let our speech spring from the very attitude that we want to produce in the judge. Will the hearer feel sorrow, when I, whose object in speaking is to make him feel it, feel none? Will he be angry, if the person who is trying to excite his anger suffers nothing resembling the emotions he is calling for? Will he weep when the speaker's eyes are dry?[15]

There is of course a difference between 'an impression of reality' and reality itself. In Cicero's dialogue *De oratore*, Antonius, the voice of untutored eloquence (and, of course, a prosopopoeia), insists that he has never tried to stir emotions without feeling those emotions himself.[16] But his argument becomes circular when he looks at how the orator can rouse his passions regularly without resorting to acting. It is, he says, the speech itself that is 'great enough to dispense with all make-believe and trickery: for the very quality of the diction, employed to stir the feelings of others, stirs the speaker himself even more deeply than any of his hearers'.[17] In even completely unreal dramatic situations we can observe actors who seem really to feel the emotions they act.[18] Antonius then goes on, giving the example of his own performance in a celebrated case: 'Do not suppose then that I myself, though not concerned to portray and reproduce in language the bygone misfortunes and legendary griefs of heroes [as an actor is], and though presenting my own personality and not representing another's [neque actor essem alienae personae, sed auctor meae], did without profound emotion the things I did.'[19] There is an especially interesting phrase here, which the translation does not quite capture: Antonius talks of being not the actor of another character ('actor . . . alienae personae') but the author of his own ('auctor meae'). Quintilian also describes the orator's craft in terms that make it sound more like fiction-making than it perhaps should, comparing the orator's ability to summon up emotions with the visionary imagination of the poet.[20] The rhetorical theorists are so interested in the ability of words to produce emotions that they approve of the idea of the orator moving himself as well as his audience, and being able to move his audience *because* he has moved himself, and moving himself not so much by the force of actual recollection as by the power of the words he has written and is uttering.

Like actors, orators perform a role, presenting a character that may be who they are or may be who they want to be thought to be. The idea of role is built into the words in Greek and Latin that describe selfhood or personhood. The Greek term *prosopopoeia*, as we have seen, means literally 'making a mask'. The Latin for mask is *persona* and from this word by metonymic extension come all words describing personhood. Cicero uses the word a great deal, and helps it come to mean both a role and a person, such as one's self.[21] To talk of speaking in one's own person is to use a dramatic metaphor: selfhood is always a mask. In just this way, Quintilian distinguishes between what Cicero has the characters in *De oratore* say, and what he says 'in his own person' ['sua ipse persona'].[22]

What the discussion of rhetorical *ēthos* emphasises is how absorbed in his performance the great orator, like the great actor, becomes. Rhetorical theorists acknowledge that prosopopoeia is a literary device brought into rhetoric, and the cumulative effect of the figure's various theoretical treatments is to align it with a related model of the creation and performance of character – *ēthos* – which is itself conceived and explained in literary terms and through use of analogies to literary creation and dramatic performance. The creation and performance of the speaking voice is both fundamentally literary – fictive – and thoroughly rhetorical – with persuasion ultimately taking priority over sincerity. If we take prosopopoeia back to its literary origins, and use it to talk about lyric voice or dramatic character, we cannot forget that it returns home fraught with new rhetorical concerns, and notably the paradoxes bound up with the rhetorical theory of *ēthos*. Most particularly, literary prosopopoeia learns from rhetoric an interest in what is involved for the performer of the voice, how that performer can become absorbed in the role he plays, can only move his audience by moving himself. When we read prosopopoeia in the light of *ēthos*, we are presented with the possibility that to perform a role is to identify with, to become, that role.

Something like this idea is found in classical poetics, in the theory of narrative. Aristotle and Plato make the following distinction between kinds of literature; it is a distinction of the mode in which things are represented. Literature may give us a single voice speaking in its own person and narrating events, with no direct speech; it may give us some narrative and some direct speech, or what Aristotle calls 'sometimes becoming someone else, as Homer does'; or it may be drama, where each person in the story is actually seen acting.[23] As Longinus puts it, describing the second kind: 'sometimes a writer, while speaking about a person [peri prosopou] suddenly turns and changes into the person himself [eis to autoprosopon antimethistatai]'.[24] For Plato, this is the problem with literature: imitating, as actor or narrator, is bad for us if the people we imitate are not the sort of people we want to be; to imitate is to risk transformation into the role one performs.[25] What is a worry for Plato, though, is an interesting potentiality in Renaissance literature. This potentiality depends on the fact that the language of selfhood in classical rhetoric and poetics offers only a set of partial views, synecdoches. We have moral character, and the face or mask. Through metonymy, we are able to talk of the creation of a speaking voice as the creation of such a moral character or mask – ethopoeia and prosopopoeia. No mask is seen, but the words spoken stand for it; there may be no real moral character but only the simulacrum of one to be inferred from those spoken words. The figure of prosopopoeia and the related doctrine of *ēthos* have an innate tendency, therefore, to ignore interiority and to elide performance with identity. Because of this inheritance, personhood as it is configured and enacted in Renaissance fictions is built on the rhetorical idea that a self is the words it speaks.

PROSOPOPOEIA IN RENAISSANCE PRACTICE

The Renaissance theorists make it much more straightforward for us to use prosopopoeia to talk about literary voice and character. Abraham

Fraunce's concise definition of prosopopoeia stresses the figure's literary basis: '*Prosopopoia* is a fayning of any person, when in our speech we represent the person of anie, and make it speake as though he were there present: an excellent figure, much used of Poets . . .'[26] It is either imperfect (i.e. indirect speech) or perfect, 'when the whole speech of anie person is fully and lively represented'. Though Fraunce goes on to give examples of dumb things being given a voice, the definition and its position in the scheme of his treatise (in a group of figures that are about voices in monologue and dialogue) clearly emphasises the usefulness of the figure for describing the creation of human character. Perhaps the most important contribution to the theory of personation by the Renaissance rhetoricians is the grouping of prosopopoeia with a number of related figures in a way that seems to recognise that they are the basic building blocks of fiction. This grouping appears to start with Erasmus, whose fifth method for the enrichment of material in Book II of *De copia* (1512) groups together kinds of description – of things, persons, places, and times – and their related figures under the heading of enargeia (vividness).[27] He recognises that 'All these topics should be dealt with separately on occasion as an exercise for our ingenuity, but a complete description contains them all', going on to give an example of a satire by Horace.[28] An Erasmian tradition of placing prosopopoeia alongside other figures of description can be traced through such writers as Joannes Susenbrotus, in his extremely influential *Epitome troporum ac schematum* [1540?], and Richard Sherry, in one of the first English rhetorics,[29] to Puttenham, who gives us, in sequence, '*Hypotyposis*, or the counterfeit representation', '*Prosopographia*, or the counterfeit countenance', '*Prosopopoeia*, or the counterfeit impersonation', '*Chronographia*, or the counterfeit time', '*Topographia*, or the counterfeit place', and '*Pragmatographia*, or the counterfeit action'.[30]

The Renaissance rhetoricians glimpse the formation from the figures of a taxonomy of fiction, a new accord between rhetoric and poetics. But they fail to take things much further, because they are still not sure if they are writing treatises on oratory with literary examples or treatises about how to read and write literature. Puttenham believes that he is doing the latter, Fraunce the former; and yet Puttenham's account of the figure by which Homer creates Achilles and Chaucer the Pardoner (prosopographia, in Puttenham's slightly confused account) is surprisingly brief when we think how central to literature character seems to us. Nevertheless, it is the continuing contact with rhetorical theory that adds a great deal of the richness and complexity to the representation of character and voice in Renaissance literature, as the example Fraunce chooses to illustrate the figure shows very clearly.

Because he is writing about oratory, Fraunce cannot quite give as his example of prosopopoeia a simple scene in which a literary character is depicted saying something. His example from the *Arcadia* is the first appearance 'Of Musidorus clad in shepheards weedes'. One of Sidney's characters, Pyrocles, comes upon another, Musidorus, whom he knows well. But that other character has disguised himself as a shepherd in order to get access to the woman he has fallen in love with. We are given through Pyrocles' eyes a first picture of the as yet unrecognised shepherd (the female pronouns are attached to Pyrocles because he is himself disguised as an amazon):

She might perceive a farre off one coming towards her in the apparaile of a shepheard, with his armes hanging down, going a kind of languishing pace, with his eyes sometimes cast up to heaven, as though his fancy strave to mount up higher; sometimes thrown down to the ground, as if the earth could not beare the burden of his paines: at length she heard him with a lamentable tune sing these few verses:

> Come shepheards weedes, become your maisters mind,
> Yeeld outward shew, what inward change he tries,
> Nor be abasht, since such a guest you find,
> Whose strongest hope in your weake comfort lies.
> Come shepheards weeds, attend my wofull cries,
> Disuse your selves from sweet Menalcas voyce,
> For other be those tunes which sorowe ties,
> From those cleare notes which freelie may rejoyce.
>   Then powre out plaints, and in one word say this,
>   Helples his plaint who spoyles himselfe of blisse.

And having ended, she might see him strike himselfe upon the breast, uttering these words. O miserable wretch, whether doo thy destinies guide thee?[31]

One of the reasons why Fraunce chooses this passage to illustrate the figure is that he is trying to keep in touch with a rhetorical rule that emphasises the elegant introduction and conclusion of the prosopopoeia – 'we must make a fit and orderly accesse too, and regresse from the same *Prosopopoeia*'.[32] The tableau of Musidorus as Dorus the shepherd has a beginning and an end. But I think Fraunce is also drawn to this passage because it is not only Sidney who is making a mask: Musidorus is creating and performing a new persona – the shepherd – and so he too is engaging in prosopopoeia, is *auctor* as well as *actor* of his persona. This is a moment when Musidorus's sense of self is rather fluid, because he is rhetorically simulating himself. His poem draws out this fluidity. He addresses the clothes he has borrowed from another shepherd, Menalcas, in an apostrophe that personifies them.

They are told to 'Yeeld' a particular 'outward shew' and to 'say' something about him – they are almost given a voice. And when they are told to 'become your masters mind', although the primary meaning is 'suit', the sense is also there of the clothes having turned themselves into his mind – what is on the inside is now identified with what is on the outside. The personation here is further complicated, because as well as the role of shepherd there is another to be performed – that of lover. Musidorus is clearly playing that part convincingly, as Sidney shows with the details of his body language – arms hanging down, eyes cast up and then down. But is the performance Musidorus's or Sidney's? We cannot tell (for now at least) if Sidney is creating a convincing lover and Musidorus is simply and sincerely being his (fictional) self, or if Musidorus is the one engaged in an act of fiction-making and is offering a convincing, dissimulative performance of a lover. The identity of the fictional character, in his borrowed clothes, falling into one new role and scripting for himself another, is made to look fragile in this scene. Prosopopoeia helps us to see how rhetorically complex the literary representation of self and voice is, because that representation is seen to operate within a network of rhetorical agendas (author's, characters') in which there are many kinds and degrees of person-making, from the author's creation of a protagonist down to a simple trick of grammar that personifies something inanimate.

Another example of how prosopopoeia can be used to relate different levels of personation is Edmund Spenser's *Prosopopoia*.[33] Spenser's poem is one of two works published in the 1590s with the name of the figure for a title. The other is Thomas Lodge's *Prosopopeia* (1596), a school exercise on a grand scale, in which Lodge imagines what the Virgin Mary would have said at the cross. Spenser's work is rather different. It works by taking one aspect of the figure – the giving of a voice to dumb things, in this case animals – and using it to interrogate some of the social and ethical issues in the very broad background of the idea of persona.

The poem is a tale, told by Mother Hubberd, about an ape and a fox. They are made to act and speak like humans in the story, one kind of prosopopoeia. And what the story is about is their efforts to make their way in the world by disguising themselves as people they are not, by adopting personae, putting on masks – another kind of prosopopoeia. Spenser chooses these animals because they are already symbols for types of human behaviour – the fox for cunning and the ape for ability to mimic. At the same time, therefore, as this tale is a rhetorical exercise in personation, it is a moral fable about dissimulation and fakery. The two animals start off disguised as soldiers, then get to be employed as a shepherd and his dog (with predictably disastrous results for the sheep), then as a priest and his parish clerk, then as a courtier and his groom. In each case, no one sees through their disguise; it proves to be enough simply to act a part. The two con-artists finally sneak off with the lion's skin while he is sleeping and the ape gets to play at being king of the animals, before they at last get their comeuppance. *Prosopopoia* is a funny story, but as well as the obvious moral there is a more difficult lesson to be learned. Spenser lives in an age in which being was all about performing, playing a role.[34] This is how Spenser's own efforts as a moral educator in *The Faerie Queene* have to be understood. In his outline of the work, the 'Letter to Ralegh', he explains that 'The generall end therefore of all the booke is to fashion a gentleman or noble person in vertuous and gentle discipline.'[35] He does this by presenting exemplary characters, like Britomart, Calidore, and the other knights; and according to the literary theory of Sidney and Spenser, the reader will try to be like these characters, will emulate them.[36] The reader will therefore be refashioned, made into an image of Spenser's idea of virtue. But how are we to distinguish the reader who has been made virtuous from the reader who apes virtue, who adopts a plausible persona but is a cunning fox underneath?

Spenser is principally worried about a society based on show and the role of the court in fostering this culture of deceit.[37] And the figure of prosopopoeia is implicated in these acts of impersonation. Milton has a rather different set of concerns when he gives an animal a voice, but he is still using what a rhetorical analysis would identify as prosopopoeia to connect the figure to worries about deceit. When Eve encounters a talking serpent, she is taken aback:

> What may this mean? Language of man pronounced
> By tongue of brute, and human sense expressed?
> The first at least of these I thought denied
> To beasts, whom God on their creation-day
> Created mute to all articulate sound . . .
> Thee, serpent, subtlest beast of all the field
> I knew, but not with human voice endued;
> Redouble then this miracle, and say
> How cam'st thou speakable of mute . . .?[38]

When prosopopoeia gives a voice to the mute it is of course an outrage against nature. What Eve does not know is that the deceit here is physical, that this is not a serpent with a voice, but a fallen angel, Satan, in the guise of a serpent. Things are rather different in the Bible, where there is no hint that the serpent is anything more than just a serpent. Chapter 3 of Genesis in the Authorised Version introduces the dialogue between Eve and the serpent with 'Now the serpent was more subtil than any beast of the field', closely following previous English translations going back to Coverdale (1535). Milton's Eve is made the origin of this observation, when she says 'Thee, serpent, subtlest beast of all the field | I knew . . .'. *The Oxford English Dictionary* quotes both passages in its definition of one obsolete sense of 'subtle': 'Of persons or animals: Crafty, cunning; treacherously or wickedly cunning, insidiously sly, wily'.[39] This is very much what Milton means by 'subtlest': as he goes on, he introduces the talking serpent as 'spirited sly snake' (613) and 'wily adder' (625). But there were other, more benign meanings of 'subtle': skilful, clever, slender, or fine. Eve cannot mean 'subtlest' quite in the sense that Milton means it, because then she might be more suspicious. Milton is showing how language itself was corrupted by the fall, how innocent meanings were replaced by more knowing ones. But what is of particular interest here is the effect of this echo of scripture at a point where the nature of a voice is at question. Satan is pretending to be a speaking snake, giving us one kind of prosopopoeia. Eve is speaking in words not her own – any reader would have spotted the scriptural quotation – and so we are more likely to remember that she is another prosopopoeia, simulated by an author with a theological agenda. If we hear that word 'subtlest' in its full Biblical sense, then Milton will seem to have failed a very basic criterion for success in prosopopoeia, 'wherein wee must diligentlie take heede, that the person thus represented have a speech fit and convenient for his estate and nature',[40] in this case a state of innocence. But if we hear Eve's speech as the product of two different rhetorical agendas, Milton's and her own, her character will look in that moment somewhat fragile – constructed on multiple layers, and the product of competing rhetorical motives. Prosopopoeia allows its users to adopt the voices of others; but it also has the potential to show them that when they think they are speaking in their own person, they are prosopopoeias themselves.

BORROWED VOICES

There was another, striking, Renaissance addition to the theory of prosopopoeia, which was a result of the grouping of fundamentally literary figures discussed above. A number of the Renaissance rhetoricians sense an interesting relation between apostrophe, the figure of address, and prosopopoeia. Both Abraham Fraunce and John Hoskyns put the two next to each other in their classifications, as, Hoskyns says, 'feigning the presence or the discourse of some such persons, as either are not at all, or if

there be, yet speake not, but by imaginacion':[41] it is a first stage to address
something, a stage which personifies, or implies the presence of the absent;
it is the next stage to find that the person created or brought forth can speak
back. Hoskyns also describes prosopopoeia evocatively as having the power
'to animate, and give life'.[42] These perspectives anticipate recent decon-
structionist reformulations of prosopopoeia, which expand the figure to
encompass any personification (even of things not given a voice), and elide
it with apostrophe.[43] Both sets of theorists see that something of very fundamental significance occurs when a voice is created, speaking in address to
another, that the power to conjure up human presences and endow them
with speaking voices is not just a momentary trick of the orator but is the
basis of the making of fictions. Whether we come at the figure from the
direction of Elizabethan rhetorical theory or from that of modern critical
theory, we can see that prosopopoeia engages with, and is implicated in,
many different degrees and forms of personation. And we can recognise
that these various shades of literary personation are being investigated continuously in many works of Renaissance English literature. We can look at
just one, a sonnet crowded with simulated presences:

> Since shunning paine, I ease can never find:
> Since bashfull dread seekes where he knowes me harmed:
> Since will is won, and stopped ears are charmed:
> Since force doth faint, and sight doth make me blind:
>
> Since loosing long, the faster still I bind:
> Since naked sence can conquer reason armed:
> Since heart in chilling feare with yce is warmed:
> In fine, since strife of thought but marres the mind,
>
> I yield, ô Love, unto thy loathed yoke,
> Yet craving law of armes, whose rule doth teach,
> That hardly usde, who ever prison broke,
> In justice quit, of honour made no breach:
>   Whereas if I a gratefull gardien have,
>   Thou art my Lord, and I thy vowed slave.[44]

This poem opens Philip Sidney's *Certain Sonnets*. It is for us to decide if the
speaker is real or imaginary, Sidney or a persona, if it is to a real or imaginary
mistress, to a particular or merely general reader. What it claims to be is
an address to Love, that is, Cupid, but that person, summoned up in the
second person address of apostrophe, is only revealed after the octave, in
line 9. Up until that moment, we might imagine that the voice of the poem
speaks to no one in particular, or to us, but the lack of personalised addressee

is weirdly compensated for by the host of personifications described: dread, force, sight, sense, reason and the rest are all to a greater or lesser degree personified, made into animate agents. The speaker is not a single being but a sort of community of faculties and qualities confronting a besieging army of Love's foot soldiers. The question to be asked about all this is very simple: when all these different things and ideas are personified, dressed up as people, where does that leave the personhood of the speaker, who exists only in this discourse and is defined only in relation to all these personifications? If you try to have a conversation with Love, what does that make you? Selfhood, the sense of identity, in this poem can only be measured in relation to various kinds of impersonation.

Sidney had died in 1586. First printed posthumously in 1598, the poem tempts its readers with the possibility that in reading it – silently or aloud – they are resurrecting a dead man, or at least his voice. For prosopopoeia – as Quintilian makes clear when he discusses schoolboys reading out great literature, or the ghost-written oration – is also something that happens when readers perform the voices that writers have created. Shakespeare is clearly interested in what is at stake when we speak or sing another's words:

DESDEMONA   She had a song of 'Willow,'
           An old thing 'twas, but it express'd her fortune,
           And she died singing it. That song to-night
           Will not go from my mind; I have much to do
           But to go hang my head all at one side
           And sing it like poor Barbary . . .
           [*Singing.*]
           'The poor soul sat sighing by a sycamore tree,
               Sing all a green willow;
           Her hand on her bosom, her head on her knee,
               Sing willow, willow, willow.
           The fresh streams ran by her, and murmur'd her moans,
               Sing willow, willow, willow;
           Her salt tears fell from her, and soft'ned the stones,
               Sing willow'
           Lay by these –
           [*Singing.*]   '– willow, willow' –
           Prithee hie thee; he'll come anon –
           [*Singing.*]
           'Sing all a green willow must be my garland . . .'[45]

Desdemona remembers the song of her mother's maid Barbary, a song that narrates and then represents, by prosopopoeia, the sad words of a jilted woman. The song itself blurs the boundaries between its narrator and the voice that narrator reports, with the refrain-lines seeming to be shared between the two; and Desdemona's performance of the song 'like poor Barbary' means that to an extent she sings with Barbary's voice: one prosopopoeia nests within another. Later in the play, Desdemona's own maid Emilia sings a snippet from the same song as she dies. For these women there is some consolation in merging their voices with each other, and with the voice represented in the song.[46] The possibility of sharing emotion and experience even with a fictive construct is both therapeutic and heuristic; the performer discovers something about herself by comparing her identity to that of another, and by putting on a mask is able to express herself more eloquently than by remaining in her own person.[47]

To return to Sidney's sonnet, we can say that if selfhood can be encapsulated – or at least brought along by metonymy – in the words a voice speaks, then that poem is Sidney and, in speaking its words, so are we. Shakespeare makes virtuoso use of this spooky side of prosopopoeia in the funeral scene of *Julius Caesar*.[48] Even before Antony starts, he is conscious that his success is partly about moving from apostrophe, addressing Caesar's corpse, to prosopopoeia, resurrecting Caesar:

> Over thy wounds now do I prophesy
> (Which like dumb mouths do ope their ruby lips
> To beg the voice and utterance of my tongue)
> A curse shall light upon the limbs of men;
> Domestic fury and fierce civil strife . . .
> And Caesar's spirit, ranging for revenge . . .
> Shall in these confines with a monarch's voice
> Cry 'Havoc!' and let slip the dogs of war[49]

Antony builds the scene that follows to a climactic prosopopoeia of Caesar, articulated into the revelation of his body and the reading of his will. Quintilian had actually used the events on which Shakespeare based his scene as an example when recommending that in the peroration the orator at a murder trial might show fragments of blood-stained clothing or even the corpse itself.[50] Antony shows the crowd each dagger entry on Caesar's toga, and finally reveals the body, moving the crowd to a fury that he quickly controls:

> I come not, friends, to steal away your hearts.
> I am no orator, as Brutus is;
> But (as you know me all) a plain blunt man
> That love my friend . . .
> For I have neither wit, nor words, nor worth,
> Action, nor utterance, nor the power of speech,

To stir men's blood; I only speak right on.
I tell you that which you yourselves do know,
Show you sweet Caesar's wounds, poor, poor, dumb mouths,
And bid them speak for me. But were I Brutus,
And Brutus Antony, there were an Antony
Would ruffle up your spirits, and put a tongue
In every wound of Caesar that should move
The stones of Rome to rise and mutiny.

(3.2.216–30)

And mutiny is what results, as Antony's rhetoric moves the crowd both emotionally and literally. His trick is a sort of prosopopoeia. Caesar's body is there, with each of its wounds a mouth to which Antony's rhetoric can give a voice, so that the crowd are offered a resurrection not only of Caesar's voice but in a way of his dead body. And Caesar's voice, or at least (in another synecdoche of selfhood) his hand, is there in the written text of the will. Brought back to rhetorical life, Caesar's presence eclipses both that of Antony – who can thus claim to be simply a straight-talking, honest man – and that of Brutus and the other conspirators, whose careful, reasoned arguments are forgotten as the crowd are swept up by the more emotive oratory that Antony practises.

CONCLUSION

The theory of rhetoric that taught authors the persuasive value of compelling characterisation also taught that any character created in words was a performance of a persona – the creation and adoption of a mask, a *prosopopoeia*. That mask could be realistic, but it was still a mask. Where we might tend to think of literary characters as believable individuals (as later Shakespeare criticism encouraged us to do),[51] the Renaissance rhetorical tradition helps us to think about them as convincing and persuasive personae. This creates interesting conundrums in drama – to what extent is the Hamlet we see a performance, and whose performance is it (Shakespeare's? Hamlet's? the actor's?)? In lyric we have the additional problem of looking at the mask and not being sure whom it represents. It might be a representation of the author or it might be a piece of fiction. And even if it is self-representation, that is still a fictive activity (the author is *auctor personae meae*). The mask is lifelike, but not alive, and because it remains a mask, we can think about putting it on ourselves, about performing (if only in our minds, as readers) the lyric 'I'. We then take over the prosopopoeia. The figure exploits its metonymic basis – it does not in fact create a person, or a mask or face, or even a voice, but rather the words that person is imagined as saying. And in doing this it suggests that it may not be possible to distinguish selfhood from the words we speak. The figure tests the ability of words, sung, spoken, or even simply read, to give the impression that a ghostly presence has been summoned into being. It helps us think about the way in which Shakespeare in his sonnets, for example, might somehow be thought of as talking to us. And about the extent to which we, in reading or performing his sonnets, are speaking in that voice, and for him.

CHAPTER 6

This exercise profitable to *Rhetorike*, is an Oracion that collecteth and
representeth to the iye, that which he sheweth.
Richard Rainolde, *The Foundacion of Rhetorike* (1563)

ENOBARBUS I will tell you,
    The Barge she sat in, like a burnisht Throne
    Burnt on the water: the Poope was beaten Gold,
    Purple the Sailes: and so perfumed that
    The Windes were Love-sicke with them[,] the Owers were Silver,
    Which to the tune of Flutes kept stroke, and made
    The water which they beate, to follow faster;
    As amorous of their strokes. For her owne person,
    It beggerd all discription, she did lye
    In her Pavillion, cloth of Gold, of Tissue,
    O're-picturing that Venus, where we see
    The fancie out-worke Nature . . .
William Shakespeare, *Antony and Cleopatra*, 2.2.190–201

Ekphrasis: painting in words

CLAIRE PRESTON

Ekphrasis, a species of vivid description, has no formal rules and no stable technical definition. Originally a device in oratory, its development as a poetic figure has somewhat confused its taxonomy, but broadly speaking it is one of a spectrum of figures and other devices falling under the rubric of enargeia ('vividness').[1] The term ekphrasis appears only belatedly in classical rhetorical theory. Discussing representation in his *Rhetoric*, Aristotle approves the 'enlivening of inanimate things' with vivid description, the 'do[ing of] something to the life' as a kind of imitation, in metaphors which 'set things before the eye'.[2] Quintilian regards vividness as a pragmatic virtue of forensic oratory: '"representation" is more than mere perspicuity, since instead of being merely transparent it somehow shows itself off . . . in a way that it seems to be actually seen. A speech does not adequately fulfil its purpose . . . if it goes no further than the ears . . . without . . . being . . . displayed to the mind's eye.'[3] The rhetor Dionysius of Halicarnassus (*fl.* 30–7 BC) makes the first surviving use of the term ekphrasis, but it was during the Second Sophistic (1st–4th c. AD), when earlier Greek rhetoric became the model for Latin practice, that the term was given firm definition and purpose. For rhetoricians of this period like Aphthonius (4th c. AD), ekphrasis (or *descriptio*) presents, as though placed before the eyes, something in life or art, a person, animal, object, event, time or place,[4] and was one of the rhetorical exercises of the 'progymnasmata'. In this context the ekphrastic description stands on its own, and as a device to be deployed almost anywhere in formal discourse it tends also to stand as a discrete, self-contained unit.[5] In his *Imagines*, Philostratus (2nd–3rd c. AD) restricted his own ekphrastic descriptions to murals, but the device was not regularly reserved in this period for art or the artificial rather than for natural objects. Thus it was inherited by the Renaissance as a usefully open device, with perhaps the single, consistent feature of discreteness and self-containment within a larger rhetorical structure.

Ekphrasis is distinctive among figures and related devices in yielding a particular kind of interpretive result. The *Rhetorica ad Herennium* specifies vivid description for the imaginary demonstration of the consequences of action, and by extension, as a prompt for action. This is a definition by outcome – however fashioned, vivid description can make a jury (for example) decide in favour of a certain verdict, so that 'freeing this defendant would be like releasing a ravenous lion among innocent citizens' is the kind of vivid ekphrastic descriptor useful to the legal orator.[6] Poetic ekphrasis capitalises on its court-room origin by insisting on interpretative responses from the reader.

Some of the most celebrated early poetic examples of ekphrasis describe artefacts or artworks: Homer's description of the shield of Achilles (*Iliad* 18), Virgil's depiction of the Trojan wars on the walls of Juno's temple (*Aeneid* I), Philostratus's ekphrastic tour of a picture gallery in *Imagines*; Longus's *Daphnis and Chloe*, a long poem purportedly describing an enormous narrative painting in Lesbos (*c.* 2nd-6th c. AD).[7] Procopius of Caesarea produces an extended ekphrasis – one which clearly looks forward to early-modern examples – of Agia Sophia (*c.* 535 AD) in Constantinople, then a relatively new building inviting astonished report. Architecturally and technically detailed, his account of the spectacular engineering and decoration as miraculous solutions to seeming physical impossibilities – the appearance of supernatural suspension from heaven, the stunningly life-like interior paintings – constantly adverts to its own inadequacy. Its indescribable beauty embodies divine influence and 'lifts the mind toward God'.[8] Claims of inexpressibility are the hallmark of the most significant Renaissance ekphrastic practice too, as is the sense of the device as portable and discrete, to be inserted at convenience into any argument, and its almost muscle-flexing, callisthenic property (the Sophists having imagined their rhetorical exercises as 'gymnastic').

Because of this looseness of classical definition, Renaissance rhetorical theorists have some difficulty in identifying ekphrasis, and even in knowing what to call it, perhaps because its use in oratory could not be translated exactly into literary practice. Puttenham (writing in around 1570) speaks of '*Hypotiposis*, or the counterfait representation', a figure 'which requireth cunning' and 'great discretion in the doer', especially in the description of artificial or unreal things, since 'to faine a thing that never was nor is like to be, proceedeth of a greater wit and sharper invention than to describe things that be true'.[9] Elsewhere he describes the figure of icon ('resemblance by imagerie or portrait'), which 'insinuate[s] under fictions with sweete and coloured speeches . . . wholesome lessons and doctrines'.[10] Henry Peacham (1593), like Puttenham, discusses icon, a 'figure of permission or concession . . . [which] commit[s] the cause in hand . . . to the consideration and judgements of others',[11] suggesting both the performative nature of ekphrasis, and the vital collusion of the reader. John Hoskins's *Directions for Speech and Style* (*c.* 1599) clearly refers to ekphrasis in his definition of 'illustration': 'the description of things living or dead; of living things, either reasonable, as of men and of personages and qualities, or unreasonable, as of horses, ships, islands, castles, and suchlike'. Hoskins's models are the 'notable and lively portraits' in *Arcadia*, where Sidney 'imagine[d] the thing present in his own brain that his pen might the better present it to you'.[12]

A minimal definition of ekphrasis, then, is 'verbal pictorialism', and the simplest kinds of ekphrasis offer only decorative, not substantive or persuasive, visual details. But ekphrastic brevity and simplicity are deceptive. Sidney often employs what feels like a casual ekphrastic phrase – one which might sensibly be called 'iconic' – to heighten our visual or spatial sense of a scene with a pictorial referent. In the revised *Arcadia* the besotted Basilius supplicates to Zelmane, 'holding up his hands, as the old governesse of Danaë is painted, when she sodainly saw the golde[n] shoure',[13] and elsewhere characters are likened to the painting of Apollo and Daphne, to Venus mourning the death of Adonis, and to the style of 'the most excellent workeman of Greece'.[14] These suggestive details are attributed but uninvestigated pictorial qualities, much as Pound's laconic line 'Mermaids, that carving' refers the reader, if cryptically, to Lombardo's carving in S. Maria dei Miracoli in Venice,[15] or Charles Olson's exclamation 'So! It was Nike' to a cotton dress blown against a girl's body.[16]

The difference between the iconic, referential ekphrasis and the fully enumerated one seems at least superficially quantitative, a matter of mapping or modelling. The first is uninterpolated, sparsely modelled, usually allusive, relying on the reader's own visual or imaginative inventory to supply the salient pictorial details; the second is (to borrow Nelson Goodman's phrase)[17] 'densely' modelled or interpolated, and assists the reader's response to visual data. The semiotic terms 'thick' and 'thin' description also describe this range of relative density or interpolation, from the heavily to the lightly detailed.[18] Sidney's iconic Basilius is 'thin': his deft allusion to the well-known vignette does not bother to enumerate pictorial items, in the expectation that the 'thick' details of the Danaë incident, and of the old man's gullibility, will be supplied by the reader. The Danaë episode in a tapestry in *The Faerie Queene* is, by contrast, thick:

And through the roofe of her strong brasen towre
Did raine into her lap an hony dew,
The whiles her foolish garde, that little knew
Of such deceipt, kept th'yron dore fast bard,
And watcht, that none should enter nor issew;
Vaine was the watch, and bootlesse all the ward,
Whenas the God to golden hew him selfe transfard.[19]

This densely modelled ekphrasis elaborates the visual details of the vignette, although it too, like Sidney's iconic version, relies on our long cultural conditioning by the classical myths, and expects that the reader will be well-rehearsed in the Danaë mytheme and in the resistless sexual energy of the gods. The power of ekphrastic passages is not, in other words, dependent on their descriptive density. The difference is that it does not matter, for Spenser's purposes, but does for Sidney's, whether the reader has actually seen a painting of this incident, or even whether such a painting exists.

Thick or thin, ekphrasis in early-modern works should also remind us of the demiurgical power Sidney claims so vigorously for the poet in the *Defence of Poetry*. For example, the Arcadian *blason* of Philoclea on the banks of the River Ladon ('What toong can her perfections tell'), in which Prince Pyrocles, disguised as a woman, watches his beloved bathing, is partly iterative, a formal vehicle for insisting on the unmatched, and perhaps inexpressible, beauty of a princess who unwittingly causes political and emotional havoc in several countries. In an earlier description of a portrait of this princess beside her mother, she is 'a yong maid, whose wonderfulnesse tooke away all beautie from her, but that, which it might seeme shee gave her backe againe by her very shadow'. In comparison with various pictures of goddesses in the same room, 'it seemd that the skill of the painter bestowed on the other new beautie, but that the beautie of her bestowed new skill on the painter'.[20] In the Ladon *blason* those tantalising, tautologous mysteries are at last figured forth with intrusive detail in a long, powerful display which paints the outward picture of virtue in the square inches of Philoclea's flesh.

Nonetheless, this minute anatomical catalogue seems to fetch up, like many *blasons*, against the impossibility of speaking except indirectly about 'the fairer guestes which dwell within', a problem familiar from Procopius's self-indicting ekphrasis of Agia Sophia. At the height of its power, ekphrastic description confesses its own failure; but this is not a failure of verbal art against the capacities of the pictorial or the real.[21] It is the failure of *any* art to capture the Platonic *idea* embodied in objects. Sidney and all the important English ekphrastists know that our 'infected will' forever denies us the perfection our 'erected wit' detects,[22] and the Ladon *blason* works by *resemblance*, a poor shadow of the truth: Pyrocles' unsated desire for Philoclea strands him on the riverbank in his inconvenient disguise, arrested by his need to picture in words what he cannot have in the flesh, uttering praise (her lips 'Rubies, Cherries, and Roses new')[23] which cannot portray her, but can only refer to her in borrowed similes, figures which cannot possibly do justice to her. This suspension is enacted by the narrative itself. The temporality of poetic description had long been presented as a deficiency of the verbal in the arguments of the paragonists (authors of debates between the arts), but here it is suddenly powerful: the *blason* stops everything in its tracks to tell us of Philoclea's overwhelmingly unrepresentable spiritual beauty.

Ekphrasis began in oratorical practice as a set piece, imposed on or tessellated in the discursive flow. As a literary device, it is similarly interruptive, suspending, a figure whose static heft enforces a particular kind of readerly attention to detail. All purely descriptive passages have this arresting quality, of course, when intruded upon active narrative progress. Ekphrastic description, however, because it purports not simply to borrow the visual but to *be* it, deliberately designs and compels scrutiny, carefully directing that attentiveness away from narrative sequence and toward precise interpretive responses to obtruded and ostentatious physical facts which encode abstract meanings. Thus the *placement* of the ekphrastic passage, as in the Arcadian *blason*, is one of its key effects: in (apparently) mimicking the spatial form of a viewed object, it operates within the narrative as a distinct panel, one which may be so located in order to insist on certain readerly responses. It may invoke our cooperation, as the Chorus of *Henry V* does so effectively in asking us to picture a war-ready nation; it may cause us to reflect, as the gaudy triumph of portraits in *Arcadia* passes before our gaze; it can present what would otherwise be technically unshowable, as does Enobarbus's spell-binding description of the royal barge in *Antony and Cleopatra*, and Gertrude's account of Ophelia's pathetic death by drowning; and it can analyse or analogise, as does Iachimo's likening of Imogen to Lucrece in *Cymbeline*. It may be, indeed, that no other rhetorical figure is so meaningful in its narrative placement.

Above all, then, ekphrasis is a trope of coercion, of enforcement – it requires interpretive notice from the reader. It is perhaps the most artificial of rhetorical moves: by attempting to make the temporal do the work of the spatial, ekphrasis advertises its own contrivance; and, as a discrete, disruptive *tour de force* imposed upon apparently organic narrative procedure and temporal sequence, that contrivance proclaims the skill and ambition of the writer at the expense of the narrative itself. That contrivance in turn compels temporal stasis, readerly contemplation, and strains belief in the mimetic probability of described ideas. It is, in other words, shamelessly self-publicising.

Ekphrasis is the maker's figure, a kind of virtual reality: it purports to describe objective, physical facts, but, unless the writer chooses, it need have no actual physical referent to which the accuracy or probability of the description might be compared. It is this unmooring of description from object, relieving it of accountability to or consistency with real objects, that offers immense possibility to writers. As Sidney says in the *Defence*, the ekphrastic poet need 'borrow nothing of what is, hath been, or shall be'.[24] The 'right poet', not hampered by the necessity of 'counterfeit[ing] only such faces as are set before them', is rather 'the more excellent, who having no law but wit, bestow[s] that in colours upon you which is fittest for the eye to see'.[25] As Sidney claims elsewhere in the *Defence*, the ekphrastic poet imitates God.

The most elaborate early-modern ekphraseis are, therefore, not necessarily those whose descriptive vividness is most intense or thick, but rather those in which the ekphrastic impulse expands upon our sense of what is imaginable, of what might be visualised by the mind's eye and what not. Thus, for example, the brief aerial view given by Edgar from his imagined Dover cliff is a functional verbal deceit which gives the mental eye of the blinded Gloucester a needful vision to precipitate his spiritual reclamation. That there is no cliff in this play is the whole point: what Edgar claims to be seeing from it could not be shown on stage; nor, indeed, is it a view which many can have experienced as 'real'. In other words, as a description it is only effective because it cannot be checked against its object; and for that reason it can persuade Gloucester and us that we *can* have such a view.

If the aim of rhetoric is persuasion, ekphrasis at its most powerful compels the reader to believe in the truth of such objects, which either cannot be imagined or cannot exist. As Sidney says of the Psalmist, and echoing Procopius, he 'maketh you, as it were, *see* God coming in His majesty . . . that unspeakable and everlasting beauty to be seen by the eyes of the mind'.[26] That the most powerful kind of visual experience should be one in which the physical eyes are not required is the culmination of the longstanding argument between the arts, originating with Plato, who placed sight atop the hierarchy of the senses, being the least mediated and therefore the least corrupt. Renaissance artists and art-theorists often claimed that poetry is hampered by its temporality, which unfolds its meaning sequentially rather than instantly. The visual, they argued, is immediate, actual, nearly mimetic, and thus more efficient, more true.[27] With its implication that words could be and ought to be as mimetic as possible as a catch-up strategy with painting, the troubled term enargeia (vividness) haunted the poets until they realised with Sidney that it is in the very immateriality of language – itself radically sundered from any transcendent connection with meanings or physical facts – that its power resides. For Renaissance neo-Platonists, verbal expression is nearest the ideal because, although untrammelled by the sensory, it 'could claim all the advantages of the visual arts while enjoying a freedom from their limitations'.[28] Painting, and sight itself, are 'tied, not to what should be but to what is, to the particular truth of things and not to the general reason of things'.[29] Ekphrasis overcomes that 'particular truth of things'.

As the foregoing discussion has already intimated, Sidney, Shakespeare, and Spenser are enthusiastic ekphrastic poets who use the figure to embody abstractions and to manipulate readerly point of view. The following examples, from the revised *Arcadia*, *The Rape of Lucrece*, and *The Faerie Queene*, show some of the ways by which ekphrasis enriches poetry and flaunts the maker's skill. Each is an ekphrasis not only in the broad sense of a set-piece description but also in the narrower sense so common in classical and Renaissance practice of a description of an artefact. Such a description presents each writer with the opportunity to write self-consciously about his own art even as he shows it off, because he is representing an act of representation.

When the wicked Cecropia comes to the cell of the virtuous Pamela to persuade her to accept the attentions of her hapless son, the narrative pattern of Book III of the *Arcadia* has until this point focused on Amphialus's tumultuous mental state, on Cecropia's busy schemes to capture the princesses by deception, and on her scuttling negotiations for Amphialus's marriage. All this alternates with the inconclusive battles and duels outside the imprisoning castle, with subplots and shifting scenes. The restlessness of Book III is quite distinct from the more placid pastoral romance of Book I and from the sequential adventure-chronicle of Book II.

Cecropia has just been visiting Philoclea, Pamela's sister, whose visible disarray in crisis (she 'suffered sorrow to distresse it selfe in her beautie') has led Cecropia to expect a similar vulnerability in Pamela. The elder sister is quite a different customer, however. In order to avoid the odious company of her gaolers, she has occupied herself with embroidery,

woorking uppon a purse certaine Roses and Lillies, as by the finenesse of the worke, one might see she had borowed her wittes of the sorow that owed them, and lent them wholy to that exercise. For the flowers she had wrought, caried such life in them, that the cunningest painter might have learned of her needle: which with so prety a maner made his careers to and fro through the cloth, as if the needle it selfe would have bene loth to have gone fromward such a mistress, but that it hoped to return thenceward very quickly againe: the cloth loking with many eies upon her, and lovingly embracing the wounds she gave it: the sheares also were at hand to behead the silke, that was growne to short. And if at any time she put her mouth to bite it off, it seemed, that where she had beene long in making of a Rose with her hand, she would in an instant make Roses with her lips; as the Lillies seemed to have their whitenesse, rather of the hande that made them, then of the matter whereof they were made; and that they grew there by the Sunnes of her eyes, and were refreshed by the most in discomfort comfortable ayre, which an unwares sigh might bestow upon them.[30]

This ekphrasis of Pamela's handiwork, like the Ladon *blason*, has a static, framed quality which arrests the frenetic pace of the preceding chapters, just as it checks Cecropia herself with its unexpected tranquillity.

Murray Krieger observes that 'ekphrastic ambition gives to the language art the extraordinary assignment of seeking to represent the literally unrepresentable',[31] and in notionally presenting the purse's 'fineness', Sidney actually seems to show Pamela's sorrow. But, we might ask, in what way could an embroidered purse *exhibit* the translated energy of Pamela's distress? The well-known emotional logic of managing psychic turmoil with disciplined concentration on a skilled manual task is credible, but the intentional fallacy of imputing emotional meaning to the *result* of such artisanal therapy is not. This purse, as a representation of Pamela's embattled spirit, is quite fantastic because her state of mind is literally unrepresentable.

The extreme, almost absurd, effort of representation which characterises this passage, and all complex ekphraseis, is extended: painters could learn of her needle which itself impersonates a besotted lover, as does the cloth in embracing the wounds she gives it. The final flourish couples the embroidered roses with her lips as she bites the thread, insists that her eyes, her breath and her white skin nourish and colour the silken lilies. Like the purse as the purported *summa* of her mental state, none of these descriptive analogies and metaphors are mimetically sustainable. At a stretch, pursed lips might resemble flowers; but the almost magical translation of whiteness from her hands to the embroidery – a whimsical extension of her actual manual handiwork – can never have material reality except in the cunning *faux*-mimesis of ekphrastic description. Pity, then, the painter who actually tries to learn from Pamela's needle, or rather, from this *description* of it.

Although characters may deliver ekphrastic passages (as Kalander does in Book I of the *Arcadia* when he tries to describe the inexpressibly beautiful daughters of his king), the extra-territorial quality of such deliveries discloses authorial command and control rather than the imagined sensibility of the speaking character. Such makerliness is flagged by the suggestion of the purse – a garden of amazingly life-like fake flowers – as a little world made cunningly and presided over by its natural deity, the demiurgical Pamela, whose eyes and sighs provide the natural elements by which it prospers; but the real star of this passage is Sidney himself, who has already daringly intimated in the *Defence* that poets are divine makers. The fantastic, extreme representation of the purse is like Edgar's rendition of Dover Cliff: the focal sensibility in this passage is clearly beyond the sensibility either of the makerly Pamela herself, or of the blunt-witted Cecropia; it can only be Sidney's, the maker's maker, and an ekphrasis of creative production.

Shortly after the description ends, our attention is shifted back to Cecropia, who like us inspects the purse (though with 'affected curiositie') and begins to dilate on its merits. The happy recipient of such an item, she says, 'shall have cause to account it, not as a purse for treasure, but as a treasure it selfe, worthie to be pursed up in the purse of his owne hart'.[32] Cecropia's insistence on the value of the purse as a material artefact, together with her crude lingering on the 'purse' pun delicately latent in Sidney's description of Pamela biting the thread, offers the reader a pointed comparison between on the one hand the meaningfully nuanced dream of a work of art that could never actually be, and, on the other, leaden clenches, trite commonplaces, and overblown rating of the actual item by someone who is quite immune to the complexities of love and devotion. The ekphrastic purse becomes a manifesto of Pamela's signal, rarefied virtues: Cecropia, a shallow rhetorician who comports herself not in poetry or embroidery but in complacent, meaningless, and dead-ended rhetorical figures, does her best to convert the delicate meanings ascribed by Sidney to the purse into the price of the money it might hold; her figures themselves figure forth her shabby soul just as clearly as the purse figures Pamela's shining virtue. To the aunt's fulsome and morally empty praise of her niece and the purse Pamela is able to smile and say, 'I valued it, even as a verie purse.'[33] This deflationary remark bears the stamp of Sidney's humour in the opening of the *Defence*, and punctures Cecropia's tedious clichés; but it also seems to devalue Sidney's own ekphrasis: despite his imaginary work, it remains a very purse and no more.

Ekphrasis was not limited in the early-modern period to works of art. Landscapes, shipwrecks, and human bodies and countenances are all, as Sidney shows throughout *Arcadia*, ekphrastic subjects. There is, however, something especially attractive about art works and artificial objects to ekphrastic poets. Where Sidney has us attend to an insignificant bit of handicraft, Shakespeare chooses an immense, elaborate painting of the siege and sack of Troy in *The Rape of Lucrece* (lines 1366–1582).[34] And where Sidney attributes impossible emotional and spiritual meaning to a thinly described flowery purse, the picture of Troy is thick and overloaded with painterly features of impossible subtlety and complexity.

'Troy's painted woes' (1492) make an ekphrasis over 200 lines long, and disrupt the final episode of an especially urgent narrative sequence. The rape has already been committed, and the agitated Lucrece has just summoned home her husband Collatine. The dreaded arrival of the implicated, shamed husband is likely to usher in the crisis of the story. We, and she, require distraction to fill the suspenseful lull in real time, a distraction supplied by her inspection, and Shakespeare's heroic rendition, of the picture. Although Lucrece searches the picture 'to find a face where all distress is stell'd' (1444), this is not a simple enumeration of items. It alludes constantly to painterly skill – 'A thousand lamentable objects there, | In scorn of nature, art gave lifeless life' (1373–4) – and these grammatical and personated interventions in the fictive 'reality' of the painting frame it as what it actually is, an artful verbal *tour de force* foregrounding the writer's skill before the imagined painter's. But the description relies heavily on conditionals which repeatedly call attention to the unreal or speculative nature of the artefact being described ('Many a dry drop *seem'd* a weeping tear' (1375); 'one *would swear he saw* [the peasants] quake and tremble' (1393)), opening up hermeneutic space for the reader's own assessment of the painting. The reader is certainly being coerced to analyse, but the analysis is radically unrestricted by authorial guidance.

The first eleven stanzas of the ekphrasis, packed with this exquisite plastic detail, constitute a caesura in our engagement with Lucrece, who in the first lines of the passage 'calls to mind where hangs a piece | Of skilful painting' (1366–7), and seeks it out to find a match for her 'distress and dolour' (1446). Her purpose, however, is delayed by all this description. In its place, the eleven stanzas intensify the direct communication from writer to reader with phrases like 'one might see' (1386), and more direct second-person address ('You might behold' (1388)), or with strangely agentless, passive constructions – 'A hand, a foot, a face, a leg, a head, | Stood for the whole to be imagined' (1428) – observed by a disembodied 'eye of mind' (1426). The bypassing of, or removing of agency from, Lucrece, the nominal 'viewer' of the work, foregrounds Shakespeare's skill rather than Lucrece's injury and mental state, and our response to the picture rather than hers.

If Sidney's Ladon *blason* displaced Pyrocles' urgent passion for Philoclea on to a poem about her, Lucrece – already objectified by her husband and his cronies as the subject of a wager – is displaced as the emotional centre of the poem. And the details which displace her are significant: these first eleven stanzas are almost exclusively concerned with the depiction of men and heroes and battles. Nestor's 'Thin winding breath which purl'd up to the sky' (1407) as he encourages the Greek troops, some of whom at the back seem to be jumping up to see him over the heads of their comrades (1414), is almost magically real, and seems to deceive the eye and cause hallucinations; the images apparently deliver undeliverable facts of intention and thought, as when the physiognomies of the Trojan mothers disclose joy 'stained' with 'heavy fear' (1435), and Achilles, standing just outside the frame of the picture, is metonymised in

> . . . his spear,
> Gripp'd in an armed hand; himself behind
> Was left unseen, save to the eye of mind.
>
> (1424–6)

The ekphrastic precision of these renditions, a precision which would in fact be unrenderable on canvas, is enthralling and commanding. What Shakespeare styles 'imaginary work' (1422) – implications like the metonym of Achilles – alludes to verbal pyrotechnics which require the cooperating imagination of the reader because it presents work which not only *does not* exist, but *could not* exist. In explicitly asking us to suspend disbelief it asks us to support the fantasy of an unrepresentable object in aid of the narrative.[35]

The receiving sensibility eventually returns to Lucrece, but her reception of the painting's visual cues is no more conceivable than Shakespeare's directly conveyed metonyms: Lucrece, herself transformed and imprisoned by her defilement, observes Hecuba gazing upon her husband's wounds:

> In her the painter had anatomiz'd
> Time's ruin, beauty's wrack, and grim care's reign;
> Her cheeks with chops and wrinkles were disguis'd:
> Of what she was no semblance did remain.
> Her blue blood chang'd to black in every vein,
> Wanting the spring that those shrunk pipes had fed,
> Show'd life imprison'd in a body dead.
>
> (1450–6)

Lucrece 'shapes her sorrows to the beldam's woes' (1457) and vows to speak for the mute Hecuba, as if supplying a subscription to an emblem, by 'tun[ing] thy woes with my lamenting tongue' (1465). Each woman, the victim of male aggression in the form of rape or military vengeance, is captured in an unrepresentable ecstasy of grief, and figures forth what Sidney calls 'the outward beauty of such a virtue'.[36] Next to the human catastrophe it depicts, the spectacular ekphrasis of the war is suddenly as paltry as the war itself.

'To see sad sights moves more than hear them told' (1324), Shakespeare informs us. Lucrece deliberately searches the Troy painting as if only some epic representational simile would be adequate to her own predicament. Spenser, by contrast, requires a longer and even more spectacular ekphrasis in *The Faerie Queene* – of the tapestries, bas-reliefs and masque in the House of Busirane (3.11–12) – in order to heighten our consciousness of point of view, narratorial command, and writerly ostentation. Although it, too, contains a fictional viewer – Britomart – she, unlike Lucrece, is one who seems almost blind to what is being shown.

At the conclusion of Book III, Britomart breaches the defences of Busirane's dreadful house, where the enchanter is holding the beautiful Amoret and applying coercive spells to force her virtue. Amoret's resistance is repaid in the physical torture (he is gradually disembowelling her) revealed in the last stanzas of the ekphrasis. But no one unless free of sexual passion can cross Busirane's threshold; the virgin Britomart alone can break in. The ekphrasis is organised as a moving panorama of Britomart's passage through two rooms as she searches within for Amoret, a structure which makes us accept her (as we do Lucrece) as the nominal or primary viewer, mediating the surrounding pictorial details. The artefacts in Busirane's rooms depict the disturbing, even horrific, casualties in '*Cupids* warres' and 'cruell battels' (3.11.29.5–6). The first room is hung with tapestries showing the loves of the great deities as perpetrated by the little winged god: Jove, Apollo and Neptune are depicted in all their various metamorphic adventures, as bestialised and demeaned as their victims. In the second room, Britomart sees walls decorated in gold relief 'Wrought with wilde Antickes . . . | In the rich metall, as they living were' (51.4–6), showing love in 'thousand monstrous formes' (7) among human beings. These bas-reliefs are hung with ruined weapons and trampled garlands of bays, indicating love's conquest of the mighty. Here on the following day Britomart witnesses a triumphal procession or masque of Cupid, with twelve personages representing the torments of love, each displaying an appropriate symbolic countenance and allegorical implements. It is at the end of this masque that the captive Amoret is displayed.

Although most of the adventures of gods in the thrall of love are catalogued rather than intensely described as pictures, Spenser at times seems to be reproducing actual images, such as the picture of Danaë and the golden shower, and praising the skill of the artist who with 'sweet wit' paints Leda asleep in daffodils, eyes only half-closed as she observes the approaching swan, images 'So lively and so like, that living sence it fayld' (46.9). For the most part, however, the tapestry is noted, episode by episode, but not *shown*. Indeed, Spenser says that these adventures are '*writ*' in the work (30.1), and later describes them as 'told' by it. (44.1). The verbs of showing ('painted', 'portrayed', 'enwoven') alternate with these other verbs of speaking or writing, and the effect of the sequence of tapestried episodes is ambivalent: are we being told what the tapestry shows (is this a proper ekphrastic rehearsal of described pictures?) or are we being told the well-known Ovidian stories to which they allude? This part of the narrative may, for all its lush detail, be iconic rather than enumerative. If so, it seems to distinguish the narrative experience of the reader from the visual experience of Britomart, the looker-on, to sideline her nominal sensibility in favour of ours, a shift which enhances the powerful indications of her sexual naiveté – Britomart (unlike Lucrece) cannot *see* the mildly pornographic images for what they are.

The shift from the two-dimensional tapestry of the first room to the almost three-dimensional 'wrought' gold of the second is a progression from a frankly artificial representation on a plane to an emerging mimetic one in space, a transition heightened by the addition of the actual spoils of war hung as trophies against the golden walls. After only a brief, if dense, ekphrasis of the bas-reliefs, the transition to this more substantial mimesis is finally supplied in the masque of Cupid, whose celebrants enter and fill the eerie emptiness and 'solemne silence'. These masquers are from Britomart's point of view real persons, not artefacts, and yet – because allegory always confuses mimesis – as impersonators of abstract qualities they inhabit what theorists of the theatre term the 'second', invented world of mimetic illusion rather than the 'first' or 'real' world of Britomart, their audience.[37] At the end of the procession, Despight and Cruelty lead the debilitated, barely ambulant Amoret, her extracted heart borne in front of her in a basin. The disclosure of Amoret, a first-world character like Britomart rather than an impersonating masquer, is shocking precisely because she appears in her own traumatised person rather than as a representation of suffering. The mimetic transition which unfolds incrementally throughout the course of the ekphrasis gradually attains full mimesis in the masquers, and full reality in Amoret.

In this sequence of rooms and displayed artefacts, Britomart, like Lucrece, is virtually absent from the account of the tapestries: for more than twenty stanzas, Spenser seems to present the loves of the gods directly to the reader, with no allusion to Britomart's presence in the scene or to her reactions. She reappears at the end of the tapestry sequence, at first dazed by the sight of the idol of Cupid on the altar, then more concerned with casting her practical 'busie eye' around the room to find the door to the second room. Her bold steps conduct us to the next room of golden bas-reliefs, and the two ekphrastic stanzas presenting the carvings and the trophies continue to exclude the warlike maid. Her response to this room, as to the previous one, is to put aside her wonder for a pragmatic domestic worry about its emptiness: 'Straunge thing it seem'd, that none was to pos-sesse | So rich purveyance, ne them keepe with carefulnesse' (3.11.53.5–9). Throughout the rendition of these two rooms, the only indication of Brito-mart's response to anything she sees, aside from unexamined puzzlement, is connected not with pictorial representations at all, but with the enigmatic commands inscribed on the walls, 'Be bold, be bold . . . Be not too bold' (54.3, 8).

It is only that night, when she encounters the masquers and Amoret, that she begins to feature as a mediating element in the narrative. Until the masquers arrive, Britomart has been, as we have been, the detached spectator of highly wrought, highly conventional vignettes whose elaborate plastic artifice is self-evident. But the masquers are not artificial in that sense, and seem, moreover, to perform a narrative of the progress of love which leads not to fulfilment but to horror. She responds like a practised theatre-goer to the grave *nuncio* figure who beckons with his hands 'In signe of silence, as to hear a play' (3.12.4.4). As she stands viewing the 'strange intendiment' (5.2),' our own position as spectators shifts: we were asked before to regard the tapestries and the bas-reliefs directly and without any interior mediation, as if we and not Britomart had been standing before them. During the masque, our vantage point becomes much like Britomart's: we too are at a play, watching mimetically realised figures. One of these figures is, of course, Britomart herself, who now becomes part of the scene we are asked to witness, much as we include Pamela herself in the ekphrasis of her needleworking. The 'rude confused rout' (25.1) of emblematic masquer figures – Strife, Sorrow, Dread, and many more whom Spenser is at a loss to name – are the phantasms of 'wauering wemens wit' (26.4), the disordered thoughts generated by the pains of love, pains Britomart herself does not yet feel. This masque, a thickly interpolated ekphrasis of a state of mind, is irrelevant to her.

This is why, when Britomart tries to become, literally, a part of that masque by intruding into the furthest room, the back-stage area (so to speak) into which the masquers disappear, she in effect destroys it, finds it vanished. Instead, only Amoret remains, not a phantasm or a representation, but a real woman chained to a pillar in the midst of further torture by Busirane, a woman to whom the allegorical masque is all too meaningful. It is only when Britomart defends Amoret's life against the enchanter and forces him to undo his spells that his lustful power is neutralised, and the decorated rooms, like the masque, are 'cleane subuerst . . . their glory quite decayd' (42.3–4).

At no point in the entire sequence does Britomart interpret, or indeed respond, to the pictures or to Amoret herself. Her pictorial illiteracy is equivalent to her sexual innocence, whereas the sexually experienced Lucrece self-consciously searches the painting for analogues of her own predicament. For both poets, ekphrastic nuance is only available to the experienced eye. It remains for Britomart to evolve as a spectator, and as a lover, a process which waits upon the events of Book V.

Originating as a weapon of forensic oratory, ekphrasis in early-modern literature becomes a subtle, insinuating instrument of narratorial patterning, authorial control, and psychological insight. At its most supple, it prompts strenuous interpretive work: characters within the fiction and readers without are asked to view and analyse the pictures on show; occasionally, differential responses from the two potential audiences become part of the meaning of the figure. Ekphrasis is not only an instantiation of Sidney's claims for poetic makerliness, but embodies a difficult, Protestant aesthetic, where understanding is won by effort.

CHAPTER 7

Ye have another manner of disordered speech, when ye misplace your words or clauses and set that before which should be behind, and *è converso*, we call it in English proverbe, the cart before the horse, the Greeks call it *Histeron proteron*, we name it the Preposterous . . .

Puttenham, *The Arte of English Poesie* (1589)

ENOBARBUS Naught, naught, al naught, I can behold no longer:
                Thantoniad, the Egyptian Admirall,
                With all their sixty flye, and turne the Rudder . . .

William Shakespeare, *Antony and Cleopatra*, 3.10.1–3

Hysteron proteron: or the preposterous

PATRICIA PARKER

Hysterologia, or Hysteron-Proteron, is a placing of that before, which should be after, and somethings after, which should be before . . .

Thomas Hall, *Vindiciae literarum* (1655)

Hysteron-proteron . . . a speaking or doing praeposterously, putting the Cart before the horse.

Elisha Coles, *An English Dictionary* (1677)

It is but an Hysteron Proteron, and preposterous conceit, to fancie wages before the work . . .

Henry More, *Annotations* (1682)

In early-modern descriptions, hysteron proteron – from the Greek for *hysteros* (later or latter) placed first and *protos* (the former or first) put after or last – was inseparable from what was known as the 'preposterous', a reversal of 'post' for 'pre', behind for before, back for front, second for first, and end or sequel for beginning. Susenbrotus's influential description of this rhetorical figure, in 1540, for example, made it a synonym for *praeposteratio*, from *posterus* (after or behind) and *prae* (in front or before).[1] In England, Puttenham used 'Preposterous' itself as his formal English equivalent for this Greek rhetorical term, ranging '*Histeron proteron*, or the Preposterous' under 'Figures Auricular working by disorder', in a chapter devoted to the general category of *Hiperbaton*, or disorders of speech.[2] Describing it as that particular form of 'disordered speech, when ye misplace your words or clauses and set that before which should be behind, and *e converso*', he remarks that 'we call it in English proverbe, the cart before the horse', and while 'the Greeks call it *Histeron proteron*, we name it the Preposterous'.[3] The instances he provides of this discursive disorder include phrases in which the expected temporal order is reversed – as when, for example, 'One describing his landing upon a strange coast, sayd thus preposterously':

When we had climbde the clifs, and were ashore,
Whereas he should have said by good order.
When we were come a shore and clymed had the cliffs
For one must be on land ere he can clime. And as another said:
My dame that bred me up and bare me in her wombe.
Whereas the bearing is before the bringing up.[4]

Puttenham's examples of hysteron proteron foreground familiar illustrations of this rhetorical figure in the period: the last of them even appears in Shakespeare's *Twelfth Night* (a play famously given to other kinds of disorder) when the Captain tells Viola that he was 'bred and born | Not three hours' travel from this very place'.[5] At the same time, Puttenham's rendering of hysteron proteron as 'The Preposterous' stands as emblematic of the conflation of these two terms in the period. Angel Day, for example, describes hysteron proteron as a preposterous reversal, putting 'that which ought to be in the first place in the second'.[6] By 1577, Henry Peacham's *Garden of Eloquence* had already described it as a preposterous placing not simply of words but of temporal order or sequence:

Hysteron proteron, when that is laste sayde, that was first done, and it differs from *Anastrophe*, for that is a preposterous placing of wordes, and this a transposition of things thus . . . the castle was made very high, the foundation layd ful deepe, here the laying of the foundation, is last said, that was first done, and the making of it high, first sayd, that was last done.[7]

Puttenham similarly distinguishes hysteron proteron from anastrophe, which he defines as 'a preposterous order, or a backward setting of words', as in 'all Italy about I went' for 'I went about all Italy' (p. 140). But what distinguishes hysteron proteron in these descriptions – and makes it available for the more general societal disorder it figured – was its inversion at the level of 'things' as well as of 'words'. Richard Sherry's *Treatise of the Figures of Grammer and Rhetorike* (1555) defines 'Hysterologia' (from Greek *hysteros* or 'later' and *logia* or 'speech') as a figure 'when the preposicion is not put unto the nowen whereunto it serveth, but to the verbe' and separates 'Hysteron proteron' from 'the figure before, because there is but transposicion of the wordes: and here is a transposicion of thinges: that is, when that in the order of speaking is set in the first place, that was not firste done but second'.[8] Here too, hysteron proteron is distinguished from anastrophe, which is simply 'a preposterous orderyng or setting of woordes', even though both come under the general heading of hyperbaton or 'troubled order'.[9] The definitional boundaries between these various forms of disordered speech do not, however, remain reliably stable in early-modern discussions. Hysterologia can be a form of hyperbaton that involves the interposition of a phrase between a preposition and its object; but also a synonym for hysteron proteron itself, as it is in one of its definitions in the *OED*.[10]

Whatever the shifting distinctions – and unstable definitions – that alternately distinguished hysteron proteron from hysterologia and made them early-modern synonyms, the common denominator remained the 'preposterous' itself and 'The Cart before the Horse', its familiar proverbial equivalent. Throughout early-modern writing, the definition of hysteron proteron as a preposterous reversal paralleled the definition of the 'preposterous' itself – as the 'out of order, overthwarth, transverted, or last done which by rule have ben first' (Huloet, 1552); and as a verb for 'to disorder, or turne arsivarsie; to put the cart before the horse' (Cotgrave, 1611).[11]

This was true not only in rhetorical discussions but also in dictionary definitions. Thomas Blount's *Glossographia* (1656) – which devotes itself to the elucidation of 'hard words' – defines 'Hysteron proteron' as 'sometimes used in derision of that which is spoken or done preposterously or quite contrary', adding, once again, that its 'common phrase is; *The Cart before the horse*'.[12] Edward Phillips defines hysteron proteron as 'a preposterous manner of speaking or writing, expressing that first which should be last'. We might also note – since it is suggestive for *King Lear*, where 'the cart draws the horse' (1.4.224) appears as a reproach to the king who has preposterously made his 'daughters' his 'mothers' (1.4.171–2) and '*Hysterica passio*' or the 'mother' (2.4.56–7) figures a parallel inversion – that he ranges it in a list that comes after the other term with which it shares a Greek root – '*Hysterical*, (Greek) as hysterical passion, a certain disease in women commonly called Fits of the Mother.'[13] It should come as no surprise, then, that one of the societal disorders it figured was the overturning of the prescribed order of female and male.

Hysteron proteron was thus a term from the discourse of rhetoric for an inversion that reversed the order of 'things' themselves, including in both temporal and logical sequence. In this sense, it appeared across a broad range of early-modern writing, as both a blemish and an exploited licence of order and style. William Barton notes, for example, in *The Choice and Flower of the Old Psalms* (1645) that 'there is not one bald phrase or ill-favoured hysteron proteron in all the book'.[14] Luke Milbourne's *Notes on Dryden's Virgil* (1698) observe in the *Georgics* what he calls 'an egregious *Hysteron Proteron*' in 'Swims down the Stream, and plunges in the deep', when if the ram 'be forc'd to leap from high, he'll plunge in the deep before he swims down the Stream'.[15] Another writer (in less negative terms) notes what he terms the 'inverted method' used by poets and orators, 'when particulars are disposed before universals' and 'the parts of a thing propounded are not handled after the same order, by which they were laid downe, which is called *Hysteron Proteron*, that is, the later former, or preposterous'.[16]

In the field of formal logic, hysteron proteron simultaneously denoted a 'preposterous' inversion, in this case 'the logical fallacy of assuming as true and using as a premise a proposition that is yet to be proved', or the proving of a proposition by reference to another one that presupposes it.[17] But it also connoted a reversal of 'cause' and 'effect'. One of the clearest articulations of such 'preposterous' reversal is provided in George Thompson's *Aimatiasis* (1670), which charges its opponent with committing 'a Hysteron Proteron in nature' by confusing 'primary precedent causes' with 'consequents of the same', observing that it is 'preposterous to take in that for a cause, which is but a meer effect, whose Posteriority plainly shews a dependency upon something going before'.[18] Much earlier, as I have detailed elsewhere, Shakespeare's *Othello* exploits the 'preposterous conclusions' that ensue when end or effect comes before cause, as part of the pervasive recourse to logical as well as other structures of hysteron proteron within the entire Shakespeare canon.[19]

Hysteron proteron itself – as 'preposterous' inversion – provides a signal early-modern instance of the premise of this entire volume, that what might seem to be simply a figure of speech could underwrite much broader cultural concerns. Early modern biblical commentators, for example, frequently remark on the importance of hysteron proteron at the local level of reading, in their analysis of particular scriptural texts. Henry Burton observes that 'hysteron proteron . . . is not unusual in Scripture story'.[20] Edward Leigh notes that Mary Magdalene's anointing of 'the feet of Jesus' before they are 'wiped . . . with her hair' in John 12:3 is to be read as a '*Hysteron proteron*, for she first wiped his feet from dust and durt, and then annointed them'.[21] Edward Calamy comments on the verse of Psalm 138 ('For thou hast magnified thy Word above all thy name') that it is to be understood 'Hysteron proteron, that is, thou hast by thy Word, (that is, by performing thy Word and Promises) Magnified thy name above all things' or 'Thy word of Promise in Christ, and thy faithfulness in performing of it, doth more exalt thy Name, than any thing by which thou art made known.'[22] But at the same time, hysteron proteron functions as an index of more fundamental issues of order, priority, and sequence. In the polemics of the Reformist bishop John Jewel, for example, it functions as a crux in the debate over transubstantiation itself, which turned on contested lines from Matthew, 26:26: 'In these woordes, *Take ye*: *Eate ye*: *This is my Bodie*, They have founde a figure called Hysteron Proteron, which is, when the whole speache is out of order, and that set byhinde, that shoulde goe before. For thus they are driven, to shifte it, and turn it: *This is my Bodie*: *Take ye*: *Eate yee*.'[23]

In other theological writing, hysteron proteron figured central issues of priority and precedence. Thomas Hall remarks in 1655 of the frequency in scripture of 'Hysterologia or Hysteron Proteron' that the 'Pen men of Scripture, doe not alwaies observe the just order of things, but the truth of the History; they set them down, in that order, in which they came to their minds, and not in that order, which they fell out in.'[24] At the level of spiritual priorities, John Reading in *A Guide to the Holy City* (1651) counsels his readers to 'Seek first the kingdome of God and his righteousnesse', warning against that '*hysteron proteron* wherein worldly desires' claim 'to be served before God'.[25] On an anagogical level, hysteron proteron could at the same time figure a focus first on the latter end of history itself. One late seventeenth-century commentary on the Book of Revelation, for example, remarks in its line-by-line reading of the prophecy of the fall of Babylon that the

voice out of Heaven to God's people, to come out of her, was uttered before the Rising of the Witnesses, and this Angel's strenuous proclaiming the fall of Babylon. This warning, I say, precedes both the partial and final overthrow of that great City. But the description of her desolation and ruines from their being haunted with Devils and unclean Birds, respects especially her final overthrow. Nor are the people of God bid to come out of her Ruines, as I have noted before, but to come out of Babylon both before her partial and consummate fall. Here there is an Hysterology.[26]

The perspective from the end – or the ultimate fall of Babylon – is thus provided by a 'hysterology' or hysteron proteron in which the end comes first, in order to give strength to those suffering in Babylon before that end is reached.

Theologically, such an assimilation of the trope is found in writing well before the early-modern period. Commenting on the second Canto of Dante's *Paradiso*, where the speed of the pilgrim's ascent to the sphere of the Moon is compared to the time it takes an arrow to 'strike, fly, and leave the bow' (*Paradiso*, 2.23–26), Charles Singleton observes that the sequence in which 'the three incidents in the flight of the arrow are arranged in inverse order' was known to ancient rhetoric by the Greek name of hysteron proteron, meaning '"the last [put] first"' and adds that Benvenuto refers to it as praeposteratio. 'Such a figure', he continues, 'suggests something *caused from the end*, since the eye is invited to consider the end first and then the action as seen from the end.'[27] When hysteron proteron or the 'last first' recurs in *Paradiso* 22 – in 'tratto e messo | nel foco il dito' ['pulled out and thrust your finger in the fire'] – it suggests nothing less than the theological underpinning of the *Divine Comedy* itself, where the perspective from the end underwrites a journey whose autobiographical narrator has already reached the end towards which his pilgrim alter-ego travels.[28]

Hysteron proteron in the larger theological sense reminds us simultaneously of the scriptural principle 'the last shall be first' and underwrites the relation of the Testaments themselves – the reversal through which the younger or New Testament claims priority over the elder or first, as in the story of Esau and Jacob and other such biblical reversals. To this we shall return – in treating of early-modern Protestant writing that characterises Papists as 'preposterating' the testaments, reversing the reversal, so to speak, by reverting from New to the Old or 'Hebrew' testament. But first we need to survey the uses of hysteron proteron itself as the familiar figure in the period for an entire series of reversals, both societal and bodily.

FROM HYSTERON PROTERON TO THE PREPOSTEROUS

> All things are Arsa versa, topsie turvie, histeron, proteron
>
> Sir Roger L'Estrange, *A New Dialogue between*
> *Some Body and No Body* (1681)

Hysteron proteron as a general figure for the topsy turvy or arsy-versy is found repeatedly in early-modern writing, making its other name – 'The Preposterous' – the bridge between rhetoric or logical order and inversions of all kinds. In Middleton's and Rowley's *A Faire Quarrell* (1617), for example, the father Russell observes that:

> Wisemen begets fooles, and fooles are the fathers
> To many wise children. Histeron, Proteron,
> A great scholler may beget an Ideot,
> And from the plow tayle may come a great scholar.[29]

Joseph Beaumont's *Psyche, or Love's mystery, in XXIV. cantos: displaying the intercourse betwixt Christ, and the soul* makes hysteron proteron the figure for an entire *mundus inversus* or upside down world: 'How wild | A Hysteron Proteron's this, which Nature crosses, | And far above the *top* the *bottom* tosses.'[30]

Such preposterous inversion, however, involved not only the turning of hierarchies upside down but also the reading of scripture itself 'backward', in the reverse of the providential direction. Henry King's 1640 royal anniversary sermon provides a particularly concentrated example of all of these 'preposterous' forms:

Great is the truth everywhere, and great this truth which extorts consent from these, and will evict it from all such who, praeposterous to God's order and method, will needs read his text backward, turning the heels to heaven, the head to earth, whiles they go about to whelm the kingdom over the king, and set the nations, that is the people, above him whom God hath set over them.[31]

Making the direct connection between the rhetorical figure writ large and the 'preposterous' inversion of the 'Physical' or carnal identified with the Hebrew testament for the 'grace' of the New, Thomas Edwards later in the century commented that 'To change the Covenant of Grace into that of Works, or cause the former in its Administration and Dispensation to depend upon the latter' was to commit 'a preposterous Hysteron Proteron'.[32]

As with its application to the reversal of the order of the scriptures, hysteron proteron could simultaneously figure multiple reversals of proper sequence, as, for example, in the reversals involving 'venus' in Thomas Cogan's *Haven of Health* (1584):

Everie man therefore that hath a care of his health as much as he may, must not onelie use a measure in those five thinges, that is to say, in labor, meat, drinke, sleepe, and venus, but also must use them in such order as Hippocrates hath proposed them, that is, to beginne the preservation of health with labour, after labour to take meate, after meate, drinke: after both, sleepe: and venus last of all. And not contrariwise using *Hysteron Proteron*, to begin with venus and to end in labour.[33]

Hysteron Proteron frequently provided an emblem not just of bodily but of political and religious disorder, and of the inverted reasoning of one's polemical opponents. John Lilburne's *An Unhappy Game at Scotch and English* (1646) – which announces on its title page that it will provide 'A full answer from England to the papers of Scotland. Wherein their Scotch mists and their fogs; their sayings and gaine-sayings; their juglings, their windings and turnings; hither and thither, backwards and forwards, and forwards and backwards again' – accuses its opponents of 'jugling Husteron Proteron tricks' in defending 'king-craft' against 'the two houses of Parliament and people of England'.[34]

At the same time, hysteron proteron provided a figure for turning the body itself back-to-front or 'arsy versy'. In Marston's *The Dutch Courtesan*, Freevill describes a character who 'thrusts his wench forth the window, and himself most preposterously, with his heels forward, follows'.[35] In *A New Dialogue between Some Body and No Body* by Sir Roger L'Estrange (1681), a bodily turning to the 'Back-Side' quickly prompts not only a reminder of hysteron proteron as a rhetorical trope but the entire range of 'backward' reversals:

SOMEBODY ... I will turn and go backward.
NOBODY Must I speak then to your Back-Side?
SOMEBODY Ay, Ay, all things are Arsa versa, topsie turvie, histeron, proteron – The Chimes go backward, the World runs backward, the Age backslides, and all things turn backward.[36]

As a figure of 'hindpart foremost' or back-to-front, such a 'preposterous' or backward turning in the period was simultaneously applied to witches who did everything backward (evoked here in 'The Chimes go backward') and to sodomy understood as 'preposterous venus' or 'preposterous amor', a turning back to front that frequently assimilated sodomitical reversals to witchcraft as well as other kinds of 'arse varse' inversion in the period.[37]

'Preposterous' in this sense is echoed in Shakespeare, in Thersites' characterisation of Achilles and his 'masculine whore' as 'preposterous discoveries',[38] while references to sexual turning back to front are frequently reflected in what was called the 'the preposterous Italian way' (Brome, 1632), as in Middleton's reference to 'an Italian world', where 'many men know not before from behind', or the 'back-door'd Italian' of Dekker's and Middleton's *The Honest Whore*.[39]

THE PREPOSTEROUS IN RELIGIOUS WRITING

The *Turks* are preposterously zealous in praying for the conversion, or perversion rather, of Christians to their irreligious Religion ...
                                        Alexander Ross, *Alcoran* (1649)

If ye spell Roma backwarde . . . it is preposterus *amor*, a love out of order or a love agaynst kynde.   John Bale, *Englysh Votaryes* (1546)

Hysteron proteron and its synonym the 'preposterous' thus connected multiple forms of inversion in the period. These included not only the reversal of elder and younger, ruler and ruled, but the hierarchies of gender, whereby the elevation of female over male, and the reversal of the teleology of gender itself – from 'imperfect' female to allegedly 'perfect' male – were figured as 'preposterous' inversions.[40] It also included the 'preposterous' reversals of witchcraft (in a tradition in which, as Stuart Clark observes, witches were said to do everything backwards),[41] reflected in the 'magicall Daunce, full of praeposterous change . . . making theyr circles backward, to the left hand' of the witches in Jonson's *Masque of Queenes*; in 'For nature so prepost'rously to err . . . Sans witchcraft could not' in *Othello*; in the backward 'charm's wound up' of *Macbeth*; and in the 'retrograde and preposterous way' of *The Late Lancashire Witches*, where wife rules husband, son commands father, servants intimidate children and the church bells are rung backward.[42] The 'preposterous' was simultaneously used in the period to characterise both Turk and Jew, identified with bewitching 'backwards' from baptism to circumcision, from Gospel liberty to the 'bondage' of the testament associated with 'Hagar' and her son Ishmael.[43] Galatians (in the Geneva Bible translation) treats of those who 'pervert the Gospel of Christ' (1:7) – a 'pervert' that corresponds to the *convertere* of the Vulgate text – providing one of the influential sources of early-modern descriptions of 'turning Turk' (or 'returning Jew') as a preposterous 'conversion' (as in Alexander Ross's claim that 'The Turks are preposterously zealous in praying for the conversion, or perversion rather, of Christians to their irreligious Religion').[44] And it was frequently combined with Romans 1 on reverting or turning back from 'truth' to 'lies', verses that coupled the 'uncleanness' of 'idolatry' with a sexual 'turning' from 'natural use' to 'that which is against nature'.

Galatians as a whole provided an important authority for the contrast between progression 'forward' and its 'backward' perversion. Throughout its Geneva glosses, turning 'backwards' or 'backe' – from the 'Spirit' to the 'lusts of the flesh', 'fornication', 'uncleannesse', 'idolatry', and 'witchcraft' – is repeatedly opposed to moving 'forward' to the (promised) 'ende'. Along with other New Testament texts, it contributed to the teleological model of reading Hebrew Scriptures 'aright', progressing in the 'right' as opposed to the 'sinister' direction, from darkness to light, flesh to spirit, 'imperfection' to 'perfection'. Galatians 3 describes the Old Testament as a *paedagogus* or 'schoolemaster' (3:24) and repeatedly stresses the importance of moving from Jewish 'Lawe' to Christian 'faith' rather than the reverse, an inversion of which the Geneva gloss comments 'this were not to goe forward, but backward'.[45] To read scripture aright was thus to move from left to right, from imperfect to perfect, spelling what it calls the ABC of the Hebrew testament in a forward direction, opposed to witchcraft, sodomy, and other forms of preposterous inversion. One early-modern text even refers to those who reverse the order of the testaments as readers who 'usen *arse*warde' (or carnally) the 'gospel' itself. Another Protestant polemic of 1607 condemns what it characterises as the '*preposterousnes*' of the Roman Church, accusing the latter of reverting to 'superstitions and opinions plainly magical' and of serving 'Satans turne' by inverting 'reason' and 'sense' (or 'will'). In its diatribe against the 'Idolatrie of the Crosse', it claims that this papist idol '*preposterateth*' in multiple fashions, placing 'a tradition of mans before Gods precept' (a '*preposteration* to renewe a Crosse so zealously'), in a passage that goes on to claim that 'wee cannot misse' such '*preposteration* in it', since 'papistes preferre their owne traditions before Gods Lawes'. It repeatedly associates such preposterous or backward turning not only with the reversion to idolatry in Romans 1, but with the 'witchcraft' of the 'devill'.[46] In the tradition of inverted right and left, another seventeenth-century text speaks (in a passage filled with echoes of Galatians' 'bewitching') of the 'dexterous sinisterity' of the 'Romish Priests' in 'seducing souls'.[47]

Within the discourse of witchcraft itself, texts such as Thomas Cooper's *The Mystery of Witch-craft* (1617) similarly identified the preposteration of the biblical testaments with the 'arsy-versy' inversion of sense over reason and the 'Popery' associated with the 'filthynesse' and 'uncleannese' of witchcraft's arseward proceedings, as reason 'turned upside down' gives way to the 'flesh'.[48] The act of turning 'backwards' from perfection to imperfection, from Gospel 'truth' to the 'lies' of Antichrist and 'dark ceremonies' of the 'Jews', assimilated both idolatry and sodomy (as part of the 'horrible uncleannesse not to be named') to a series of figures for preposterous inversion. At the same time, 'preposterating' or turning backward to the testament of 'Arabian' Hagar (associated with both Turk and Jew) was conflated with the biblical figure of muddying the pure water of Abraham's wells (understood as purified by Isaac/Christ), adding a racialised imagery of 'pollution' to the 'uncleanliness' of sodomy and idolatry from Romans 1.[49]

Reading in the right direction, from Hebrew 'imperfection' to the 'perfection' of the Gospel – rather than hysteron proteron – was further conflated with the teleology of progression from 'imperfect' to 'perfect' male, contrasted to 'preposterous amor' as well as to the 'eunuch' who 'gelded hym selfe into a preposterous offyce of Venery' in the work of John Bale.[50] I will end, then, with the importance of all such 'preposterous' inversions in the writing of the 'bilious Bale' because his work provides such a striking early-modern instance. As a convert from the Church of Rome, Bale draws attention to anxieties surrounding the reversibility of conversion itself, not only for the individual convert but for England, whose post-Reformation history provided repeated instances of turning (and re-turning) in both directions. Bale's writings graphically demonstrate why it matters to reread early-modern understandings of 'the preposterous' across a spectrum broad enough to encompass the preposteration of the testaments themselves as an 'arseward' or 'sodometical' reversal.[51] In Bale's anti-Papist writings, *Roma* as 'Praeposterous' *Amor* is not only a gloss on the 'turning' of Romans 1 to 'unclean' idols and a 'preposterous offyce of Venery' but a polemic against the Judaising of 'Hebrew' ceremonies that reverse the teleological movement of the testaments themselves from 'perfection' to 'imperfection' – moving not 'forward' but 'backward' as the Geneva gloss would later put it. New Testamental figures of backsliding (the return of 'a dogge, to his vomyte' and 'the sowe that was washed, into hys olde fylthy puddle') constitute what Bale terms (in another graphic, bodily image) '*arsewarde* procedynges', a reversal of the 'perfeccion of the Gospell' by reversion to the 'imperfeccion' of Antichrist. The term in Bale that connects all of these forms of inversion is the 'preposterous', including not only the inseparable couple of sodomy and idolatry but the Galatians figure of Christians 'bewitched' into turning 'backwards', to 'circumcision' and the Jewish 'testament' of 'Agar' the 'bondwoman'. In *The Image of Both Churches*, the 'proude bishop of Rome' – condemned by Bale as 'the preposterouse vycar of the lambe' – is associated with 'buggerye and other carnall beastlynesse', part of the Roman Church's 'subtyle witche craftes' and 'dayly sacryfyce to the devyll'. The Luciferic inversion Bale terms 'the monstruouse nature of that malignant churche of Antichrist' underwrites not only the *mundus inversus* of 'Anti-cristes kyngedome' but preposterous inversions of all kinds, tellingly characterised by Bale as 'all' in the 'femynine' gender: 'manye excellent writers in discribinge Anti-cristis kyngedome / hath called yt a false / fylthye / Fleshlye / whoryshe / preposterouse / . . . promiscuouse / and abhominable generacion. Here is the childe sayd to begett his father / or the sonnes childe his grandefather / and all in the femynine gendre.'[52]

Since Bale himself began as a Roman votary, his subsequent Protestant polemics became a re-righting both of his personal history and of the history of England, turned back (as he represents it, in a clear echo of Romans 1) to 'Romyshe lyes' and 'Italyshe beggerye' (the word in early-modern English so often conflated with 'buggery'), identified with the Roman Church and the Italian Polydore Vergil, whose history of England Bale both rewrites and rerights.[53] Re-righting in every sense becomes in Bale the rectifying of the 'backward' turning (or 'Roma spelled backwards') of the preposterous *amor*, idolatry and 'witchcraft' of Rome itself. In his play *Three Laws* (in another clear echo of Romans 1), the 'Necromantic' character of 'Idolatry' (dressed in the habit of 'an olde wytche') is inseparable from 'bestyall Sodomye'. The sinister or backward inversions of witchcraft are conflated in this play with the converting or turning of male into female, 'he' into 'she'; while the rerighting associated with scriptural right reading becomes the teleological or left-to-right progression of the 'three Laws' of the play's title (from

'Natura Lex' to 'Moseh Lex' to 'Christi Lex'), a progression associated with movement to the 'perfect' male from the 'imperfect' or female (including all that Bale designated by the 'femynine gendre'), from the 'sodomye' or 'olde buggerage' of Rome to the 'Evangelium' who is both 'a man of the new learning and a married man'.[54]

The 'true faythfull churche' of England is proclaimed in *Three Laws* – by 'Deus Pater' himself – to be 'clensed by the power of our ryght hand', from the pollution and 'fylth' of Papistry and its sodometical 'infeccyons'.[55] Reading from left to right, 'imperfect' to 'perfect', involves throughout Bale's writings the re-righting of the 'preposterous' inversions of Papists condemned repeatedly (as in other Protestant polemicists) as the 'Synagogue of Satan'. The preposteration of the testaments which in Bale is inseparable from 'preposterous amor' is thus paralleled by the sinister inversion of the right reading of Scripture and the right writing of the history of England itself. The 'ryght hond' of scripture – turned or 'wrast(ed)' in the wrong direction by the Roman 'Clergye' in Bale's English history play *King Johan* – is ultimately restored by the proto-Protestant King John, in a play in which the false writing of English history is identified with the sinister 'rites' of the Pope whose excommunicating 'curse' associates him with the witchcraft of 'Satan the Devyll'.[56] Turning 'back' from the truth of the 'Gospell' (or the 'right invocacion of God' contrasted with the 'ydolatries' of that 'most detestable sodomite')[57] is characterised by Bale as the inverse of reading 'scripture a ryght', or the 'right handelinge' of scripture, opposed to the 'filthie buggeries' of the Church of Rome.[58] In *King Johan*, 'Veritas' or Truth (echoing Romans 1 on truth 'turned' back to 'lies') enters to right (and re-write) the reputation of this king, perverted by the 'Romane' Polydore Vergil, in lines on the 'lying' of this 'Romane' in multiple senses ('Thynke yow a Romane with the Romans can not lye?').[59]

Everything is righted by the end of *King Johan*, especially in Bale's revised ending celebrating Elizabeth's reclaiming of England from the papistry of Mary's reign, with its 'abhomynacyon / Of supersticyons, witchecraftes and hydolatrye'.[60] But England (and Englishmen) had already several times converted or 'turned' in opposite directions, seduced (as Bale himself put it) by the 'sophisticall sorceryes' of friars who replaced the true 'Christen churche' with the idolatrous 'images' of the 'filthye sinagoge of Sathan' and its 'monstruouse buggery'.[61] The writing that in Bale could re-right multiple forms of 'preposterous' reversal remains subject (like the 'contraries' of the discourse of witchcraft, as Stuart Clark describes them, or the reliance of Bale's own theatre on the idolatrous images they simultaneously condemn) to the ever-present possibility of unstable reversal.

The true English or Protestant Church is not only characterised by Bale as reading 'scripture a ryght' but as 'clean' and 'unspotted', in contrast to the 'fylthy gloses and dyrty exposycyons' of Papists whose turning, perverting, or 'wrastynge the text' of Scripture is combined (as in Tyndale and others) with muddying the clear water of Abraham's wells (purified by 'Christ oure spirituall Isaac').[62] Bale's use of this passage – whose 'muddying' was often combined with the 'puddle' of the New Testament figure of backsliding, as well as the maculate 'spottedness' or 'blackness' of the 'Ethiope' and the 'uncleanness' of Romans 1 – makes clear that what modern apprehensions might separate into bodily, religious, and 'racial' are here combined, in a teleology whose hysteron proteron-like reversal threatens precisely such sullying.[63] What we might be tempted to think of as an exclusively scriptural emblem of 'backward' inversion was inseparable not only from the 'uncleanness' and 'sodometrye' of idolatry but also from the 'bondage' of return to a 'testament' figured by 'Arabian' Hagar, whose 'bond brat' figured both 'Turk' and 'Jew'.[64] The role of the 'preposterous' in the polemics of John Bale might thus serve as a striking early-modern reminder of what was at stake – far beyond the local discourse of rhetoric – in preposterous or hysteron proteron-like reversals of all kinds.

CHAPTER 8

Paradiastole, or the Curry favell . . . when we make the best of a bad thing, or turne a signification to the more plausible sence: as, to call an unthrift, a liberall Gentleman: the foolish-hardy, valiant or couragious: the niggard, thriftie . . .

Puttenham, *The Arte of English Poesie* (1589)

None of these poyntes would ever frame in me.
My wit is nought, I cannot lerne the waye:
And much the lesse of thinges that greater be,
That asken helpe of colours of devise
To joyne the mene with eche extremitie,
With the neryst vertue to cloke always the vise;
And as to pourpose like wise it shall fall
To presse the vertue that it may not rise;
As dronkenes good felloweshippe to call,
The frendly Foo with his dowble face
Say he is gentill and courtois therewithall;
And say that Favell hath a goodly grace . . .

Sir Thomas Wyatt, 'Myne owne John Poyntz'

Paradiastole: redescribing the vices as virtues

QUENTIN SKINNER

The earliest English rhetorical handbooks in which the figure of paradiastole is named and defined are Henry Peacham's *Garden of Eloquence* (1577) and George Puttenham's *Arte of English Poesie* (1589).[1] Peacham places paradiastole in the third order of the rhetorical schemates,[2] and thus among the figures of amplification used to 'garnish matters and causes'.[3] He turns to consider it immediately after discussing meiosis, to which it is said to be 'nye kin', and defines it as follows: '*Paradiastole* . . . is when by a mannerly interpretation, we doe excuse our own vices, or other mens whom we doe defend, by calling them vertues.' 'This figure is used', he summarises, 'when vices are excused.'[4]

Puttenham pursues the comparison between meiosis and paradiastole at greater length. If, he argues, 'you diminish and abbase a thing by way of spight or mallice, as it were to deprave it', this is an instance of meiosis. The contrast with paradiastole is said to be as follows: 'But if such moderation of words tend to flattery, or soothing, or excusing, it is by the figure *Paradiastole*, which therfore nothing improperly we call the *Curry-favell*, as when we make the best of a bad thing, or turne a signification to the more plausible sence . . . moderating and abating the force of the matter by craft, and for a pleasing purpose.'[5] Puttenham later reiterates that, whereas the figure of meiosis – which he labels 'the Disabler'[6] – has the effect of denigrating what is described, the figure of paradiastole or Curry-favell is used to exculpate.[7]

Both Peacham and Puttenham are self-conscious about the need to rework the conventions of classical rhetoric for a Tudor audience, an aspiration most clearly reflected in Puttenham's efforts to domesticate the outlandish names for the figures and tropes inherited by the Roman rhetoricians from their Greek authorities. But at the same time they remain heavily dependent on the body of ancient treatises in which the full range of the figures and tropes had already been anatomised and discussed. Within this ancient literature, the earliest work in which the figure of paradiastole had been defined and illustrated under that name was the *De figuris senten-tiarum et elocutionis* attributed to P. Rutilius Lupus and dated to *c.* 20 AD. Rutilius's handbook was printed in Venice as early as 1519, and subsequently republished in the Aldine collection of rhetorical texts edited by George of Trebizond in 1523, as well as in several editions later in the century.[8] The full entry on paradiastole reads as follows:

This *schema* distinguishes between two or more things that seem to have the same force, and teaches us how far they are distinct from each other by assigning the right meaning to each of them. Hyperides: For when you attempt to deceive the opinion of others, you frustrate yourself. You are not able to show that you should be understood as wise rather than crafty, or courageous rather than reckless, or careful in family matters rather than niggardly, or severe rather than ill-willed. There is no vice in which you are able to glory by praising it as a virtue. The same *schema* can readily be used yet more impressively when a reason is added to the judgment. This can be done in the following way: Hence do not so often call yourself frugal when you are avaricious. For someone who is frugal makes use of what is sufficient; you on the contrary, because of your avarice, want more than you have. So what will follow will not be the fruits of thrift but rather the miseries of destitution.[9]

Although this is the earliest discussion of paradiastole to have survived, the quotation from Hyperides (an Attic orator of the fourth century BC) indicates that, as we shall later see, the figure was already well-known at a much earlier date.

Rutilius may also have been indebted to the popular handbook generally known as the *Rhetorica ad Herennium*. This had been produced by a con-temporary of Cicero's, and until the ascription was disproved by Raphael Regius in the 1490s it was frequently attributed to Cicero himself.[10] The *Ad Herennium* never uses the term paradiastole, but in the course of Book III we are treated to some hyperbolical advice about how to employ the technique in a court of law. Sometimes, we are told, it may even be possible to redescribe the cardinal virtues as instances of vice: 'What the person speaking against us calls justice we shall demonstrate to be cowardice, and a lazy and corrupt form of liberality; what he names prudence we shall say is inept, indiscreet and offensive cleverness; what he speaks of as temperance we shall speak of as lazy and dissolute negligence; what he names courage we shall call the heedless temerity of a gladiator.'[11] Like Rutilius, the author of the *Ad Herennium* is interested in rhetorical redescription as a means of challenging and undermining those who claim to be acting virtuously.

Rutilius's analysis was subsequently taken up, in an abbreviated form, in the most influential of all the surveys of the figures and tropes, that of

Quintilian in his *Institutio oratoria* of *c.* 90 AD. At the same time, however, Quintilian modifies Rutilius's account in one fundamental respect. Rutilius had treated paradiastole as the name of the figure we employ when we seek to unmask someone for deceitfully laying claim to a virtue, and attempt to show that they deserve to be condemned. The ultimate aim is to denigrate our rivals and adversaries. Quintilian, by contrast, thinks of paradiastole as the figure in play when we seek to defend someone against an accusation of vice, and attempt to show that they deserve to be praised. The ultimate aim is to excuse, and normally to excuse ourselves.

Quintilian's revision, or perhaps misunderstanding, of Rutilius's argument becomes clear as soon as he turns to his examples. For Rutilius, it is an instance of paradiastole when we criticise someone for trying to claim that he is wise when he is merely crafty, or courageous when he is merely reckless, and so on. But for Quintilian, the figure is in use 'whenever you call *yourself* wise rather than crafty, or courageous rather than reckless, or careful rather than niggardly' ['Cum te pro astuto sapientem appelles, pro confidente fortem, pro illiberali diligentem'].[12] Although Quintilian takes over Rutilius's illustrations, he reverses their direction in every case.

When the *ars rhetorica* was revived in the Renaissance, it was Quintilian's view of paradiastole that largely prevailed. The earliest Renaissance text in which the figure is defined and illustrated is Antonio Mancinelli's *Carmen de Figuris*, which was printed in Venice as early as 1493 and frequently republished.[13] As he admits, Mancinelli is wholly reliant on Quintilian,[14] and simply quotes him to the effect that 'it is an instance of *paradiastole* when you call yourself wise rather than crafty, or courageous rather than reckless'.[15] His analysis served in turn as a major source for Johann Susenbrotus in his *Epitome Troporum ac Schematum*, perhaps the most widely used treatise on *elocutio* of the later sixteenth century. First printed in Germany, it was republished in London as early as 1562 and went through at least four editions in the next generation.[16] Susenbrotus summarises by noting that 'according to Mancinelli, it is said to be *paradiastole* when, instead of crafty, we say wise'.[17] His own list of examples begins by repeating Quintilian word-for-word: 'when you call yourself wise rather than crafty, or courageous rather than reckless, or careful rather than niggardly'.[18] It was largely through the conduit of Mancinelli's and Susenbrotus's treatises that Quintilian's analysis passed into the writings of the English rhetoricians of the sixteenth century, to whom we next need to turn.

The distinction of being the first to comment on rhetorical redescription falls to Thomas Wilson, whose neo-Ciceronian *Arte of Rhetorique* was first published in 1554.[19] Wilson never uses the term paradiastole, but in anatomising 'the firste kinde of Amplification', which is said to occur 'when by changing a woorde, in augmentynge we use a greater, but in diminishynge we use a lesse', he notes that this is the device we use whenever 'we give vices, the names of vertue'.[20] As we have already seen, the earliest English handbooks in which this technique is named as paradiastole are those of Peacham and Puttenham, after which the term passed into general currency. When, for example, Peacham reissued his *Garden of Eloquence* in an extended version in 1593, he defined paradiastole as 'a fit instrument of excuse' by means of which the vices are disguised as virtues.[21] Angel Day writes in similar terms in his *Declaration* of 1592, listing paradiastole among the 'schemes syntaxical' and explaining that this is the figure we deploy whenever 'with a milde interpretation' we palliate our own or other people's faults.[22]

The principal way in which the Tudor rhetoricians reveal their dependence on the Roman tradition lies in their choice of examples. As we have seen, the first illustration used by Rutilius and Quintilian had been that of trying to characterise yourself not as crafty (*astutus*) but rather as wise (*sapiens*). Mancinelli and Susenbrotus repeat the example, and Peacham likewise declares it an instance of paradiastole 'when we call him that is craftye, wyse', or when we justify 'deepe dissimulation' as 'singuler wisdome'.[23] Day slightly varies the vocabulary, speaking of calling 'a subtill person, wise',[24] but Peacham in the revised version of his text reverts to the standard formula, referring to those who defend 'craft and deceit' by redescribing it as 'wisdome and pollicie'.[25]

By similar lines of descent other examples suggested by Rutilius reappear as standard paradiastolic pairings in Renaissance handbooks: careful/niggardly, frugal/avaricious, stern/spiteful, just/cruel. Rutilius's final example is the most familiar of all, and subsequently resurfaces in almost every Renaissance rhetorical text: that of a man who praises himself as *fortis* or courageous when he is in fact *confidens* or *temerarius*, a man of recklessness. Quintilian appropriates it, as do Mancinelli and Susenbrotus, and here again the Tudor rhetoricians follow suit. Peacham even suggests that one might justify a murder by calling it a manly deed,[26] while Puttenham writes of excusing 'the foolish-hardy' as 'valiant or couragious', and Day similarly notes that one can call 'a bold fellow, couragious' and 'a man furious or rash, valiant'.[27]

This last case is of particular significance. By contrast with the others I have examined, all of which appear for the first time in Roman sources, this example can already be found in a number of ancient Greek texts. Among these, undoubtedly the most influential was Aristotle's *Art of Rhetoric*.

Aristotle's treatise became widely known after it was translated into Latin in the latter part of the fifteenth century, and by the end of the sixteenth century there were four separate Latin versions in print: those of George of Trebizond (1523), Ermolao Barbaro (1544), Carolo Sigonio (1565), and Antonio Maioragio (1591).[28] George of Trebizond introduces Aristotle's discussion by making him say that, if we aspire to speak persuasively, we must ensure that, 'when it comes to praise and blame, those things which are close to being morally worthy are accepted as having the quality itself' ['Ea quoque accipienda sunt, quae honestis propinqua sunt, tanquam ad laudem, vel vituperationem conferentia'].[29] One of his illustrations is that of trying to claim that someone who is merely *ferox* or savage is actually *fortis* or brave. This choice of terminology was closely followed by other sixteenth-century translators of Aristotle's text, which no doubt helps to explain why the example came to be one of the most frequently cited instances of paradiastole.[30]

Behind Aristotle's discussion, however, lies the celebrated analysis in Book III of Thucydides' *History* of how evaluative terms begin to be misapplied when communities fall into civil war. Thomas Nicolls published an English translation of Thucydides as early as 1550, in which Thucydides is made to say that, as soon as sedition and conflict broke out in the cities of Greece, 'all the evylles whiche they committed, they disguised and named by newe and unaccustomed names'. His first illustration is that 'temeritie and rashnes, they named magnanymytie and noblenes of courage, so that the rashe were named vertuous defendors of theyr frendes'.[31] Soon after the appearance of Nicolls's version, Thucydides' discussion caught the attention of Justus Lipsius, writing his *Politicorum libri sex* in Leiden in the 1580s at the height of the Dutch religious wars. When William Jones translated Lipsius's text into English in 1594, he rendered the passage by saying that, in the predicament described by Thucydides, 'whatsoever is rash and headie, that is deemed by them to be couragiously and valiauntly enterprised'.[32]

The excusing of rashness as courage may thus be said to constitute an unambiguous case in which an ancient Greek example of rhetorical redescription was taken up into Roman rhetorical theory and eventually came to be classified as an instance of paradiastole. It is striking, however, that there is no other case in the extant sources of such a transmission taking place. The Greek discussion appears to have remained a largely distinct strand of thought, illustrated with a distinct range of examples. It was only in the course of the sixteenth century that a number of rhetoricians began to enrich the discussion of rhetorical redescription (now universally known as paradiastole) by drawing examples eclectically from ancient Greek sources as well as from the Roman handbooks on which I have so far concentrated.

As I have intimated, the main conduit through which these additional examples flowed was undoubtedly Aristotle's *Art of Rhetoric*. But we also need to consider the remarkable discussion of rhetorical redescription in Book VIII of Plato's *Republic*, a discussion to which Aristotle's observations owe an obvious debt. Plato's analysis does not appear to have been known to the rhetorical theorists of the early Renaissance, but this situation was transformed after the appearance of Marsilio Ficino's *Platonis Opera*, his Latin version of the principal dialogues. Ficino's translation was printed in Venice in 1517, and repeated republications throughout the sixteenth century finally brought Plato's *oeuvre* to the attention of a wider audience.[33]

Plato examines the phenomenon of rhetorical redescription in the course of reflecting on how the soul adjusts itself from an oligarchic to a democratic form of life. One sign of this psychological decline is that many forms of behaviour previously recognised as corrupt begin to be exonerated. For instance, pride and insolence are redescribed as nobility and greatness. As Ficino's translation phrases it, 'they speak of insolence as the behaviour of those who have been nobly brought up'.[34] Aristotle repeats the example in his *Art of Rhetoric*, in which he argues – in the vocabulary developed by his sixteenth-century translators – that an arrogant, proud, or contumacious person can always hope to represent himself as magnificent, honourable, splendid, and great.[35] Among Renaissance rhetoricians, Susenbrotus is the first to pick up the example, which he duly classifies as an instance of paradiastole and describes by saying that a man who is haughty or *fastidiosus* can always hope to claim that he is really noble or *magnanimus*.[36] His way of formulating the distinction was thereafter widely adopted. Angel Day, for example, notes in his *Declaration* of 1592 that it is a standard case of paradiastole to say of 'him that is proud' that he is really a man of magnanimity.[37] According to Plato, other consequences of the corruption of the soul under democracy are that prodigality comes to be redescribed as magnificence and unbridled behaviour as an expression of liberty, and that brazen and shameless persons begin to be praised for their courage and strength.[38] Aristotle omits this last example, but several Tudor rhetoricians nevertheless treat it as a standard case of paradiastole.[39]

One further contrast between the Greek and Roman discussions of rhetorical redescription needs to be emphasised. According to the understanding that eventually came to predominate in Roman thought, the point of using the technique is always to exonerate and excuse. Among the Greek writers, however, it is always assumed that the same device can equally well be employed to question and denigrate the virtues. It is true that Rutilius had adopted something like this perspective in treating paradiastole as a means of unmasking hypocrisies. Like the author of the *Ad Herennium*, however, Rutilius is chiefly interested in the complex possibility of criticising rivals and adversaries by countering and undermining their efforts to commend themselves. By contrast, the Greek writers focus on the simpler strategy of casting doubt on forms of behaviour normally regarded as unquestionably worthy of praise. One instance offered by Thucydides is that of impugning 'prudent consultation and deliberating in causes' as an expression of 'sensed and cloked deceate'.[40] A second possibility mentioned by Thucydides – and repeated by Plato – is that of ridiculing modesty of demeanour as nothing more than 'covered pusillanimytie or cowardenes'.[41] To which Thucydides adds – and Aristotle repeats – that 'an honest fear' can similarly be dismissed as mere slackness and faintness.[42]

One might finally ask what the Tudor rhetoricians managed to add to these earlier accounts. The answer is that they contribute almost nothing of their own at all. Wilson proposes one new example, which Peacham repeats: that of excusing gluttony and drunkenness as good fellowship.[43] Peacham adds two more, both of which gesture at his puritan sympathies: one is excusing idolatry as 'pure religion', the other excusing pride as 'cleanlynesse'.[44] Apart from this, however, the Tudor rhetoricians are little more than mouthpieces – in the case of this figure at least – of their ancient authorities.

Although the writers I have been examining undoubtedly isolate a distinct rhetorical technique, it remains to show how it could ever be practised with success. The numerous treatises on the good life circulating in early Tudor England all point to the obvious difficulty: that the virtues and vices appear to be names of diametrically opposed qualities. As John Larke, for example, puts it in his *Boke of Wysdome* of 1532, moral conflict is always between 'contraries':[45] between prudence and folly, chastity and lechery, liberality and covetousness, and even more antithetically between temperance and intemperance, constancy and inconstancy, justice and injustice.[46] But if the virtues and vices are such clearly opposed principles, how can we ever hope to redescribe the one as the other without being instantly accused of playing an obvious rhetorical trick?

By way of answer, the rhetoricians of the next generation appealed to one of the governing assumptions of Aristotelian moral philosophy: that every virtue consists in a mean between two opposed vices. Among the moral treatises of the early Elizabethan period, Sir Thomas Hoby's translation of

Castiglione's *Cortegiano* furnished perhaps the most influential discussion of the claim. As Lord Octavian explains in Book IV, virtue is always 'placed in the middle between two extreme vyces, the one for the overmuch, and the other for the overlitle'.[47] Soon afterwards Cornelius Valerius, whose treatise on the virtues appeared as *The Casket of Jewels* in 1571, went on to add an explicit reference to the source of the argument. Agreeing that 'vertue is a meane in middes degree', he informs us that this insight is owed to Aristotle, by whom virtue is defined as 'a custome of the minde enterprised through reason situated in mediocritie'.[48]

If virtue is a mean, it follows that many of the vices, far from being 'contraries' of the virtues, will be likely to appear disconcertingly close to them. Castiglione draws the inference by invoking an image of neighbourliness. For every vice, he argues, there will always be a 'nexte vertue' and for every virtue a 'nexte vice'.[49] To which Valerius adds, still more troublingly, that in some cases the virtues and vices may turn out to be members of the same family. A number of vices, as he expresses it, are 'cousin germain to Vertue'.[50]

Castiglione and Valerius both acknowledge that, once this implication is recognised, it is easy to see how the vices can often be redescribed as virtues. As Aristotle had originally noted in the *Art of Rhetoric*, it will only be necessary to claim that (in the words of Sigonio's translation) 'those qualities which are in the neighbourhood of those actually present have an identical force'.[51] Both Castiglione and Valerius explicitly refer to the figure of paradiastole by way of making the point. As the Count observes in Book I of the *Cortegiano*, the neighbourly relationship between virtue and vice is such that we can always call 'him that is saucye, bolde: hym that is sober, drie: hym that is seelye, good: hym that is unhappye, wittie: and lykewyse in the reste'.[52] Valerius draws the same conclusion in still more anxious tones. He accepts that the distinction between virtue and vice can sometimes be 'apertly perceived'; we can readily see the difference, for example, 'when ignorance is set against wisdom, wrong against Justice, cowardnesse agaynst Fortitude'.[53] But there are other cases in which the vice 'is not so easely espied, as when craftinesse or subtiltie is gaiged agaynst wisedome, cruelty against Justice, lewdhardinesse agaynst manlinesse'.[54]

The power of paradiastole to disorder the vices and virtues is encapsulated by the rhetoricians in two favourite metaphors. One speaks of clothing and disguising the vices to lend them an outward appearance of good qualities. The Count in the *Cortegiano* observes that we can always hope to 'cover' a vice 'with the name of the nexte vertue' and to 'cover' a virtue 'with the name of the nexte vice'.[55] Henry Peacham in *The Garden of Eloquence* turns the image into the very definition of paradiastole, which he describes as the figure we use 'to cover vices with the mantles of vertues'.[56]

The other metaphor speaks of colouring the vices in such a way as to make them appear 'colourable' or excusable. Sometimes this image is more broadly applied to characterise the figures of speech as a whole. Angel Day, for example, says of the figures at the start of his *Declaration* that they comprise 'the ornament, light and colours of Rhetorical speech'.[57] But the same metaphor is also used to refer more specifically to the power of paradiastole to make the vices seem more acceptable. Day defines paradiastole as the figure we employ 'when with a milde interpretation or speech, wee color others or our owne faultes'.[58]

It remains to consider what attitude the rhetoricians adopt towards the figure of paradiastole and its power to colour the vices. Classical writers on the *ars rhetorica* had always taken pride in the ability of powerful orators to make us change our minds about the right way of 'seeing' particular actions and events. Cicero had even put into the mouth of Crassus in the *De oratore* the view that this may be the highest rhetorical skill of all. There will always be two sides to any question, and the aim of the orator should be to show that a plausible argument can always be constructed *in utramque partem*, on either side of the case. 'We ought', as Crassus expresses it, 'to have enough intelligence, power and art to speak *in utramque partem*' on all the leading issues in the moral sciences: 'on virtue, on duty, on equity and goodness, on dignity, benefit, honour, ignominy, reward, punishment and all similar things.'[59]

If one of the aims of eloquence is to make us examine the same question from different perspectives, then a skilful use of paradiastole will obviously be a valuable art to cultivate. Once the *ars rhetorica* was incorporated into Christian culture, however, this possibility came to be viewed with much greater nervousness, even by the rhetoricians themselves. They are anxious to insist that the question as to whether any given action ought properly to be described as virtuous can always be settled with finality. As they are obliged to recognise, however, this is precisely the kind of certainty that the figure of paradiastole tends to undermine. Susenbrotus concludes that this is one of the moments at which the art of rhetoric may be said to overreach itself: '*Paradiastole* is used whenever, by means of an excessively polite interpretation, we speak ingratiatingly so as to express approval of our own vices or those of others, as the wrong-headed reprobates of our own time are accustomed to do, who scratch each other's backs in exactly this way, as the proverb has it.'[60] Thomas Wilson[61] and especially Henry Peacham strongly endorse Susenbrotus's doubts. Although Peacham offers a neutral analysis of paradiastole in the 1577 edition of his *Garden of Eloquence*, his expanded edition of 1593 violently denounces the figure as a 'vice of speech'.[62] We are left confronting an ironic spectacle: that of the rhetoricians condemning the art of rhetoric for possessing the very power they generally liked to celebrate.

To those, however, with a professional interest in demonstrating that it is always possible to argue *in utramque partem*, the lure of paradiastole proved irresistible. So it is hardly surprising to find that, in the years immediately following the publication of the rhetorical handbooks I have been examining, there was a growing awareness of its literary as well as its forensic possibilities. John Lyly employs the figure in several of his orations in *Euphues*, and even alludes to Nicolls's translation of Thucydides when lamenting that the modest and shamefast are nowadays likely to be reviled for cowardice.[63] Marlowe was aware of this example, which he puts to dramatic use in Part II of *Tamburlaine*, in which the tyrant kills his own son for excusing his refusal to fight as 'manly wise' when Tamburlaine regards it as cowardly.[64] Shakespeare likewise displays an interest in such redescriptions from an early stage, and it is especially striking to find him making use of both the metaphors favoured by the rhetoricians to explain how it is possible for vices to be excused.

As we have seen, one of these metaphors had spoken of 'colouring' the vices to make them look like virtues. These are precisely the terms in which the politic Cardinal Beaufort responds to Queen Margaret in *2 Henry VI* when she proposes that Gloucester be summarily killed:

> That he should die is worthy policy;
> But yet we want a colour for his death.
> 'Tis meet he be condemned by course of law.[65]

It is ironic that Richard Gloucester should later complain – as he does when Catesby presents him with the head of the murdered Hastings – that he himself has been deceived by this very rhetorical trick:

> I took him for the plainest harmless creature
> That breathed upon the earth, a Christian,
> Made him my book wherein my soul recorded
> The history of all her secret thoughts.
> So smooth he daubed his vice with show of virtue.
> (*Richard III*, 3.5.24–8)

As the use of 'daubed' implies, the colouring may not even have to be very skilful to be rhetorically effective.

Shakespeare also likes to invoke the image of 'covering' the vices to make them more pleasing to the eye. There are several instances in the early plays,[66] but the most elaborate occurs in *The Merchant of Venice* at the moment when Bassanio is trying to choose between the three caskets. Turning to the golden one, he sets it aside with these words:

> So may the outward shows be least themselves.
> The world is still deceived with ornament.
> In law, what plea so tainted and corrupt
> But, being seasoned with a gracious voice,
> Obscures the show of evil? In religion,
> What damned error but some sober brow
> Will bless it and approve it with a text,
> Hiding the grossness with fair ornament?
> There is no vice so simple but assumes
> Some mark of virtue on his outward parts.
>
> (3.2.73–82)

When speaking of the verbal ornaments that deceive, Bassanio is partly referring in a general way to the *ornamenta*, the figures and tropes of speech. But when he speaks of hiding grossness with fair ornament, he appears to be referring more specifically to the power of paradiastole to 'cover' the vices by giving them an outward appearance of goodness.

Of far greater importance is the fact that Shakespeare is deeply interested in the dramatic exploration of paradiastole as (in Peacham's phrase) an instrument of excuse.[67] As we have seen, an instance of the technique given by Castiglione had been that of calling 'him that is saucye, bolde'. With this in mind, it is worth reconsidering the scene from *The Second Part of Henry the Fourth* in which Mistress Quickly informs the Lord Chief Justice that Falstaff has broken his promise to marry her. The Chief Justice rounds on Falstaff in tones remarkably reminiscent of Castiglione's Count, reproving him for his 'confident brow' and 'impudent sauciness' (2.1.113–15). But Falstaff responds by quoting Castiglione back at him: what you call 'impudent sauciness', he retorts, is really 'honourable boldness'.[68] It is part of the comedy, however, that Falstaff avails himself with such effrontery of one of the stock examples of paradiastole, and the Chief Justice knows too much about the art of rhetoric to let him to get away with it. He even appears to know about the specific objection that Henry Peacham had raised against the use of paradiastole: that it 'opposeth the truth by false tearmes'.[69] As the Chief Justice likewise objects, Falstaff is simply 'wrenching the true cause the false way' (112–13). He is instantly exposed for trying to play a well-known rhetorical trick.

A further stock example of paradiastole had been that of seeking to commend oneself for 'good husbandry', for being careful and thrifty, when one is in fact avaricious and covetous. This being so, it is similarly worth reconsidering the scene at the beginning of *The Merchant of Venice* in which Antonio and Bassanio meet Shylock to seal their bargain. As soon as he enters, Shylock declares his hatred of Antonio for lending out money gratis, for attacking his own taking of interest, and for accusing him, he later adds, of cut-throat practices (1.3.42, 49, 110). Reacting to Antonio's rebukes, Shylock offers precisely the account of himself that the rhetoricians had recommended. First he redescribes his alleged avarice as thrift:

> He hates our sacred nation, and he rails,
> Even there where merchants most do congregate,
> On me, my bargains, and my well-won thrift –
> Which he calls interest.
>
> (46–9)

Next he tells the story of Jacob's good husbandry in grazing his uncle Laban's sheep. Jacob was promised all the lambs that were born parti-coloured, and found a way to increase their number:

> The skilful shepherd peeled me certain wands,
> And in the doing of the deed of kind
> He stuck them up before the fulsome ewes
> Who, then conceiving, did in eaning time
> Fall parti-coloured lambs; and those were Jacob's.
> This was a way to thrive; and he was blest;
> And thrift is blessing, if men steal it not.
>
> (83–9)

Shylock not only excuses his conduct; he redescribes it as positively virtuous: he has found a way to thrive without stealing, a form of increase sanctified by the Bible itself.

Shylock's use of paradiastole may at first sight seem a world away from Falstaff's effronteries. He not only pleads his case in passionate verse, but his sincerity is much harder to doubt. As in the case of Falstaff, however, he is playing a familiar rhetorical trick, and as before the trick is immediately exposed. Susenbrotus had warned that 'we have an example of *paradiastole* when vices show themselves under the guise of virtue, and by these means even the Devil himself can be transfigured into an Angel of light'.[70] Antonio reacts to Shylock's story of Jacob's good husbandry in remarkably similar terms:

> Mark you this, Bassanio?
> The devil can cite Scripture for his purpose.
> An evil soul producing holy witness
> Is like a villain with a smiling cheek,
> A goodly apple rotten at the heart.
> O, what a goodly outside falsehood hath!
>
> (96–101)

Antonio not only echoes Susenbrotus's view of paradiastole as a devilish force; his remark about giving falsehood a goodly outside alludes to one of the metaphors most frequently invoked by the rhetoricians to describe this specific figure of speech.

Modern readers of this scene are perhaps more likely to sympathise with Shylock than with his attackers. This makes it all the more important to recognise how unsympathetically the use of such redescriptions would have been viewed even by the rhetoricians themselves at the end of the sixteenth century. Seven years before the publication of *The Comical History of the Merchant of Venice* in 1600, Henry Peacham in his *Garden of Eloquence* had offered, as a standard case of paradiastole, the attempt to defend 'insatiable avarice' by calling it 'good husbandrie'.[71] But Peacham had immediately gone on to denounce such redescriptions as an 'instrument of excuse serving to selfe-love, partiall favour, blinde affection, and a shamelesse person'.[72] For all his nobility of utterance, Shylock's self-justification is precisely the sort of thing to be expected, according to Peacham, from someone who is not merely shameless but whose basic purpose is 'the better maintenance of wickednesse'.[73]

Shakespeare's interest in paradiastole as a means of exculpation is not confined to these comedies of the late 1590s. To the same period belongs *Julius Caesar*, in which the tragic possibilities inherent in rhetorical redescription are profoundly explored. This aspect of the tragedy begins to unfold at the start of Act 2, when Brutus meditates on his intention to assassinate Caesar and then shares with the other conspirators his sense of how this action might be justified. In his soliloquy he reflects that Caesar 'would be crowned' and thus that, if Rome is to avoid this possible 'abuse of greatness', 'It must be by his death' (2.1.10, 12, 18). As he is obliged to admit, however, Caesar has not so far done anything to make him deserving of such a violent end (28–9). This in turn means that, as Brutus warns the conspirators later in the scene, they are liable to appear envious if they kill Caesar, and will be open to an accusation of sheer butchery (164, 166, 178).

If there is no possibility of justifying Caesar's assassination by considering – as Brutus puts it – 'the thing he is', how can it ever be justified? Brutus recognises that his own behaviour and that of his fellow conspirators will have to be rhetorically redescribed:

> Since the quarrel
> Will bear no colour for the thing he is,
> Fashion it thus.
>
> (28–30)

As he acknowledges – drawing on the distinctive vocabulary of the rhetoricians – he will need to 'fashion' his act, to give it an appealing rhetorical shape; more specifically, he will need to 'colour' it, to disguise and brighten it to yield a more attractive appearance.

How can this be done? Henry Peacham had suggested that murder can perhaps be excused by calling it a manly deed. As Brutus begins to converse with the conspirators, he appears for a moment to gesture at this possibility. One way, he suggests, to prevent the killing of Caesar from looking merely envious will be to 'kill him boldly, but not wrathfully' (172). Brutus's main suggestion, however, comes from a much more elevated source, the justification of Caesar's assassination to be found in Book III of Cicero's *De officiis*. Cicero had appealed to the familiar image of the body politic and the importance of maintaining its health. To cite the earliest English translation, that of Robert Whytinton of 1534, tyrants are said to be 'poysonfull' and in need of being expelled from the body if it is to survive.[74] William Baldwin subsequently elaborated the image in his *Treatice of Morall Philosophy*, by far the most widely printed work on moral theory in later sixteenth-century England.[75] A good ruler, Baldwin declares, 'is lyke a common fountaine or springe'; if he becomes impure and poisonous, the people will be left without remedy 'untill the fountaine be purged'.[76]

This image of purgation is exactly the one that Brutus adopts to justify his killing of Caesar. In his soliloquy he compares Caesar with a serpent's egg, a source of venom that needs to be crushed in the shell if the body of Rome is to avoid being poisoned (14, 16, 32–4). In his speech to the conspirators he places the same image at the heart of the rhetorical redescription on which he finally takes his stand:

> This shall make
> Our purpose necessary, and not envious;
> Which so appearing to the common eyes,
> We shall be called purgers, not murderers.
>
> (177–80)

Purgers, not murderers. So convinced is Brutus by his redescription that he not only commends it to his fellow conspirators but predicts that it will be accepted without question by the people at large.

By contrast with Falstaff and even Shylock, Brutus's use of paradiastole owes nothing to the rhetoricians and their stock examples. He takes his redescription from one of the most widely respected works of moral philosophy of his own as well as Shakespeare's age. Nor is Brutus instantly challenged, as happens to Falstaff and Shylock alike. The conspirators silently accept his justification, and after the assassination it is shown to have exactly the power that Brutus had promised of making their action seem acceptable. Addressing the plebeians, Brutus explains that Caesar was ambitious, and that this is why he slew him (3.2.26–7). He does not repeat his earlier reference to purging the body politic of poison, but this is precisely how the plebeians spontaneously construct his act. 'This Caesar was a tyrant' declares the First Plebeian; to which the Third Plebeian adds 'We are blessed that Rome is rid of him' (70–1). They agree that the conspirators have rid the city of something noxious: they are purgers, not murderers.

Brutus's victory, however, is a rhetorical one, open to the danger that an orator adept at arguing *in utramque partem* may be capable of questioning and undermining his version of events. This is what Cassius dreads (3.1.234–7), and this is what Antony achieves with his intensely rhetorical response to Brutus's prose address to the people. Antony persuades them that Caesar was *not* ambitious: that 'Ambition should be made of sterner stuff' (3.2.93). He is consequently able to insist that the conspirators *were* merely envious: 'See', he shows the people, 'what a rent the envious Casca made' (173). By this stage they have already repudiated Brutus's justification for his act. As soon as Antony refers to 'the honourable men | Whose daggers have stabbed Caesar' (152–3), the Fourth Plebeian suddenly shouts: 'They were villains, murderers' (156). Murderers, not purgers. Brutus's redescription is fatally inverted, and the next we hear of him is that he and Cassius 'Are rid like madmen through the gates of Rome' (262). We are left with a final, ironic play on the idea of purgation: they have rid through the gates, and Rome is rid of them.

Unlike Falstaff, or even Shylock, Brutus cannot simply be dismissed for attempting, in Peacham's phrase, to oppose the truth by false terms. But nor is he able to provide an unassailable justification of his act. Was he a purger or merely a murderer? It is part of his tragedy, we are made to realise, that this is a question without an answer: it will always be possible to argue in *utramque partem*, on either side of the case. Such is the power of rhetoric; more specifically, such is the power of paradiastole.

CHAPTER 9

A Comparison, is a certain Oracion, shewyng by a collacion the wor-
thines, or excellencie of any thing: or the naughtines of the same,
compared with any other thyng or thynges, either equalie, or more
inferiour.

Richard Rainolde, *The Foundacion of Rhetorike* (1563)

If I would compare him with *Shakespeare*, I must acknowledge him
the more correct Poet, but *Shakespeare* the greater wit. *Shakespeare* was
the *Homer*, or Father of our Dramatick Poets; *Johnson* was the *Virgil*,
the pattern of elaborate writing; I admire him, but I love *Shakespeare*.

John Dryden, *Of Dramatick Poesie. An Essay* (1668)

Syncrisis: the figure of contestation

IAN DONALDSON

In a famous scene in *Le Bourgeois Gentilhomme*, Molière's Monsieur Jourdain learns to his delight that there is a technical term to describe the style
in which he has spoken unwittingly throughout his life: that he has always
spoken in *prose*. 'Really?', he says in excitement to his tutor; 'You mean I've
been speaking prose for over forty years without knowing it?' And he goes
off at once to announce this important fact to his wife. 'Do you know what
I'm speaking right now? *Prose.*' Many Renaissance terms of rhetoric might
be thought to offer a similar satisfaction, furnishing us with formal terms –
amphibologia, tautologia, insultatio, barbarismus – to describe styles of
speech we had already effortlessly mastered without their aid. Syncrisis
may look at first sight like a term of this kind. Unfamiliar nowadays not
just to the general public but to many scholars as well, absent from almost
every modern dictionary, syncrisis is the name of an exercise that once
served throughout Europe as a central element in the school curriculum,
in the training of orators, and in the formation of principles of literary and
moral discrimination. Yet despite its curious erasure from modern consciousness, syncrisis is still widely practised today by writers who would no
doubt be as startled as M. Jourdain to discover there is a formal term to
describe what they do, when they assess side-by-side the achievements of
(let us say) Mozart and Haydn, or of Matisse and Picasso, or of Auden and
Eliot, or of Churchill and Thatcher, or of George Michael and Boy George,
or of Chelsea and Manchester United, or of Dell and Apple, or Pepsi and
Coke.

For syncrisis is a word which simply denotes a bringing-together for
comparative analysis (Greek *syn* = 'together' plus *krisis* = 'decision, judgement') of objects, events, institutions, of artists, writers, warriors, foot-
ballers, politicians, elephants, charioteers – the categories are almost without limit – in order to arrive at a final adjudication of their relative merits,
and to persuade the reader or listener that one of these elephants or writers or warriors is superior to the other.[1] Syncrisis was widely practised in

167

classical times, the exercise being commended especially in the writings of Quintilian and Cicero and the Greek scholar of mysterious identity known simply as 'Longinus', who in his treatise on the Sublime, written in the first or second century AD, formally compares and contrasts Plato with Demosthenes, Demosthenes with Cicero, *The Iliad* with *The Odyssey*, and so on. For Quintilian, the practice was an essential part of a student's moral education, 'the comparison of the respective merits of two characters' being closely allied to 'the praise of famous men and the denunciation of the wicked', and the ability to distinguish between virtue and vice. For all of these writers, syncrisis serves as an exercise in comparison and discrimination, but also (critically) in persuasion, and in this respect may be seen as fundamental to the art of rhetoric.[2]

Syncrisis was equally familiar throughout the Renaissance, when the writings of Cicero and Quintilian and the classical school exercises played a major role in rhetorical training.[3] The exercise served, as ever, to formalise the manner in which critical judgements were offered, and to sharpen natural habits of comparative assessment. It offered a binary view of the world, a choice of moral pathways, an imperative to distinguish between two persons or objects or categories of a seemingly similar nature. Shakespeare's Hamlet, fresh from his studies at Wittenberg, vigorously applies the strategies of this art in conversation with his mother, as he contrasts the qualities of Gertrude's first husband with those of her second:

> Look here upon this picture, and on this,
> The counterfeit presentment of two brothers.
> See what a grace was seated on this brow,
> Hyperion's curls, the front of Jove himself,
> An eye like Mars to threaten and command . . .
> This was your husband. Look you now what follows.
> Here is your husband, like a mildewed ear
> Blasting his wholesome brother.[4]

Shakespeare is likely to have encountered this style of argumentation in rhetorical instruction at his grammar school in Stratford upon Avon.[5] At St Paul's School, London, the young John Milton was obliged to perform oratorical exercises derived from Quintilian and Cicero 'in which one likens one thing with another, showing one of the things to be either equal or superior to the other'; exercises that allowed the student flexibly to argue for or against the proposition that night was superior to day, wisdom to ignorance, or work to pleasure, and the mature poet to compose such satisfyingly antithetical works as *L'Allegro* and *Il Penseroso*.[6] Many years later,

Coleridge followed a similar educational programme at Christ's Hospital under the tuition of the Reverend James Boyer, who, as Coleridge recalls in the opening chapter of *Biographia Literaria*, 'early moulded my taste to the preference of Demosthenes to Cicero, of Homer and Theocritus to Virgil, and again of Virgil to Ovid'. Boyer required his students to read Shakespeare and Milton 'as lessons' while studying the Greek tragic poets, thus encouraging a comparative assessment of the great English and classical authors.[7]

John Dryden evidently underwent a similar rhetorical training at Westminster School under the legendary Dr Busby, for his literary judgements are characteristically expressed through contrast and comparison. Dryden habitually groups the writers he discusses in pairs in order to demonstrate the differences between them and to arrive at a final verdict on their merits. In his Preface to *Fables Ancient and Modern* (1700), for example, Dryden compares the achievements of Homer and Virgil, concluding his analysis in this way:

But to return: our two great poets, being so different in their tempers, one choleric and sanguine, the other phlegmatic and melancholic; that which makes them excel in their several ways is that each of them has followed his own natural inclination, as well in forming the design as in the execution of it. The very heroes shew their authors: Achilles is hot, impatient, revengeful,

impiger, iracundus, inexorabilis, acer, etc.

Aeneas patient, considerate, careful of his people, and merciful to his enemies; ever submissive to the will of heaven,

quo fata trahunt retrahuntque, sequamur.

I could please myself with enlarging on this subject, but am forced to defer it to a fitter time. From all I have said, I will only draw this inference, that the action of Homer, being more full of vigour than that of Virgil, according to the temper of the writer, is of consequence more pleasing to the reader. One warms you by degrees; the other sets you on fire all at once, and never intermits his heat. 'Tis the same difference which Longinus makes betwixt the effects of eloquence in Demosthenes and Tully; one persuades, the other commands.[8]

In that final nod to Longinus, Dryden acknowledges the rhetorical model he has chosen to follow, and moves at once to a comparison of another pair of writers, Ovid and Chaucer. In his *Discourse Concerning the Original and Progress of Satire* (1693) Dryden compares and contrasts in a similar way the achievements of Horace and Juvenal, finding Horace the more urbane and good-mannered of the two satirists, but Juvenal the more vigorous and spirited.

so that, granting Horace to be the more general philosopher, we cannot deny that Juvenal was the greater poet, I mean in satire. His thoughts are sharper; his indignation against vice is more vehement; his spirit has more of the commonwealth genius; he treats tyranny, and all the vices attending it, as they deserve, with the utmost rigour; and consequently, a noble soul is better pleased with a zealous vindicator of Roman liberty than with a temporizing poet, a well-mannered Court slave, and a man who is often afraid of laughing in the right place; who is ever decent, because he is naturally servile.[9]

In the passages just quoted, Dryden appears to move in a curious, not to say reckless, manner between literary criticism and biographical speculation. About the historical 'Homer', virtually nothing is known, but this does not prevent him from confidently declaring Homer's temper was choleric and sanguine, while that of Virgil was phlegmatic and melancholic. He imagines the characters of the two authors to resemble those of the principal characters they create: 'The very heroes show their authors: Achilles is hot, impatient, revengeful . . . Aeneas patient, considerate, careful of his people, and merciful to his enemies; ever submissive to the will of heaven.' In this curiously circular manner of reading from the text to the life, from literary to psychological appraisal, Dryden is typical of his age. Alexander Pope, pursuing a similar contrast in the Preface to his translation of *The Iliad* some years later, argues in similar fashion: 'When we behold their Battels, methinks the two Poets resemble the Heroes they celebrate: *Homer*, boundless and irresistible as *Achilles*, bears all before him, and shines more and more as the Tumult increases; *Virgil* calmly daring like *Aeneas*, appears undisturb'd in the midst of the Action . . .'[10] The comparisons which Pope and Dryden offer here are not merely aesthetic, but relate also to human temperament and conduct.[11]

For syncrisis was an exercise practised in relation not merely to literary texts but also to the lives of the famous. When Plutarch wrote his lives of illustrious men in the first century AD, he grouped most of his subjects in pairs in order to compare and assess their respective qualities.[12] It was through the example in particular of Plutarch that English Renaissance writers discovered the excitements of comparative biography; of studying lives *in parallel*. 'Parallel' is actually a somewhat inaccurate term to describe these exercises, in which it was as necessary to note divergences of career and character as to record similarities. Sir Henry Wotton, modelling his biographical procedures explicitly on those of Plutarch, examined paired figures from the classical past, such as Pompey and Caesar, and also from nearer times and places, looking 'by way of Parallel' at the two royal favourites, the Earl of Essex and the Duke of Buckingham, noting 'their diversities' as well as 'their Conformities' in 'Fortunes and Fames', '*Person* and *Mind*', '*Actions* and *Ends*'.[13]

Parallel biography rested on the same large theory of historical repetition that underpinned the comparative work of Plutarch: the belief that certain kinds of events and people tended to recur from one historical era to another, and that corresponding typologies of conduct and character might therefore be constructed. Renaissance writers often chose to narrate the lives of famous characters from the ancient world or from the Old Testament – of Caesar, Alexander, Cleopatra, David, Absalom, Achitophel – in such a manner as to imply the existence of some present-day equivalent shadowed or paralleled in the earlier life. In certain contexts the syncrisis might be offered teasingly, hintingly, through ambiguity and innuendo, in clear awareness of the penalties accompanying more overt statement. In Ben Jonson's Roman tragedy *Sejanus* the historian Cremutius Cordus is accused of disparaging the Emperor Tiberius in precisely this manner, 'By oblique glance of his licentious pen' (3.414), having written admiringly about Brutus and Cassius, the assassins of Julius Caesar, thus appearing to suggest that Tiberius might merit a fate identical to that of Caesar. Cordus's offence – for which his writings are burnt, and he himself is condemned to death – is to have planted this hint through the covert exercise of syncrisis:

> To have a Brutus brought in paralell,
> A parricide, an enemie of his countrie,
> Rank'd, and preferr'd to any real worth
> That *Rome* now holds.[14]

Cordus's situation as presented in the published text of the play may be intended in part to reflect that of Jonson himself, who had been brought before the Privy Council on apparent suspicion of having practised a similar form of historical parallelism in the original version of the play, when it was first performed. It may also reflect on the situation of the historian John Hayward, whose account of *The Life and Raigne of King Henrie IIII*, dedicated suspiciously to the Earl of Essex and daringly reporting a successful coup against an earlier English monarch, had triggered the ban on the printing of English histories on 1 June 1599 and led to Hayward's own confinement in the Tower of London. In each of these cases, syncrisis proved to be a politically hazardous exercise.[15]

Syncrisis of a more overt and less inflammatory kind was also commonly practised within the period. Samuel Daniel, in dedicating his *Tragedie of Cleopatra* to Mary Herbert, Countess of Pembroke, praises his patroness's personal accomplishments (which are as great, it is implied, as those of

Cleopatra herself), and the achievements of English writers in relation to
those of modern Italy, which, for all its collective talents, 'cannot shew a
Sidney':

> Let them produce the best of all they may
> Since Rome left bearing, who bare more than men
> And we shall parallel them every way
> In all the glorious actions of the men.[16]

'Elizaes blessed peace' in Daniel's vision will rival that of Augustus; to
write about Cleopatra is to be reminded of one's happiness in living in
the present age. Shakespeare, a close reader both of Plutarch's *Lives* and of
Daniel's tragedy, turns the comparison another way in his own tragedy of
Antony and Cleopatra. Here is Charmian speaking of her now-dead mistress
at the end of this play:

> Now boast thee, Death, in thy possession lies
> A lass unparalleled. Downy windows, close;
> And golden Phoebus never be beheld
> Of eyes again so royal.[17]

A lass unparalleled: the adjective is carefully chosen. Shakespeare's achievement is to persuade us of the uniqueness of Cleopatra's character – its sharp
particularity, its literally unmatchable nature – while subtly reminding us
that she is in fact not wholly unparalleled in history and mythology. The
play discreetly reminds us of resemblances between the fate of Antony and
Cleopatra and that of Aeneas and Dido, and of Mars and Venus, of Bacchus
and Venus, of Hercules and Omphale. Cleopatra's story at times runs close
to that of Eve, and of Delilah.[18]

It has been suggested furthermore that Shakespeare in his depiction
of Cleopatra may have been thinking quite precisely about Elizabeth I,
drawing numerous parallels between the characters and circumstances of
the two queens.[19] Elizabeth, like Cleopatra, was subject to fits of rage and
liable to treat her counsellors and maids of honour in much the same
style that Shakespeare's Cleopatra treats messengers from Rome. On one
occasion Elizabeth had flung a slipper at Walsingham which hit him in
the face, while on another she broke the finger of one of her maids of
honour, whom she was accustomed to striking freely. Both Cleopatra and
Elizabeth affected illness and other shams to get their way; both were
adept at languages; both liked revelry and amusement and lavish dress;
both were witty. Both rode splendidly in their royal barges; both enjoyed

participating personally in warfare; both ruled small kingdoms with the help of their navies; both staked their thrones on a decisive battle, Elizabeth's navy successfully routing the Spanish Armada, Cleopatra failing disastrously at the Battle of Actium.

Shakespeare's syncrisis might not have been well received had the play been performed or published during Elizabeth's lifetime. *Antony and Cleopatra* is a natural sequel to *Julius Caesar*, which had been performed at the Globe in 1599. One explanation that has been advanced for Shakespeare's delay in completing the later play, which was probably written and performed in 1606/7, is political caution: the Queen who was so quick to detect historical parallels on other occasions ('I am Richard II, know ye not that?') might well have been displeased at the manner, however subtle, in which the implied comparisons between herself and the Egyptian monarch had been developed.[20] During Elizabeth's lifetime Fulke Greville had suppressed his own play on Antony and Cleopatra out of fear that it would be read as an account of the relationship between Essex and Elizabeth; while Francis Bacon, addressing James VI and I in *The Advancement of Learning* years after the death of Elizabeth, chose still to speak of her warily as 'a princess that, if Plutarch were now alive to write lives by parallels, would trouble him, I think, to find a parallel amongst women'.[21] Yet James, troubled by popular nostalgia for Elizabeth during the early years of his reign, would scarcely have been offended by an implicit comparison of his predecessor with Cleopatra. *Antony and Cleopatra*, it has been suggested, might indeed have been performed originally at court in James's presence, and intended as a deliberate compliment to him, playing on certain parallels that James himself had attempted to encourage between his own reign and that of Octavius Caesar, later to become known as the Emperor Augustus.[22]

The figure of syncrisis may thus be employed in either a subversive or a panegyrical mode, or indeed with complete neutrality, as the two subjects for comparison are weighed equably against each other. But as the title of this chapter suggests, the style which syncrisis seems naturally to encourage is that of contestation. It is a figure that looks always for a comparator, choosing always to rank one subject directly or indirectly against another. It thrives on competition and enmity, on conflict and battle. The Latin verb *committere* which is frequently used in relation to these exercises means to commit or bring together for the purposes of formal comparison. The same word is used for the bringing together of armies or gladiators or fighting cocks to engage in battle. Here is how Juvenal in his misogynistic sixth Satire describes a female critic employing the art of syncrisis:

Illa tamen gravior, quae cum discumbere coepit,
laudat Vergilium, periturae ignoscit Elissae,
committit vates et comparat, inde Maronem
atque alia parte in trutia suspendit Homerum.
cedunt grammatici, vincuntur rhetores, omnis
turba tacet, nec causidicus nec praecox loquetur,
altera nec mulier; verborum tanta cadit vis,
tot partier pelves ac tintinnabula dicas
pulsari.

(434–42)

[But most intolerable of all is the woman who as soon as she sits down to dinner commends Virgil, pardons the dying Dido, and pits the poets against each other [committit vates et comparat], putting Virgil in the one scale and Homer in the other. The grammarians make way before her; the rhetoricians give in; the whole crowd is silenced; no lawyer, no auctioneer will get a word in, no, nor any other woman; so torrential is her speech that you would think all the pots and bells were being clashed together.]

Juvenal's female critic is a stirrer, a trouble-maker, a proposer of invidious comparisons. In an epigram (7.24) addressed to a critic who had attempted in a similar style to *commit* his verses against those of Juvenal, Martial angrily denies the possibility of enmity existing between the two poets, seeking to quieten the competitive spirit which this exercise has set in train.

The competition which syncrisis proposes is often not merely personal, but national, too. Quintilian's and Plutarch's comparisons are largely designed to measure the relative achievements of Greece and Rome: Homer and Virgil serve as cultural champions of these nations, and Alexander and Caesar as exemplars of their military prowess. By the Renaissance, English writers begin with equal care to measure native talent against that of the classical world. The analyses of poetical form and rhetorical figures set out in George Puttenham's *Arte of English Poesie* (1589) are inspired by the simple comparative question: 'why should not Poesie be a vulgar Art with us aswel as with the Greeks and Latines, our language admitting no fewer rules and nice diversities than theirs?'[23] In *Palladis Tamia* (1598) Francis Meres attempts an elaborate syncrisis of English and classical literary achievement: 'A COMPARATIVE DISCOURSE OF OUR ENGLISH POETS WITH THE GREEKE, LATINE, AND ITALIAN POETS'.

As Greece had three poets of great antiquity, Orpheus, Linus, and Musaeus, and Italy other three auncient poets, Livius Andronicus, Ennius, and Plautus: so hath England three auncient poets, Chaucer, Gower, and Lydgate.

As Homer is reputed the Prince of Greek poets, and Petrarch of Italian poets: so Chaucer is accounted the God of English poets.

As Homer was the first that adorned the Greek tongue with true quantity: so *Piers Plowman* was the first that observed the true quantitie of our verse without the curiositie of rime.

And so on, through a long and increasingly attenuated list of cultural comparisons: 'As Euripedes is the most sententious among the Greek Poets: so is Warner among our English Poets'; 'As Hesiod writ learnedly of husbandry in Greeke: so hath Tusser very wittily and experimentally written of it in English'; 'As Anacreon died by the pot: so George Peele by the pox.'[24]

By the late seventeenth century these comparative exercises moved into a more belligerent mode, as the great debate concerning the relative achievements of the Ancients and the Moderns got under way. In France Charles Perrault published his *Parallele des anciens et des modernes* (1688), an energetically chauvinistic onslaught on the much-vaunted achievements of the ancients, attacking Homer in particular for the puerile and barbarous nature of his work. Against Homer and the ancients Perrault ranges the great modern writers of France – Boileau, Racine, Corneille – whose achievements, Perrault ringingly declares, surpass those of the classical world. This is open and declared warfare. Certain editions of Perrault's work actually included battle-maps showing the major writers of ancient and modern times drawn up in military formation on either side of the River Helicon, awaiting the decisive combat. The so-called quarrel of the ancients and moderns, a huge exercise in cross-cultural syncrisis, raged on for many years, engaging the controversial energies of such writers as Fontenelle in France and William Wotton and Sir William Temple in England, and forming the background to Jonathan Swift's satirical work, *The Battle of the Books*.[25]

The army of the Moderns, as Swift depicts it, is considerable in its numbers but uncertain in its choice of leaders:

The difference was greatest among the horse, where every private trooper pretended to the chief command, from Tasso and Milton to Dryden and Withers . . . The army of the Ancients was much fewer in number; Homer led the horse, and Pindar the light-horse; Euclid was chief engineer; Plato and Aristotle commanded the bowmen; Herodotus and Livy the foot; Hippocrates the dragoons. The allies, led by Vossius and Temple, brought up the rear.[26]

Yet for many in England the choice of leaders among the Moderns was beyond dispute: it was none other than William Shakespeare. In his great poem 'To the Memory of My Beloved, The Author, Mr William Shakespeare, and What He Hath Left Us' standing at the head of the 1623 First

Folio – a powerful feat of literary syncrisis, methodically *committing* and comparing Shakespeare against his modern and ancient rivals – Ben Jonson had made the matter clear.

> For, if I thought my judgement were of yeeres,
>   I should commit thee surely with thy peeres,
> And tell, how farre thou didst our *Lily* out-shine,
>   Or sporting *Kid*, or *Marlowes* mighty line.
> And though thou hadst small *Latine*, and lesse *Greeke*,
>   From thence to honour thee, I would not seeke
> For names; but call forth thund'ring *Aeschilus*,
>   *Euripides*, and *Sophocles* to us,
> *Paccuvius*, *Accius*, him of *Cordova* dead,
>   To life againe, to heare thy Buskin tread,
> And shake a Stage: Or, when thy Sockes were on,
>   Leave thee alone, for the comparison
> Of all, that insolent Greece, or haughtie Rome
>   Sent forth, or since did from their ashes come.
> Triumph, my *Britaine*, thou hast one to showe,
>   To whom all Scenes of *Europe* homage owe.
>
> (27–42)

No one until this time had spoken of Shakespeare in such magisterial terms, placing him confidently above his English peers and 'all, that insolent Greece, or haughtie Rome' had hitherto achieved.[27] Jonson's poem helped to shape and articulate the verdict that, by the late eighteenth century, would be regarded as axiomatic: that Shakespeare was a writer whose creative powers defied and transcended routine comparison, and who was indeed, as Jonson put it, 'not of an age, but for all time!' (43). By a curiously ironical twist, however, the Romantic consensus regarding the nature of Shakespeare's genius was arrived at through a further process of syncritic evaluation, by which Shakespeare's qualities were defined through a series of sustained contrasts with those of the very writer who had pronounced his uniqueness: Ben Jonson. Shakespeare (in this conspectus) was wild, artless, and untutored, the poet of fancy and imagination, where Jonson was laboured, learned and pedantic, the poet of correct yet chilly judgement. The one was a true original, whose writings embraced the world of nature, the other a bare imitator, whose writings merely mirrored the world of books. Shakespeare's formal irregularities spoke of English freedoms, while Jonson's more organized art signalled his subservience to foreign models. The personal character of Shakespeare, as deduced from a selective reading of his work, emerged as generous, gentle, and amiable, while Jonson's, through the application of similar tests, appeared as envious, saturnine, morose.[28]

Few examples better illustrate the rhetorical power of syncrisis and its critical limitations than this routine contrast of these two supreme English writers of the early-modern period. The elevation of Shakespeare led inevitably, by the repeated application of these literary commonplaces, to the denigration of Jonson and the progressive dismissal of his work. In such an exercise there could be only one winner. While one contestant had been crowned, the other lay on his back, unconscious in the ring. It was Jonson's fate to be perceived as the man-who-was-not-Shakespeare; as the writer whose supposed qualities served merely to define, through negatives, the qualities that England's national genius was assumed to possess.

By the early eighteenth century at least one judicious critic was inclined to regard this favoured contrast, and the larger rhetorical exercise which it exemplified, with a wary eye. In his Preface to *The Works of Shakespeare* Alexander Pope attributed the familiar opposition of Shakespeare and Ben Jonson to 'the zeal of the Partizans' on either side. 'It is ever the nature of Parties to be in extremes; and nothing is so probable, as that because *Ben Johnson* had much the most learning, it was said on the one hand that *Shakespear* had none at all; and because *Shakespear* had much the most wit and fancy, it was retorted on the other that *Johnson* wanted both.'[29] 'Nothing is more absurd or endless, than the common method of comparing eminent writers by an opposition of particular passages in them, and forming a judgement from thence of their merit upon the whole', Pope wrote elsewhere, focusing now on another all too-familiar contrast:

We ought to have a certain knowledge of the principal character and distinguishing excellence of each: It is in *that* we are to consider him, and in proportion to his degree in *that* we are to admire him . . .

No Author or Man ever excell'd all the World in more than one Faculty, and as *Homer* has done this in Invention, *Virgil* has in Judgment. Not that we are to think *Homer* wanted Judgment, because *Virgil* had it in a more eminent degree; or that *Virgil* wanted Invention, because *Homer* possest a larger share of it: Each of these great Authors had more of both than perhaps any Man besides, and are only said to have less in Comparison with one another.[30]

No stranger himself to the quarrels and contests of authors, Pope was aware of the critical simplifications they might provoke, and the perils that lay in the art of comparison.

CHAPTER 10

All suche testimonies maie be called sentences of the sage, whiche are brought to confirme anye thyng, either taken out of olde authours, or els suche as have bene used in this commune life. As the sentences of noble men, the lawes in anie realme, quicke saiynges, proverbes, that either have bene used heretofore, or bee nowe used. Histories of wise philosophers, the judgementes of learned men, the commune opinion of the multitude, old custome, auncient fashions, or anie suche like.

Thomas Wilson, *The Rule of Reason, Conteinyng the Arte of Logique* (1551)

CANTERBURY   Then heare me gracious Soveraign, and you Peers,
That owe your selves, your lives, and services,
To this Imperiall Throne. There is no barre
To make against your Highnesse Clayme to France,
But this which they produce from *Pharamond*,
In terram Salicam mulieres ne succedant,
No Woman shall succeed in Salike Land . . .

William Shakespeare, *Henry V*, 1.2.33–9

Testimony: the artless proof

R. W. SERJEANTSON

The argument from testimony is not formally a figure of speech. But it is closely related, as we shall see, to several of the figures of speech, and testimonies can themselves contain the whole gamut of schemes and tropes. Like the figures, testimony is extremely widespread in all forms of Renaissance literature. It is most important in the literature of argument: writing, usually in prose, in which an author is arguing in praise or defence of something, or for a particular course of action, or for the truth of an opinion or event. But testimony also appears in poetry and drama; in any genre, in short, in which the resources of Renaissance rhetoric were used to persuade an audience, raise a hearer's passions, or give a reader pleasure.

It is well worth trying to understand the ways in which Renaissance authors used the argument from testimony. Renaissance writing is often governed by conventions derived from formalised arts of argument, of which the art of rhetoric is the most pervasive. To draw attention to these conventions came to be regarded as unskilled and jejune – like a swimmer using a bladder, as one later seventeenth-century image had it.[1] Yet that Renaissance readers were highly conscious of the different forms of logical and rhetorical argument is evident not only from the innumerable handbooks of those arts that formed a staple of the curriculum of the grammar-schools and the early years of a university education, but also from the printed and manuscript analyses that survive of classical, biblical and vernacular literature. William Temple's analysis of Sir Philip Sidney's *Apology for Poetry*, for instance, paid careful attention to Sidney's use of testimony.[2] To understand the arguments Renaissance authors used, then, may deepen our appreciation of the effects they hoped to bring about in their audiences, and also, perhaps, enable us to conjecture how those audiences might have taken them.

THEORIES OF TESTIMONY

Renaissance rhetoricians, following the Latin orator and rhetorical theorist Cicero, commonly divided the art of rhetoric into five 'parts': invention (*inventio*), arrangement (*dispositio*), style (*elocutio*), memory (*memoria*) and delivery (*pronuntiatio*).[3] The figures of speech fell within the province of style. Testimony, however, was not a figure of speech but a form of argument, and the part of rhetoric that considered arguments was not style, but invention – the 'most important part of all' according to Cicero.[4] Yet most Renaissance writers on rhetoric emphasised the congruence of *inventio* and *elocutio*, regarding them as parallel means to the same end: invention 'discovered' the subject-matter (the *res*) of an argument, while *elocutio* amplified and varied its words (*verba*).

Invention, the art of finding out arguments, had a slightly unusual status. It fell into the province not only of rhetoric, but also of the other Renaissance discipline of argument, rhetoric's more abstract and rigorous sister art: logic. Some Renaissance theorists of argument, and particularly the Ramists, made testimony exclusively a part of logic, while others allowed that it (also) belonged to rhetoric. But all agreed that, in technical terms, testimony was one of the 'topics' or 'common-places' (*loci communes*) of argumentative invention. These 'topics' had a formal and well-defined sense, from which the more general and less precise modern use of the word derives. They were conceived as 'seats of argument': places, as it were, to which the orator might go to find or 'discover' (*invenire*) material for an oration. In the Renaissance they formed a vital argumentative resource. Their purpose was to help speakers win credit for their arguments: in a very widely quoted definition, Cicero had defined an argument as a 'plausible invention to produce belief'.[5]

The topics of logic (to begin with them) tended to be strongly abstract and comparative in nature. As Thomas Wilson put it in his popular vernacular *Arte of Rhetorique* (1553), the logician 'talketh of things universally, without respect of person, time, or place'.[6] The assumptions that informed the logical topics were often those of neo-Aristotelian philosophy, which emphasised relations between cause and effect, which regarded the world as being ordered according to a hierarchy of *genera* and *species*, and which prized syllogistic argument founded upon essential definitions of things. Hence the places from which logicians were instructed to draw their arguments included such topics as definition, cause, effect, contraries, the greater, and the less.[7] King Lear's warning to Cordelia that 'Nothing will come of nothing' may be regarded as an argument drawn from the topic of the cause (as well as being a vernacular rendering of the philosophical maxim *ex nihilo nihil fit*). Similarly, Brutus's answer for his actions in *Julius Caesar* – 'not that I loved Caesar less, but that I loved Rome more' – is (among other things) an instance of argument from the topic of the greater.[8]

The rhetorical 'topics', by contrast, were much more specific and circumstantial in nature. Rhetoricians were warned of the 'folly' of not taking into account the time and place of their speeches, and the audiences to whom they were delivered.[9] They might therefore seek arguments from the more moral and human topics of honesty, possibility, greatness and pettiness; or consider the 'circumstances' of an action – who, what, when, where, why, with what help.[10] In a demonstrative oration praising a person, for instance, the orator was encouraged to draw material from the topics of their birth or death, the kingdom or town in which they lived, and their parents and ancestors.[11]

In both the arts of logic and rhetoric, then, testimony served as one further 'place' to which speakers might go to in order to find material for their arguments. In the same way that a logician might draw material from causes or effects, and a rhetorician might draw material from the justice or injustice of a particular cause, so both forms of argument appealed to the topic of testimony to find further material for their speeches. For logicians, testimonies could provide a source of propositions for syllogisms or enthymemes, whilst for rhetoricians testimonies were a further and important means of imparting credit (*fides*) to their arguments.[12]

An exemplary genre – the funeral oration – suggests some of the uses of the topic of testimony in practice.[13] In this genre it serves as a particularly valuable source of praise; one deployed by John Donne, for instance, in the sermon he preached at the funeral of Sir William Cokayne on 12 December 1626. Donne's witness here is none other than King James I, himself very recently deceased. Donne writes that he had 'sometimes heard' James 'say of' Cokayne, 'That he never heard any man of his breeding, handle businesses more rationally, more pertinently, more elegantly, more perswasively.'[14] This conventionally laudatory function of testimony could be exploited in more self-consciously original ways; above all, perhaps, in the speech Antony gives to the plebeians over Caesar's body in Shakespeare's *Julius Caesar* (1599). Here Antony deftly turns around the convention of citing testimonies to the deceased when he sets all his reasons for Caesar's virtuous nature – his fidelity, his justice, his military success, and his refusal of the 'kingly crown' – against Brutus's opposing testimony: 'Yet Brutus says he was ambitious.'[15] The disjunction between what Brutus says and

the expected conventions of the funeral genre highlights the falseness of
Brutus's position and begins the rhetorical work of turning Antony's audience against Caesar's assassins.

Yet there was one way in which testimony was regarded as being a slightly
unusual form of argument: in contrast to the other topical arguments, the
kind of proof it provided was regarded as 'artless'. ('Art', in this context,
implies 'skill' or 'technique', rather than imaginative inspiration; rhetoric
was conceived as an *ars*, a set of practical skills, rather than a *scientia*, or body
of knowledge.) In its formal classification, the theorists suggested no particular skill was necessarily required to discover or 'invent' testimonies, because
they already existed. For this reason Aristotle, in his *Art of Rhetoric*, had
called these sorts of proof *atechnoi*, 'without art', and Quintilian, following
Aristotle closely here, had coined the Latin term *inartificialis*.[16] Following
these authors, Renaissance rhetoricians commonly classified judgements,
rumours, fame, information obtained by torture, oaths, and testimonies all
as 'artless' proofs.[17] Of these, testimonies were the most general and, for
Renaissance authors, the most useful. Moreover, as we shall go on to see,
although these proofs were formally classified as 'artless', in practice a large
body of precepts grew up about how to use and present them.

Quintilian's term *inartificialis* was picked up very widely in the sixteenth century, owing above all to its adoption by Petrus Ramus in his
influential *Dialectic* (1556).[18] Ramus was a high-profile French convert to
Protestantism, who had the misfortune to be murdered in the course of
the St Bartholomew's Day massacre of 1572, in which a large number of
Huguenots were slaughtered by their fellow Roman Catholic citizens. This
shocking event became immediately notorious among European protes-
tants. Christopher Marlowe's play *The Massacre at Paris* (1593) dramatises
it, and towards the beginning of the play Marlowe actually depicts Ramus's
murder at the hands of the dukes of Guise and Anjou.[19] Guise is represented
as taunting Ramus for some of the things for which he was most notorious:
his shallow learning, his tendency to analyse any subject-matter by means
of dichotomies, and his fondness for epitomes. Most strikingly, Guise then
goes on to mock Ramus's account of testimony:

> And he forsooth must goe and preach in *Germany*:
> Excepting against Doctors axioms,
> And *ipse dixit* with this quidditie,
> *Argumentum testimonii est inartificiale*
> [argument from testimony is artless].
> To contradict which, I say, *Ramus* shall dye:
> How answere you that? your *nego argumentum* [I deny the argument]
> Cannot serve, sirra, kill him.[20]

This scene, characteristically for Marlowe, is a learned joke. Guise's speech is a parody of the genre of the philosophical disputation, with its formal procedures of proposition and counter-argument; it also has the disputation's self-consciousness about the arguments being employed. Moreover, in his account of inartificial argument, Ramus had described it as having 'but little strengthe to prove or disprove'.[21] This characterisation of the argument from authority underlies Guise's charge that Ramus is hostile to 'Doctors axioms' and their authoritative pronouncements; *ipse dixit* ('he himself said so') was the expression disciples of the Greek philosopher Pythagoras conventionally used to introduce their master's words.[22] Guise's '*I* say', furthermore, is a mocking parody of the *ipse dixit* formula. Overall, the passage is a prime case of a literary text working in dynamic relation to the rhetorical instrument it is employing. It is also, in the end, a piece of dark wit about the inefficacy of verbal argument in the face of physical violence.[23]

Testimony, then, was one of the topics of argumentative invention in rhetoric and dialectic. At one level its relationship to other arguments corresponds to the well-established distinction in medieval philosophical and theological discourse between reason (*ratio*) and authority (*auctoritas*). Yet it would be misleading to suggest that the distinction was as sharply drawn as this in the Renaissance. Precisely because of the profound impact in this period of neo-classical rhetoric – the reach of which even extended (via the tradition of humanist dialectic) to the discipline of logic – forms of Renaissance argument, including Renaissance philosophy, are less inclined to draw this distinction between reason and authority rigorously, tending rather to be more self-consciously eloquent, and also more inclined to draw upon historical and poetic resources, than their late medieval precursors. They were also, as we shall now see, extremely self-conscious about how testimonies should be presented and amplified.

PRESENTING TESTIMONY

For all that its 'artless' nature made testimony a slightly unusual form of argument, it had one fundamental use: to prove a point. In this sense, testimony functioned rather like a witness in a law-court. There is nothing surprising about this: the classical theories of oratory from which Renaissance rhetoric developed were written above all for the benefit of pleaders in law-courts and popular political orators.[24] Hence it would be a mistake to conclude that simply because they classified testimony as an 'artless' proof the rhetorical theorists of antiquity or their Renaissance heirs regarded it as unimportant. Quintilian, in fact, had even gone so far as to say that the greatest part of legal cases were made up of inartificial proofs, and he went on to assert that although these inartificial proofs lacked art in themselves, nevertheless 'the highest powers of eloquence are generally required to uphold or refute them'.[25]

Yet for a Renaissance philosopher, and much more so for an orator or a poet, it was usually not enough simply to cite a testimony like a witness at the bar. As Renaissance rhetoric became increasingly directed towards written rather than oral art, the precepts that Roman orators had formulated for the treatment of witnesses came to be applied to the use of more literary and philosophical testimony. One important consequence of this was that the manuals on good Latin style that proliferated in the Renaissance commonly devoted space to teaching their readers how to 'bring in' (*citare*) textual witnesses in an elegant and classically sanctioned manner.[26] The godfather of all these works was Lorenzo Valla's *Elegancies of the Latin Language* (1444); its worthy successor was Desiderius Erasmus's *On the Twofold Abundance of Words and Things* (1512). Erasmus's book is celebrated among scholars of humanism for giving a hundred-and-forty-six different variations on the phrase 'your letter pleased me greatly', but Erasmus is scarcely less copious on the subject of how to introduce authorities, as this extract suggests: 'As Cicero has it; on Plato's authority; as Varro bears witness; if we accept what Terence says; as we find reported in Pliny; . . . according to Epicurus, happiness lies in pleasure; . . . Livy witnesses to the truth of this.'[27]

The effect of remorseless accumulation that Erasmus encouraged was further developed by Renaissance rhetoricians in a variety of different ways. One of the principal forms that this encouragement took was in the doctrine of 'amplification': the technique of augmenting and magnifying one's case in order to arouse the passions of the audience.[28] Most authors agreed that logical argument in itself should not be amplified; the thought was that bare reason did not need to be embellished.[29] In contrast, as Thomas Wilson put it, it was precisely 'by large amplification and beautifying of his cause' that 'the rhetorician is always known'.[30] The Danzig pedagogue Bartholomew Keckermann, whose works were widely studied in the early seventeenth-century English universities, made clear that after all the resources of the 'artificial' techniques of dilation had been exploited, there was also available dilation by 'inartificial argument', that is to say, by 'testimony or sententia, which we cite to extend [*dilato*] the argument we have put forward, and to develop or prove our main point'.[31] In his popular *Index rhetoricus* (1625), the famous English schoolmaster Thomas Farnaby similarly proposed testimonies 'crowded and crushed together' as the eighth and final technique for amplifying demonstrative rhetoric.[32]

Amplification could also be used to enhance the authority of testimony. Keckermann recommended praising both the author and indeed the testimony itself. He also suggested lingering over its delivery – a form of dilation known as *expolitio*.[33] Donne introduces James I's testimony in praise of Sir William Cokayne by first praising James himself, in a notable piece of amplification, as 'the greatest Master of Language and Judgement, which these times, or any other did, or doe, or shall give'.[34] Thomas Wilson similarly gives a particularly impressive example of how an orator may 'commend the authority which he alledgeth':

> . . . he might say thus. These wordes are no fables uttered among men, but an assured truth left unto us by writing, and yet not by any common writing, but by such as all the world hath confirmed and agreed upon that it is authentic and canonical; neither are they the words of one that is of the common sort, but they are the words of a doctor in the Church of God; and yet not the words of a divine or doctor of the common sort, but of an Apostle; and yet not of one that is the worst, but of Paul, that is the best of all others and yet not Paul's, but rather the words of the Holy Ghost, speaking by the mouth of Paul.[35]

Testimony may formally have been classified as an 'artless' proof. But the import of Wilson's impressive crescendo here is that the rhetorician could nonetheless do a very great deal to amplify its authority and power. Yet even the convention of praising the source of a testimony could cut both ways. We have already seen how, in *Julius Caesar*, Antony's use of Brutus's testimony to Caesar's ambition upsets the conventional expectations of the funeral oration. Shakespeare heightens this effect still further by Antony's repeated, and increasingly hollow amplification of Brutus's own character as 'an honourable man'.[36]

TESTIMONY AND ITS NEIGHBOURS

Although testimony was formally an aspect of logical or rhetorical 'invention', in use – like much in Renaissance rhetoric – it shaded into a range of other rhetorical features. In this way testimony came to be directly associated with the figures of speech. One important 'testimonial' figure – one which bears witness, cites authority, or reports a speech – is that of prosopopoeia.[37] Prosopopoeia is a figure of rhetorical amplification, defined by the author of the *Rhetorica ad Herennium* (who calls it *conformatio*) as being 'when a person not present is feigned in some way as if they were, or when something silent or formless is made to speak'.[38] It is as if, says Thomas Wilson, 'we imagine a talk for someone to speak'.[39] It was a figure that was regarded as having particular force at persuading and inflaming the mind to the emulation of virtue, and its testimonial character is evident, even if its power of proving was less secure.[40]

In his *Garden of Eloquence*, Henry Peacham gathered together four different 'figures of moderation' that also bore some relation to the argument from testimony – as is indicated by his suggestion that they, like the testimony of witnesses,[41] are particularly valuable 'to confirm or confute'. Peacham defined the eye-witness figure martyria, called *testatio* in Latin, as 'a forme of speech by which the Orator or Speaker confirmeth some thing by his owne experience'. Apodixis (*experientia* or *evidens probatio*) similarly appealed not to the orator's own experience but to common and irrefutable experience. Apomnemonysis (*dicti commemoratio*) recalled for the audience 'some saying or sentence of another worthy of remembrance and observation'; whilst antirrhesis, by contrast, involved the rejection of 'the authority, opinion or sentence of some person'.[42]

As these definitions suggest, the overarching rhetorical figure that was perhaps closest to testimony is the sententia or 'moral sentence'. A sententia, which had overtones of its classical Latin sense of 'judgement', was a pithy and memorable phrase: a 'recitall of some grave matter' which both beautified and graced a style.[43] Several writers were clear that testimony could take the form of a 'Notable sentence' or was a 'sententia of a witness'.[44] Richard Sherry, in his *Treatise of Schemes and Tropes* (1550), closely associated the sententia with the argument from testimony or authority when he defined it as one of the seven kinds of figure called '*Indicacio*, or authoritie'.[45] Other writers, however, also explain that a sententia did not necessarily have to be a testimony *per se*: as a 'notable saying or sentence' it might (in the distinction drawn by Angel Day) be either 'by common custom admitted, or by some author delivered'.[46]

A number of further rhetorical figures clustered around the sententia. One was the proverb, which was sometimes regarded, following Aristotle and Quintilian, as a form of testimony. Another was the chria, which Sherry defined as 'very short exposition of any dede or worde', with 'the name of the author recited'.[47] Closely related to both was the gnome, which John Smith described in 1657 as 'when we bring in a sentence or such a remarkable saying of anothers to the same purpose with the Author, he being not named'.[48] Perhaps the most extraordinary literary product of the Renaissance fascination with testimonies was the genre of the cento: a text composed entirely of quotations taken from other authors (the Latin word *cento* originally meant a patchwork garment). This genre went in the course of the Renaissance from being a copious source of moral instruction to simple parody.[49] Justus Lipsius's *Politica* (1589) is woven very largely from testimonies taken from the notoriously concise and sometimes obscure Roman historian Tacitus.[50] In Renaissance England the cento was often also known by its Greek name of 'rhapsody': John Florio, for instance, translated Montaigne's 'centons qui se publient pour centons' as 'mingle-mangles of many kinds of stuffe, or as the Grecians call them *Rapsodies*'.[51] Edmund Bolton asserted that Geoffrey of Monmouth was 'nothing else but a meer Satyra, Rhapsodie, or Cento' pieced together out of Welsh ballads.[52] And Robert Burton wrote of his *Anatomy of Melancholy* (1621–51) that he had 'laboriously collected this *Cento* out of divers Writers'; indeed, one list of remedies for the grievances of melancholy simply consists of an undigested list of 'Sentences selected out of humane authors'.[53] Perhaps for this reason the cento could also serve as a caution for rhetorical theorists. Bartholomew Keckermann, for instance, warned that the orator should not overuse sententiae. They should serve as the seasoning of the orator's meal, not as the food; otherwise the oration risked becoming a mere cento.[54]

Not every quotation, however, had the force of a testimony. When the purpose was illustrative, rather than probative, we are in the realm not of testimony but of the example (*exemplum*).[55] Examples differed from testimonies in their function, which was to shed light on a point, not to attempt to prove it. Francis Bacon cited a conventional maxim to this effect in the first of the letters of advice he wrote in the name of the Earl of Essex to the youthful Earl of Rutland: 'examples illustrate, they do not prove'. Yet Bacon went on to note that examples may indeed 'make things plain that are proved'.[56] Robert Sanderson similarly commented in his popular *Compendium of the Art of Logic* (1615) that the example is the least efficacious of all arguments: 'for it illustrates more than it proves; it does not so much compel as persuade'.[57]

Testimonies often took the form of what would now be called quotations, and the rhetorical function of verse quotations in particular was something that Renaissance authors were explicitly conscious of. Yet it is striking that in this period there seems to have been no secure conception of the 'quotation' in its modern sense that was distinct from the different arguments and figures discussed here. Here again, there were classical precedents. An instance that was sometimes noted in the Renaissance was the passage in Cicero's oration *Pro Sestio* in which Cicero defends himself from the charge of levity after having introduced a quotation from a verse drama into a judicial oration.[58] Cicero reassures his audience he has not simply plucked *flosculi* ('little flowers') from any kind of indecorous source. Cicero's faithful elaborator Quintilian similarly noted in his *Institutio oratoria* that even philosophers, who think everything else inferior to their own writings, sometimes condescend to repeat verses from the poets for the authority they confer.[59] Sir Philip Sidney noted in his *Apology for Poetry* (*c.* 1582), that Cicero 'taketh much pains, and many times not without poetical helps, to make us know the force love of our country hath in us'.[60] And in his *Arcadian Rhetorike* (1588), Sidney's admirer Abraham Fraunce advised his reader as follows: 'In prose avoid verse, unless now and then a verse bee brought in out of some author, either for proof or pleasure.'[61]

The wide range of rhetorical figures associated with testimony, then, demonstrates the creative instability of both Renaissance rhetorical theory and practice. Historians of rhetoric have often noted the fluidity of the figures and tropes.[62] Here we have a further instance of rhetorical instability: testimony was a form of argument, and therefore fell into the province of *inventio*; but it also shaded into the figures, the province of *elocutio*.

TESTIMONY AND 'TRUE VALUE'

Testimony was used to prove, to persuade, to amplify, and to give pleasure. Yet it also had a further vital function: to establish value and to confer merit. If an author needed to prove the importance or worth of their subject, testimony was often the best means of doing so. One of the most impressive and thoroughgoing instances of this phenomenon in the English Renaissance is found in Book 1 of Francis Bacon's *Of the Proficience and Advancement of Learning* (1605). In form a judicial oration addressed directly to James I, it contains all the Ciceronian components of the exordium, proposition, division and enumeration of the case, and, most importantly, the proof and confutation.[63] Bacon's subject in Book 1 is the 'excellencie of learning and knowledge', and in order to prove this case and refute objections to it he draws extensively on testimony. In fact, he asserts that his purpose throughout the first book is, 'without varnish or amplification, justly to weigh the dignitie of knowledge in the ballance with other things, and to take the true value thereof by testimonies and arguments divine, and humane'. Bacon's testimonies were particularly calculated to appeal to his audience, James I. To the British Solomon Bacon invokes the testimony of the biblical Solomon's authorship of the book of Proverbs and of his putative work of natural history (see I Kings 4:33). Later on Bacon also cites to his philosophical monarch Plato's testimony that '*Then should people and estates be happie, when either Kings were Philosophers, or Philosophers Kings.*'[64]

Throughout the book the majority of Bacon's arguments are drawn from the topic of testimony, and the authority of his witnesses is upheld in the ways recommended by the Renaissance rhetoricians.

The use of testimony to establish the worth or power of something is similarly dramatised in the debate in John Milton's *Comus* (1634) over the power of virtue. The Lady, a 'hapless virgin' (line 349) lost in the night, is apprehensively sought by her two brothers.[65] As they go, the men debate her safety, with the Second Brother in particular fearing that the fruits of her beauty are in danger from 'the rash hand of bold Incontinence' (396). The Elder Brother argues the contrary case. He acknowledges that her state is not secure beyond 'all doubt, or controversy' (408). But he musters a number of arguments in defence of the likelihood of her safety: her virtue, her wisdom, and her capacity for contemplation (372–7). Yet her strongest defence, he insists, lies in a further virtue that is specifically her own: her chastity. He defends the 'hidden strength' of chastity – and condemns its obverse, lust, (462–74) – in a self-consciously demonstrative oration; an oration, in effect, in praise of the power of chastity. At the heart of this oration are a set of arguments drawn from testimony. First the anonymous testimony of native folklore is invoked: 'Some say' that 'No goblin, or swart faëry of the mine, | Hath hurtful power o'er true virginity' (431, 435–6). But it appears that this testimony may be insufficiently persuasive; so the Elder Brother turns to a still more credit-worthy set of authorities, the Greek mythographers:

> Do ye believe me yet, or shall I call
> Antiquity from the old schools of Greece
> To testify the arms of chastity?
>
> (438–40)

The witness offered by the 'stern frown' of Diana and the 'chaste austerity' of Minerva both serve to confirm his case for the steel-clad armour of chastity, and they do so with such eloquence that it draws from the Second Brother the admiring exclamation 'How charming is divine philosophy!' (475).

This use of testimony to establish value depended fundamentally on its source being authoritative. Whether it was proving a case or turning a point, it was important that the authority of the testimony be recognised by its audience if it was to have its persuasive effect. This phenomenon is recognised in a comment recorded in the table-talk of the lawyer, scholar, and parliamentarian, John Selden (1584–1654). Under the heading of *Bookes Authors*, his compiler recorded Selden as recommending that 'In quoting

of Books; quote such Authors; as are usually read; others you may read for
your owne satisfaccion but not name them.'[66] This view was entirely in
accordance with a school and university curriculum that emphasised the
thorough reading of what one tutor called 'antient classick Authours . . .
of the best note'.[67] Selden himself went on to draw an analogy that also
indicated the close relationship between literary testimony and the law-
court: 'To quote a Moderne Dutchman where I may use a Classick Author;
is as if I were to Justifie my reputacion; And I neglect persons of note and
quality that know me; and bring the Testimoniall of the Scullion in the
kitchien.'[68]

The Renaissance conception of testimony, then, had a two-fold aspect. Its
primary function was to bear witness to something, to prove an author's case
and to confer value on the thing being argued for. In its secondary function,
however, it also served as a testimonial to the author himself, demonstrating his participation in a shared intellectual culture. The authority of the
testimony was also conferred on the author who cited it.

THE FORTUNES OF TESTIMONY

As the seventeenth century progressed, developments in a range of fields – in
natural philosophy, mathematics and rhetoric – served to bring about some
fundamental changes in the way that testimony was conceived and used.
One important development occurred in the field of philosophical argument, and above all in natural philosophy. The experimental philosophers
were working to get away from the hitherto-dominant academic conception of natural philosophy, which hoped to explain what happened 'all, or
most of the time', and to replace it with circumstantial accounts of specific
'matters of fact' derived from individual experiments. To do this they had
to confront the received view of how testimony functions in philosophical
argument, which emphasised that the testimony of reputed authorities was
principally to *confirm* arguments already proved by topics of reason. But
the experimental philosophers found themselves forced to insist that what
they wished to do with their testimonies was in fact to *inform* their readers
of what they had witnessed.[69] The crisis of authority this provoked has been
interpreted in a variety of ways – as the incorporation of legal methods into
natural philosophy, or as the infiltration of gentlemanly codes of civility
into scientific practice[70] – but at its heart lies a profound reconfiguration
of received modes of argument. One consequence of this crisis was that the
evidence of testimony finally became separated from the argument from
authority in philosophical reasoning.[71]

By their celebrated attacks on the principle of authority, the 'new philosophers', or *novatores* of the seventeenth century, such as René Descartes, Thomas Hobbes and John Locke, exposed the paradox at the heart of Renaissance philosophical argument. Sixteenth and earlier seventeenth-century theorists of proof were united in the principled view that argument from testimony could not provide demonstrative certainty. The demands of scientific knowledge prohibited so fallible a proof. Yet in practice the argument from testimony was extremely commonly used. Rhetoricians eagerly cited and amplified ancient (and, increasingly, modern) testimonies; and even philosophers cited each other and, most commonly, drew upon the authority of *the* philosopher, Aristotle. It was this practice of testimonial argument that came to be attacked by the anti-authoritarian 'new philosophers'.

The most comprehensive English attack on the use of testimony in the seventeenth century came in the 'Reviewe, and Conclusion' of Thomas Hobbes's *Leviathan* (1651). Hobbes noted that the habit of 'quoting ancient Poets, Orators, and Philosophers' was an established 'custom of late time', but it was one that he himself had 'neglected'. Hobbes went on to give 'many reasons' (eight in total) why he had denied himself this particular rhetorical weapon. Taken as a whole, these reasons constitute a powerful attack on the Renaissance conception of testimonial argument: it confuses fact with right; ancient authors contradict both themselves and each other; to cite another author's testimony betrays a lack of judgement and suggests argumentative 'Indigestion'. Moreover (and more pointedly) Hobbes asserted that it was often with fraudulent motives that 'men stick their corrupt Doctrine with the Cloves of other mens Wit'; and (bitingly) that 'the praise of Ancient Authors' proceeds simply 'from the competition, and mutuall envy of the Living'.[72] An account of moral and political philosophy that was founded – as that of Hobbes's humanist predecessor Hugo Grotius had been – on 'testimonies of philosophers, historians, poets and finally orators', is here condemned entirely.[73]

The Renaissance practices and arts of argument were highly formal in nature. But by the end of the seventeenth century this formality had come to appear increasingly forced and, at worst, formulaic. In his *Peri Bathous* (1728), for instance, Alexander Pope parodied the argumentative topics by proposing the construction of 'a *Rhetorical Chest of Drawers* . . . divided into *Loci*, or *Places*, being repositories for Matter and Argument in the several kinds of oration or writing'.[74] One aspect of this attack on the topics was that the overuse of testimony, or even its use at all, came to be regarded as a sign of pedantry. The function of testimony as amplification and ornament was passing. In his 'Rules to be observed by young Pupils and Schollers in the University', for instance, James Duport – a fellow of Trinity College, Cambridge, between 1627 and 1668 – instructed his students not to 'stuffe and loade your Speeches and Declamations with Greek, and Latine sentences, Apothegmes, Verses or scrapps of Poets' (although it should be noted that he permitted them in familiar letters, and himself went on to publish a popular Homeric gnomology).[75] In 1670 John Aubrey accused the times of Elizabeth I and James I as having had a 'stile pedantique, stuff't with Latin, and Greeke sentences, like their Clothes'.[76] And in 1697 William Wotton, a 'modern' in the *querelle des anciens et des modernes* noted that young men in the universities were now taught 'to laugh at that frequent Citation of Scraps of *Latin*'.[77] The 'artless proof', in short, was becoming something else again: in an age of mathematics it appeared insufficiently demonstrative; in an age of experimental philosophy it was becoming a source of information rather than a mode of confirmation; and in an age of literary 'politeness' it appeared pedantic. The sententia was becoming merely sententious.

CHAPTER II

Hyperbole of *Cicero* called *Superlatio*, of *Quintilian Superiectio*, and it is a sentence or saying surmounting the truth onely for the cause of increasing and diminishing, not with purpose to deceive by speaking untruly, but with desire to amplifie the greatnesse or smalnesse of things by the exceeding similitude.

Henry Peacham, *The Garden of Eloquence* (1593)

Oft a flood
Have wee two wept, and so
Drownd the whole world, us two; oft did we grow
To be two Chaosses, when we did show
Care to ought else; and often absences
Withdrew our soules, and made us carcasses.

But I am by her death, (which word wrongs her)
Of the first nothing, the Elixer grown . . .

John Donne, 'A nocturnall upon S. *Lucies* day,
Being the shortest day.'

Hyperbole: exceeding similitude

KATRIN ETTENHUBER

BIRON Taffata phrases, silken terms precise,
  Three-pil'd hyperboles, spruce affection,
  Figures pedantical – these summer flies
  Have blown me full of maggot ostentation.
  I do forswear them . . .
                    William Shakespeare, *Love's Labour's Lost*, 5.2.406–10

Biron's resolve to abjure the temptations of rhetorical excess is a turning-point in his wooing of Rosaline. It marks the end of an elaborate display of courtship rituals which culminates in Biron's dressing up as a 'Muscovite', only to receive a good dressing down at the hands of Rosaline who, throughout the play, evinces an uncanny ability to see through the disguises and 'vizards' presented to her. The language of the extract brings rhetorical and theatrical artifice into close, and by no means comfortable, contact with one another: the precious over-refinement of 'Taffata phrases' and 'silken terms' is a comment on Biron's recent histrionic exploits, but it also reminds the audience of their association with a linguistic habit that may be less easy to shed.

Biron's indictment of stylistic affectation crystallises around one specific figure: hyperbole.[1] In the definition prefaced to this chapter, the sixteenth-century theorist Henry Peacham describes it as 'a sentence or saying surmounting the truth';[2] Richard Lanham, in his influential modern update of the rhetoric handbooks, refers to hyperbole as 'exaggerated or extravagant terms used for emphasis'.[3] The Greek term meant literally 'a throwing beyond'.[4] Its Latin synonyms, *superlatio* (literally, 'the raising to a higher degree') and *superiectio* ('the action of transcending a limit'), help to illustrate hyperbole's trajectory: it covers a broad spectrum of exaggeration and intensification, from the mildly implausible to the downright impossible.[5]

Readers of classical and early-modern rhetoric handbooks may have recognised in Biron's speech a familiar note of distrust: throughout the history of rhetoric, hyperbole's reputation has been unprepossessing to say the least. Most theoretical treatments of the figure are far from straightforward; hyperbole's usefulness is rarely taken for granted and, once established, almost invariably hedged about with elaborate instructions, caveats, and qualifications. Some writers even argue that hyperbole can become a stylistic vice, and advise the orator to dispense with its services altogether.[6]

This chapter will start by examining some of the most trenchant critiques of hyperbole, showing how the distrust of rhetorical exaggeration is implicated in larger aesthetic, philosophical and moral concerns. It will then map out two alternative narratives of hyperbolical language, which portray the device in a more positive light. The first of these re-evaluates the discourse of exaggeration by redefining the limits of decorum: as the range of appropriate rhetorical subjects is extended, theorists reconsider hyperbole's place in the world of figures. The second takes on the problem of audience response: by offering a fresh interpretive approach to the problem of linguistic excess, early-modern rhetoricians manage to convert hyperbole's extravagant conceits to edifying uses.

PEACOCKS, FOOLS, AND THINGS IN BETWEEN

John Prideaux's *Sacred Eloquence* (1659) starts its account of hyperbole by reporting a taxonomic peculiarity. Some 'modern Rhetoricians', he claims, class hyperbole among the 'affections of a *Trope*, rather than *Tropes* themselves'.[7] In the view of these theorists, hyperbole is a bad imitation of a rhetorical figure, embarrassing and slightly vulgar in its ostentatious display of linguistic ornament: 'there is no *Trope*, but may be . . . screwed up too high in hyperbolicall expressions'. Prideaux's discussion also reminds us of Biron's suggestion that excessive artifice compromises the orator's ability to impress and persuade his audience: stylistic affectation frequently fails to affect. As a rhetorical strategy, exaggeration intrinsically involves risk: if an idea is 'screwed up too high in hyperbolicall expressions' – if the rhetorical volume is cranked up too much – it will draw attention to itself, and the audience may become rather too aware of the fact that its perceptions are being manipulated as a result. As with a magician's trick, if you see the wire the effect is ruined.

In Prideaux's account, hyperbole's most vehement detractors are to be found among the 'modern Rhetoricians', but to understand their concerns properly we must turn to a key document in ancient rhetorical theory, Demetrius's *On Style*. In this treatise, hyperbole is identified as the characteristic feature of one particular type of writing: the 'frigid' style.[8] Once again, the reference is far from flattering. 'Frigidity' is a rhetorical fault,

Demetrius maintains, a 'distorted' reflection of the grand, elevated, or epic style: 'frigidity is defined by Theophrastus as "that which exceeds its appropriate form of expression," for example "an unbased cup is not tabled," instead of "a cup without a base is not put on the table" . . . The trivial subject does not allow such magniloquence.'[9] There are two key phrases in this analysis that deserve further consideration. Demetrius's account pivots on the word 'exceeds' (*hyperballon* in Demetrius's Greek), establishing a clear etymological connection between frigidity and hyperbolic rhetoric. In both cases the orator, by employing excessive artifice, overshoots the mark and ends up alienating his audience; rather than moving them, he merely alerts his listeners to the fact that he is trying too hard. While elevated language lifts our spirit and carries us wherever the orator wants us to go, the frigid style – like frost – falls flat, and ruins all pretensions to grandeur.

But it is the other main criterion discussed in his exposition, 'the appropriate form of expression', which helps us to see why so many theorists struggle to integrate hyperbole into their rhetorical systems. What Demetrius refers to here is one of the foundational principles of the art of rhetoric: the idea of decorum, commonly defined as the fitting conjunction of style and subject matter. In order to be persuaded by a rhetorical performance, the audience must be able to establish a plausible link between content and form, between what is being said and the linguistic means used to express it. According to Demetrius, hyperbole deals in the 'impossible' and the 'extravagant'; it pushes rhetorical artifice to the limits of credibility and thus represents a fundamental infringement of the rules of decorous, plausible speech. Hyperbole breaks the boundaries of good style. This argument has its weaknesses. Demetrius is particularly eccentric in smoothing over the difference between technical prescription and personal preference; it often seems as though he is opposed to all forms of linguistic extravagance, regardless of their context. Nevertheless, hyperbole would have a hard time recovering from this verdict.[10]

Rhetorical and poetic styles do not exist in a cultural vacuum. This is a commonplace of literary theory: as Seneca reminds his correspondent Lucilius in the *Epistulae Morales* – a text that makes frequent allusions to the interdependence of good speaking and good living – 'style has no fixed laws; it is changed by the usage of the people, never the same for any length of time'.[11] The same is true of the figures which, as Demetrius has shown us, form an integral part of stylistic patterns, movements, and modes.[12] The applications and functions of any given rhetorical device are thus, to a considerable degree, contingent on the larger aesthetic and cultural templates of their historical moment. It is important to remember this when we move on to considering one of the most influential early-modern critiques of hyperbole, in George Puttenham's *Arte of English Poesie* (1589). Puttenham's account builds on some of the familiar categories of the classical rhetorical tradition – the terms of decorum, the distrust of linguistic excess – but also subtly recalibrates them so that they can be made suitable for his own purposes:

> I for his immoderate excesse cal him the over reacher right with his originall or [*lowd lyar*] and me thinks not amisse: . . . this maner of speach is used, when either we would greatly advaunce or greatly abase the reputation of any thing or person, and must be used very discreetly, or els it will seeme odious, for although a prayse or other report may be allowed beyond credit, it may not be beyond all measure.[13]

In Puttenham's analysis, moderation and discretion still figure prominently as the benchmarks against which the successes and failures of hyperbole can be measured. At the same time, however, the place and objectives of hyperbolic rhetoric are subjected to a thorough, and very specific, process of reinterpretation. Puttenham's account of hyperbole is genre-specific: the main province of hyperbole is now epideictic, the rhetorical form in which reputations can be made or destroyed ('when we would greatly advaunce or greatly abase the reputation of any thing or person').[14] The connection between hyperbole and epideictic was frequently observed in classical manuals of rhetoric, but when we view it against the background of Puttenham's contemporary models – such as Castiglione's *The Courtier* – it acquires special significance.[15]

Unlike many classical accounts of rhetoric, which have their roots in the forensic debates of the law courts, Castiglione's treatise focuses on a different kind of court culture: his aim is to teach the Renaissance courtier how to make friends and influence people. Gaining expertise in how to 'advaunce or . . . abase the reputation of any . . . person' is a crucial aspect of this endeavour. Castiglione's courtier spends a great deal of time repositioning himself in the shifting and fluid networks of power; one of his key skills is to portray friends and enemies in the most strategic light. In Puttenham's version of this rhetorical philosophy, hyperbole represents a severe liability. Extravagant praise, the *Arte* suggests, is incompatible with prudence and discretion and thus often sabotages our aspirations to power and influence; unless it is used with extreme caution, it can make the speaker look like 'a grosse flattering foole'.[16] Once again, the notion of boundary-breaking looms large, as hyperbole soars beyond the limits of political decorum.

Puttenham's description presents hyperbole as the most uncourtly and politically inept of all the devices: it is loud, clumsy, and heavy-handed, and possesses none of the qualities of elegance, sophistication and intellectual sharpness that Puttenham values so much in his Italian model. The examples given in the treatise make it abundantly clear that his concerns about hyperbole's inefficiency have nothing to do with the potential moral complexities of excessive praise. Puttenham is more than happy to work with figures that lie, and speaks admiringly of allegory, or, as he terms it, the *false semblant*. His problem with hyperbole is that it is a '*lowd lyar*', and a loud liar will never be able to counsel and persuade a king. As the drama of political intrigue unfolds around Puttenham's courtly figures, hyperbole is banished to the sidelines as an oafish, bumbling fool.

When literary writers take on these issues in rhetorical theory, they rarely follow the handbooks to the letter. As each of the three literary case studies in this chapter shows, the story of hyperbole in the dramatic, poetic, and prose works of the period was determined by a process of creative – and often highly selective – transformation and adaptation. One of the main aims of this chapter is to shed some light on this process. Throughout the discussion, therefore, I will not only attend to the local rhetorical purposes of hyperbolic language, but will try to say something about *how* a given writer puts the figure through its paces.

I want to start by following Puttenham's trail to one of the textbook cases of hyperbole in early-modern dramatic writing: Shakespeare's Hotspur. The opening scenes of *Henry IV, Part 1* – a play which saw its first performance seven years after Puttenham's treatise was published – use hyperbole as an important means of characterisation, drawing on many of the aesthetic and social connotations it had accumulated in its theoretical treatments.[17] Hotspur's language exceeds the bounds of decorum, and demonstrates a conspicuous absence of strategic intelligence and Machiavellian flair. But despite these similarities, Shakespeare's reading of hyperbole is more complicated than Puttenham's. As rhetorical choices come to be associated with some of the play's decisive moral and political dilemmas, hyperbole takes on a set of broader philosophical and structural functions.

In Act I, Scene 3, Worcester outlines his plan to incite the Scots, the Welsh, and the Archbishop of York to rebellion against the King. This is eagerly endorsed by his co-conspirators and kinsmen, Northumberland and Hotspur. However, whilst Northumberland agrees that the best path towards success lies in stealth, cunning, and intrigue – in what is 'ruminated, plotted, and set down' – Hotspur is confident of his ability to triumph in a direct confrontation with the royal forces:[18]

HOTSPUR By heaven, methinks it were an easy leap,
    To pluck bright honor from the pale-fac'd moon,
    Or dive into the bottom of the deep,
    Where fadom-line could never touch the ground,
    And pluck up drowned honor by the locks,
    So he that doth redeem her thence might wear
    Without corrival all her dignities;
    But out upon this half-fac'd fellowship.
                                    (1.3.201–8)

Hotspur's schemes for pursuing honour and glory alternate between grasp-
ing for the moon and diving to the bottom of the ocean; his speech, in
fact, presents precisely the kind of 'extravagant and impossible conceits'
that Demetrius had identified in the worst types of hyperbolical excess.
Even more significant than this, however, are the comments that Hotspur's language elicits from his partners in crime. His father, Northumber-
land, remarks that 'Imagination of some great exploit | Drives him beyond
the bounds of patience' (199–200) and goes on to call Hotspur a 'wasp-
stung and impatient fool' (236), while Worcester disapproves of his 'quick-
conceiving discontents' (189). In a rhetorical manoeuvre that resonates
richly with Puttenham's account of hyperbole, Hotspur's co-conspirators
forge a close link between linguistic and political indecorousness. The key
phrase 'beyond the bounds' brings together a host of assumptions designed
to discredit Hotspur's character: he is too 'quick' in 'conceiving' visions of
poetic and military prowess, and impassioned to the point of delusion –
he rushes in where more experienced plotters fear to tread. Hotspur's incom-
petence, in short, emerges from his refusal to respect the limits of rhetorical
prudence and emotional restraint.

    One purpose of this profile is to confine Hotspur to the role of junior
partner: he may be a useful prospect, but his energies need to be channelled
and contained if they are to be made useful for the present task. In this
respect, too, Hotspur's rhetoric plays into the more senior pair's hands. In
the *Rhetoric*, Aristotle had noted that 'there is something youthful about
hyperboles; for they show vehemence. Wherefore those who are in a passion most frequently make use of them.'[19] At one level, then, hyperbole is
the defining feature of the juvenile hothead. In the context of Northumberland's and Worcester's larger strategic plan, however, it also encapsulates
a very different mindset. Although he is tender in years, in the minds of
his partners Hotspur has already grown into a full-blown political anachro-
nism, a dinosaur, a thing of the past. Where Worcester and Northumberland emphasise the need for cunning and flexibility, a rhetorical and moral

realpolitik that can adapt itself to changing circumstances and demands, Hotspur adheres to a single set of values and commands only one rhetorical register: war is the appropriate response to a political crisis; soldiers adhere to a code of honour and aspire to epic heroism – in language as well as in action.

Hotspur's co-conspirators are keen to denigrate this vision of politics, and, once again, the rhetoric handbooks give them all the weapons they need. The soaring hyperbolic imagery of Hotspur's speech, Northumberland argues, belongs to the realm of 'Imagination', and Worcester clinches this reading: 'He apprehends a world of figures here', he says of his nephew, 'But not the form of what he should attend' (1.3.209–10). Hotspur's hyperboles are a symptom of his inability to live in the real world, where people 'attend' to pragmatic political business in ways that are simultaneously less ostentatious and more effective. His partners are concerned that by soaring too high he will bring the whole scheme crashing down (a familiar anxiety from Demetrius's account of 'frigid' rhetoric); that is why they prefer to creep along stealthily. With every moment of overt rhetorical swagger, they become more firmly convinced of the value of covert operations.

It is important to remember the purpose that lies behind the exchanges depicted in this scene. If Hotspur falls victim to a courtly version of bullying here, this is because Northumberland and Worcester need to bring him around to their way of thinking; if their ambitions of rebellion are to be fulfilled, the group must adopt a coherent policy. But in the global context of the play and its sequel, their clash of rhetorical philosophies also serves to make a larger point. The devaluation of Hotspur's hyperbolic register coincides with an attack on his politics: Worcester and Northumberland seek to define the tone of the conspiracy in more ways than one. From this moment onwards, the strategic and linguistic proceedings are dominated by stealth, intrigue, and ruthless opportunism – qualities embodied not by Hotspur but by the leader-in-waiting, Prince Hal. But the demise of big words implies also the disappearance of big ideals – honour, glory, and valour – and this may be a loss to be deplored. At the end of Act I, having put an army of anti-hyperbolists at Northumberland's and Worcester's disposal, Shakespeare leaves us with a rather more ambivalent sense of the figure's implications. Hotspur's extravagant visions of heroism may not represent the most successful model of political engagement, but they imply an honesty of purpose that is missing from the rest of the play.[20]

Most of the texts I have looked at so far present hyperbole as a rhetorical device with a less than respectable pedigree. Among the many shortcomings listed by the theorists, its persistent disregard for the rules of decorum and the connected failure – through affectation or clumsiness – to move the audience, count most gravely in hyperbole's disfavour. Aristotle, Demetrius, Puttenham and Prideaux's 'Moderne Rhetoricians' mount powerful arguments against hyperbole but, like any good advocate, they only really shine when they get to plead their side of the case. In the next section, we encounter an alternative view of hyperbolic language: one that rethinks the cultural contexts and applications of rhetorical exaggeration and thereby ultimately redefines its place in the 'world of figures'.

VERSIONS OF THE SUBLIME

To understand how the next part of the story develops, we need to take a brief look at Quintilian's comments on hyperbole in the *Institutio oratoria*. Here, Quintilian offers a partial solution to one of the gravest objections raised in previous accounts of hyperbolic rhetoric: the charge that hyperbole 'suggests something impossible'.[21] This problem involves the subjects of rhetoric (although it also engages a number of other, more complicated issues in post-Aristotelian rhetorical theory) – a category, according to Quintilian, that merits rethinking from a hyperbolical perspective: 'Hyperbole . . . has positive value when the thing about which we have to speak transcends the ordinary limits of nature. We are then allowed to amplify, because the real size of the thing cannot be expressed, and it is better to go too far than not to go far enough.'[22] Quintilian argues that, at least where rhetorical *inventio* is concerned, the notion of what is 'possible' is of distinctly limited value. If eloquence is to capture the excessive, the extravagant, and the transcendent, he suggests, it should also be allowed to enlist the boundary-breakers among the figures of speech.[23]

Quintilian provides a tantalising glimpse of how hyperbole might be put to more positive and constructive uses, but it took a rather more radical rethinking of rhetorical principles to bring out the potential ramifications of his views. This is provided by the treatise *On the Sublime*, traditionally ascribed to Longinus. The main objective of this text is to delineate 'the [rhetorical] means by which we may be enabled to develop our natures to some degree of grandeur'; the orator's task is to take the audience beyond the limits of ordinary human experience.[24] As he redefines the broader purposes of rhetoric, Longinus also offers a thorough consideration of some of its key categories. Subject matter (or *inventio*) is one of these. Longinus is not concerned with mundane concepts such as 'wealth, position, reputation': these things merely possess an 'outward show of grandeur'.[25] The true sublime touches a part in us that is at once loftier and more profound: 'the whole universe is not enough to satisfy the speculative intelligence of human thought; our ideas often pass beyond the limits that confine us'.[26] This rhetorical philosophy also has a significant impact on the role of *dispositio*, or the arrangement of an argument: unlike many of his predecessors, Longinus does not aim to convince his audience through a plausible argument that builds on the gradual, cumulative marshalling of facts; his orator builds up to a sudden, 'well-timed flash of sublimity'.[27] And finally, Longinus eschews modes of persuasion that are based on *logos* (argument) and *ethos* (character), and instead appeals exclusively to the emotions of his audience:

> For the effect of genius is not to persuade the audience but rather to transport them out of themselves. Invariably what inspires wonder, with its power of amazing us, always prevails over what is merely convincing and pleasing. For our convictions are usually under our own control, while these things exercise an irresistible power and mastery, and get the better of every listener.[28]

All these changes have a direct bearing on the question of hyperbolic decorum. In Longinus's model, rational persuasion is replaced by ecstatic rapture. As the orator seeks to inspire, enthrall, and transport the audience into a world of sublimity, hyperbole receives a new lease of life. It is a serial breaker of boundaries, as countless theorists attest, and thus ideally suited to create the flashes of transcendental insight that take us 'beyond the limits that confine us'. Hyperbole can be a vehicle of sublime ecstatic experience precisely because it represents 'that which is thrown beyond' the frontiers of knowledge.

The influence of Longinus's treatise on the literary theory and practice of the early-modern period is a complex and fascinating issue. For the purposes of this discussion, I am going to focus on two very selective aspects of this reception history: first, I want to examine how Longinus's ideas can be used to illuminate a particular strand of Renaissance rhetorical thought by looking at a group of writers who assign hyperbole an important part in their theory of Christian eloquence. I will then discuss the implications of this revaluation for literary practice; my case study will be Richard Crashaw's elegy 'Upon Mr *Staninough's* Death'.[29]

John Prideaux's *Sacred Eloquence* (1659) appeared in print less than a decade after the first English translation of Longinus's treatise was published.[30] Prideaux's handbook is devoted entirely to Christian – and, more specifically, scriptural – rhetoric; its principal aims are homiletic and pedagogic: 'Sacred Eloquence . . . is to be used in Prayer, Preaching, or Conference; to the glory of God, and the convincing, instructing, and strengthning our brethren.'[31] 'Sublime Hyperboles' take pride of place in Prideaux's list of rhetorical figures. The term 'sublime' is a crucial help in understanding Prideaux's approach to rhetoric. Hyperbole matters because it enables us to make contact with God, and shows us a world in which the rules of human reason and communication are suspended. Once again, it goes beyond 'the limits that confine us'. Prideaux cites a passage from the Gospel of Matthew in illustration of this model: 'It is easier for a camel to go through the eye of a needle, than for a rich man to enter into the kingdom of God' (19:24).[32] If we follow Demetrius's view of rhetoric, this is simply an impossible conceit which would make an audience lose faith in the speaker. But for Christian theorists of eloquence, hyperbole shores up faith and points the way to God precisely because it defies the laws of probability: as it breaks through the limits of human cognition, it provides a brief glimpse into a world where a camel fitting through the eye of a needle is an entirely reasonable idea – the kingdom of God. The scriptural verse that follows Prideaux's example reminds us of this principle: 'Jesus said unto them [the Apostles] . . . with men this is impossible; but with God all things are possible' (19:25). Matthew's account turns the universe upside down. In the revised rhetorical system that accompanies this worldview, hyperbole can become a means of readjusting our spiritual perspective and an instrument of faith. It is part of a Christian grand style that brings 'into captivity every thought to the obedience of Christ'.[33]

By reconstructing this mindset, we can also identify one of the salient differences between secular and religious versions of the sublime. While for Longinus the rhetoric of transcendental ecstasy is proof of the orator's power and 'genius', the Christian orator reserves such reverence for the subject of his hyperbolic praise – God. The desire to glorify God, in other words, always already entails the diminution and abjection of the human artist and his strategies of figuration: this is why Thomas Traherne – another Christian hyperbolist – is adamant that 'All Hyperbolies are but little Pigmies, and Diminutiv Expressions, in Comparison of the Truth.'[34] Hyperbole can put us in touch with the highest things, but in order to do this it must first acknowledge its own insignificance. Unlike Demetrius's frosty figures, therefore, the Christian version of hyperbole rarely becomes a victim of its own hubris: an orator who puts himself at the service of the almighty, as Traherne insists, 'can never Exceed, nor be too high' – and this in turn means that his rhetoric is far less likely to fall flat.

The Christian rhetorical tradition gives hyperbole a chance to redeem itself. Where Demetrius's account of stylistic frigidity constructs a narrative of vaunting ambition and inevitable failure, Prideaux and Traherne offer a more optimistic outlook. Extravagant praise of God, these theorists suggest, can be a vital means of spiritual reorientation: by giving us an intimation of God's unlimited power, hyperbole helps to instil humility and faith. In Crashaw's elegy 'Upon Mr *Staninough's* Death', we encounter both of these versions of hyperbole. We are also confronted with a familiar set of issues: the poem's speaker reflects on the spiritual implications of death to reassess man's place in the world. As the text develops its central conceit, the verdict initially looks far from encouraging:

> Come then, youth, Beauty, and Blood, all ye soft powers,
> Whose silken flatteryes swell a few fond houres
> Into a false Eternity, come man,
> (Hyperbolized nothing!) know thy span.
> Take thine own measure here, downe, downe, and bow
> Before thy selfe in thy Idæa, thou
> Huge emptinesse contract thy bulke, and shrinke
> All thy wild Circle to a point! ô sinke
> Lower, and lower yet; till thy small size,
> Call Heaven to looke on thee with narrow eyes . . .[35]

The speaker's diagnosis focuses on the phrase 'hyperbolized nothing' – a complicated conceit at the centre of an involved and difficult set of couplets. One of the first things to note about Crashaw's metaphor is that it faces in two directions simultaneously. On the one hand, 'hyperbolized nothing' provides a summary evaluation of the preceding lines. 'Man' has constructed a misguided image of his own importance; although the transitory attractions of life ('youth, Beauty') may provide illusions of status and grandeur ('a false Eternity'), they are ultimately self-destructive. The text articulates the dangers of vanity through an image of tumescence: Crashaw's vision of human life sees us 'swell' with pride before we fall. Hyperbole – with its connotations of extravagant over-inflation – becomes a symbolic shorthand for this whole nexus of concerns. One might say that in the elegy 'Upon Mr *Staninough's* Death', mankind's career proceeds along the trajectory of Demetrius's unreconstructed hyperboles: we are puffed up with ambition and end up terminally deflated.

But whilst it sums up this bleak picture of the human condition, the phrase 'hyperbolized nothing' also looks forward to the next stage of the poem's argument, which proceeds to take man's true 'measure'. In classical accounts of the figure, hyperbole was frequently associated with the grammatical superlative, and it is this connection between rhetoric and grammar that Crashaw exploits here.[36] Once we abandon the self-centred perspective mapped out in the previous lines and consider our place in the universal context of God's creation, the poem argues, there is only one conclusion: that 'man' is the nothingest form of nothing.[37] This superlative or – to shift disciplines – exponential sense of our insignificance is at once awe-inspiring and patently absurd: 'nothing' multiplied by itself a million times still yields nothing. The effect of this image is to direct us, in typically hyperbolic fashion, to the limits of what we can conceive, and that is its point: 'man's' irrelevance emerges most clearly in his failure to comprehend his own ignorance. The following six lines pursue this conceit through a series of perspectival modulations until they finally arrive at a familiar thought. At the end of this section, Crashaw presents an almost disconcertingly literal take on Traherne's idea that rhetorical exaggeration implies a process of diminution: his hyperbole reduces men to 'pigmies' by shrinking them almost to the point of invisibility – God himself is forced to squint, and looks upon them 'with narrow eyes'.

Yet this, the lowest possible point, is exactly where the text wants us to be. The best way of looking at the world is (metaphorically, for the time being) from the grave: 'This posture is the brave one: this that lyes | Thus low stands up (me thinkes) thus, and defyes | The world' (27–29). Unless we crouch down low, we will miss the things that really matter. It is no accident, then, that in advocating this philosophy of steadfast humility, Crashaw's poem finds rich resonances in the resurrection myth. Christ's voluntary self-abasement is consummated only in death, but this decision to lie low contains its own reward: at the moment of triumph, he 'stands up . . . and defyes the world'. If we become dead to the distractions of human existence and acknowledge our own 'nothingness', the text suggests, we too may be raised into a better world.

In the elegy 'Upon Mr *Staninough's* Death', hyperbole becomes the symbol of this ascetic stance. Having begun life as an expression of man's overweening ambition, the figure subsequently develops into an agent of mortification that brings our 'nothingness' into the sharpest possible focus. In Crashaw's text, hyperbole no longer carries associations of sinful overreaching: the language of exaggeration has been translated into a means of achieving humility and put into the service of Christ. From its new-found position of rhetorical merit, hyperbole can hold out legitimate hopes of salvation.

Crashaw's hyperbole thus offers a microcosmic version of the poem's central narrative. As a doubly oriented conceit, it rehearses the process of spiritual reorientation the text demands from its audience. The 'hyperbolised nothing' of Crashaw's elegy, in other words, is not a simple rhetorical set piece, a moment of high figurative intensity that illuminates one particular corner of the text. It structures the poem's argument, shapes its thought patterns at every turn, and thus becomes a valuable tool of philosophical and religious inquiry. Hyperbole also holds together two potentially divergent movements: the sequential articulation of ideas on the one hand, and the vertical dynamic of devotional reform on the other. It is nothing less than the instrument that enables Crashaw to put humanity in perspective.

POETIC LIARS AND VIRTUOUS TRUTHS

Longinus, Traherne and Prideaux have offered us some versions of the sublime; there are significant differences between these narratives, but they concur in their overall evaluation of hyperbole's merits and uses. Extravagant conceits can challenge the boundaries of language and give us a glimpse of the truths that lie beyond the frontiers of human knowledge. Theorists of the Christian sublime also particularly reflect on the orator's role in this process: without a good dose of humility and self-abnegation, Traherne insists, no rhetorician can find the 'true way' towards God. Yet for all their instructive value, these accounts remain somewhat incomplete. Rhetorical transactions always involve an audience – spectators, listeners, or readers that interact with the material presented to them. And hyperbole, as the author of the *Rhetorica ad Herennium* recognized, is a figure that – more than others – depends on the audience's response: it leaves, he suggests, 'more to be suspected than has been actually asserted'.[38] I want to spend the remainder of this chapter trying to unpack this somewhat cryptic assertion, thereby supplying some of the missing links in hyperbole's story thus far. This will take us back to the secular incarnations of early-modern rhetorical thought.

Thomas Wilson, the most Ciceronian of the Renaissance theorists, offers two definitions of hyperbole. The first of these, in the 1553 *Arte of Rhetorique*, sounds familiar enough, not least in its focus on the orator's point of view. Here, the figure is described as a 'Mountyng above the truthe', 'when we set furthe thynges excedyngly and above all mennes expectacion'.[39] Wilson's second account of hyperbole can be found in a slightly more unusual place: his logic manual *The Rule of Reason*, printed two years earlier. In this work, by contrast, the main emphasis lies on the audience's response: 'we must diligently take hede, when such [i.e. hyperbolical] speches are used', Wilson advises, 'that we take not them as they be spoken, but as they are ment'.[40] Wilson's analysis distinguishes between two different levels of interpretation: (1) the surface layer (what is 'spoken') – this corresponds to the literal meaning, and encompasses the obvious, the common sense, the

factual or the experiential (or, in modern linguistic terminology, the deno-
tative sense); and (2) the Layer beneath (what is 'ment') – this corresponds
to the figurative (or connotative) meaning, and refers to the emotional or
ideological associations a statement is designed to evoke. To comprehend
the full import of a hyperbolic expression, the audience must learn to nego-
tiate these semantic distinctions. If the reader remains at the literal level, as
we will see, hyperbolic statements often yield nonsensical results. But how
do we get at the figurative meaning?

Peacham's discussion in the second edition of *The Garden of Eloquence*
(1593) suggests that the problem might be overcome through an act of
imaginative self-extension. The most extreme forms of hyperbole break the
rules of literal truth to advance insights of a higher order; hyperbole deploys
'large speech' to convey ideas and emotions that everyday experience cannot
comprehend. In Peacham's most instructive example – the tale of a woman
whose grief was so profound that 'it rent her heart in sunder' – the absurdity
of the statement is intended to function as a trigger: by entertaining notions
that were previously inconceivable, we can translate figurative language into
emotional meaning, and bridge the gap between 'what is spoken' and 'what
is ment'.

Peacham's account of hyperbole's operations is patterned on one of its
most familiar metaphors. By asserting that hyperbole can convey larger
truths, he invites the reader to reach out towards a world that lies beyond
the boundaries of fact, a place where moral and emotional perceptions are
purified and intensified. In the case of the grieving woman, this implies a
projection of empathy that, by definition, never quite manages to catch up
with the feeling it pursues. Having literalised the emotion of grief to the
point of absurdity, hyperbole (once again) takes us back to the abstract, the
intangible, and the elusive. In Peacham's example, retaining this residue of
the unimaginable is particularly important, since the act of expressing pain
also implies the risk of trivialising it (as might be the case when a hyperbole
becomes a cliché). In this sense, hyperbole asserts the importance of partial
blindness and functional ignorance; the notion of complete comprehension
devalues the thought or feeling that hyperbole evokes. At the same time,
however, Peacham foregrounds hyperbole's ability to draw attention to
the complexities of rhetorical representation. By highlighting the limits
of figuration and productively destabilising the reader's views of linguistic
norms and conventions, it encourages active reflection on the different
ways in which meaning is constructed and communicated. This is, perhaps,
the most complete rebuttal of the notion that hyperbole fails by drawing
attention to itself.

How, then, can the idea of active readerly engagement be used to bring out the virtues of hyperbole in literary practice? Sidney's *Defence of Poesy* provides one particularly interesting response to this question. If Peacham shows us that hyperbole can further our understanding of the unimaginable by presenting it in incomprehensible form, Philip Sidney makes the daring case that hyperbole can in fact transform its audience. From the beginning of the treatise, Sidney's portrait of the poet, and of the ideal literary worlds he creates, resonates with the now-familiar rhetoric of hyperbolic sublimity:

the heavenly Maker of that maker [the poet] . . . set him beyond and over all the works of that second nature; which in nothing he showeth so much as in poetry, when, with the force of a divine breath, he [the poet] bringeth things forth surpassing her doings . . .

Nature never set forth the earth in so rich a tapestry as divers poets have done, neither with so pleasant rivers, fruitful trees, sweet-smelling flowers, nor whatsoever else may make the too-much-loved earth more lovely: her world is brazen, the poets only deliver a golden.[41]

Sidney's *Defence* offers many examples of extravagant language, but this passage puts the idea of hyperbolic rhetoric on a much grander scale. It uses hyperbole as a figure of thought in the broadest possible sense, as a conceptual tool that helps to construct the basic outlines of the argument. Sidney's poet occupies a realm 'beyond and over' the limits that restrict lesser writers; his works, likewise, far surpass the boundaries of the 'natural', plausible, and experiential, evoking a high-resolution, glossy, artificially enhanced version of reality.

The *Defence* also addresses a problem that would have been familiar to many theorists of hyperbole: the accusation that 'they [the poets] should be the principal liars'.[42] (Peacham and Puttenham deal with this problem, as does their model, Quintilian.) Sidney's answer to this charge initially looks conventional enough: he begins by disclaiming all interest in the factual or literal dimensions of writing. But he then proceeds to introduce a new idea which substantially modifies the interpretive grid set out by Wilson and Peacham. Sidney still operates with the concepts of the literal and the figurative sense (or denotation and connotation), but in the *Defence*, the relationship between these terms is not merely semantic but also ethical and performative. To put the issue more simply, it is not just a question of what a hyperbolic conceit means, but of what it can do: since 'the poet . . . never affirmeth . . ., not labouring to tell you what is or is not, but what should or should not be. . . . so in poesy, looking but for fiction, they [the audience] shall use the narration but as an imaginative ground-plot of a profitable invention.'[43] Sidney's poetry shows us what 'should . . . be', but it aspires to being more than just 'fiction'. Its idealised worlds have specific practical designs on the audience: they want to fire the moral imagination and encourage us to reinvent ourselves in their image. This is the 'profitable' lesson at the heart of Sidney's argument: 'not only to make a Cyrus, which had been but a particular excellency as nature might have done, but to bestow a Cyrus upon the world to make many Cyruses, if they [the readers] will learn aright why and how that maker made him'.[44] Cyrus represents the embodied form of a golden universe that operates according to the patterns of hyperbolic rhetoric: it presents us with exaggerated, extreme versions of characters and events that break the boundaries of the plausible, thereby encouraging us to transcend our own limitations. Hyperbole, then, drives the process of poetic idealisation, but it also provides the dynamic moral principle – the process of *moving beyond* the boundaries of our own old moral self – that forms the foundation of Sidney's defence. The idea of an active reader, who is capable of seeing beyond the literal and willing to till the ground-plot of virtuous self-improvement, forms a crucial part of this endeavour. Once again it is important to realise that the gap between the real and the ideal cannot be closed entirely – nor should it be. We cannot cross the boundary into Sidney's golden world and be transformed into a blueprint of rectitude (it has often been noted that in Sidney's own poetic works, Cyruses are in rather short supply), but we can aspire to become a better version of who we are.

CONCLUSION

Hyperbole tests boundaries: in rhetorical thought, in literary practice, and in the cultural and philosophical discourses associated with figurative language. This boundary-testing takes a variety of forms, all of them contingent on forces that lie outside the remit of theory, and all of them engaging the reader's ethical and intellectual sensibilities. Demetrius protects the boundaries of good style by invoking the broader aesthetic categories of aptness and propriety. Shakespeare's *1 Henry IV* transposes these concerns into a political register to contain Hotspur's heroic momentum. In Sidney, by contrast, hyperbole is used to stretch the limitations of the moral self. Peacham aims at nothing less than expanding the boundaries of comprehension.[45]

Hyperbole also fosters a sense of perspectival mobility, and an enhanced awareness of the ways in which boundaries, norms, and conventions are constructed. In Crashaw's elegy, for instance, salvation itself is made dependent on our ability to see things from a different point of view and to acknowledge the limits of human perception. As it shrinks and magnifies, elevates and depresses, inflates and deflates, the rhetoric of exaggeration can correct or destabilize our perspective on the world of figures, and on what lies beyond.

CHAPTER 12

Metalepsis, when we goe by degrees to that which is shewed, a fygure sildom used of Oratours, and not ofte of Poets, as to saye, he lyeth in a darcke Dungeon. Now in speaking of darcknesse, we understand closeness, by closeness, blacknesse, by blacknesse deepenesse. *Virgil* by eares of Corn, he signifyeth harvestes, by harvestes, sommers, and by sommers, yeares.

Henry Peacham, The Garden of Eloquence (1577)

Metalepsis: the boundaries of metaphor

BRIAN CUMMINGS

> To morrow, and to morrow, and to morrow,
> Creepes in this petty pace from day to day,
> To the last Syllable of Recorded time:
> And all our yesterdayes, have lighted Fooles
> The way to dusty death.[1]

Macbeth's reaction to his wife's death and his meditation on time and mortality are characteristic of later Shakespeare in combining epigrammatic grandeur with extreme figurative complexity. The verse is readily remembered but not easy to explain. This sense of linguistic difficulty is not counterproductive, however; one of the features that makes these lines memorable is that it is not possible to catch the sense straightaway, so that it remains mysterious and complex in the same way that the idea Macbeth is expressing is mysterious and complex. His mind is caught at the moment of the most intense effort to explain and understand what his life has been like and how it is going to end, yet it cannot complete its thought or comprehend its own sense. His meaning, like his premonition of death, is haunted by an apprehension of incompleteness.

A quick reflection on the make-up of the sentence shows that it is the figurative sequence, rather than the syntax or diction, that creates a sense of complexity. None of the words individually is difficult or philosophical. Macbeth's sentence presents instead a concatenation of figures which pile quickly on top of each other. His speech refers overtly to the mathematical reckoning of time, measured in terms of speed ('this petty pace'). Time passes by inexorably, indifferent to the course of a single life. Macbeth longs for the space to mourn his wife but time will not let him. This figure is conflated with a figure of an individual lifetime made up like a book with 'syllables', in particular the book of record which the angel keeps at the last judgement. Time itself seems infinite but each life within it is limited, like a sentence that must end in its own period. These are perhaps the primary figures we have to keep in mind. Yet we also note that there is

217

no explicit connection made between them. The figure transfers itself from one referent to the other without elucidation. Time measured in relation to speed and time imagined as a book of words are conflated together, but the link between them is left to the auditor to make out. To cloud the picture further, there are other figurative undercurrents. The phrase 'creepes in' can be interpreted in two different ways, one in terms of slow progress and the other in terms of a narrow space.[2] This suggests a new connection with a third figure of a passageway, a sense supported by the Elizabethan meaning of 'pace' as a narrow road, passage or strait.[3] Although submerged as a meaning the connection is natural in that it associates the finitude of time with burial, perhaps in a catacomb beneath the ground. In turn, this creates a link with a fourth, final figure that emerges at the end of the sentence, where a person's past is represented as a funeral procession ('The way to dusty death'), lit by torches held by fools.

It may be objected that such an analysis complicates what is in theatrical terms a sudden apprehension of meaning or even a mere intuition. Nicholas Brooke's editorial despair seems just in the circumstances: 'a line too complex in its resonances for commentary to be anything but reductive'.[4] Yet at some level every hearer picks up four associated thoughts: the passage of time, the rites of mourning, interment in the earth, and the last judgement. Why is it, then, that we feel that rhetorical analysis can take us only so far here? Partly, it is because figures of speech have traditionally been studied in isolation, one figure or example at a time. No single act of interpretative equivalence can explain what is going on in Macbeth's sentence. Nor, perhaps, will an explanation in terms of metaphor as substitution of one meaning for another. Macbeth's line holds its fascination because it sets up metaphors in chain with one another, and allows the hearer to 'see' more than one figure at a time. Shakespeare multiplies metaphors out of each other, duplicates and reduplicates a figure in different guises. He lets one figure stand out, then shifts into another, then continues where he left off from before, then (without showing us what he is doing) in the same sentence substitutes another figure yet behaves as if he is still referring to the same one all along. In this process, a theory of semantic equivalence fails to register the way that this sentence takes risks with its own meaning, risks indeed that it will emerge as meaningless. The speaker shares with us a powerful sense of living on the edge, of life and reason under threat of collapse.

Renaissance rhetoricians have no figure in their catalogues that fully accounts for the linguistic form of this passage, which exemplifies what Alastair Fowler has called 'the Shakespearean conceit'.[5] But they had a term, which they borrowed from their classical masters, that seems to capture the process of figuration I have described: metalepsis (also known in English as 'transumption'). Though variously defined and applied, metalepsis was a term that was used to describe a process of transition, doubling, or ellipsis in figuration, of replacing a figure with another figure, and of missing out the figure in between in order to create a figure that stretches the sense or which fetches things from far off. Yet like the thing it was trying to describe, it was not an easy figure to explain. This is George Puttenham's definition: 'But the sence is much altered and the hearers conceit strangly entangled by the figure *Metalepsis*, which I call the farfet, as when we had rather fetch a word a great way off then to use one nerer to expresse the matter aswel and plainer.'[6] Puttenham catches the way that Shakespeare's line travels great distances and merges ideas together. He also catches the way in which Shakespeare thereby appears to stretch the sense so far that we strain to reach it. The reasoning is far-fetched, and the hearer's understanding is 'entangled' or perhaps momentarily bewildered. Puttenham cannot quite make sense of the figure himself: he hesitates between according metalepsis an honourable place among the more complex elaborations of speech, or consigning it to the detritus of wasted words and failed figures. This essay, then, will consider a variety of questions: what metalepsis is, whether it explains what is going on in classical and Renaissance literary masterpieces, and how it helps us to understand the metaphoric process more widely.

Metalepsis can hardly be counted amongst the most glamorous of the flowers of rhetoric. Indeed the redoubtable nineteenth-century German scholar Richard Volkmann called it a 'very obscure and difficult figure' which owes its origin to a simple error of interpretation of a line in Homer.[7] Despite these unprepossessing beginnings great claims have been made for it. Metalepsis was one of the key models cited in Paul de Man's theory of figuration as 'the element in language that allows for the reiteration of meaning by substitution'.[8] In 1975, at the height of the fashion for the Yale school of deconstruction, Harold Bloom called metalepsis 'the largest single factor in fostering a tone of conscious rhetoricity in Romantic and post-Romantic poetry'.[9] A few years later, John Hollander concluded his influential book *The Figure of Echo* with a chapter on metalepsis and provided a historical appendix to explain the term's meaning.[10] Most recently, Gérard Genette has developed his influential application of metalepsis to narratology in a full-length book, *Métalepse*.[11]

Somewhere between these poles of opinion, the rhetorical treatises of the humanists almost always found a place for metalepsis, although as often as not with some note of caution or distaste. In what follows it transpires that modern interest in metalepsis has been as it were a digression or transumption from its classical and Renaissance origins. Metalepsis in modern theory has become a figure of the figure, a figure of literary influence or legacy (in Bloom and Hollander) or of the presence of authorship in narrative (in Genette). Metalepsis in Renaissance theory, I suggest, is more precise than this and yet also more general. However mysterious its function or however cameo its appearance in theoretical treatises, it is a figure which takes us to the heart of the humanist concern with the nature of language.

For a definition, I turn, then, to Desiderius Erasmus. In the first book of *De duplici copia verborum ac rerum commentarii duo* ('Two books on the twofold copiousness of words and things'), first published in 1512, metalepsis is, Erasmus says, very close to catachresis (for which he prefers the Latin term, *abusio*).[12] In metalepsis 'we move by stages towards what we mean to say'.[13] In effect, some of the stages of meaning are left out. This is the example he gives from the *Aeneid*: 'sed pater omnipotens speluncis abdidit atris' ['the omnipotent father hid them in lustreless caves'].[14] By *ater* Erasmus says we understand 'blackness', hence 'obscurity', hence 'hidden depths'. We could call this a kind of metaphorical ellipsis, in which one or more middle terms are excluded. Perhaps not surprisingly, Erasmus considers such a figure more likely to be of use in poetry than in prose. Metalepsis functions as a kind of figurative compression, and by making the process of meaning more indirect, more compacted, and less definite, seems akin to those features of imaginative language which are indeed commonly called 'poetic'.

After considering the meanings of metalepsis, and its place in the history of rhetorical theory and of literary practice, I will return to Erasmus to formulate a more general account of its significance. This may help to explain why, although Erasmus was the founding father of Renaissance rhetoric, he also became in time its forgotten master. Already we can see something of the obscure fascination that metalepsis can excite. It is a figure associated with a deeply metaphoric process, the process by which one word or meaning can be substituted for another. It raises questions about how such transference can take place, and the conditions under which the transference can be held to be successful. Yet it is also associated with metaphoric failure, or with that most deadly of linguistic sins, the mixed metaphor. Its nearest kin is catachresis, the improper use of words. Failure and success seem to be very close together here. The reason for this is that metalepsis deliberately leaves the process of transference implicit. Much of the interest in metalepsis lies indeed in what it leaves out. Therefore, if the reader or listener fails or refuses to take the connection, we are left with an uncomfortable or even embarrassing sense of a breakdown of communication. Either the original speaker is too clever for her own good or more stupid than he thinks. Yet if a metalepsis comes off, part of the sheer thrill of success is precisely this sense of a sharing of something recondite or mysterious, the way language pulls things together which seem in principle to be far apart.

THE FIGURE IN THEORY

What is the origin of metalepsis? There is no mention of the figure in the *Rhetorica ad Herennium*. Although the word is older, the earliest trace I have found of it in a taxonomy of rhetorical terms is among the Greek treatises on tropes in the first century BC, most conspicuously in the work attributed to the Alexandrian grammarian Tryphon.[15] From there it found its way into Quintilian's *Institutio oratoria* around 95 AD where it comes seventh in order among the tropes in Book VIII, following metaphor, synecdoche, metonymy, antonomasia, onomatopoeia, and catachresis. Quintilian defined metalepsis as *transumptio*, the last and perhaps least of the figures that involve a change of meaning. He gives as the simplest example in common Latin usage *cano* ('I sing') used in place of *dico* ('I say').[16] A missing term, *canto* (which can carry either meaning), is understood to lie between them. In this way Quintilian seems to confirm the suggestion in Tryphon that metalepsis involves turning a synonym into a homonym.[17] Indeed its effect is similar to what in English is called a pun.[18] In everyday language-use, the closest analogy may be in rhyming slang, where *have a butcher's* (from *have a butcher's hook*) means 'have a look'.

Metalepsis, then, appears to be a highly specialised type of rhetorical figure, and this is how it is described when it is adopted from Quintilian into Renaissance theory, as indeed also in many modern handbooks of rhetorical terms.[19] Erasmus in *De copia* imitates closely the description found in *Institutio oratoria*. Philipp Melanchthon also followed Quintilian in placing metalepsis among the tropes but in the most developed form of his theory in *Elementa rhetorices* (first published in 1531), gave it greater prominence by placing it second after metaphor.[20] From these sources, metalepsis found its way, often word for word, into most of the rhetorical texts of the sixteenth-century humanists, such as Johannes Susenbrotus and

Cyprianus Soarez, and in England into the handbooks of Richard Sherry, Thomas Wilson (who used Quintilian's Latinate term 'transumption'), Henry Peacham, and George Puttenham.

Susenbrotus's enormously influential treatise, *Epitome troporum ac schematum et Grammaticorum et Rhetorum arte rhetorica libri tres* (Zurich, [1540?]), restored the categorical order found in Quintilian, and defined metalepsis in terms almost exactly copied from Quintilian and Erasmus. To illustrate the figure the rhetoricians used a similarly narrow corpus of literary examples from classical literature. Quintilian followed Tryphon in using a single line from Homer's *Odyssey*; Erasmus borrowed the line from the *Aeneid* from late classical grammarians; Susenbrotus added a line from Virgil's *Eclogues* which was then also adopted by Soarez and Peacham.[21] Susenbrotus develops the view that metalepsis is distinguished by its involving a step-by-step process of similitude, that it signifies a transition, in which a medial step is inferred.[22] Susenbrotus also adds, striking out a little perhaps from Quintilian, that this transition takes the figure 'further away from its proper signification'. Melanchthon observes something similar: metalepsis is a trope of likeness, but the likeness is less in degree than with metaphor proper. This is why he places metalepsis immediately after metaphor, as if thereby to make an important distinction about the process of similitude. Clearly there is a paradox here, to which I will return. The whole linguistic purpose of a trope, according to Quintilian, is 'a shift of a word or a phrase from its proper meaning to another'.[23] Tropes involve treating the unlike as alike. Yet different tropes involve a different degree of unlikeness. Metaphor, Melanchthon says, transfers a name to something unlike but not so unlike itself, something still similar to the original.[24] Metalepsis stretches the analogy further, finding likeness in something rather more different, perhaps even something utterly unlike.[25]

The implication is that metalepsis stretches metaphor a little further than we want to go, perhaps even to breaking point. Yet the handbooks are divided about this. Sometimes metalepsis is seen as a doubling of metaphor, a metaphor within a metaphor. Sometimes, as in Melanchthon and (in English) in Sherry, Puttenham, and the 1593 edition of Peacham, it is defined rather differently, as the substitution of a cause for an effect (or vice versa), effectively a species of metonymy. Heinrich Lausberg deduces from this that there are two distinct types of metalepsis.[26] Perhaps, rather, metalepsis raises questions about the relationship between metaphor and metonymy, and also about what we think the processes of substitution or reduplication in language are. Metalepsis is a miniature language game: with a little patience the figure can be worked through, perhaps even with some pleasure in the ingenuity of the effort. But at other times metalepsis seems to question the possibility of ever figuring it out. Metalepsis is a borderline figure, one that sometimes goes beyond the bounds, or strains the understanding and the patience of the reader or auditor. As we shall see, it therefore provokes questions about the boundaries of metaphor itself.

METALEPSIS AND FAILURE

Perhaps it is not surprising, then, that metalepsis has often been considered as a type of failed figure. Its closest relative is catachresis which, as we have seen, Erasmus calls abusio. Catalogues of rhetorical tropes hesitate between calling catachresis a figure or else an attempt at a figure which has gone wrong. The word in Greek means literally 'misuse, misapplication', and Erasmus defines catachresis as where 'we resort to misapplication where a proper word does not exist'.[27] He seems to be hedging his bets, undecided between, shall we say, Hamlet's calculatedly clumsy barb, 'I will speak daggers to her', and Alexander Pope's open lampoons of exaggerated figures going wildly wrong in his mock-Ars poetica *Peri Bathous, or the Art of Sinking in Poetry* ('Shave the Grass', 'Nail my sleeve').[28] The same ambivalence appears to surround metalepsis. It is not altogether clear if metalepsis really belongs in the handbook, if it cuts the mustard. The Jesuit rhetorical master Soarez declared in *De arte rhetorica* (1562) that 'this trope is very unusual and out of place'.[29] There is something about the figure that jars the ear or catches the mind of the listener off balance as to whether something very clever is being said or else something pretentious and naff. Later in the century Puttenham (cited above) remarked that metalepsis 'entangled' the sense, which is not entirely a compliment.[30] Metalepsis is a form of extravagance; it draws attention to itself rather than makes art by showing it less. Quintilian argued that it was easier to pull off in Greek than in Latin and recommended that it should not be used often and perhaps only for comic effect.[31] In the less winning grace of Puttenham's English it is said, like all things exotic and dearly bought, to be one for the ladies.

To consider the difference between catachresis and metalepsis let us take another example from *Macbeth* (1.7.35–6). As the married couple begin to devise their plan for Duncan's murder, Lady Macbeth works to screw her husband's courage to the sticking-place, because he keeps wavering. Macbeth vows 'to proceed no further in this business', arguing that it has taken him many years to acquire the good standing in which he now appears. His lady then asks: 'Was the hope drunk, | Wherein you dress'd yourself?'

Hope appears in two different guises, as a persona who has got drunk and is no longer in possession of sober reason, and as a piece of clothing which has been donned and now discarded. Editors have attempted to avoid the mixed metaphor by emending 'dress'd' either to an elided form of 'address'd' or to the altogether different 'bless'd'. But as Kenneth Muir shrewdly observed in his Arden edition, if this is an example of catachresis it is Shakespeare's and not the compositor's. Indeed, both drinking and clothing metaphors are endemic to the play. The idea of drunken clothes is part of a metaphoric reflex which overtakes the play from its beginning to its end. It seems better to take the line as a metalepsis, whereby Lady Macbeth presents her husband both as a fake and as one who is not in full control of his faculties. She wants him instead to be a proper man. By contrast, the editorial alterations are examples of thinking which is too literal-minded and clumsily straightforward for a drama which aims to stretch the boundaries of the figurative as far as possible.

Indeed it may be that it is in the risk of failure that we come to what is the most interesting feature of metalepsis and its place in rhetorical theory. For figurative failure raises also the issue of figurative success, and of what are understood to be the criteria of this success. Can any word be substituted for another? Consider here de Man's comment on Bloom's account of figuration that 'substitution is always, by necessity, a falsification'.[32] Yet the concept of catachresis implies that some modes of substitution are more false than others, or at least that sometimes we register when false coin has been given. De Man is too certain of his ground here, since 'falsification' implies in reverse that we know what it has been falsified from. Metalepsis exists in a metaphorical hinterland where we do not know in advance what has been substituted for what, or what is false and what is true.

To explain metalepsis at all we have to explain a larger theory of figuration that can accommodate it. In this essay I am interested in examining not the incidental features which make metalepsis stand out from other figures, its peculiar habitats and lifestyle, but its place within an overall Renaissance theory of the rhetorical figures. In what follows I will pay particular attention to such a theory in Erasmus: an idea which may itself elicit some surprise, since it is commonly understood that Erasmus is not interested in theory. I want to show something not just about how this figure works, but about how Erasmus understands the process of figuration to work, and thereby also perhaps in some way how Erasmus thinks about language more largely.

ERASMUS'S THEORY OF FIGURATION IN *DE COPIA*

It is in a theory of figures that Erasmus comes to important insights into how language is generated and at the same time how its usage comes to be regulated. *De copia* constitutes both a theory of how figures work and a case study of those figures in practice. Indeed, it makes itself a figure for the very thing it is claiming to describe – the richness of the language – while offering a commentary, not only on the process of figuration, but on its own implication in figurativeness. In this theory, metalepsis plays a significant part, although that part is embedded in a complex layering of arguments that is not completely articulated. We can tell something about the significance of metalepsis within Erasmus's scheme by noting the terms that surround it in Book I. It is preceded by accounts of various types of metaphor or metaphorical process: metaphor itself comes first, glossed by its Latin name *translatio*, 'so called because a word is transferred away from its real and proper signification to one that lies outside its proper sphere'.[33] This is followed by discussion of something Erasmus calls *metaphora reciproca*, in which he makes a fascinating series of remarks on how metaphors may be reversible in some cases but in others are not. Next come allegory (which he defines as metaphor extended beyond the boundary of single words), catachresis, and onomatopoeia (which he calls *fictio nominis* ['word-making']). Metalepsis, which comes next, is immediately followed by metonymy, synecdoche and (a term he leaves in Greek) *isodunamia*, which he glosses 'equivalence'. Metalepsis, then, is part of a sequence of terms that he uses to discriminate between what we might see as degrees of metaphoricity, and at the same time also different ways of constructing metaphoricity. Whether we are talking primarily about differences of scale or of type is indeed one of the things I am most interested in discovering.

Quintilian had already offered some account of the distinction between metalepsis and what we might call metaphor proper in the *Institutio*. Yet he has some trouble in making himself clear. *Translatio*, the Latin term for the Greek *metaphora*, is called by Quintilian 'by far the most beautiful of tropes'.[34] Quintilian's love of metaphor may seem odd to those who have been brought up in the post-Enlightenment tradition of disparaging figurative language, beginning with Locke's *An Essay Concerning Human Understanding*.[35] Whereas Locke regards metaphor as an accretion on and deviation from natural language, Quintilian calls it a 'gift from nature'. This reflects two different kinds of thinking about metaphor. According to one version, metaphor is a given within the language, like an *objet trouvé* which confers delight through discovery but which is not the achievement of the speaker himself. The illiterate have as much access to metaphor as the learned, Quintilian says, because the users of metaphor can readily be unconscious of its use. On the other hand, metaphor is praised as one of the principal signs of a correct style and one of the most pleasing adornments of eloquence. Giving sugar to his own medicine he adds a metaphor: metaphor is so 'elegant' that 'it shines by its own light however splendid its context'. In the first sense, metaphor acts almost like an extension of the literal sense. The language itself cannot put it properly, so a word is transferred 'from a place in which it is proper' to a place where there is no proper word or where the figurative word works better than the proper one would.[36] In the second sense, metaphor acts instead as 'ornament'.[37] It is something strictly superfluous to the language, an affect of style.

This is a subtle and ingenious account of metaphor, one that is more open than Locke to ways in which 'proper' and 'non-proper' forms of meaning are hard to distinguish. Yet this difficulty, while it is one that is embraced and cherished by Quintilian, also plays havoc with his categories. As a 'natural' metaphor of the first type he cites the Latin word *gemma* when used by farmers to refer to a vine-bud: he cannot restrain his pleasure, and cries out 'What else could they say?'[38] There is no literal word for a vine-bud, so the figure takes its place. Yet by an irony of philology, Quintilian may have taken the figure in the reverse direction from the truth: modern historians of Latin believe the sense of 'jewel' to be derived from the similarity of a precious stone to a bud. Once again, we could ask, how would we know? Is not every word a figure in some original sense to which we no longer have access? As others have found before and since, the 'proper' sense proves more elusive than at first sight.

Etymology cannot provide an incontrovertible guide here to a figurative genealogy. The figure escapes from Quintilian's grasp as he attempts to capture it. The complexity becomes clearer when he comes to define metalepsis as a form of defective or etiolated metaphor. In a sentence which gave his sixteenth-century editors some difficulty, he compares metalepsis to a process of transition, perhaps even a transition from one trope to another: 'quae ex alio [tropo] in aliud velut viam praestat' ['which, as it were, makes a path from one thing [one trope] to another']. The Aldine edition of 1512, and sixteenth-century editions of Quintilian thereafter, deleted the word *tropo*.[39] It was therefore hard for a sixteenth-century reader to see the difference between metalepsis and any other kind of metaphor: metalepsis in its simplest sense 'makes a path from one thing to another'. After all, the definition of metaphor, going back to Aristotle, is that it is a shortened form of simile; in simile we compare one thing with another, while in metaphor (in Quintilian's phrase) 'one thing is substituted for the other'.[40] By a strange process of transference, in fact, it could be that the most philosophically complex thinking in all of Quintilian on the subject of metaphor comes in his analysis of metalepsis. He calls metalepsis 'a sort of intermediate step between the term transferred and the thing to which it is transferred; it does not signify anything in itself, but provides the transition'.[41] Once again (reflecting the difficulty of the passage) the manuscript transmission at this point is uncertain, and at one point is supplied only in a single Paris exemplar. The full sentence was not available in any sixteenth-century edition. Yet its interest can be seen from the fact that this is the source for Erasmus's definition of metalepsis as an intermediary process (what Quintilian calls 'an intermediate step'). The figure does not signify in itself, but it 'provides the transition'. For a moment, we have come face to face with the deepest mystery in metaphor altogether: the hinge between the term transferred and 'the thing to which it is transferred', or that between word and thing.

RES AND VERBA

As Terence Cave argued in what is by far the most brilliant essay on the *Copia*, from its full title onwards the work is concerned with the relationship between *res* (matter, things) and *verba* (words): *De duplici copia verborum ac rerum commentarii duo*.[42] The division into two books, the first apparently on the copiousness of words, and the second on the copiousness of things, perhaps gives the impression of some simple division between the two. At times Erasmus also appears to endorse the implied (and sometimes explicit) hierarchy in classical rhetoric in which words are organised according to their correspondence to what is assumed to be a pre-existing order of things. This is the doctrine made explicit in Cicero's *De oratore*: 'a full supply of facts [rerum] begets a full supply of words'.[43] Erasmus, however, whatever his lip service to this doctrine, in effect reverses its tenet by beginning with a book on *verba*, words. In addition, as Cave judiciously observes, in Erasmus 'it is not reality that is imitated, but other writers; not ideas, but texts'.[44] We can continue in this vein to observe that, to an extent that is extraordinary in relation to other Renaissance handbooks, Erasmus's work does not even pretend to be about an art of speaking: it is entirely an art of writing. And in this respect it does not merely take its examples from writing, it makes principles of writing its generative order of analysis.

The organising principles of Book I work outward from the language, from the way words work, and not inward from the meanings they purport to represent. Of course, there is no absoluteness of distinction that can work here; Erasmus has not, any more than anyone, discovered some philosopher's stone to break apart signifier and signified. At one point Erasmus abandons his usual methods and even hazards a little philosophy: 'It might be thought that these two aspects are so interconnected in reality that one cannot easily separate one from the other, and that they interact so closely that any distinction between them belongs to theory rather than practice.'[45] Cave is tempted to say that as a result Erasmus collapses the distinction between *res* and *verba*: '*Res* and *verba* slide together to become "word-things"; the notion of a single domain (language) having a double aspect replaces that of two distinct domains, language and thought.'[46] Yet we are clearly on difficult ground here. Cave is absolutely right, I think, to notice that Erasmus almost scrupulously avoids the term 'rhetoric' and the kinds of easy classificatory distinctions which its history has allowed to develop. Cave is also right to observe that in replacing 'rhetoric' with *copia* he is consciously using a word which is more figurative, less easy to decipher. Erasmus has embarked on an essay in figurativeness but the language he has available to him is also figurative.

I want therefore to conclude by suggesting two ways in which Erasmus attempts to re-order the rules of rhetoric according to linguistic principles. One is a scale of sameness in relation to difference. We could call this his principle of mimesis. The simplest form of *varietas*, he says, and the easiest way to create *copia* in writing, is to use 'different words which indicate the same thing', what grammarians call synonyms.[47] This terminology causes him some anxiety. Aristotle, in the *Categories*, he notes, identified synonyms and homonyms as opposite logical terms.[48] Boethius in his Latin translation of Aristotle used the terms *aequivoca* and *univoca*. Erasmus is unhappy with this: it implies a distinction by means of *res* rather than *verba*. Of course he can hardly find a terminology for synonyms which avoids any contamination of referentiality, but he wants to find some way of categorising what is going on between synonyms which does not beg the question right from the outset. To do so he prefers as his own terms 'isodynamic' and 'polysemous'. The chapter in Book I dealing with synonyms, chapter 11, is as a consequence one of those which underwent the greatest expansion from the first edition in 1512 to the last Erasmus oversaw in 1534. He adds a whole series of captions to describe different ways of generating synonyms, and tries his level best to treat them as a category of words rather than as a set of pre-defined meanings. He then attempts to set synonymity on some kind of scale. For, he says, 'you will hardly find two words anywhere so isodynamic that they are not kept apart by some distinction'.[49] The next type of *varietas* following synonyms is thus enallage, or 'related forms of words which differ only slightly'.[50] Enallage involves the substitution of a case or number in a noun, or a tense or mood in a verb; it is of course a very common form of elegant variation in inflected languages. Thus *bibax* and *bibulus, bibosus* and *bibo*, can all be used to describe a person who is (shall we say) a little the worse for drink.

Erasmus is beginning here to propose a hypothesis of language as a theoretical construct in which at one end of the spectrum there is an infinite set of synonyms with the same meaning, at the other a single word, a master homonym, with an infinite set of meanings. In either case, language is tending towards what for Erasmus are unconscionable vices, a linguistic hell: endless tautology, or even worse, homoiologia or 'identical repetition'.[51] Metaphor, or something like it, is the key process which enables language to avoid either of these extremes, by allowing one word to be exchanged for another. A language with only literal senses is condemned always to say the same thing or else to say nothing. Figuration provides the horizon of possibility for a language that can make sense of anything. Figures of speech allow a language to make things up, and thus (paradoxically) also create the conditions for mimesis. A language with figures is creative and productive (as Erasmus would say, copious), by enabling exchange to take place, and at the same time representational (mimetic) by providing the conventions of acceptance by which one word is used in place of another.

This suggests that beneath the concentration on synonyms that appears to be *De copia*'s key feature there is a subtler argument at work concerning the relation of synonymity to metaphor. This makes some account for the extraordinary register of minute gradations in his descriptions of different kinds of metaphor. I am arguing that he does not deal with metaphor as one figure of speech among many, but as a way of explaining how language comes to be able to create figures in the first place. Metalepsis, like related figures such as synecdoche and metonymy, represents a crucial stage in this analysis. Chomarat feels that Erasmus consciously misunderstands Quintilian's definition of metalepsis: we might rewrite this to say that he misapplies it to form a larger figurative scheme.[52]

Indeed, it turns out that, whereas the terminology of metalepsis or metonymy suggests at first a precise taxonomy in which each figure stands for a distinct procedure, instead there is a continuous flux of different figures which slide into one another. Erasmus recognises this elasticity between the figures by saying that metalepsis is 'a form of synecdoche', as is also metonymy. At times it seems when reading the rhetorical treatises of the humanists that both the terms and the examples used to describe the tropes are almost interchangeable. Thus Melanchthon cites the celebrated epithet *pallida mors* ('Pale Death') from Horace's *Odes* as a case of metalepsis, adjoining the analysis that death is described by reference to its effect.[53] The substitution of cause for effect (or vice versa) is conventionally ascribed of course to metonymy, which is where it is found in Erasmus (following Quintilian), using the same citation from Horace to demonstrate a different figure. Yet this is not to say that so learned a commentator as Melanchthon got it wrong. It shows instead how the paradoxical energies of similitude refract and convert as they pass through a new medium. Each figure as it were contains the next, in a process that is itself a kind of metonymy; except that since (according to figurative logic) container is always substitutable for contents, the exchange can occur in both directions. Thus synecdoche appears in Erasmus as a more general term than metonymy (since it allows the derivation of the many from the one, the whole from the part, a class from an example, subsequent actions from previous ones) yet in another sense appears to be another example of metonymy. The definition of synecdoche in Erasmus at one point appears to lend to metaphor an overwhelming power in language to create and transform the world: 'In short, whenever one thing is understood from another in any way whatsoever.'[54]

This shows that the process of substitution can be repeated, and that not all the terms of likeness need to be evident. The peculiar power of metalepsis in Renaissance theory is precisely that it leaves certain steps in the exchange invisible. It makes space for imagination, for language as fiction or fantasy. In this figure we do not know how we have got to where we are, as if we have been transported by an unseen mechanism. This is the effect of all metaphor; yet in metalepsis the process is doubled. By leaving out the intervening metaphor, metalepsis sets figuration into a self-replicating chain: 'In a *metalepsis*, a word is substituted metonymically for a word in a previous trope, so that a *metalepsis* can be called, maddeningly but accurately, a metonymy of a metonymy.'[55] But Erasmus is not saying, as deconstruction seemed to be saying when it became interested in metalepsis a few years ago, that anything can be substituted for anything. Some metaphors are reciprocal, Erasmus says, so that the two terms of exchange are interchangeable; but others are not. And metalepsis leaves the sensation that the figure is not perfectly alike, that the distance travelled is too far or its difference too great. Thus figuration retains many mysteries of qualification which he cannot entirely elaborate.

This brings me in conclusion to the second principle Erasmus discovers in metaphor, which we might call one of quantification rather than qualification. This is his principle of copiousness itself. The idea of metaphor allows Erasmus the licence to expand the language more or less at pleasure. This is the object of *copia*: that there is no end of ways of saying things, so that an eloquent person will be able to make a sentence out of anything. An unkind observer might see this as a licence for prolixity. Yet Erasmus might be suggesting something more precise than this. A language that is non-finite is not the same as one that is infinite. From the beginning of Erasmus's work he is not only encouraging linguistic exuberance, he is also setting out boundaries. The very first sentence of *De copia* is a warning about *copia*: 'The adoption of the copious style involves risk.'[56] Copiousness is 'carried too far by some writers' (1.iv). He is always on the guard against figures which overreach themselves. One kind of figure is like 'adding garlic to . . . Greek confections' (1.x) (does he mean baklava?); another is like 'putting sweet oil on lentils' (1.xi) (here, if he is using Puy lentils, sweet oil might of course be rather successful). The most common of all Erasmus's figures for complaint is one of quantity. Quintilian censures Stesichorus for 'over-abundant and extravagant expression' (1.iv). Ovid 'has been taxed with not knowing when to stop' (1.iii). The ideal of *De copia* is not, then, more is better, but enough is enough: the best writing, he says, is where 'nothing is lacking' and yet 'nothing is redundant' (1.vi). But how far can you go? In this respect, too, metalepsis turns out to be a measure of the boundaries in Erasmus's ideas of figuration. For metalepsis is a metaphor which may have gone too far, one which is far-fetched, one which needs to be brought back within the bounds of sense. Metalepsis sets the imagination free and yet also pulls it in, showing as if in relief what might after all be the limits of language.

Rather than identifying metalepsis as a precise form of rhetorical figure, then, we could see it as a way of understanding a wider phenomenon in figuration. The Greek rhetoricians refer not only to a figure called metalepsis but to a way of thinking which they call *metaleptikōs*. No writer, we may feel, is more metaleptic than Shakespeare. Hardly any figure in Shakespeare appears on its own or in a single guise. His figures typically leave out an intervening metaphor, making the process of figuration more oblique or mysterious. And more than any other writer, perhaps, his figures appear to link themselves in replicating chains, double up on themselves, invert themselves, or merge into each other. *Macbeth* begins with a string of these imaginative metalepses, and once they are set in motion, the figure can only end in death.

The witches conjure into being 'Strange images of death'[57] which pass from one person to the next, and from one speech to the next, without any respect to ordinary processes of referentiality. They put ideas into our heads, which once there cannot be removed. Early in the play, Macbeth himself comments on this rule of the imagination, and as if in afterthought or else in horrible premonition (it is hard to say which) he becomes the first to utter the word 'murder' in the play:

> Present Feares
> Are lesse then horrible Imaginings:
> My Thought, whose Murther yet is but fantasticall,
> Shakes so my single state of Man,
> That Function is smother'd in surmise,
> And nothing is, but what is not.[58]

Is 'murther' here a figure? And if so, is it a tortured ellipsis ('a thought of murder') or a terrifying prolepsis (an inadvertent prophecy)? The border-line between imagining terrible things ('but fantasticall'), and doing them, is the great ethical and political crux of the play. Macbeth cannot help imagining things, and once imagined, cannot stop himself doing them. The explanation for this is caught between a traditional tragic canopy of fate and a complex motivational psychology of moral behaviour. Yet it also follows a logic of figures which (according to the analysis here) we may call metaleptic. This logic is caught nowhere more fully than in some of the most famous lines in the play:

> If it were done, when 'tis done, then 'twer well,
> It were done quickly: If th' Assassination
> Could trammell up the Consequence, and catch
> With his surcease, Successe: that but this blow
> Might be the be all, and the end all. Heere,
> But heere, upon this Banke and Schoole of time,
> Wee'ld jumpe the life to come.[59]

The lines are like a metalepsis in explanation of metalepsis, not in some reductive self-referential *aporia* but in a recognition of the way that every life is lived in an interplay between language and action. In the play's continuous passage between *figura* and *res* it finds its 'be all, and . . . end all'. The boundaries of a fantasy happening on stage and the actors and spectators who are caught in the apprehension of their own mutual mortality are never more fragile than here. Yet the figures provide fictive pleasure and relief as well as remorseless self-commentary. As the figures double up on themselves, they provide for us at least an illusion that in the act of making up our own language we can (at least fleetingly) anticipate the shape of our existence and 'jumpe the life to come'.[60]

CHAPTER 13

It hath bene said before how by ignorance of the maker a good figure may become a vice, and by his good discretion, a vicious speech go for a vertue in the Poeticall science. This saying is to be explaned and qualified, for some maner of speaches are always intollerable and such as cannot be used with any decencie, but are ever undecent namely barbarousnesse, incongruitie, ill disposition, fond affectation, rusticitie, and all extreme darknesse, such as it is not possible for a man to understand the matter without an interpretour . . .

Puttenham, *The Arte of English Poesie* (1589)

The vices of style

WILLIAM POOLE

Style is corrupted in as many ways as it can be ornamented.

Quintilian, *Institutio oratoria*

Catachresis (in English *Abuse*) is nowe growne in fashion (as most abuses are) . . .

John Hoskyns, *Directions for Speech and Style* (*c.* 1599)

Some enigma, some riddle; come, thy l'envoy, begin.

William Shakespeare, *Love's Labour's Lost*

If rhetoric is the art of speaking well, then presumably formalised rhetoric should recognise what it is to speak *badly*. In other words, for any taxonomy of the virtues of style there must be, either formally or by implication, a parallel taxonomy of the vices of style. These vices are the subject of the present chapter, first in terms of their taxonomy, and then in their literary application.

What is the merit of studying the vices of style? The first answer turns on the correlation between, on the one hand, the relation between bad and good rhetoric, and on the other, the relation between good rhetoric and 'common' discourse. For if the vices of style represent deviations from licit rhetoric, might this return us to the prior problem that rhetoric is itself a deviation from common speech? As George Puttenham confessed in his *Arte of English Poesie* (1589): 'As figures be the instruments of ornament in every language, so be they also in a sorte abuses or rather trespasses in speech, because they passe the ordinary limits of common utterance.'[1] Here, it is important to register Puttenham's terminology, because Puttenham's treatise proposed English equivalents to replace the entire classical tongue-twisting rhetorical lexicon.[2] And in his lexicon, 'abuse' and 'trespass' are precise names for two figures central to any discussion of rhetorical deviancy. First, 'the abuser' is Puttenham's term for catachresis, or distorted lexis; and secondly, 'the trespasser' is his term for hyperbaton, or distorted syntax – two of the basic manoeuvres of rhetoric, but both right on the border of vicious style, as the headnote quotation from Hoskyns insinuates.[3]

The second response concerning the study of the vices is connected to the first: talking about how to identify and categorise the vices of style is by implication a discussion about the entire business of stylistic taxonomy – or, to employ rhetorical terminology, it is a discussion about how the third part of rhetoric, *elocutio*, the dominant subject of this book, can function at all. Accordingly, this chapter will address first the most general problems of definition between rhetoric, logic, and grammar, and secondly the internal problems of classification within rhetoric itself. Richard Sherry's vernacular taxonomy of the vices will then be elucidated, following which the various techniques for identifying such breaches of 'discretion'[4] will be appraised. The second part of this essay will survey the literary application of the vices in a variety of different genres. One tentative conclusion is this: early-modern writers grew more tolerant of certain vices than were the theorists of antiquity. Certain moves inadmissible in classical speech became licit in early-modern text.

PROBLEMS OF DEFINITION

The myriad terms chaperoned under *elocutio* are themselves of complex origin;[5] and grammar, encountered in the curriculum before rhetoric, intro-duced many terms that rhetoric would later reintroduce. Rhetoricians there-fore treated several of the vices as members simultaneously of grammatical and rhetorical categories.[6] Within rhetoric itself, problems of taxonomy were sure to arise because of the variety of authorities available. To take the two most popular authorities, Quintilian and the earlier *Rhetorica ad Herennium*, the former praises while the latter rebukes certain figures.[7] In other cases, Quintilian reclassifies many of the earlier treatise's schemes as really figures of thought, ejects some terms altogether, and is in general critical of 'those authors who have set almost no limit to the invention of technical terms'.[8] He also regards some of the tropes included in the *Ad Herennium* as puerile.[9] Any student versed in both works could not miss these discrepancies.

Quintilian himself supplied what is the first formal list of the vices in his eighth book, but even in this originary list certain borders were contested. Of ellipsis (omission of a word or short phrase), for instance, he comments that when it is done deliberately, it is a figure not a vice, and is also sometimes termed epanalepsis, an orthodox figure. Of periphrasis (circumlocution), inserted into the middle of the list of vices immediately after macrologia (longwindedness), Quintilian merely comments that it is extremely close to the former, but held to be a virtue. Virgil is cited under the vice of pleonasm (redundancy) as an example nevertheless of a 'good' pleonasm, because done for the sake of assertion (*adfirmatio*). Outside the list of vices, similar ambiguities can occur. Metalepsis (the 'far-fetched') is only grudgingly endorsed by Quintilian, who considers it to be 'very rare and highly incorrect', unless occurring in comedy. Hyperbole (exaggeration) is left until late in the discussion because it is a 'bolder' (*audacior*) usage than rhetoric normally permits. *Audax* is a term often encountered on the border between the virtues and the vices.[10]

Such tensions could not but inform early-modern systems, all of which were more or less redactions of the classical corpus.[11] But the early-modern rhetoricians had inherited a technical vocabulary that was originally developed for a language that was highly inflected, in which word order was correspondingly more flexible, and whose prosody relied on the length of syllables rather than stress. Hence some classical ideas required redefinition. Various style manuals, for instance, apply the terminology of the orthographical schemes (a division introduced by Melanchthon) to issues that in retrospect look as if they are reacting to problems of dialect, obsolescence, and standardisation. Henry Peacham's examples of antistoecon or the replacing of one letter in a word by another (e.g. 'warke' v. 'worke'; 'wull' v. 'will') correspond to Scottish or northern spellings versus southern (and later standard) forms.[12] Metathesis or the switching of two letters in a word prompts the example 'aksed' for 'asked' (*ask* < OE axian), a form witnessed by the *Oxford English Dictionary* for the late sixteenth century, though fast becoming obsolete.[13] The style manuals also contain redundancies, and, as Peter Mack has pointed out, these are on occasion marked as such, for instance Peacham again on the obscure ecthlipsis (elision of the *-um/-am/-em* termination in Latin).[14] This is quite inapplicable to English, as Peacham admits: 'this fygure is not used in our English tongue, and therefore I cannot geve it an Example'.[15] Peacham is thus a good example of a rhetorician who can both acknowledge the imperfect fit of the imported Latin system, as well as reform it where he can. More generally, the occasional clumsiness of this transition and the practical difficulty posed by a complex and obscure vocabulary are visible in the problems Peacham's compositors evidently faced: an errata note reveals that they were dealing with unfamiliar terms which led to basic mistakes in deciphering Peacham's handwriting: hence 'cacosmtheton', 'polysmdeton', 'polyploton'.[16] So the virtues were themselves unstable as a group, intermittently vicious, and that instability was passed on: like the two surfaces of a single sheet of paper, any flexion affects both sides.

A CATALOGUE OF VICES

We now turn to the vices themselves. The standard Latin term is *vitium* (*vitia* in the plural), translated in English rhetorical discussions of the terms variously as 'vice', 'faute', or 'abuse'. The vices themselves can be encountered in rhetorical treatises in a number of ways, although their most systematic presentation was in lists, either directly from Quintilian, or in mediated forms, most notably the popular *Tabulae* of Mosellanus, a continental work dating from 1516, but which was also printed in England (there are extant editions of 1573 and 1577).[17] It was prescribed at Eton ('mosellanys figures or Copia rerum et verborum of Erasmus') and subsequently at other English grammar schools.[18] It was through Mosellanus's tables that many educated people especially in the first half of the sixteenth century would have first encountered the vices, and Mosellanus provided the base for vernacular lists such as that found in Richard Sherry's *Treatise of Schemes and Tropes* (1550), which contains a list of 'fautes' sequenced exactly as in Mosellanus. In a typical move, Sherry categorises the vices as vicious in prose, though not necessarily in verse: 'Of Scheme, the second parte is in speech as it were a faute, which though it be pardoned in Poetes, yet in prose it is not to be suffered.'[19] Here are Sherry's 'Fautes', which he subdivides into the Obscure, the Inordinate, and the Barbarous, glossed with definitions, using Sherry's phrasing where possible. Illustrative examples from Shakespeare have been added:[20]

1. Obscure ('darknes thorow faut')

Acyrologia: word in improper signification, as in 'you shall have syxe strypes you *longe* for'. (As Sherry's example suggests, the word used is often directly opposite in meaning to the 'proper' choice for the context. This is a notable feature of Dogberry's language: 'O villain! thou wilt be condemn'd into everlasting *redemption* for this.')[21]

Pleonasmus: superfluity, as in 'he spake it *wyth his mouthe*'. (Juliet's Nurse uses it as a form of emphasis: 'I saw the wound, I *saw* it *with mine eyes*.')[22]

Perissologia: as pleonasmus, but applied to a whole sentence, not just a word.

Tautologia: vain repetition, as in Cicero's 'Therefore that judgement was not lyke a judgement O Judges.' (Antony answers Lepidus's request for a description of the crocodile with a series of uninformative tautologies, such as: 'it is as *broad* as it hath *breadth*'.)[23]

Homiologia: monotony. (This is a constant feature of Justice Shallow's speech: 'Where's the roll? where's the roll? where's the roll? Let me see, let me see, let me see.')[24]

Amphibologia: grammatical ambiguity, as in 'Hys father loveth him better then hys mother.' (Quince's prologue to the play of Pyramus and Thisbe is an extended exercise in grammatical ambiguity caused by alternative punctuation;[25] further examples of this device will be discussed in the penultimate section below.)

Periergia/Macrologia: straining for eloquence, but falling into superfluity.

2. Inordinate ('when eyther order or dignitie lacketh in the wordes')

Tapinosis: 'when the dygnitye of the thyng is diminyshed by basenes of the worde'. (Pandarus defames Achilles by this means: 'Achilles! A drayman, a porter, a very camel.')[26]

Aischrologia: obscenity, 'when the words be spoken, or joyned together, that they may be wronge [wrung] into a fylthye sence'. Sherry adds 'Of thys it nedeth not to put any example, when lewde wanton persons wyl soone finde inowe.'

Cacozelia: affectation, 'as when affectyng copy [copiousness], we fall into a vayne bablynge'. (This is a vice committed by Osric and parodied by Hamlet: 'Sir, his definement suffers no perdition in you, though I know to divide him inventorially would dozy th' arithmetic of memory.')[27]

Aschematiston: no tropes and figures whatsoever.

Cacosyntheton: faulty syntax, 'when wordes be naughtelye joyned together, or set in a place wher thei shuld not be'. (Often taking the form of adjective-noun reversal, this is a vice of affectation, rather than ignorance, as when Holofernes greets the entrance of Jaquenetta with: 'A soul feminine saluteth us.')[28]

Soraismus: the introduction of foreign words into English. (Holofernes is again an offender, as in: '*Allons!* we will employ thee.')[29]

3. Barbarous (faults initially encountered in the grammar curriculum)

Barbarismus: words written or pronounced abnormally by addition, contraction, alteration or transposition. This, Sherry notes, has been partially addressed in previous sections on the figures. (It is common in

Shakespeare's representations of foreigners' English, as in Sir Hugh Evans's Welsh pronunciation: 'Fery goot. I will make a prief of it in my note-book.')[30]

Solecismus: grammatical error, 'whych because it is used of famous authores, in stede of fautes, be called figures'. (This is often represented as a vice of ignorance, as in Mistress Quickly's confusion of adjective and noun: 'her husband will be *absence* from his house . . . He's a very *jealousy* man.')[31]

We will have occasion to return to some of the problems such a list presents us with, but before that I want to make some general observations on how vice can be defined.

There are broadly speaking two techniques for identifying vice: either by taxonomy, as above; or by pairing to a virtue. As Quintilian said, 'Style is corrupted in as many ways as it can be ornamented', so in the ideal taxonomy of rhetoric, every term would have its vicious inflection.[32] And although these two approaches turn up rather similar lists (the terminology having been settled in advance), there is a difference in approach and effect, especially in pedagogic terms: taxonomy can dissociate vice from virtue, whereas pairing presupposes proximity. This encourages the sense that the distinction between a virtue and a vice is as much a matter of aesthetics as of lists, a conclusion that we shall reach again in this essay.

The second method, by pairing, works by comparison with virtue usu-ally in terms of excess; as Quintilian said, 'all vice is too much'.[33] Hence not a few manuals phrase their discussions in terms of a virtue and its cor-responding vice. Erasmus opened his *De copia* by stressing the proximity of rhetorical success to rhetorical failure: 'a good many mortal men who make great efforts to achieve this godlike power of speech fall instead into mere glibness'; and the second edition of Peacham's *Garden of Eloquence* concluded the discussion of each figure with a 'use' and a 'caution'.[34] Tax-onomy of itself is thereby revealed to be insufficient to the task of finally deciding what is licit and what is not. Likewise, George Puttenham's dis-cussion of the vices is headed 'Some vices in speech and writing are always intollerable, some others now and then borne withall by licence of approved authors and custome.'[35] Such a method is obviously similar to the Aris-totelian idea of the mean, in which case licit rhetoric is the path between, on the one hand, homoeologia or aschematiston (sometimes aschema-tismus), the two vices that effectively mean no ornation at all, and on the other, the shifting bank of exaggerated styles, such as bomphilogia and so forth.[36]

As suggested, the arbitration between *virtus* and *vitium* turns quickly into an aesthetic decision rather than one supplied by definition alone: the countless lists of figures retailed in the early-modern period inevitably if tacitly appeal to an extra-systematic understanding of style. Yet even across a few decades, style could appear a matter of fashion, and so not something that could be permanently stabilised by taxonomy. John Hoskyns, whose 'Direccions For Speech and Style' (c. 1599) provides the most intelligent appreciation of how style and fashion interact, reflected candidly on the influence of non-rhetorical activities on contemporary style:

It is true that we studie according to the predominancie of courtly inclynacions, whilest mathematiques were in requests all our similitudes came from lynes, circles, and Angles, whilest morall philosophie is nowe a while spoken of, it is rudenesse not to be sententious, and for my parte, I'le make one, I have used and outworn several styles since I was first a Fellow of New College, and am yet able to beare the fashion of writing companie, let our age therefore onlie speake morally, and let the next age live morrally.[37]

Hoskyns here identifies something the elaborate lists of figures could not confess so openly: that literary taste also controlled what figures were in and out of fashion, and that changes in literary taste were influenced by extra-literary concerns, here a shift in 'courtly' interests from mathematics to moral philosophy.

SHIFTING VALUES

This leads us to some more issues concerning the vices arising out of taxonomy versus taste and fashion. The first and most obvious point is that lists and judgements differ – we have seen disagreements over classification within antiquity and we shall conclude with an example of a disagreement of valuation between antiquity and the early-moderns. A second issue is that of clarity – some textbooks so intermingle what others separate as vices and virtues that the precise borders between the categories, indeed the categories themselves, are breached. For instance when Johannes Susenbrotus produced his *Epitome troporum ac schematum*, a work that gradually but decisively eclipsed Mosellanus in England, he abandoned any formal classification of the vices, and instead sprinkled them throughout his other categories.[38]

An interesting example of such intermingling is provided by Peacham's 'orders' or groups of figures, taking as an example from his first edition the order of 'the schemes syntactical'. The interest here is the intermixture of licit and illicit figures, and the status of the supportive citation. Peacham opens his discussion with a reflection, again, on the overlap between the material of the grammarian and that of the rhetorician:

although al these fallowing, be fygures of construction, yet some of them be used of Oratours, among the figures of Rhetorick, and because I would not disapoynt the Gramarrian of his fygures, which I know he will looke for, nor the Rhetorician of those which he dayly useth, I will set them down in both places brieflye, so that neyther of them, shall have cause to fynde faulte for their wante.[39]

Of the schemes syntactical, the 'fyrst Order' (eclipsis, aposiopesis, zeugma, syllepsis, prolepsis, anapodoton) involves cutting away something, 'which want is yet pleasaunte, for that it doth marvelously serve to brevity, both in wryting and speaking'. The 'second Order', however, which involves some type of excess, comprehends devices that 'are reckened among vices, of the ungarnished order, called Pleonasmus'. Yet under pleonasmus we find not only Ovid cited as an example, but also Job, 'Loe all this have I seene with mine eyes and hearde with mine eares' – and Peacham can hardly be counselling us to regard Job as vicious. Epanalepsis, too, includes illustrations from Virgil and Isaiah; 'This is also a figure of Rhetoric', Peacham adds, repeating Quintilian. The 'third order' is governed by hyperbaton, and its contents (hyperbaton itself, anastrophe, hysterologia, hysteron proteron, tmesis, parenthesis, hypallage, synchisis, and amphibologia) 'doe make the oration very darke and obscure', although these figures are not explicitly classed as vicious. But under the heading for hyperbaton itself, 'right and lawfull order' is displaced by 'unproper placing', hardly a positive-sounding phrase, although Cicero is immediately cited for an 'apte and prettie' example. Anastrophe again looks like vice – 'a preposterous order' – although Peacham's gloss does not arbitrate. Synchisis, though, is unequivocally condemned: 'it is unprofitable, and rather to be avoyded, then at any tyme to be imitated'.

The fourth order is explicitly negative: 'Fygures of the forth order be those, which either by want of aptnesse and dignitie, or els by to muche curiositie and finenesse, doe make the oration faultie, and be also reckened among the vices of the ungarnyshed order, which are permitted to Poets, when necessitie compelleth, but evermore unlawfull to Oratours.' Here is where we get a list that more obviously resembles the Quintilian–Mosellanus–Sherry set – tapinosis, bomphilogia, cacozelon, cacemphaton, paroemion, periergia, cacosyntheton and soroesmus. Next, the fifth order 'compryseth those Figures, which compound a sentence altogeather of one colour'. These are asyndeton, polysyndeton, scesis onomaton, hyrmos, epitheton, periphrasis, emphasis and lyptote. Despite the phrase 'of one colour', which smacks of homoeologia, this is a respectable neighbourhood. But it has some peculiar residents. Hyrmos, for example, is defined as 'an unfashioned order of speech . . . long continued, and as it were, stretched out to the ende, still after one sorte, voyde of all round and sweete composition'. Emphasis is again a citizen of two states: 'some recken this among tropes, and others put it among fygures of construction'. The sixth and final order stresses the distinction (though here not an absolute distinction) between poetic and prosaic decorum: 'Fygures of the sixt Order, be those which do consist in chaunging of cases, genders, numbers, moodes, tences, and persons, propper to Poets onely, yet sometyme used of Oratours.' Examples from both Terence and Cicero are then given.

If we consider this taxonomy from the point of view of a typical sixteenth-century student, using Peacham either as a crib for Latin rhetoric or as a directive for vernacular reading, it is obvious that Peacham gives off rather mixed signals about what is licit and illicit usage. Some terms in virtuous surrounds, such as eclipsis, are in other lists classed as vices. Some are ambidextrous, such as epanalepsis. Some, such as hyrmos, are glossed in rather negative terms, but are placed in the company of positive figures.

SOME LITERARY APPLICATIONS

Let us now turn to the literary ramification of what we have so far surveyed. First, any reader of early-modern rhetorics (in the plural) would have an inevitable involvement with the difficulties of rhetorical taxonomy. Such texts also would heighten awareness of generic considerations, poetry being identified as the zone where the rules were slackened. One approach to relating the style of Donne, for instance, to that of his contemporaries is to note how he exacerbates certain aspects of the vices. Consider the following lines from Donne's Holy Sonnet 'What if this present were the worlds last night?' Donne asks his opening question – can he be damned? – in the octave, only to reply in the sestet:

> No, no; but, as in my idolatorie
> I said to all my profane mistresses,
> Beauty, of pitty, foulnesse onely is
> A signe of rigour . . .[40]

Donne here uses zeugma (more precisely hypozeugma) to obfuscate what is after all a deeply inappropriate sentiment in a sonnet on the Last Judgement – 'beauty [is a sign of] pity, only foulness is a sign of rigour', an argument drawn from the chat-up line (to his 'profane mistresses'), 'all the nice girls say yes, all the ugly ones say no; what kind of girl are you?' (Note that this is also paradox within paradox: the nice girls, so Donne's mistresses would have assumed, are traditionally the ones who *deny*.) But to employ such an argument in order to insist upon his own salvation is perverse. Donne's hypozeugma, which would have been licit in Latin syntax, produces cacosyntheton in English, deliberately evading understanding upon a first reading – and fittingly so, as the persona of Donne's poem attempts a questionable argumentative move. With respect to English word order, these lines exploit both zeugma, cacosyntheton, and hyperbaton, Puttenham's 'Trespasser' – the very root, we recall, that Puttenham used to describe rhetoric itself: 'trespasses in speech'.

The vices also had application in the drama. As one might expect, the academic drama – that is, the plays written and acted in the universities – was obsessed with the trivium (grammar, rhetoric and logic, the lower division of the seven liberal arts). Several of the plays written in the sixteenth and early seventeenth centuries satirise the grammar-school classroom the students had so recently escaped. *Susenbrotus*, a Cambridge neo-Latin play of 1616, is titled after the textbook rhetorician we have already encountered, who is in this cruel little comedy a deluded schoolmaster, babbling reconstituted snippets of Lily's *Grammar*, the legally stipulated textbook of the age, but failing to notice that the girl he is courting is really a boy in disguise. A more sophisticated piece of work is Richard Zouche's *Sophister* (published in 1639, but written much earlier), in which all the characters are named after pieces of grammar, rhetoric, and logic, and speak as they are named. The play opens with Fallacy (i.e. a being from the world of logic) and his servant Ambiguity (from the world of rhetoric) on a dark stage, Fallacy carrying a 'darke Lanthorne' – a perversion of logic is thus paired with a vice of style, and the governing metaphor of the rhetorical vices (darkness), is rendered literal.

One advantage of drama is that a play can contain ineloquent characters without itself being ineloquent – characters who are supposed to be perceived as deluded or deficient can be marked as such because they are rhetorically vicious. An example of this occurs in a fragmentary Oxford play of about 1615, in which a septuagenarian codger named Demea – a stock figure from the Roman comedies of Plautus – plans to woo a girl a quarter of his age:

Or were she sett as guerdon for desarte
In tilting chivalry or feircest feight;
I stately mounted clad in silver Azur
With stately plumes crowneing my stately mazor
Maugre there force, before ten thousande eyes
   From all defendants I would bare the prize.

Up-to-date literary people with good memories reading or hearing these lines would recognise in them a garbled recollection of a passage from Josuah Sylvester's popular verse translation of Du Bartas' *Divine Weeks and Works*, which in the 1605 edition contained the following simile:

As HARDY LAELIUS, that Great GARTER-KNIGHT . . .
Most bravely mounted on proud RABICAN,
All in guilt armour, on his glis'tring Mazor
A stately Plume, of Orange mixt with Azure,
In gallant Course, before ten thousand eyes
From all Defendants bore the Princely Prize.[41]

The problem is that Demea has fallen into the vice of cacozelia, with admixtures of homoeologia – in straining so hard to paint a picture of himself as a lusty knight he bungles his language, repeating 'stately' three times in two lines, 'as when affectyng copy, we fall into a vayne bablynge', in Sherry's words.[42]

The vices of course had a part to play on the London stages too, as most if not all the popular playwrights had at least a grammar school education. Shakespeare, for instance, knew the precise rhetorical vocabulary of abuses, as the phrase 'Some enigma, some riddle' in *Love's Labour's Lost* demonstrates – 'riddle' is Puttenham's English term for aenigma. In *The Merry Wives of Windsor* Sir Hugh Evans is shocked at Pistol's 'He hears with ears' because it is 'affectations' – and also the standard example across the textbooks for pleonasmus, as Baldwin noted.[43] In *Hamlet*, Polonius, in praising brevity, utters perhaps the best known example of macrologia in the language: 'I will be brief', he lies.[44]

The use of letters on the stage – texts that can be seen, sometimes heard, but never read by the audience – also provided a fertile ground for exploiting rhetorical vices, notably that of amphibologia or ambiguity. An early, celebrated example from a school play occurs in Nicholas Udall's *Ralph Roister Doister*, written some time before 1553. We can so date and attribute this seminal fusion of classical and native comic traditions precisely because Udall's ambiguous letter was cited in a logic textbook of 1553 as an example of 'doubtfull writyng, whiche by reason of poinctyng, maie have double sense', and there attributed to the well-known schoolmaster and translator Udall. The widow Christian Custance is ambiguously wooed by letter:

> Swete maistresse, whereas I love you nothyng at all,
> Regardyng your richesse and substaunce chief of all,
> For your personage, beautie, demeanour, and witte,
> I commende me unto you never a whitte.
> Sorie to heare reporte of your good welfare . . .

– and so on, for some three dozen virtuosic verses.[45] Read enjambed, with appropriate punctuation and pausing, the letter flatters; but read with the line and rhyme, the sense inverts. Later examples on the public stage also take us back to the classroom. In 2 *Henry VI*, York, reading out an ambiguous letter, quotes a well-known example of the duplicity of the Oracle in order to signal that he knows he is being tricked by a devious *amphibologia*:

> 'The duke yet lives that Henry shall depose;
> But him out-live, and die a violent death.'
> Why, this is just
> '*Aio te, Aeacida, Romanos vincere posse.*'[46]

This was the very example given by Mosellanus for that vice in his textbook; here Shakespeare may be directly recalling his time in the classroom.[47] The same kind of written *amphibologia* is used by Mortimer near the end of Marlowe's *Edward II*:

> *Edwardum occidere nolite timere bonum est.*
> Feare not to kill the king tis good he die.
> But read it thus, and thats another sence:
> *Edwardum occidere nolite timere bonum est.*
> Kill not the king tis good to feare the worst.
> Unpointed as it is, thus shall it go.[48]

If the 'point' is to be taken after *nolite*, the instruction is not to kill; if after *occidere*, then the instruction is to kill. Only in voicing this *amphibologia*, as Mortimer is doing for us, is it resolved one way or the other.

Finally, there is also a certain playfulness generated from the taxonomic instabilities discussed in this chapter. Noel Malcolm has written brilliantly on nonsense verse in this period, identifying it as a highly literary phenomenon, drawing on, in his analysis, *impossibilia*, parody, and 'translinguistic foolery'.[49] But nonsense, especially via parody, might further be thought of as one by-product of the friction generated between competing rhetorical systems, and exploitation of that which is classified as vicious. This brings us into the territory of fustian, parody, mock-oration, and bomphilogia. As an example of this I shall cite an anonymous seventeenth-century mock epistle to a wordy parson from his exasperated flock, adopting the very style for which the parson is being criticised: 'To the most Deutero-nomicall PoliDoxologist and Pantifilogicall Linguist Mr A. C. Arch-Rabbi, Sophi, Phanodandi, Diotrophis de Hontbye. The unanimous, and humil-lious desiderations, as well of your Parochian, as hic et ubiquitavian, illiter-ate, semipaganian Auditors.'[50] This letter is another, extended example of cacozelia, which Quintilian called the worst of vices because it, unlike the other faults of style, is sincerely if disastrously intended. Here, it is artfully and wittily intended. The letter proceeds to apologise that the 'Agrico-lated Intellects' of the rural congregation are not managing to understand the 'Caliginous Sublimity' of their learned leader with his 'Cicophronian Cothurnes' – 'Cico' hovering between 'Ciceronian' and 'Caco-', the rhetor-ical prefix for a vice; and a *cothurnus*, of course, is a buskin, the tragic actor's boot, a final reminder that the heights of aspiration frequently turn into the depths of affectation, the sentiment once more of the opening paragraph of Erasmus's *De copia*.

The broader literary conclusion, however, is that many of these problems were arising now in the context of written as opposed to spoken discourse. The Elizabethan style manuals constantly oscillate between verbs of speak-ing and hearing, or of writing and reading. But although the oratorical vocabulary persists, the use of such manuals is obviously for reading – for 'the exposicion of good authoures', as Sherry wrote in his epistle.[51] The Renaissance interest in the dark and the difficult accompanied the rehabil-itation of what was in origin an art of speaking to what had become not just an art of writing, but a technique of reading.

Nowhere is this more prominent than in the Renaissance genres of para-dox and aenigma. The former was in the early-modern period not strictly a part of rhetoric at all, but was understood as a generic marker following Cicero's *Paradoxa Stoicorum*, and it was deployed in learned discourse in order to interrogate, to render systems mobile, to be free.[52] Aenigma, which was a figure of speech, had been banned by Quintilian on the grounds that it merely confused speakers: the good speaker, Quintilian counselled, will avoid hyperbaton, aenigma, ambiguity or obscurity of any kind. He recalled with disapproval the orator whose only advice to his students was *skotison!* – 'darken it!'[53] For Quintilian the crime here lies in placing the burden of interpretation on the *ingenium* of the recipient. But aenigma, usually dis-cussed as the last excess of allegoria, was rehabilitated in the early-modern period for the very reason that it exercised the intelligence. Thus we observe a shift in the assumed capacity and intellectual interests of the audience of stylised speech. Erasmus, the authority, was unequivocally supportive: 'This is no bad thing if you are speaking or writing for an educated audience, and even if you are writing for the general public, for one should not write so that everyone can understand everything, but so that people should be compelled to investigate and learn some things themselves.'[54] Peacham starts off sounding disapproving, but ends up sympathetic. Aenigma is:

> a sentence of which for the darknesse, there can be no certaynty gathered, this Trope is more agreeable to Poets, then to Orators, for every Aenigmaticall sentence is obscure, and every Oratour doth in speaking, flye obscurity, and darck speeches, in whome the facillity and perspecuity of the speech, is a goodly vertue, notwithstanding sometime, darcknesse is delectable, as that which is understood of wyse and learned men, for when men fynde at last, by long consyderation, the meaning of some darcke riddle, they much delight and rejoyce, that their capacity was able to compasse so hard a matter, and commende highly the devysers wit, therefore it may be in an oration, where wise men be hearers.[55]

Angel Day repeated the metaphor of darkness, again appreciatively: aenigma is 'a darke sentence, or as we ordinarily say, used in high and deepe mysteries, otherwise conveyed sometime in pleasant fancies, and accustomed in other writings'.[56] This was the opinion of Susenbrotus, who added what had become the clinching argument: the Bible deploys aenigma, especially in the prophets and in Revelation.[57]

   This points to a decisive factor in the reworking of classical rhetorical standards: the application of rhetorical analysis to biblical text.[58] As the influential educator Joachim Camerarius noted, Revelation ('Apocalypse') was so called 'because in Greek *kalupsai* has the meaning of hiding and veiling'.[59] Christ too used aenigma, in the form of parable. As the Suida defined it, says Camerarius, parable is 'speech intended for practical understanding, employing ambiguity, obscurity, and abstruseness'. So it is partially owing to its biblical use that aenigma was promoted out of the vices, and identified as a way of sorting out the sheep from the goats: aenigma employs 'oblique' means in order to evade vulgar understandings and entice further cogitation. As Justin remarked, parable is used 'lest it be understood by all, and so that work and diligent enquiry is needed in order to discover and learn'.[60] St Paul, too, in the phrase usually translated as 'now we see through a glass darkly' used the term aenigma ('darkly' translates 'en ainigmati'), causing Augustine to remark that this passage must remain misunderstood by those ignorant of Greek rhetorical vocabulary.[61] No higher authorities could be sought to emphasise not only the rhetorical nature of scripture, but its habitual use of the rhetoric of obscurity and seeming confusion. As the prominent Jacobean scholar John Hales wrote, invoking the figure of hysteron proteron or inverted syntax, 'there are in Scripture of things that are *ustera protera, seemingly confus'd* . . . there are I say in Scripture more of them, then in any writing that I know secular or Divine'.[62] So much for the evangelical Protestant fiction that scripture was uniformly easy to understand.

CONCLUSION

In terms of the history of rhetoric, study of the vices operates not just as a discussion *e contrario* of the virtues, but of the presuppositions unvoiceable in taxonomic form of just what makes virtues virtuous and vicious vices. Secondly, the shifts in what counts as a vice – I have ended on the example of aenigma, but it applies to the whole governing class of hyperbaton – highlight once again the basic problems of applying a classical art of speaking to a Renaissance culture of writing and reading, and a classical vocabulary to a modern and increasingly vernacular environment. If, as the editors of this volume state, *elocutio* was the part of rhetoric that 'most readily transplanted from oratorical to literary theory',[63] then it did not remain unchanged in that process.

Notes

INTRODUCTION

1. Neil Rhodes, *The Power of Eloquence and English Renaissance Literature* (London: Harvester Wheatsheaf, 1992), p. vii. For an influential formulation of a similar view, see C. S. Lewis, *English Literature in the Sixteenth Century Encluding Drama* (Oxford: Clarendon Press, 1954), p. 61.
2. For more detailed accounts of Renaissance rhetoric and its background see 'Suggestions for further reading' below, e.g. works by Skinner, Vickers, Mack and Kennedy. For further bibliography see the reference works edited by Plett and by Murphy and Green.
3. Richard Rainolde, *The Foundacion of Rhetorike* (1563).
4. Lee A. Sonnino, *A Handbook to Sixteenth-Century Rhetoric* (London: Routledge and Kegan Paul, 1968), p. 7.
5. Mabbott, quoted by D. L. Clark in *John Milton at St Paul's School: A Study of Ancient Rhetoric in English Renaissance Education* (New York: Columbia University Press, 1948), pp. 176–7.
6. Cicero, *De oratore* ['On the Orator'], 1.16.70.
7. *Critical Essays of the Seventeenth Century*, ed. J. E. Spingarn, 3 vols. (Oxford: Clarendon Press, 1908), vol. 1, p. 210.
8. William Shakespeare, *Troilus and Cressida*, 3.2.60–5, in G. Blakemore Evans (ed.), *The Riverside Shakespeare* (Boston: Houghton Mifflin, 1974); further Shakespeare quotations are from this edition.
9. Henry Peacham, *The Garden of Eloquence* (1593), p. 118.
10. See, e.g., on hyperbaton ('Longinus', *On the Sublime*, 22.1).
11. Quintilian, *Institutio oratoria*, 3.2.3.
12. Lady Mary Wroth, *The Countesse of Mountgomeries Urania* (1621), sig. s4v.
13. A point rediscovered in modern cognitive linguistics. See G. Lakoff and M. Johnson, *Metaphors We Live By* (Chicago: University of Chicago Press, 1980).
14. Demetrius, *On Style*, 263 and 267.
15. Quintilian, *Institutio oratoria*, 9.1.17.
16. Peacham, *The Garden of Eloquence* (1593), p. 110.
17. Quintilian, 9.1.7–9; 9.1.16.
18. Richard A. Lanham, *A Handlist of Rhetorical Terms*, 2nd edn (Berkeley and Los Angeles: University of California Press, 1991), p. 79.

19. *Julius Caesar*, 3.2.24–9.
20. Lines 7–12, in Colin Burrow (ed.), *Metaphysical Poetry* (London: Penguin, 2006), p. 134.
21. Cf. Puttenham: 'it may as well be called the *clyming* figure, for *Clymax* is as much to say as a ladder'; *The Arte of English Poesie* (1589), p. 173.
22. Demetrius, *On Style*, 270.
23. Baldassare Castiglione, *The Book of the Courtier*, trans. Thomas Hoby, ed. Virginia Cox (London: Everyman, 1994), p. 360.
24. *1 Henry IV*, 5.4.83–7.
25. On aposiopesis and death in *Hamlet* see Michael Neill, *Issues of Death: Mortality and Identity in English Renaissance Tragedy* (Oxford: Oxford University Press, 1997). *Antony and Cleopatra* is another play in which Shakespeare uses the figure for his protagonists' deaths.
26. Samuel Shaw, *Words Made Visible: Or Grammar and Rhetorick Accommodated to the Lives and Manners of Men* (1678–9), pp. 98–9.
27. *Ibid.*, pp. 156–7, 114–15.

1 SYNONYMIA: OR, IN OTHER WORDS

For their comments and suggestions during the preparation of this chapter, I am grateful to Gavin Alexander, Anthea Fraser Gupta, Jane Hodson, Goran Stanivukovic and John Woolford.

1. Henry Peacham, *The Garden of Eloquence* (1577), sig. P4r–v [editorial layout].
2. Quintilian, *Institutio oratoria*, 9.3.47 recognises both lexical synonymia and synonymia of thought.
3. On the vices of style, see William Poole's chapter in this volume.
4. For a (consciously polemical) overview of both traditions, see Brian Vickers, *In Defence of Rhetoric* (Oxford: Clarendon Press, 1988), pp. 435–79.
5. Ruth Rendell, *The Babes in the Wood* (London: Random House, 2003), pp. 43, 45.
6. In Scaliger's *Poetices libri septem* (Lyon, 1561), synonymia is 'the opposite of tautologia' because it 'gives variety'. The relevant passage is quoted by Lee Sonnino, *A Handbook to Sixteenth-Century Rhetoric* (London: Routledge and Kegan Paul, 1968), pp. 116–17.
7. *2 Henry IV*, 3.2.96–8; 5.1.4–6. All quotations from Shakespeare are from G. Blakemore Evans (ed.), *The Riverside Shakespeare* (Boston: Houghton Mifflin, 1974).
8. Graham Chapman *et al.*, *Monty Python's Flying Circus: Just the Words*, 2 vols. (London: Methuen, 1989), vol. 1, p. 105.
9. *Rhetorica ad Herennium*, 4.28.38; Quintilian, *Institutio oratoria*, 8.4.27.
10. F. W. Bateson, *English Poetry and the English Language*, 3rd edn (Oxford: Clarendon Press, 1973), chapter 2. First published in 1934.
11. *Ibid.*, p. 30.
12. *Ibid.*, p. 51. The passage is *The Faerie Queene*, 2.8.5.1–4.

13. C. S. Lewis, 'Variation in Shakespeare and Others', in *Selected Literary Essays*, ed. Walter Hooper (Cambridge: Cambridge University Press, 1969), p. 87. The essay was first published in 1939.
14. *Richard II*, 2.1.33–7, *Hamlet*, 1.2.133–7; in Lewis, pp. 82–3.
15. *Ibid.*, pp. 82, 87, 75–6.
16. Desiderius Erasmus, *De copia*, in *Literary and Educational Writings 2*, ed. Craig R. Thompson, Collected Works of Erasmus, 24 (Toronto: University of Toronto Press, 1978), p. 303 [hereafter *CWE*]; Vickers, *In Defence of Rhetoric*, p. 258.
17. Notably in the works by Baldwin, Joseph, Kennedy, Skinner and Vickers listed in this volume's 'Suggestions for further reading'.
18. J. W. Binns, *Intellectual Culture in Elizabethan and Jacobean England* (Leeds: Francis Cairns, 1990), p. 3.
19. See J. B. Altman, *The Tudor Play of Mind: Rhetorical Inquiry and the Development of Elizabethan Drama* (Berkeley and London: University of California Press, 1978).
20. See Ian Donaldson's chapter in this volume.
21. See R. W. Serjeantson's chapter in this volume.
22. *Love's Labour's Lost*, 4.2.3–7 (my italics).
23. John Hoskins, *Directions for Speech and Style*, ed. Hoyt H. Hudson (Princeton: Princeton University Press, 1935) p. 24.
24. Veltkirchius, quoted in T. W. Baldwin, *William Shakespere's Small Latine and Lesse Greeke*, 2 vols. (Urbana: University of Illinois Press, 1944), vol. 1, p. 185.
25. A concise account of these developments is offered in the preface to the *CWE* edition.
26. Erasmus, *On Copia of Words and Ideas*, ed. Donald B. King and H. David Rix (Milwaukee: Marquette University Press, 1963), p. 17 (hereafter K and R).
27. For an account of the printing history of John of Garland's text and of Erasmus's hostility towards its author, see R. H. Schram, 'John of Garland and Erasmus on the Principle of Synonymy', *University of Texas Studies in English* 30 (1951), pp. 24–39.
28. *CWE*, p. 285.
29. K and R, p. 20. Echoing Quintilian, *Institutio oratoria*, 10.1.5–9. To compare the categories distinguished by modern scholars, see Roy Harris, *Synonymy and Linguistic Analysis* (Oxford: Basil Blackwell, 1973) pp. 14–15.
30. K and R, p. 24.
31. Veltkirchius, as quoted in Baldwin, *Small Latin*, vol. 1, pp. 177–8.
32. K and R, p. 38.
33. Joshua Poole, *Practical Rhetorick* (1663), p. 170.
34. Ian Michael, *The Teaching of English From the Sixteenth Century to 1870* (Cambridge: Cambridge University Press, 1987), p. 275.
35. K and R, p. 16.
36. Lewis, p. 80.
37. K and R, pp. 16–17; Quintilian 10.5.9.
38. For an excellent brief account see Elaine Sisman, 'Variations', in L. Macy (ed.), *Grove Music Online*, www.grovemusic.com. For a discussion of 'varying'

as a literary aesthetic, see Sylvia Adamson, 'Literary language', in Roger Lass (ed.), *The Cambridge History of the English Language, Volume III, 1476–1776* (Cambridge: Cambridge University Press, 1999), pp. 549–70.

39. Henry Peacham, *The Garden of Eloquence* (1593), ed. W. G. Crane (Gainesville: Scholars' Facsimiles and Reprints, 1954), pp. 149–50.
40. See p. 73.
41. George Puttenham, *The Arte of English Poesie* (1589), ed. Gladys Willcock and Alice Walker (Cambridge: Cambridge University Press, 1936), p. 196.
42. The latter suggestion is confirmed by the general pattern of Peacham's revisions noted by Crane in Peacham, *Garden* (1593), p. 10; he weeds out of his garden many figures based on orthographical and syntactic patterning.
43. Hoskins, *Directions*, pp. 2–3, 24–5.
44. *Ibid.*, p. 24.
45. *Ibid.*, p. 22.
46. See pp. 20, 48, 68–9.
47. John Locke, *An Essay Concerning Humane Understanding* (1690), 2.11.2.
48. *Ad Herennium*, 4.28.38. It is unfortunately beyond the scope and word-limits of this chapter to discuss the questions raised by this passage and by its relation to Quintilian's use of the terms *interpretatio* and *synonimia*.
49. For discussion of these difficulties, see Harris, *Synonymy*, chapter 1; D. A. Cruse, *Lexical Semantics* (Cambridge: Cambridge University Press, 1986), pp. 265–8; S. Tanskanen, *Collaborating Towards Coherence* (Amsterdam: John Benjamins, 2006).
50. Matthew 21: 1–7 (*King James Bible*).
51. Matthew 21: 4–5, referring to Zechariah 9:9.
52. Peacham, *Garden* (1577), sig. p4v (my italics).
53. For the relevant figures, see P. Pahta and S. Nevanlinna, 'On Markers of Expository Apposition', *NOWELE* 39 (2001), pp. 3–51.
54. Sisman attributes the first example to Frescobaldi and 1627 ('Variations').
55. Francis Bacon, 'Of Truth', in *The Essayes or Counsels* (1625), p. 2.
56. *Macbeth*, 3.4.20–4.
57. Simon Palfrey, *Doing Shakespeare* (London: Arden Shakespeare, 2005), p. 131.

2 COMPAR OR PARISON: MEASURE FOR MEASURE

1. Richard Lanham, *The Motives of Eloquence* (New Haven: Yale University Press, 1976), p. 1. To begin with this principle is not to ignore the counter-tradition of the 'art that conceals art'; for the most part, however, such apparent artlessness was itself a means of artistic self-display.
2. Henry Peacham, *The Garden of Eloquence* (1593), p. 58.
3. R. Warwick Bond (ed.), *The Complete Works of John Lyly*, 3 vols. (Oxford: Clarendon Press, 1902), vol. 1, p. 184.
4. Marvin Spevack (ed.), *Julius Caesar*, New Cambridge Shakespeare (Cambridge: Cambridge University Press, 1988). On this speech see above, Introduction, pp. 8–9.
5. Quintilian, *Institutio oratoria*, 9.3.75.

6. George Puttenham, *The Arte of English Poesie*, ed. Baxter Hathaway (Kent, Ohio: Kent State University Press, 1970), p. 222.

7. Brian Vickers, *Francis Bacon and Renaissance Prose* (Cambridge: Cambridge University Press, 1968), p. 96.

8. See, for example, Puttenham, *The Arte of English Poesie*, p. 19, and Philip Sidney, *The Defence of Poesy*, in Gavin Alexander (ed.), *Sidney's 'The Defence of Poesy' and Selected Renaissance Literary Criticism* (London: Penguin, 2004), pp. 8–9.

9. Peacham, *The Garden of Eloquence*, sig. 'AB'2v.

10. Puttenham, *The Arte of English Poesie*, p. 312.

11. Christy Anderson, 'Learning to Read Architecture in the English Renaissance', in Lucy Gent (ed.), *Albion's Classicism* (New Haven: Yale University Press, 1995), p. 251.

12. Henry Wotton, *Elements of Architecture* (1624), pp. 20–1.

13. Heinrich Lausberg, *Handbook of Literary Rhetoric: A Foundation for Literary Study*, ed. David E. Orton and R. Dean Anderson (Leiden: Brill, 1998), p. 417.

14. John Shute, *The First and Chief Groundes of Architecture*, fol. 4r.

15. *Ibid.*, sig. A2r.

16. Quintilian, *Institutio oratoria*, 9.3.76.

17. Peacham, *The Garden of Eloquence*, p. 54.

18. John Hoskins, *Directions for Speech and Style*, ed. Hoyt H. Hudson (Princeton: Princeton University Press, 1935), pp. 37–8 [editorial italics]. In debating terminology it is worth remembering that the Renaissance rhetoricians were by no means consistent in the naming of figures. For example, Hoskins refers to a sentence with similar words at the end of each clause as illustrating *similiter cadens*, where the ancients would have reserved that term for words with similar case endings.

19. Cf. Sylvia Adamson's chapter on synonymia in this volume.

20. Peacham, *The Garden of Eloquence*, p. 59.

21. Edmund Spenser, *The Faerie Queene*, ed. J. C. Smith, 2 vols. (Oxford: Clarendon Press, 1909), 1.4.29.

22. Andrew Gurr (ed.), *Richard II*, New Cambridge Shakespeare (Cambridge: Cambridge University Press, 2003), 4.1.203–14.

23. Thomas Kyd, *The Spanish Tragedy*, ed. Philip Edwards (London: Methuen, 1959), 2.2.24–31.

24. As Jonas Barish has pointed out, Kyd's flagrant pleasure in rhetoric represents a mature, sophisticated attitude compared, for example, to that of the author of *The Rare Triumphs of Love and Fortune*, and other such 'naïve' drama. See '*The Spanish Tragedy*, or The Pleasures and Perils of Rhetoric', in John Russell Brown and Bernard Harris (eds.), *Elizabethan Theatre* (London: Edward Arnold, 1966), 59–85 (pp. 72–4).

25. Puttenham, *The Arte of English Poesie*, p. 104.

26. Francis Bacon, *The Advancement of Learning* and *New Atlantis*, ed. Arthur Johnston (Oxford: Clarendon Press, 1974), p. 26.

27. G. C. Moore Smith (ed.), *Gabriel Harvey's Marginalia* (Stratford-upon-Avon: Shakespeare Head Press, 1913), p. 115.

28. Albert Feuillerat, *John Lyly: Contribution a l'histoire de la renaissance en Angleterre* (New York: Russell and Russell, 1910), p. 450.

29. T. W. Baldwin, *William Shakespere's Small Latine and Lesse Greeke*, 2 vols. (Urbana: University of Illinois Press, 1944), vol. I, p. 274.

30. See especially Vickers's chapter, 'Syntactical symmetry', in *Francis Bacon and Renaissance Prose*, pp. 96–140. It is noteworthy, moreover, that in the indictment of Ascham cited above, Bacon permits himself a lengthy and fairly glittering series of parallel phrases.

31. Roger Ascham, *Toxophilus, The Schole of Shootinge* (1545), p. 7.

32. Alvin Vos, 'Form and Function in Roger Ascham's Prose', *Studies in Philology* 55 (1976), 305–22 (309).

33. The phrase is that of Thomas Greene, 'Roger Ascham: The Perfect End of Shooting', *ELH* 36 (1969), 609–25 (624).

34. Ascham, *Toxophilus*, p. 16.

35. 'Roger Ascham: The Perfect End of Shooting', 616.

36. Thomas Elyot, *The Boke Named the Governour* (1580), pp. 64–5.

37. David Norbrook, 'Rhetoric, Ideology, and the Elizabethan World Picture', in Peter Mack (ed.), *Renaissance Rhetoric* (London: St Martin's, 1994), pp. 140–64 (p. 141).

38. Janel Mueller, *The Native Tongue and the Word: Developments in English Prose Style, 1380–1580* (Chicago: University of Chicago Press, 1984), p. 337.

39. *The New York Times*, 8 January 2006: Section 2, p. 35. In a longer version of this essay, I hope to look more closely at writers who themselves undertook building projects, notably Mary Sidney Herbert at Houghton Conquest.

40. *The Elements of Geometry*, tr. H. Billingsley (1570), sig. d4r.

41. Wotton, *Elements of Architecture* (1624), p. 53.

42. Shute, *The First and Chief Groundes of Architecture*, fol. 3r.

43. Eric Mercer, *English Art 1553–1625* (Oxford: Clarendon Press, 1962), p. 39.

44. David Evett, *Literature and the Visual Arts in Tudor England* (Athens: University of Georgia Press, 1990), p. 210.

45. John Summerson, *English Architecture, 1530–1830* (New Haven: Yale University Press, 1953), p. 61. My description of the appearance of Longleat refers to its third remodelling, overseen by Robert Smythson and influenced certainly by his work in London on William Cecil's Somerset House in the Strand.

46. William Alexander McClung, *The Country House in English Renaissance Poetry* (Berkeley: University of California Press, 1977), p. 58.

47. Illustrated in Paula Henderson, *The Tudor House and Garden* (New Haven: Yale University Press, 2005), p. 24.

48. Mark Girouard, *Robert Smythson and the Elizabethan Country House* (New Haven: Yale University Press, 1983), p. 32.

49. Henderson, *The Tudor House and Garden*, p. 26.

50. Quoted in Emily Sophia Hartshorne, *Memorials of Holdenby* (London, 1868), pp. 15–16.

51. 'At Longleat . . . the right-angle of the corner of the house juts out between the right angles of the bay windows to either side – leading to a three-dimensional

effect of stepping, or receding right angles, which is exceedingly effective' (Girouard, *Robert Smythson and the Elizabethan Country House*, p. 72).

52. Henderson, *The Tudor House and Garden*, p. 19.

53. Andrew Boorde, *A Compendyous Regyment or a Dyetary of Helth* (1542), p. 238.

54. Roger Ascham, *The Schoolemaster*, ed. Lawrence V. Ryan (Charlottesville: The University Press of Virginia, 1967), pp. 110–11.

55. Jonas Barish, *Ben Jonson and the Language of Prose Comedy* (New York: W. W. Norton, 1970), p. 48.

56. Evett, *Literature and the Visual Arts in Tudor England*, p. 204.

57. Vickers, *Francis Bacon and Renaissance Prose*, p. 115.

3 PERIODOS: SQUARING THE CIRCLE

I am grateful to the late Master, Professor Malcolm Bowie, and to the Fellows of Christ's College, Cambridge, for appointing me a distinguished visiting scholar in 2005–6 and thereby enabling the work that appears here. Special thanks to Gavin Alexander and Katrin Ettenhuber, Fellows in English, and to Professor David Sedley, Fellow in Classics, for their colleagueship and assistance. I am indebted to Professor Sylvia Adamson of the University of Sheffield for timely encouragement and invaluable editorial intervention.

1. Aristotle, *Rhetoric*, 3.9.2–3.

2. *Ibid.*, 3.9.3.

3. Aristotle does, however, note in passing a 'simple period that consists of only one clause' (*Rhetoric*, 3.9.5) but does not elaborate. This remark seems aimed at acknowledging the linguistic fact of simple sentences while implying that the artful composition associated with periodos requires larger, more complex sentences.

4. *Ibid.*, 3.9.6.

5. Demetrius, *On Style*, 11.

6. Quintilian, *Institutio oratoria*, 9.4.22–3, 32.

7. *Ibid.*, 9.4.122–3.

8. *Ibid.*, 9.4.123. Quintilian is here developing Cicero's allusion to the 'joints and limbs' of composition (*De oratore*, 3.43.171–48.186). Cicero's alternative images for proper periodic construction are the pitched frontal of a temple pediment, for a sentence with two members and a marked 'turn', and a leafy, branching tree, for a sentence with more than two members (3.46.179–80).

9. Quintilian, *Institutio oratoria*, 9.4.122–3. Contrast the *Rhetorica ad Herennium* 4.19.27, long ascribed to Cicero, in which the preferred synonym for periodos is *continuatio* and this markedly different definition is offered: 'A period is a close-packed and uninterrupted group of words embracing a complete thought.' The *Rhetorica ad Herennium*, importantly, classifies periodos as a figure of speech or scheme.

10. Quintilian, *Institutio oratoria*, 9.4.128–30.

11. I excerpt and summarise the Latin in *Joannis Lodovici Vivis Valentini de ratione dicendi libri III* (Cologne, 1537), pp. 59–60. The colophon records the completion of the work at Bruges in 1532. Other editions of *De ratione dicendi* appeared at Louvain in 1533, and at Basel in 1536 and 1555. In later editions, the discussions of periodos and *ordo* occur in chapters 7 and 8, respectively, of Book 1.

12. Cf. Russ McDonald's chapter on compar in this volume.

13. Vives, *De ratione dicendi*, pp. 59–60, 61–2. The assemblage of pronouncements by Aristotle, Cicero, Alexander, and George of Trebizond on periodos, *cola*, and *commata* in Book 4, ch. 25 of Julius Caesar Scaliger's *Poetices Libri Septem* (Lyons, 1561, pp. 196–8) does not challenge the singularity of Vives' probing reflections. Scaliger's interests lie chiefly in the taxonomy of types and components of periodic sentence composition, although he does grant it pride of place in his catalogue of figures of speech that 'adorn language and heighten the effectiveness of a rhetor's utterance'.

14. [Edward Hall], *The Union of the Two Noble and Illustre Famelies of Lancastre and Yorke* (1548), excerpted in Karl Julius Holzknecht, *Sixteenth-Century English Prose* (New York: Harper, 1954), p. 132. For a concise listing of the principal syntactic resources of periodic composition in English, see Sylvia Adamson, 'Literary Style', in *The Cambridge History of the English Language III, 1476–1776*, ed. Roger Lass (Cambridge University Press, 1999), p. 586. For an account of the humanist system of punctuation used in the examples in this chapter, see Malcolm Parkes, *Pause and Effect: An Introduction to the History of Punctuation in the West* (Aldershot: Scolar Press, 1992), pp. 81–91.

15. Raphael Holinshed, *Chronicles of England, Scotlande, and Irelande*, 2nd edn (1586), excerpted in Holzknecht, *Sixteenth-Century English Prose*, p. 324.

16. Francis Bacon, *The Advancement of Learning*, Book 1, ch. 4, section 2, in *Advancement of Learning and New Atlantis*, ed. Arthur Johnston (Oxford: Clarendon Press, 1974; rpt. 1988), p. 26.

17. *Ibid.*, Book 2, ch. 14, section 12, 'De analogia demonstrationum'. The Aristotle reference is to the *Prior Analytics*, 2.5.

18. A voluminous literature has existed for some time on the impact of Ramistic thought in England generally and on Bacon's mixed response to it. See W. S. Howell, *Logic and Rhetoric in England, 1500–1700* (Princeton: Princeton University Press, 1956), pp. 247–317, 364–75, and references given at p. 146 n.

19. Bacon, *Advancement*, Book 2, ch. 17, section 2.

20. *Ibid.*, sections 2, 7.

21. The motive and implications of Bacon's opposition of magistral and probational method have been much discussed, but, as far as I am aware, the identification of the magistral with the periodic sentence has not been made before. See, further, Karl R. Wallace, *Francis Bacon on Communication and Rhetoric* (Chapel Hill: University of North Carolina Press, 1943); Brian Vickers, *Francis Bacon and Renaissance Prose* (Cambridge: Cambridge University Press, 1968), pp. 116–19, who lays a positive emphasis of his own on Bacon's 'syntactical

symmetry'; and Lisa Jardine, *Francis Bacon: Discovery and the Art of Discourse* (Cambridge: Cambridge University Press, 1974), pp. 174–8.

22. On 'clausal spread' as a defining feature of 'authoritative' prose style, see Janel M. Mueller, *The Native Tongue and the Word: Syntax and Style in English Prose, 1380–1580* (Chicago: University of Chicago Press, 1984), pp. 203–4.

23. Bacon, *Advancement*, Book 2, ch. 17, section 7.

24. On Cranmer's collects, see Mueller, *The Native Tongue and the Word*, pp. 226–43.

25. John Donne, *Sermons*, ed. George R. Potter and Evelyn M. Simpson (Berkeley and Los Angeles: University of California Press, 1953–62), vol. VI, p. 172.

26. Aphoristic effect, in this instance, can equally well be analysed in terms of 'sense parallelism', a powerful stylistic resource, Semitic in origins, that transposes effectively into other languages and is a conspicuous mode of biblical expression. See Mueller, *The Native Tongue and the Word*, pp. 34–35.

27. Thomas Farnaby's *Index rhetoricus* (1625), pp. 17–19, continued to circulate in a highly popular distilled form – 10 editions before the end of the century – instructions on periodic sentence composition from classical sources (Aristotle, Cicero) and Renaissance authorities (Sturm, Scaliger, Keckermann, Soarez). Significantly, Farnaby makes no mention of the turn or the circuit. He highlights two-membered periods, describing one of their possible modes of relation as that of *protasis-apodosis*, or the 'if–then' relation of formal logical entailment.

28. Two representative, later seventeenth-century treatises that eliminate any mention of a circuit from their discussions of periodic sentence composition are [Thomas Hobbes], *A Compendium of the Art of Logick and Rhetorick in the English Tongue* (1651), pp. 257–8; and [Bernard Lamy], *The Art of Speaking: written in French by Messieurs du Port Royal: In pursuance of a former Treatise, Intituled, The Art of Thinking. Rendered into English* (1676), pp. 134 [for 150]–138 [for 154].

29. Ben Jonson, *Timber: or Discoveries* (publ. 1641), in C. H. Herford, and Percy and Evelyn Simpson (eds.), *Ben Jonson*, 11 vols. (Oxford: Clarendon Press, 1925–52), vol. VIII, pp. 620–1. The editors date Jonson's composition of this text to the period 1628–35.

30. *Ibid.*, p. 623.

31. Vives, *De ratione dicendi*, p. 61.

32. Jonson, *Timber*, 626, 628.

33. See, respectively, Thomas N. Corns, *The Development of Milton's Prose Style* (Oxford: Clarendon Press, 1982), pp. 39–41; and Martine Watson Brownley, *Clarendon and the Rhetoric of Historical Form* (Philadelphia: University of Pennsylvania Press, 1983), pp. 45–6.

4 PUNS: SERIOUS WORDPLAY

I am grateful to the editors of the *Cambridge Quarterly*, in whose journal a section of this chapter appeared in an earlier form.

1. Joseph Addison, *Spectator*, ed. Donald F. Bond, 5 vols. (Oxford: Clarendon Press, 1965), vol. 1, p. 260 (no. 61, 10 May 1711).

2. The term 'pun' is in itself almost infinitely slippery, as Walter Redfern concludes in one of the few monographs on the subject: 'punning overspills any boundaries placed around it'. *Puns*, 2nd edn (Oxford: Blackwell, 2000), p. 96.

3. [John Taylor], *Mercurius Aquaticus* (Oxford, 1643 [1644]), quoted in Catherine Bates, 'The Point of Puns', *Modern Philology* 96 (1999), 421–38 (425–6 n.).

4. Sister Miriam Joseph, in her classic study *Shakespeare's Use of the Arts of Language* (New York: Columbia University Press, 1947), identifies a fourth, asteismus, 'a figure of reply in which the answerer catches a certain word and throws it back to the first speaker with an unexpected twist, an unlooked for meaning' (p. 167). This discussion will, for simplicity's sake, confine itself to the other three devices.

5. It is possible to find licence for the use of syllepsis in this sense in contemporary rhetorical handbooks. George Puttenham calls it the figure of 'double Supplie', and gives as one of his examples a play on the word 'requite': 'Where ye see this word [*requite*] serve a double sence: that is to say, to revenge, and to satisfie.' (Gladys Doidge Willcock and Alice Walker (eds.), *The Arte of English Poesie* (Cambridge: Cambridge University Press, 1936; repr. 1970), p. 165.) Angel Day, too, allows this understanding – 'when one verb supplieth two clauses, one person two rooms, or one word serveth to many sences' – though the two examples he gives are both of the first type he mentions, a grammatical turn that is closely related to zeugma. (*A Declaration of . . . Tropes, Figures or Schemes* (1592), p. 87.) This slightly more restrictive definition, whereby one word (a verb or preposition) governs two others in different senses, seems in fact to have been the prevailing one in the period, and a popular one thereafter: see, for example, J. A. Cuddon, *The Penguin Dictionary of Literary Terms and Literary Theory* (Harmondsworth: Penguin, 1992), p. 938. Its effect is the smart sort of pun of which Alexander Pope was particularly fond, as these instances from *The Rape of the Lock* (1714) demonstrate: 'Or stain her Honour, or her new Brocade' (II.107); 'Or lose her Heart, or Necklace, at a Ball' (II.109); 'Here Thou, Great *Anna*! whom three Realms obey, | Dost sometimes counsel take – and sometimes *Tea*' (III.7–8). John Butt (ed.), *The Poems of Alexander Pope* (London: Routledge, 1963), pp. 225, 227.

6. *Mr William Shakespeares Comedies, Histories, and Tragedies* (1623), facsimile reprint (London: Routledge, 1997), Act 5, scene 2; all subsequent references are to this edition, and will be given in the form (5.2) in parentheses in the text (the first folio is unlineated). Where this edition misses out act and scene divisions, these will be supplied in square brackets from the Riverside edition (Boston: Houghton Mifflin, 1974).

7. Stephen Booth, 'Shakespeare's Language and the Language of Shakespeare's Time', *Shakespeare Survey* 50 (1997), pp. 1–17 (12).

8. Henry Peacham, *The Garden of Eloquence* (1593), p. 57.

9. XCVI. *Sermons by the Right Honourable and Reverend Father in God, Lancelot Andrewes, Late Lord Bishop of Winchester* (1629), p. 204. Subsequent references are to this edition, and the page numbers will appear in parentheses in the text.

10. Peacham, *Garden of Eloquence*, p. 56.
11. Andrewes, *XCVI. Sermons*, p. 146.
12. Robert South, *Sermons Preached Upon Several Occasions*, 5 vols. (Oxford: Oxford University Press, 1842), vol. III, p. 359.
13. See 'Lancelot Andrewes' (1926), in T. S. Eliot, *For Lancelot Andrewes: Essays on Style and Order* (London: Faber and Gwyer, 1928), pp. 13–32 (p. 14).
14. Samuel Johnson, *Preface to Shakespeare's Plays, 1765*, facsimile edn (Menston: Scolar Press, 1969), pp. xxiii–xxiv.
15. Molly Mahood, *Shakespeare's Wordplay* (London: Methuen, 1957), p. 9.
16. Johnson, *Preface*, p. xxiii.
17. Kenneth Muir, 'The Uncomic Pun', *Cambridge Journal* 3 (1950), 472–85 (484).
18. Sylvia Adamson, 'Literary Language', in Roger Lass (ed.), *The Cambridge History of the English Language Vol. 3, 1476–1776* (Cambridge: Cambridge University Press, 1999), pp. 539–653 (p. 610).
19. Thomas Sprat, *The History of the Royal-Society of London for the Improving of Natural Knowledge* (1667), p. 113.
20. Puttenham, *Arte of English Poesie*, p. 207. His alternative name for the figure is 'the Rebounde'.
21. Andrewes, *XCVI. Sermons*, p. 232.
22. Compare the levels of awareness as Leontes is given the same pun in *The Winter's Tale* (1.2): 'Goe play (Boy) play; thy Mother playes, and I | Play too'. The theatricality of the situation is acknowledged, the fissures emphasised, in a way that would be impossible for Andrewes.
23. Andrewes, *XCVI. Sermons*, p. 232.
24. *Ibid.*, p. 46.
25. Peter McCullough (ed.), *Lancelot Andrewes: Selected Sermons and Lectures* (Oxford: Oxford University Press, 2005), p. xxvi.
26. Andrewes, *XCVI. Sermons*, p. 15.
27. *Ibid.*, p. 48.
28. *Ibid.*, p. 112.
29. On the vices of style see William Poole's essay in this volume.
30. Mahood, *Shakespeare's Wordplay*, p. 170.
31. Muir, 'The Uncomic Pun', 474.
32. E. E. Kellett, 'Some Notes on a Feature of Shakspere's Style', in *Suggestions: Literary Essays* (Cambridge: Cambridge University Press, 1923), pp. 57–78 (p. 74).
33. See *OED*, 'red' *a.* and *n.*, senses 3a and 3b.
34. T. Hawkes (ed.), *Coleridge on Shakespeare* (Harmondsworth: Penguin, 1969), pp. 175, 250.
35. *Carry On Cleo*, dir. Gerald Thomas (1964).
36. Russ Mcdonald, *Shakespeare and the Arts of Language* (Oxford: Oxford University Press, 2001), p. 150.
37. Peacham, *Garden of Eloquence*, 'Epistle Dedicatory'. For an account of the division between civic and religious rhetoric, see Quentin Skinner, *Reason and Rhetoric in the Philosophy of Hobbes* (Cambridge: Cambridge University Press, 1996), pp. 66–8.

38. Adamson, 'Literary Language', p. 555.
39. Kellett, 'Some Notes on a Feature of Shakespeare's Style', p. 67.

5 PROSOPOPOEIA: THE SPEAKING FIGURE

1. Sir Philip Sidney, *The Defence of Poesy* (*c.* 1580), in Gavin Alexander (ed.), *Sidney's 'The Defence of Poesy' and Selected Renaissance Literary Criticism* (London: Penguin, 2004), p. 14.
2. Richard Rainolde, *The Foundacion of Rhetorike* (1563), sig. N2v. This was the first English version of the progymnasmata.
3. Quintilian, *Institutio oratoria*, 3.8.50–1.
4. The figure is classified as a figure of thought; Latin names for it include *conformatio*, *fictio personae* and *sermocinatio*.
5. Quintilian, *Institutio oratoria*, 1.8.3.
6. *Ibid.*, 9.2.31–2 ('Nam certe sermo fingi non potest, ut non personae sermo fingatur'). Though I follow Russell's 2001 translation elsewhere, in this passage I use the translation in the earlier Loeb edition of H. E. Butler (4 vols., 1920–2), which makes better sense of the Latin.
7. Aphthonius calls the speech in character *ethopoeia*, and distinguishes three sub-categories: *ethopoeia* proper, where a character (*ēthos*) is imagined for a person (such as Hercules) already known; *eidolopoeia*, where both person and character are known (as when we represent the voice of someone dead); and *prosopopoeia*, where 'everything is made' ['quando finguntur omnia et mores et personae']: Aphthonius, *Progymnasmata* (1572), sig. Y8v.
8. For further detail on etymology and the early theory of the figure see ch. 1 of James J. Paxson, *The Poetics of Personification* (Cambridge: Cambridge University Press, 1994).
9. Henry George Liddell, Robert Scott, *et al.* (eds.), *Greek–English Lexicon* (Oxford: Clarendon Press, 1996), *prosōpon* and *ēthos*.
10. Aristotle, *Poetics*, 1450b
11. Aristotle, *Rhetoric*, 1.2.3–5.
12. *Ibid.*, 2.1.3.
13. *Ibid.*, 3.7.4.
14. Thomas Wright, *The Passions of the Minde in Generall* (1604), sigs. M6v–7r.
15. Quintilian, *Institutio oratoria*, 6.2.26–28. For another English version of this topos cf. Thomas Wilson, *The Arte of Rhetorique* (1553), in Brian Vickers (ed.), *English Renaissance Literary Criticism* (Oxford: Clarendon Press, 1999), p. 118.
16. Cicero, *De oratore*, 2.45.189.
17. *Ibid.*, 2.45.191.
18. *Ibid.*, 2.45.193
19. *Ibid.*, 2.47.194.
20. Quintilian, *Institutio oratoria*, 6.2.29.
21. See Charlton Thomas Lewis, Charles Short, and E. A. Andrews (eds.), *A Latin Dictionary* (Oxford: Clarendon Press, 1969), *persona*, B.1 and 2.
22. Quintilian, *Institutio oratoria*, 10.5.2.

23. *Poetics*, 1448a, in the translation in D. A. Russell and M. Winterbottom (eds.), *Ancient Literary Criticism: The Principal Texts in New Translations* (Oxford: Clarendon Press, 1972); cf. Plato, *Republic*, 393–4.

24. Longinus, *On the Sublime*, 27.1

25. Plato, *Republic*, 395.

26. Abraham Fraunce, *The Arcadian Rhetorike* (1588), sig. G2r.

27. Desiderius Erasmus, *Literary and Educational Writings 2*: *De Copia and De Ratione Studii*, ed. Craig R. Thompson, Collected Works of Erasmus, 24 (Toronto: University of Toronto Press, 1978), pp. 577–89.

28. *Ibid.*, pp. 588–9.

29. Joannes Susenbrotus, *Epitome troporum ac schematum et grammaticorum et rhetorum* (1562), sigs. F4v–F6r (the first English printing); Richard Sherry, *A Treatise of Schemes and Tropes* (1550), sigs. E1v–E3r.

30. *The Art of English Poesy* (1589), in Alexander (ed.), *Selected Renaissance Literary Criticism*, pp. 182–4.

31. Fraunce, *The Arcadian Rhetorike*, sigs. G3v–G4r; taken from manuscript, his text corresponds to Sir Philip Sidney, *The Countess of Pembroke's Arcadia: The Old Arcadia*, ed. Jean Robertson (Oxford: Clarendon Press, 1973), pp. 39–40.

32. Fraunce, *The Arcadian Rhetorike*, sig. G2v.

33. Published in *Complaints* (1591). For a modern edition see Edmund Spenser, *The Shorter Poems*, ed. Richard A. McCabe (London: Penguin, 1999).

34. The classic account here remains Stephen J. Greenblatt, *Renaissance Self-Fashioning: From More to Shakespeare* (Chicago: University of Chicago Press, 1980).

35. Edmund Spenser, *The Faerie Queene*, ed. Thomas P. Roche (Harmondsworth: Penguin, 1978), p. 15.

36. See Alexander (ed.), *Sidney's 'The Defence of Poesy' and Selected Renaissance Literary Criticism*, Introduction, esp. pp. lviii–lxii, and the text of Sidney's *Defence*, passim.

37. On the disguising of vice see further Quentin Skinner's chapter in this volume.

38. *Paradise Lost*, 9.553–63, in Stephen Orgel and Jonathan Goldberg (eds.), *John Milton*, The Oxford Authors (Oxford: Oxford University Press, 1991).

39. J. A. Simpson and E. S. C. Weiner (eds.), *The Oxford English Dictionary*, 2nd edn, 20 vols. (Oxford: Clarendon Press, 1989), subtle, †10.

40. Fraunce, *The Arcadian Rhetorike*, sig. G2r.

41. 'Direccions for Speech and Style', in Louise Brown Osborn, *The Life, Letters and Writings of John Hoskyns, 1566–1638* (New Haven: Yale University Press, 1937), p. 162. Fraunce, *The Arcadian Rhetorike*, sig. F7v. In this, as in most of his treatise (though not the examples), Fraunce follows the *Rhetorica* (1548) of Audomarus Talaeus. Cf. the earlier English digest of Talaeus in Dudley Fenner, *The Artes of Logike and Rhethorike* ([Middelburgh], 1584).

42. 'Direccions for Speech and Style', p. 163.

43. See Paul de Man, 'Autobiography as De-Facement', *Modern Language Notes* 94 (1979), 919–30: 'the figure of prosopopeia, the fiction of an apostrophe to an absent, deceased, or voiceless entity, which posits the possibility of the

latter's reply and confers upon it the power of speech' (926). De Man develops these ideas further in 'Hypogram and Inscription', in *The Resistance to Theory* (Minneapolis: University of Minnesota Press, 1986), pp. 27–53; first printed as 'Hypogram and Inscription: Michael Riffaterre's Poetics of Reading', *Diacritics* 11 (1981), 17–35. They are taken up in a number of pieces by J. Hillis Miller, including 'Prosopopoeia and *Praeterita*', in Laurence Lockridge, John Maynard, and Donald D. Stone (eds.), *Nineteenth-Century Lives* (Cambridge: Cambridge University Press, 1989), pp. 125–39. For an important response to de Man see Michael Riffaterre, 'Prosopopoeia', *Yale French Studies* 69 (1985), 107–23.

44. Text from William A. Ringler, Jr (ed.), *The Poems of Sir Philip Sidney* (Oxford: Clarendon Press, 1962).

45. *Othello*, 4.3.28–51, in G. Blakemore Evans (ed.), *The Riverside Shakespeare* (Boston: Houghton Mifflin, 1974). Barbary's song is mentioned in passing in the first quarto edition of 1622, but the singing of it is found only in the Folio text of 1623. The portions in quotation marks here are italicised in the Folio text.

46. It is notable too that they may have adapted a song that in other versions describes a jilted *male* lover. See Ross W. Duffin, *Shakespeare's Songbook* (New York and London: W. W. Norton, 2004), pp. 467–70.

47. For the connection between solo song and prosopopoeia, see the younger Henry Peacham's *The Compleat Gentleman* (1622): 'Yea, in my opinion no rhetoric more persuadeth or hath greater power over the mind; nay, hath not music her figures, the same which rhetoric? What is a revert but her antistrophe? her reports, but sweet anaphoras? her counterchange of points, antimetaboles? her passionate airs, but *prosopopoeia*s? with infinite other of the same nature?' (Oliver Strunk, Leo Treitler, and Gary Tomlinson (eds.), *Source Readings in Music History: The Renaissance* (New York and London: Norton, 1998), p. 73). On the figures and music see further Brian Vickers, 'Figures of Rhetoric/Figures of Music?', *Rhetorica* 2 (1984), 1–44.

48. Cf. Samuel Shaw's play *Words Made Visible: Or Grammar and Rhetorick Accommodated to the Lives and Manners of Men* (1678–9), where the personified figure itself declares its ability to 'raise the dead as familiarly as any *Conjurer*' (p. 171).

49. *Julius Caesar*, 3.1.259–73, in Evans (ed.), *The Riverside Shakespeare*.

50. Quintilian, *Institutio oratoria*, 6.1.30–1.

51. For the classic statement of Shakespeare's ability as a creator of dramatic character see Samuel Johnson, *Mr. Johnson's Preface to his Edition of Shakespear's Plays* (London, 1765), esp. pp. viii–xiii.

6 EKPHRASIS: PAINTING IN WORDS

1. Some of its near relations are icon, chronographia, topographia, pragmatographia, and hypotyposis.

2. Aristotle, *Art of Rhetoric*, 3.11.1; and *Aristotle's Rhetoric* (1686), pp. 191–192.

3. Quintilian, *Institutio oratoria*, 8.3.62; for his discussion of enargeia, see 8.3.61–71.

4. Aphthonius, *Progymnasmata* (1572), sig. 2A7v–8v; see also Murray Krieger, *Ekphrasis: The Illusion of the Natural Sign* (Baltimore: Johns Hopkins Press, 1992), p. 7.

5. Richard A. Lanham, *A Handlist of Rhetorical Terms*, 2nd edn (Berkeley: University of California Press, 1991), p. 61, p. 120.

6. *Rhetorica ad Herennium*, 4.39.51.

7. The poem claims to be an ekphrasis, although after its explanatory proem its ekphrastic status is not maintained, and the pastoral narrative lacks the interestingly self-conscious effects that would mark it out as other than simple description: Longus, *Daphnis and Chloe*, trans. George Thornley (1657), ed. J. M. Edmonds (London: Heinemann, 1962), p. 7.

8. Procopius, *Buildings*, 1.1.24ff. (vol. 7 of the Loeb *Procopius*).

9. George Puttenham, *The Arte of English Poesie*, ed. Gladys Doidge Willcock and Alice Walker (Cambridge: Cambridge University Press, 1936), p. 238.

10. *Ibid.*, p. 196.

11. Henry Peacham, *The Garden of Eloquence* (1593), pp. 110–11.

12. John Hoskins, *Directions for Speech and Style*, ed. Hoyt H. Hudson (Princeton: Princeton University Press, 1935), p. 41–2.

13. Philip Sidney, *The Countesse of Pembroke's Arcadia*, ed. Albert Feuillerat (Cambridge: Cambridge University Press, 1912), p. 254.

14. *Ibid.*, p. 17.

15. Canto 83, in *The Poems of Ezra Pound* (London: Faber and Faber, 1975), p. 529.

16. Song 4 in 'The Songs of Maximus', *Maximus Poems*, ed. George F. Butterick (Berkeley: University of California Press, 1983), p. 19.

17. Nelson Goodman, *The Languages of Art: An Approach to a Theory of Symbols* (London: Oxford University Press, 1969), p. 136.

18. The terms were first proposed by the philosopher Gilbert Ryle and adapted by the anthropologist Clifford Geertz for the description of objects and ceremonies.

19. Edmund Spenser, *The Faerie Queene*, ed. A. C. Hamilton (London: Longman, 1977), 3.11.31.3–9. All further citations in the text refer by book, canto, stanza and line to this edition.

20. Sidney, *Arcadia*, p. 18.

21. As suggested – puzzlingly – by Wendy Steiner (*Pictures of Romance: Form against Context in Painting and Literature* (Chicago: University of Chicago Press, 1988), p. 13).

22. See *A Defence of Poetry*, in Katherine Duncan-Jones and Jan van Dorsten (eds.), *Miscellaneous Prose of Sir Philip Sidney* (Oxford: Clarendon Press, 1973), p. 79.

23. Sidney, *Arcadia*, p. 219.

24. Sidney, *A Defence of Poetry*, p. 81.

25. *Ibid.*, p. 80.

26. *Ibid.*, p. 77.

27. For example, Leonardo, *Trattato della Pittura* (*c.* 1498), Paolo Lomazzo, *The Artes of Curious Painting* (1598), and Lodovico Dolce, *Aretino* (1557). But see W. T. J. Mitchell on the fallacy of such a distinction between temporal and spatial narrative (*Iconology: Image, Text, Ideology* (Chicago: University of Chicago Press, 1986), pp. 100–3).
28. Krieger, *Ekphrasis*, p. 2.
29. Sidney, *A Defence of Poetry*, p. 85.
30. Sidney, *Arcadia*, p. 402.
31. Krieger, *Ekphrasis*, p. 9.
32. Sidney, *Arcadia*, p. 403.
33. *Ibid.*
34. *The Rape of Lucrece*, in William Shakespeare, *The Poems*, ed. F. T. Prince (London: Methuen; Cambridge, MA: Harvard University Press, 1960). Further citations in the text refer to this edition.
35. That this, like all other ekphrastic descriptions, is wholly fictive is obvious in the fruitless attempts of many commentators to find the 'original' of the Troy painting.
36. Sidney, *Defence*, p. 81.
37. See Harry Berger, Jr, 'Theater, Drama, and the Second World: A Prologue to Shakespeare', *Comparative Drama* 2.1 (1968), 3–20.

7 HYSTERON PROTERON: OR THE PREPOSTEROUS

1. Joannes Susenbrotus, *Epitome troporum ac schematum* (Zurich, [1540?]), pp. 32–3.
2. See George Puttenham, *The Arte of English Poesie* (1589), p. 141.
3. *Ibid.*, p. 141.
4. *Ibid.*, p. 142.
5. *Twelfth Night*, 1.3.22–3. The edition used for this and all subsequent references to Shakespeare is G. Blakemore Evans (ed.), *The Riverside Shakespeare* (Boston: Houghton Mifflin, 1974).
6. Angel Day, *A Declaration of . . . Tropes, Figures or Schemes* (1599), p. 83.
7. See Henry Peacham, *The Garden of Eloquence* (1577), sig. F4r–v.
8. Richard Sherry, *Treatise of the Figures of Grammer and Rhetorike* (1555), sig. C4r.
9. *Ibid.*, sig. C2v.
10. See *OED*, hysterology 1 = hysteron proteron; and Richard A. Lanham's *A Handlist of Rhetorical Terms*, 2nd edn (Berkeley: University of California Press, 1991), p. 89.
11. See Richard Huloet, *Abecedarium* (1552), sig. 2A3r under 'Preposterous'; Randle Cotgrave, *Dictionarie of the French and English Tongues* (1611), sig. 3S2r under 'Préposterer'.
12. Thomas Blount, *Glossographia* (1656), sig. U3r.
13. Edward Phillips, *The New World of English Words* (1658), sig. T1r.
14. William Barton, *The Choice and Flower of the Old Psalms* (1645), sig. A1v.
15. Luke Milbourne, *Notes on Dryden's Virgil* (1698), pp. 188–9.

16. Thomas Granger, *Syntagma logicum. Or, The Divine Logike* (1620), pp. 318–19. On the reversal of 'general' and 'particular' see my *Literary Fat Ladies: Rhetoric, Gender, Property* (London: Methuen, 1987), pp. 85–9.

17. This – after its rhetorical sense as a 'figure of speech in which the natural or rational order of its terms is reversed' – is part of the definition of hysteron proteron provided in *The American Heritage Dictionary of the English Language*, 4th edn (Boston: Houghton Mifflin, 2000).

18. George Thompson, *Aimatiasis* (1670), pp. 45, 77.

19. See Parker, *Shakespeare from the Margins* (Chicago: University of Chicago Press, 1996), ch. 1.

20. Henry Burton, *A Vindication of Churches* (1644), p. 64.

21. Edward Leigh, *Annotations upon all the New Testament* (1650), p. 157.

22. Edmund Calamy, *The Godly Mans Ark, or, City of Refuge* (1658), p. 143.

23. John Jewel, *A Replie unto M. Hardinges Answeare* (1565), p. 476.

24. Thomas Hall, *Vindiciae literarum* (1655), p. 163.

25. John Reading, *A Guide to the Holy City* (Oxford, 1651), p. 243.

26. S. E., Mennonite, *An Answer to Several Remarks upon Dr. Henry More, his Expositions of the Apocalypse and Daniel, as also upon his Apology* (1684), pp. 155–6.

27. See Dante Alighieri, *The Divine Comedy*, translated, with a commentary, by Charles S. Singleton, *Paradiso*, vol. 2: Commentary (Princeton: Princeton University Press, 1975), p. 43; and C. S. Singleton, 'The Vistas in Retrospect', *MLN* 81 (1966), 55–80, esp. 63–4.

28. For a brilliant series of analyses that include consideration of this structure, see John Freccero, *Dante: The Poetics of Conversion*, ed. Rachel Jacoff (Cambridge, Mass.: Harvard University Press, 1986).

29. Thomas Middleton and William Rowley, *A Fair Quarrel*, ed. R. V. Holdsworth (London: Ernest Benn, 1974), 1.1.404–7.

30. Joseph Beaumont, *Psyche*, 2nd edn (Cambridge, 1702; originally published 1648), 1.85.

31. Henry King, *A Sermon Preached at St. Pauls March 27* (1640), reprinted in Mary Hobbs (ed.), *The Sermons of Henry King* (Rutherford: Scolar Press, 1992), pp. 227–8. I am grateful to David Cressy for this example.

32. See Thomas Edwards, *The Paraselene Dismantled of Her Cloud* (1699), p. 8.

33. Thomas Cogan, *The Haven of Health* (1584), p. 4r.

34. John Lilburne, *An Unhappy game at Scotch and English* (Edinburgh [i.e. London?], 1646), title page and pp. 13–14.

35. See William Barksted and Lewis Machin (from a draft by John Marston), *The Insatiate Countess*, in Martin Wiggins (ed.), *Four Jacobean Sex Tragedies* (New York and London: Oxford University Press, 1998), 1.1.29–38.

36. Sir Roger L'Estrange, *A New Dialogue Between Some Body and No Body, or, The Observator Observed* (1681), number 2 (dated November 29, 1681).

37. On sodomy and witchcraft, see Alan Bray, *Homosexuality in Renaissance England* (London: Gay Men's Press, 1982); on preposterous venus or preposterous amor, see Jonathan Goldberg, *Sodometries: Renaissance Texts, Modern*

Sexualities (Stanford: Stanford University Press, 1992), pp. 4ff., 180–1, 184, 188, 192, 279 n. 4; and my 'Preposterous Events', *Shakespeare Quarterly* 43 (1992), 186–213.

38. *Troilus and Cressida*, 5.1.17, 23–4.

39. Richard Brome, *Covent-Garden Weeded*, in *Five New Playes* (1659), p. 13; Thomas Middleton, *Michaelmas Term*, 3.1.18 (cf. *A Mad World, my Masters*, 3.3.59: 'after the Italian fasion, backward'); Middleton and Thomas Dekker, *The Honest Whore* (1604), sig. D4v, and the entry under 'Italian fashion' in Gordon Williams, *A Dictionary of Sexual Language and Imagery in Shakespearean and Stuart Literature*, 3 vols. (London: The Athlone Press, 1994).

40. George Sandys, for example, insists in his discussion of changes from 'female' to 'male' that no examples of the reverse may be found, since 'it is preposterous in Nature . . . when men degenerate into effeminacy', in *Ovids Metamorphosis Englished, Mythologiz'd and Represented in Figures* (1640), p. 184.

41. See Stuart Clark, *Thinking with Demons: The Idea of Witchcraft in Early Modern Europe* (Oxford and New York: Oxford University Press, 1997).

42. Ben Jonson, *The Masque of Queenes* (1609), sig. D1v-2r; Shakespeare, *Othello*, 1.3.62–4; *Macbeth*, 1.3.37; Richard Brome, *The Late Lancashire Witches* (1634), sig. B4v.

43. See especially Galatians 3 (which begins 'O Foolish Galatians, who hath bewitcht you . . .?'); and the allegory of the testaments in Galatians 4:21–31, where 'Hagar' the bondwoman (mother of Ishmael) is read as a figure of the testament of the Jews, in contrast to the legitimate line of Sarah and the promise of Abraham fulfilled in the New Testament. In early-modern writing on Galatians this reading of Hagar (mother of Ishmael, and hence also progenitor of the 'Turks') is frequently used to conflate 'Turks' and 'Jews' in the opposition Galatians presents between baptism and circumcision, Gospel liberty and Old Testament 'bondage'. Turning Turk (and re-turning Jew, as Papists in the period were also accused of doing in continuing the ceremonies of the Hebrew scriptures) were both presented as 'preposterous', as was backsliding or being 'bewitch'd' backwards from Gospel freedom. For the importance of this biblical paradigm to representations of the Turk in early-modern writing, see my 'Preposterous Conversion: Turning Turk and its "Pauline" Righting', *Journal for Early Modern Cultural Studies* 2.1 (2002), 1–34.

44. See Alexander Ross, *The Alcoran of Mahomet, Translated out of the Arabique into French by the Sieur Du Ryer* (1649), sig. 2F1r–v.

45. See the Geneva Bible gloss to Galatians 3:3 ('Are ye so foolish, that after ye have begun in the Spirit, ye would now be made perfit by the flesh?'): 'If the Lawe be to be joyned with faith, this were not to goe forward, but backward.'

46. See Robert Parker, *A Scholasticall Discourse against Symbolizing with Antichrist in Ceremonies: Especially in the Signe of the Crosse* (1607), e.g. pp. 146–7.

47. The quotation is from Thomas Fuller, *The Appeal of Injured Innocence* (1659), Part II, p. 101 ('The activity of the Romish Priests to gain Proselites: their dexterous sinisterity in seducing Souls').

48. Thomas Cooper, *The Mystery of Witch-craft* (1617), pp. 88–124.

49. See Parker, *A Scholasticall Discourse against Symbolizing with Antichrist*, p. 146.
50. See John Bale, *Acta Romanorum pontificum* (Basel, 1558), trans. by John Studley into English and published as *The Pageant of Popes* (1574).
51. Alan Stewart, in *Close Readers: Humanism and Sodomy in Early Modern England* (Princeton: Princeton University Press, 1997) uses the sodomitical as a conceptual framework to read the work of Bale. But the 'preposterous' as a keyword that connects 'sodometrye' with idolatry and both with the preposteration of the testaments, as well as with Papist reversion to Hebrew ceremonies and Law, enables a reading of multiple interconnections with the sodomitical.
52. Bale, *A Mysterye of Inyquyte* ('Geneva' [i.e. Antwerp], 1545), p. 2.
53. The 'perfeccyon' (line 1286) of the Gospel is awaited by 'Moseh Lex' (or the Law of Moses, described as not only 'blind' but 'lame') in Bale's *Three Laws* [1548] ('Now wyll I to Christ, that he maye me restore / To more perfeccyon than ever I had afore', lines 1285–6).
54. Stewart, *Close Readers*, p. 68.
55. *Three Laws*, lines 1868–71 and 1873–6, in Peter Happé (ed.), *The Complete Plays of John Bale*, 2 vols. (Cambridge: D. S. Brewer, 1985–6), vol. II.
56. *King Johan*, lines 434–70, in *The Complete Plays of John Bale*, vol. I, pp. 40–1. In response to the Clergye's citing Psalm 44:10 ('Astitit Regina a dextris tuis in vestitu | deaurato circumdata varietate. | A quene, sayth Davyd, on thy ryght hond, lord, I se, | Apparrellyd with golde and compassyd with dyversyte') which it reads wrongly as the 'diverse' sects of the Roman church, the contrary reading is provided by King John ('Davyd meanyth vertuys by the same diversyte, | As in the sayd psalme yt is evydent to se | And not munkysh sectes; but yt is ever yowre cast | For yowre advauncement the Scripturs for to wrast').
57. Peter Happé and John N. King (eds.), *The Vocacyon of Johan Bale* (Binghamton, New York: Renaissance English Text Society, 1990) p. 54: 'I preached the Gospell of the knowledge and right invocacion of God' against the 'ydolatries' of the 'fylthie adulterer' and 'most destable sodomite' (p. 55), citing as his text Romans 1.
58. See *The Vocacyon of Johan Bale*, p. 83 on 'the right handelinge' of the scriptures as opposed to the 'filthie buggeries' of the Church of Rome.
59. See *King Johan*, p. 86: 'Veritas. I assure ye, fryndes, lete men wryte that they wyll | Kynge Johan was a man both valeaunt and godlye. | What though Polydorus reporteth hym very yll | At the suggestyons of the malicyouse clergye? | Thynke yow a Romane with the Romans can not lye?' (lines 2193–7).
60. See *King Johan*, p. 98 (lines 2671–84). In *King Johan*, 'Englond' is a widow whose spouse (God) is exiled, replaced by the 'Usurped Power' of the Pope.
61. *The Vocacyon of Johan Bale*, p. 37.
62. See *Three Laws*, p. 97 (lines 1091–105).
63. In the play *God's Promises*, 'idolatrye', associated with 'the devyls illusion', appears together with reference to 'vyle Sodomytes' that 'lyve so unnaturallye' (Act 3, lines 315–18, in *The Complete Plays of John Bale*, vol. 2, p. 13).
64. On the excluded 'bond brat', see John Prime, *An Exposition and Observations upon Saint Paul to the Galatians* (Oxford, 1587), p. 239. Bale himself – for

whom the Pope and the Turk were the Gog and Magog of Revelation – writes of 'Turkes religious buggerers to this present day' in *English Votaryes* (1546), fol. 20v.

8 PARADIASTOLE: REDESCRIBING
THE VICES AS VIRTUES

I should like to express my particular thanks to Gavin Alexander, Stephen Greenblatt, Susan James, and Jason Scott-Warren.

1. There is also a definition (but an unilluminating one) in Richard Sherry, *A Treatise of the Figures of Grammer and Rhetorike* (1555), fol. 39v. For recent discussions of paradiastole see Frank Whigham, *Ambition and Privilege: The Social Tropes of Elizabethan Courtesy Theory* (Berkeley: University of California Press, 1984), pp. 40–2, 204–5; Virginia Cox, 'Rhetoric and politics in Tasso's *Nifo*', *Studi Secenteschi* 30 (1989), 3–98 (53–5); Quentin Skinner, 'Thomas Hobbes: Rhetoric and the Construction of Morality', *Proceedings of the British Academy* 76 (1991), 1–61 (esp. 4–40) and 'Moral Ambiguity and the Renaissance Art of Eloquence', *Essays in Criticism* 44 (1994), 267–92; Conal Condren, *The Language of Politics in Seventeenth-Century England* (Basingstoke: Macmillan, 1994), pp. 78–84; Quentin Skinner, *Reason and Rhetoric in the Philosophy of Hobbes* (Cambridge: Cambridge University Press, 1996), pp. 142–80; Richard Tuck, 'Hobbes's Moral Philosophy', in Tom Sorell (ed.), *The Cambridge Companion to Hobbes* (Cambridge: Cambridge University Press, 1996), pp. 175–207 (pp. 195–9).

2. See Henry Peacham, *The Garden of Eloquence* (1577), sig. B1r for his classification of the figures, which are divided into Tropes and Schemates, with the latter subdivided into grammatical and rhetorical schemes.

3. *Ibid.*, sig. N2r.

4. *Ibid.*, sig. N4v.

5. George Puttenham, *The Arte of English Poesie*, ed. Gladys Doidge Willcock and Alice Walker (Cambridge: Cambridge University Press, 1970), pp. 184–5.

6. *Ibid.*, p. 185, marginal gloss.

7. *Ibid.*, p. 220. 'To curry favell' [lit. = 'to groom the chestnut horse'] is the original of the modern idiom 'to curry favour', which developed from it, by folk etymology, during the 16th century. Puttenham's readers would have been familiar with its use in the proverb linking flattery with success at Court: 'He that wylle in courte abyde Must cory favell back and syde.' (For this and other versions, see M. P. Tilley, *Dictionary of the Proverbs in England in the Sixteenth and Seventeenth Centuries* (Ann Arbor: University of Michigan Press, 1950), p. 724.)

8. The Bibliothèque Nationale records editions in 1530 (Paris), 1540 (Lyon), and 1541 (Paris).

9. Publius Rutilius Lupus, *De figuris sententiarum et elocutionis*, ed. Edward Brooks (Leiden: Brill, 1970), p. 8.

10. For the debate over the authorship see Skinner, *Reason and Rhetoric*, pp. 32–3.

11. *Rhetorica ad Herennium*, 3.3.6.
12. Quintilian, *Institutio oratoria*, 9.3.65 (italics added).
13. The British Library records four editions published between 1493 and 1503.
14. Mancinelli explicitly states that he is writing 'teste Fabio libro nono', that is, according to the authority of Quintilian in Book IX of his *Institutio oratoria*: Antonio Mancinelli, *Carmen de figuris* (Venice, 1493), sig. HIr.
15. *Paradiastole* 'sit . . . quum te pro astuto sapientem appelas, pro confidente fortem' (*ibid.*). But in the same passage Mancinelli also contrasts being *fortis* with being *temerarius*.
16. The British Library lists London printings (all in Latin) in 1562, 1570, 1572, 1608, and 1621.
17. Johann Susenbrotus, *Epitome troporum ac schematum* (1562), p. 46: 'Mancin. Pro astuto sapiens sit Paradiastola dictus.'
18. *Ibid.*: 'cum pro astuto sapientem appelles: pro confidente, fortem: pro illiberali, diligentem'. Following Mancinelli, however, Susenbrotus also contrasts *fortis* with *temerarius*.
19. The title-page states that the work was published in January 1553, i.e. 1554 our style. On Wilson as rhetorician see Cathy Shrank, *Writing the Nation in Reformation England, 1530–1580* (Oxford: Clarendon Press, 2004), pp. 182–219.
20. Thomas Wilson, *The Arte of Rhetorique* (1554), fols. 66v, 67r.
21. Henry Peacham, *The Garden of Eloquence* (1593), p. 168.
22. Angel Day, *A Declaration of . . . Tropes, Figures or Schemes* (1592), p. 90.
23. Peacham, *The Garden of Eloquence* (1577), sig. N4v.
24. Day, *A Declaration of . . . Tropes, Figures or Schemes*, p. 90.
25. Peacham, *The Garden of Eloquence* (1593), p. 168.
26. Peacham, *The Garden of Eloquence* (1577), sig. N4v.
27. Puttenham, *The Arte of English Poesie*, p. 185; Day, *A Declaration of . . . Tropes, Figures or Schemes*, pp. 62–3.
28. Subsequent references will be by name of translator and to the following editions: *In Tres Rhetoricorum Aristotelis Libros* in *Rhetoricorum libri quinque*, trans. George of Trebizond (Venice, 1523), fols. 109–35; *De Arte Dicendi Libri III*, trans. Ermolao Barbaro (Paris, 1559); *De Arte Rhetorica Libri Tres*, trans. Carolo Sigonio (Bologna, 1565); and *De Arte Rhetorica Libri Tres*, trans. Antonio Maioragio (Venice, 1591).
29. George of Trebizond, fol. 114v.
30. See George of Trebizond, fol. 114v on *ferox/fortis*; cf. Barbaro, p. 32 on *temeritas/fortitudo*; Sigonio, p. 49 on *audax/fortis*; and Maioragio, fol. 70r, col. 1 on *temerarius/fortis*.
31. Thucydides, *The Hystory*, trans. Thomas Nicolls (1555), fol. 200r.
32. Justus Lipsius, *Six Bookes of Politickes or Civil Doctrine*, trans. William Jones (1594), p. 69.
33. There were later sixteenth-century printings in Basel, Frankfurt and Lyon as well as Venice.
34. Plato, *De republica vel de iusto* in *Platonis Opera*, trans. Marsilio Ficino (Venice, 1517), fol. 259v.

35. See George of Trebizond, fol. 114v on *arrogans/magnificus atque honestus*; Barbaro, p. 32 on *superbus/magnificus & splendidus*; Sigonio, p. 49 on *contumax/magnificus ac grandis*; and Maioragio, fol. 70r, col. 1 on *contumax/magnificus & gravis*.
36. Susenbrotus, *Epitome troporum ac schematum*, p. 46.
37. Day, *A Declaration of . . . Tropes, Figures or Schemes*, p. 63.
38. See Plato, *De republica*, trans. Ficino, fol. 259v on *prodigalitas/magnificentia*, *licentia/libertas*, and *impudentia/fortitudo*.
39. See Peacham, *The Garden of Eloquence* (1577), sig. N4v and Puttenham, *The Arte of English Poesie*, p. 185.
40. Thucydides, *The Hystory*, fol. 200r.
41. Thucydides, *The Hystory*, fol. 200r; cf. Plato, *De republica*, trans. Ficino, fol. 259v on *pudor/fatuitas*.
42. Thucydides, *The Hystory*, fol. 200r (Nicoll, however, reverses the direction of the example); for Aristotle cf. George of Trebizond, fol. 114v on *moderatus/timidus & insidiator*; and Barbaro, p. 32, Sigonio, p. 49, and Maioragio, fol. 70r, col. 1 on *cautus/insidiosus*.
43. The example already occurs in Sir Thomas Wyatt, 'Myne own John Poyntz', line 64, in R. A. Rebholz (ed.), *The Complete Poems* (Harmondsworth: Penguin, 1978): 'As dronkenes good felloweshippe to call'. It became popular: William Fulbecke deplores the fact that nowadays 'a confederate in venereous practises' will be 'accounted immediatly a good fellow' (*A Booke of Christian Ethicks or Moral Philosophie* (1587), sig. E2r).
44. Peacham, *The Garden of Eloquence* (1577), sig. N4v.
45. John Larke, *The boke of wysdome folowynge the auctoryties of auncyent phylosophers* (1532), fols. 7v, 9v, 27v, 45r, 50r, 56r.
46. *Ibid.*, fols. 9v, 27v, 56r; fols. 7v, 46v , 50r.
47. Baldassare Castiglione, *The Courtyer . . . Done into Englyshe by Thomas Hoby* (Edinburgh, 1899), p. 330.
48. Cornelius Valerius, *The Casket of Jewels: contaynynge a playne description of morall philosophie* (1571), sig. D1r–v.
49. Castiglione, *The Courtyer*, p. 44.
50. Valerius, *The Casket of Jewels*, sig. F2v.
51. *De Arte Rhetorica Libri Tres*, trans. Sigonio, p. 49.
52. Castiglione, *The Courtyer*, p. 44.
53. Valerius, *The Casket of Jewels*, sig. F2v.
54. *Ibid.* .
55. Castiglione, *The Courtyer*, p. 44.
56. Peacham, *The Garden of Eloquence* (1593), p. 169.
57. Day, *A Declaration of . . . Tropes, Figures or Schemes*, p. 77.
58. *Ibid.*, p. 90.
59. Cicero, *De oratore*, 3.27.107.
60. Susenbrotus, *Epitome troporum ac schematum*, p. 46.
61. Wilson, *The Arte of Rhetorique*, fol. 69r.
62. Peacham, *The Garden of Eloquence* (1593), pp. 168–9.

63. John Lyly, *Euphues. The Anatomy of Wit*, ed. Edward Arber (London, 1868), p. 115.
64. Christopher Marlowe, *Tamburlaine the Great* Parts 1 and 2, ed. David Fuller, The Complete Works of Christopher Marlowe, vol. 5 (Oxford: Clarendon Press, 1998), 4.1.17 and 4.1.91.
65. 3.1.235–7, in William Shakespeare, *The Complete Works*, ed. Stanley Wells and Gary Taylor (Oxford, 1988). All further references to Shakespeare are to the texts in this edition.
66. So too in Shakespeare's poetry of the 1590s. See, for example, *The Rape of Lucrece*, line 246: Tarquin is said to speak in such a way that 'what is vile shows like a virtuous deed'.
67. Peacham, *The Garden of Eloquence* (1593), p. 168.
68. 2.1.125–6; Castiglione, *The Courtyer*, p. 44. Editors of *2 Henry IV* do not seem to have spotted the source of the remark.
69. Peacham, *The Garden of Eloquence* (1593), p. 167.
70. Susenbrotus, *Epitome troporum ac schematum*, p. 46.
71. Peacham, *The Garden of Eloquence* (1593), p. 168.
72. *Ibid.*, p. 169.
73. *Ibid.* .
74. Cicero, *The thre bookes of Tullyes offices both in latyne tonge and in englysshe lately translated by Roberte Whytinton* (London, 1534), sig. Q8r.
75. Baldwin's treatise, first published in 1547, was reprinted at least three times in the 1550s. The text was enlarged by Thomas Palfreyman in 1567, and in this version, further enlarged in 1579, it went through at least ten further printings by the end of the century. The edition here used is that of 1579.
76. William Baldwin, *A Treatice of Morall Philosophy* (1579), fol. 72v.

9 SYNCRISIS: THE FIGURE OF CONTESTATION

1. *Syncrisis* as a term for extended comparison is found in the Greek texts on school exercises, though it is used in a more restricted sense by Aristotle (Henry George Liddell, Robert Scott, *et al.* (eds.), *Greek–English Lexicon* (Oxford: Clarendon Press, 1996)). It is closely related to the classical topics of *similitudo* and *comparatio*, and the three terms are often used more or less interchangeably in late Latin writing and during the Renaissance. For discussions of *similitudo* and *comparatio*, see Cicero, *Topica*, 10.41–11.46 and 18.68–71; and *Rhetorica ad Herennium*, 4.45.59–48.61. For later interpretations of *syncrisis*, see *A Glossary of Later Latin to 600 AD*, compiled by Alexander Souter (Oxford: Clarendon Press, 1949). For syncrisis as a figure, operating on a smaller scale, see for example Henry Peacham, *The Garden of Eloquence* (1593), p. 162: '*Syncrisis*, is a comparison of contrary things, and diverse persons in one sentence.' For extended discussions of the various forms of rhetorical comparison see John Hoskins, *Directions for Speech and Style* [1599], ed. Hoyt H. Hudson (Princeton: Princeton University Press, 1935), pp. 17–21; and John Smith, *The Mysterie of Rhetorique Unvail'd* (1657), pp. 207–10. Smith's definition, lifted from Peacham, serves as the source

for that of the *Oxford English Dictionary*: 'Comparison; *Rhet*. A figure by which diverse or opposite things are compared'. Syncrisis might equally aim however to reveal similarity as well as difference in the matters brought together for comparison.

2. D. A. Russell (ed.), *'Longinus' on the Sublime* (Oxford: Clarendon Press, 1964), 12.2–13 (Plato and Demosthenes, Demosthenes and Cicero), 32.8 (Lysias and Plato); Quintilian, *Institutio oratoria*, 2.4.20–21; cf. 3.7; Cicero, *Brutus*, 36ff.

3. The school exercise is discussed in English in Richard Rainolde's *The Foundacion of Rhetorike* (1563), fols. xlvi–viii. Rainolde's discussion of Comparison follows that in the *Progymnasmata* of the late fourth century AD Greek sophist and rhetorician Aphthonius of Antioch. In certain Latin translations of Aphthonius published in England the Latin and Greek terms *comparatio* and *syncrisis* are placed side by side. (I am grateful to Gavin Alexander for this information.)

4. William Shakespeare, *Hamlet*, ed. Harold Jenkins, The Arden Shakespeare (London: Methuen, 1982), 3.4.53–7, 63–5.

5. T. W. Baldwin, *William Shakspere's Small Latin and Lesse Greeke*, 2 vols. (Urbana: University of Illinois Press, 1944), esp. vol. II, ch. 37 and p. 133.

6. Donald Lemen Clark, *John Milton at St Paul's School* (New York: Columbia University Press, 1948), p. 242.

7. Samuel Taylor Coleridge, *Biographia Literaria*, ed. George Watson (London: Dent, 1956), p. 3.

8. John Dryden, *Of Dramatic Poesy and Other Critical Essays*, ed. George Watson, 2 vols. (London: Dent, 1962), vol. II, p. 276.

9. *Ibid.* pp. 131–2. In his *Life of Plutarch* (*ibid.* pp. 11–12), Dryden develops a similar series of contrasts between Plutarch and Seneca, but in order to reject the traditional comparison of these two writers. 'If I had been to find out a parallel for Plutarch, I should rather have pitched on Varro, the most learned of the Romans, if at last his works had yet remained; or with Pomponius Atticus, if he had written.'

10. Alexander Pope, *The Iliad of Homer*, Books I–IX, ed. Maynard Mack *et al.*, The Twickenham Edition of the Poems of Alexander Pope (London: Methuen, 1967), vol. VII, *Translations of Homer*, Preface, p. 12. It is not surprising that Samuel Johnson, who was well acquainted with the methods of syncrisis – he compares Homer and Virgil in *Rambler* 121 – should have ventured in similar fashion in his *Life of Pope* a 'parallel' assessment of the merits of Pope and Dryden: Samuel Johnson, *Lives of the English Poets*, ed. George Birkbeck Hill, 3 vols. (Oxford: Clarendon Press, 1905), vol. III, pp. 222–3.

11. 'It is true', Pope confesses elsewhere, 'that in this way of turning a *Book* into a *Man*, this reasoning from his Works to himself, we can at best but hit off a few outlines of a Character': 'An Essay on the Life, Writings, and Learning of Homer', Mack (ed.), *The Iliad of Homer*, p. 51.

12. Forty-six out of the surviving fifty biographical accounts are paired in this way. For analysis, see C. B. R. Pelling, 'Synkrisis in Plutarch's Lives', *Quaderni del Filologico Ferrarese* 8 (1986), 83–96; D. A. Russell, *Plutarch* (London: Duckworth, 1972); Timothy E. Duff, *Plutarch's Lives: Exploring Virtue and Vice*

(Oxford: Clarendon Press, 2002). (I am grateful to Professor Duff for his careful reading of the present essay.)

13. 'The Great Action between Pompey and Caesar, Extracted out of the Roman and Grecian Writers, by H.W. K^r. For an Historical Exercise'; 'Of Robert Devereux, Earl of Essex, and George Villiers, Duke of Buckingham: Some Observations by way of Parallel in the time of their estates of Favour'; 'The Difference and Disparity Between the Estates and Conditions of George Duke of Buckingham and Robert Earl of Essex Written by the Earl of Clarendon in his younger dayes', in Henry Wotton, *Reliquiae Wottonianae* (1685), pp. 239–42, 161–83, 184–202. Dedicating this volume to Wotton's grand-nephew, Philip, Earl of Chesterfield, Wotton's friend and fellow-biographer Izaac Walton modestly notes a 'Parallel' between Wotton's character and his own (sig. a4).

14. Ben Jonson, *Sejanus His Fall*, 3.396–9, in C. H. Herford and Percy and Evelyn Simpson (eds.), *Ben Jonson*, 11 vols. (Oxford: Clarendon Press, 1925–52), vol. IV. Cordus practises history along Plutarchian lines; contemplating the fortunes and character of Germanicus, he declares: 'I thought once, | Considering their formes, age, manner of deaths, | The neerenesse of the places, where they fell, | T'have paralelled him with great Alexander; | For both were of best feature, of high race, | Yeer'd but to thirtie, and in forraine lands, | By their owne people, alike made away' (1.136–42).

15. Ben Jonson, *Conversations with Drummond*, 326–7, in Herford and Simpson (eds.), *Ben Jonson*, vol. I; John Hayward, *The Life and Raigne of King Henrie IIII, the first and second parts*, ed. John J. Manning (London: Royal Historical Society, 1991); cf. Annabel Patterson, *Censorship and Interpretation: The Conditions of Writing and Reading in Early Modern England* (Madison: University of Wisconsin Press, 1984); Ian Donaldson, '"Misconstruing Everything": *Julius Caesar* and *Sejanus*', in Grace Ioppolo (ed.), *Shakespeare Performed: Essays in Honor of R. A. Foakes* (Newark: University of Delaware Press, 2000), pp. 88–107.

16. The Epistle Dedicatorie, 78–86, 94, in M. Lederer (ed.), *Daniel's The Tragedie of Cleopatra* (Louvain: A. Uystpruyst, 1911; repr. Vaduz: Kraus Reprint, 1963). Daniel's 1611 text (quoted here) differs significantly in wording, though not in sentiment, from his original text of 1594. Such fulsome praise of the glories of Elizabeth's reign so deep into the reign of her successor conveys its own indirect but unmistakable message.

17. William Shakespeare, *Anthony and Cleopatra*, ed. Michael Neill, The World's Classics (Oxford and New York: Oxford University Press, 1994), 5.14.50–4.

18. See Barbara J. Bono, *Literary Transvaluation: From Vergilian Epic to Shakespearean Tragicomedy* (Berkeley: University of California Press, 1984); Janet Adelman, *The Common Liar: An Essay on 'Antony and Cleopatra'* (New Haven: Yale University Press, 1973); David Bevington (ed.), *Antony and Cleopatra*, The New Cambridge Shakespeare (Cambridge: Cambridge University Press, 1990), Introduction; Robert S. Miola, *Shakespeare's Rome* (Cambridge: Cambridge University Press, 1983).

19. See Helen Morris, 'Queen Elizabeth I "Shadowed" in Cleopatra', *Huntington Library Quarterly* 32 (1969), 271–8; Keith Rinehart, 'Shakespeare's Cleopatra and England's Elizabeth', *Shakespeare Quarterly* 23 (1972), 81–6.

20. Geoffrey Bullough (ed.), *Narrative and Dramatic Sources of Shakespeare*, vol. v, The Roman Plays (London: Routledge and Paul, 1964), pp. 215–17.

21. *A Dedication to Sir Philip Sidney* ('The Life of Sidney', written *c.* 1610), in John Gouws (ed.), *The Prose Works of Fulke Greville, Lord Brooke* (Oxford: Clarendon Press, 1986), p. 93; Francis Bacon, *The Advancement of Learning*, ed. G. W. Kitchin (London: Dent, 1954), The First Book, To the King, p. 47.

22. William Shakespeare, *Antony and Cleopatra*, ed. Emrys Jones, New Penguin Shakespeare (Harmondsworth: Penguin, 1977), Introduction; Howard Erskine-Hill, *The Augustan Idea in English Literature* (London: Edward Arnold, 1983); H. Neville Davies, 'Jacobean *Antony and Cleopatra*', *Shakespeare Studies* 17 (1985), 123–58.

23. George Puttenham, *The Arte of English Poesie* (1589), ed. Edward Arber (London: A. Constable and Co., 1895), Book i, chapter 2, p. 21.

24. Francis Meres, *Palladis Tamia*, in G. Gregory Smith (ed.), *Elizabethan Critical Essays*, 2 vols. (Oxford: Clarendon Press, 1904), vol. ii, pp. 308–24.

25. See Richard Foster Jones, *Ancients and Moderns: A Study of the Rise of the Scientific Movement in Seventeenth-Century England*, 2nd edn (St Louis: Washington University Press, 1961).

26. Jonathan Swift, *The Battle of the Books*, in *Gulliver's Travels*, etc. (London: Oxford University Press, 1919), pp. 555–6.

27. Jonson echoes lines 38–9 in *Discoveries* 916–18 when praising Bacon, who has 'perform'd that in our tongue, which may be compar'd, or preferr'd, either to insolent *Greece*, or haughty *Rome*'. The formula is borrowed from Seneca the Elder, *Controversiae*, i, preface, 6. Cf. Bacon's own belief 'that this third period of time will far surpass that of the Grecian and Roman learning', Kitchin (ed.), *The Advancement of Learning*, p. 208.

28. For a fuller account of this development, see Ian Donaldson, 'Jonson and the Tother Youth', ch. 2 in *Jonson's Magic Houses* (Oxford: Clarendon Press, 1997).

29. Preface to Alexander Pope (ed.), *The Works of Shakespeare*, 6 vols. (London, 1725), vol. i, pp. ix–x.

30. Pope, *The Iliad of Homer*, ed. Mack, Preface, p. 12.

10 TESTIMONY: THE ARTLESS PROOF

1. Samuel Butler, *Prose Observations* [*c.* 1670?], ed. Hugh de Quehen (Oxford: Clarendon Press, 1979), p. 128.

2. William Temple, *Analysis of Sir Philip Sidney's Apology for Poetry*, trans. John Webster (New York: Centre for Medieval and Renaissance Studies, 1984), pp. 70, 118, 136, 150, 152.

3. J. J. Murphy and R. A. Katula, *A Synoptic History of Classical Rhetoric*, 2nd edn (Davis, CA: Hermagoras Press, 1995), pp. 117, 137, 183.

4. Cicero, *De inventione*, 1.7.9.

5. Cicero, *De partitione oratoria*, 2.6.

6. Thomas Wilson, *The Art of Rhetoric (1560)*, ed. P. E. Medine (University Park: Pennsylvania State University Press, 1994), p. 46.

7. See e.g. J. H. Alsted, *Encyclopaedia*, 2 vols. (Herborn, 1630), vol. II, p. 2339.

8. *The Tragedy of King Lear*, 1.1.90; *The Tragedy of Julius Caesar*, 3.2.21–2; in William Shakespeare, *The Complete Works*, ed. Stanley Wells and Gary Taylor (Oxford: Clarendon Press, 1988), pp. 945, 614.

9. Wilson, *Art of Rhetoric*, p. 53.

10. Wilson, *Art of Rhetoric*, p. 60. On the *circumstantiae*, see further Kathy Eden, *Hermeneutics and the Rhetorical Tradition: Chapters in the Ancient Legacy and its Humanist Reception* (New Haven: Yale University Press, 1997), esp. pp. 88, 95–97.

11. Wilson, *Art of Rhetoric*, p. 54. See also G. J. Vossius, *Rhetorices contractae* (Amsterdam, 1666), pp. 8–9.

12. John Rainolds, *Oxford Lectures on Aristotle's Rhetoric*, trans. L. D. Green (London: Associated University Presses, 1988), p. 178. See also Thomas Wilson, *The Rule of Reason* (1551), sig. M5v.

13. Vossius, *Rhetorices contractae*, pp. 112–16.

14. John Donne, *The Sermons*, ed. George R. Potter and Evelyn M. Simpson, 10 vols. (Berkeley: University of California Press, 1953–62), vol. VII, p. 274.

15. Shakespeare, *Julius Caesar*, 3.2.97, 87, 94, 99.

16. Aristotle, *Art of Rhetoric*, 1.15.1; Quintilian, *Institutio oratoria*, 5.1.1.

17. See e.g. Richard Sherry, *A Treatise of Schemes and Tropes* (1550), pp. 78–9; Cypriano Soarez, *De arte rhetorica libri tres* (Rouen, 1614), p. 49. See also Rainolds, *Oxford Lectures*, p. 166.

18. See further F. Muller, 'Le *De inventione dialectica* d'Agricola dans la tradition rhétorique d'Aristote à Port-Royal', in F. Akkerman and A. J. Vanderjagt (ed.), *Rodolphus Agricola Phrisius (1444–1485)* (Leiden: Brill, 1988), pp. 281–92 (esp. pp. 290–1).

19. On the actual circumstances of Ramus's murder, see W. J. Ong, *Ramus, Method, and the Decay of Dialogue: From the Art of Discourse to the Art of Reason* (Cambridge, MA: Harvard University Press, 1983), p. 29.

20. Christopher Marlowe, *The Massacre at Paris*, ed. Edward J. Esche, in *The Complete Works of Christopher Marlowe*, vol. V (Oxford: Clarendon Press, 1998), p. 334, but adopting all of Dyce's emendations and further emending the octavo's reading '*ipsi dixi*'.

21. Petrus Ramus, *Dialecticae libri duo* (1574), p. 98. Translation from *The Logike of the Moste Excellent Philosopher P. Ramus Martyr*, trans. Roland Makilmayne (1574), p. 65.

22. Cicero, *De natura deorum*, 1.5.10.

23. Contrast the interpretation offered by T. A. Goeglein, '"Wherein hath Ramus been so offensious?": Poetic Examples in the English Ramist Logic Manuals (1574–1672)', *Rhetorica* 14 (1996), 73–102, esp. 75.

24. George A. Kennedy, *Classical Rhetoric in its Christian and Secular Tradition from Ancient to Modern Times* (Chapel Hill: North Carolina University Press, 1980), p. 18.

25. Quintilian, *Institutio oratoria*, 5.1.2.
26. Lorenzo Valla, *Elegantiae*, in *Opera omnia*, ed. Eugenio Garin, 2 vols. (Turin: Bottega d'Erasmo, 1962), vol. I, pp. 1–235 (p. 198). See also Anthony Grafton, 'The New Science and the Traditions of Humanism', in Jill Kraye (ed.), *The Cambridge Companion to Renaissance Humanism* (Cambridge: Cambridge University Press, 1996), pp. 203–23 (p. 212).
27. Desiderius Erasmus, *De copia*, trans. Betty Knott, in *Literary and Educational Writings 2: De Copia and De Ratione Studii*, ed. Craig R. Thompson, Collected Works of Erasmus, 24 (Toronto: University of Toronto Press, 1978), p. 438; Erasmus, *De copia verborum ac rerum*, ed. B. Knott, *Opera omnia*, vol. 6 (Amsterdam: North-Holland, 1988), p. 132.
28. See further Quentin Skinner, *Reason and Rhetoric in the Philosophy of Hobbes* (Cambridge: Cambridge University Press, 1996), pp. 133–7.
29. Bartholomew Keckermann, *Systema rhetoricae*, in *Opera omnia*, 2 vols. (Geneva, 1614), vol. II, cols. 1426–7.
30. Wilson, *Art of Rhetoric*, p. 65.
31. Keckermann, *Systema rhetoricae*, col. 1427. On Keckermann, see further Howard Hotson, *Johann Heinrich Alsted, 1588–1638: Between Renaissance, Reformation, and Universal Reform* (Oxford: Clarendon Press, 2000), pp. 29–32; J. S. Freedman, 'The Career and Writings of Bartholomew Keckermann (d. 1609)', *Proceedings of the American Philosophical Society* 141 (1997), 305–64; Kenneth Charlton, *Education in Renaissance England* (London: Routledge and Kegan Paul, 1965), p. 148.
32. Thomas Farnaby, *Index rhetoricus* (1625), sig. A6v (but see also sig. B3r). See further R. W. Serjeantson, 'Thomas Farnaby', in E. A. Malone (ed.), *British Rhetoricians and Logicians, 1500–1660: First Series*, Dictionary of Literary Biography, 236 (Detroit: Gale, 2001), pp. 108–16.
33. Keckermann, *Systema rhetoricae*, col. 1427. Sherry, *Treatise*, pp. 93–4, similarly treats 'Expolicion' immediately after authority.
34. Donne, *Sermons*, vol. VII, p. 274.
35. Wilson, *Arte of Rhetoric*, p. 153.
36. Shakespeare, *Julius Caesar*, 3.2.83, 88, 95, 100, etc.
37. See Gavin Alexander's chapter on prosopopoeia in this volume.
38. *Rhetorica ad Herennium*, 4.53.66.
39. See Wilson, *Art of Rhetoric*, p. 204. See also Henry Peacham, *The Garden of Eloquence* (1577), sig. D3r.
40. Joannes Susenbrotus, *Epitome troporum ac schematum* (1562), p. 87.
41. *Rhetorica ad Herennium*, 1.10.18; Quintilian, *Institutio oratoria*, 5.7.8.
42. Henry Peacham, *The Garden of Eloquence. Conteyning the Figures of Grammar and Rhetorick* (1593), pp. 86, 85, 87, 88. Peacham's account of the figure of apomnemonysis, which he also calls a 'place' (or topic), is very close to such descriptions of the topic of testimony as Wilson's, at the head of this essay.
43. Angel Day, *The English Secretary* (1599), Book 2, p. 99. D[aniel]. T[uvil]., *The Dove and the Serpent* (1614), p. 89.
44. Dudley Fenner, *The Artes of Logike and Rethorike* ([Middleburg], 1584), sig. B4v. William Walker, *De argumentorum inventione libri duo* (1672), p. 47.

45. Sherry, *Treatise*, p. 93.
46. Day, *English Secretary*, p. 99.
47. Sherry, *Treatise*, p. 93.
48. John Smith, *The Mysterie of Rhetorique Unvail'd* (1657), p. 244.
49. Theodor Verweyen and Gunther Witting, 'The Cento: A Form of Intertextuality from Montage to Parody', in H. F. Plett (ed.), *Intertextuality* (Berlin: de Gruyter, 1991), pp. 165–78.
50. Justus Lipsius, *Politica*, ed. Jan Waszink (Amsterdam: Van Gorcum, 2004). See further Anthony Grafton and Lisa Jardine, *From Humanism to the Humanities: Education and the Liberal Arts in Fifteenth- and Sixteenth-Century Europe* (London: Duckworth, 1986), pp. 198–9; also Peter Burke, 'Tacitism', in T. A. Dorey (ed.), *Tacitus* (London: Routledge and Kegan Paul, 1969), pp. 149–71 (p. 162).
51. Michel de Montaigne, *Essais*, ed. Alexandre Micha, 3 vols. (Paris: Garnier-Flammarion, 1969–79), vol. i, p. 195; Montaigne, *Essays* [1603], trans. John Florio, 3 vols. (London: Dent, 1980), vol. i, p. 151.
52. Edmund Bolton, 'Hypercritica, or a Rule of Judgement for Writing or Reading our History's (1618?)', in J. E. Spingarn (ed.), *Critical Essays of the Seventeenth Century*, 3 vols. (Bloomington: Indiana University Press, 1957), vol. i, pp. 87–8.
53. Robert Burton, *The Anatomy of Melancholy*, ed. T. C. Faulkner *et al.*, 6 vols. (Oxford: Clarendon Press, 1989–2000), vol. i, p. 11; vol. ii, pp. 203–206. See also Skinner, *Reason and Rhetoric*, pp. 118, 267.
54. Keckermann, *Systema rhetoricae*, col. 1475.
55. Compare J. D. Lyons, *Exemplum: The Rhetoric of Example in Early Modern France and Italy* (Princeton: Princeton University Press, 1986), esp. pp. 29–31; see also the superior Timothy Hampton, *Writing from History: The Rhetoric of Exemplarity in Renaissance Literature* (Ithaca: Cornell University Press, 1990).
56. Francis Bacon (attrib.), 'To the Earl of Rutland – Letter I', in James Spedding *et al.* (eds.), *Works*, 14 vols. (London: Longman, 1862), vol. ix, pp. 6–15 (p. 14).
57. Robert Sanderson, *Logicae artis compendivm (1618)*, ed. E. J. Ashworth (Bologna: Clueb, 1985), p. 152.
58. Thomas Hobbes, *Leviathan*, ed. Richard Tuck (Cambridge: Cambridge University Press, 1996), p. 490. Cicero, *Pro Sestio*, 55.119; see further Harald Hagendahl, 'Methods of Citation in Post-Classical Latin Prose', *Eranos* 45 (1947), 114–28.
59. Quintilian, *Institutio oratoria*, 5.11.39.
60. Philip Sidney, *An Apology for Poetry*, ed. Geoffrey Shepherd, 2nd edn (Manchester: Manchester University Press, 1973), p. 107.
61. Abraham Fraunce, *The Arcadian Rhetorike* (1588), sig. c4v.
62. See further Brian Vickers, 'Rhetorical and Anti-rhetorical Tropes: On Writing the History of *Elocutio*', *Comparative Criticism* 3 (1981), 105–32 (esp. 105–9).
63. See esp. *Rhetorica ad Herennium*, 1.3.4. See also J. M. Steadman, 'Beyond Hercules: Bacon and the Scientist as Hero', *Studies in the Literary Imagination* 4 (1971), 3–47 (20–3).
64. Francis Bacon, *The Advancement of Learning*, ed. Michael Kiernan, The Oxford Francis Bacon, 4 (Oxford: Clarendon Press, 2000), pp. 5, 33, 36, 39. On James's

use of the model of Solomon, see Alan Stewart, *The Cradle King: A Life of James VI and I* (London: Chatto and Windus, 2003), esp. p. 147.

65. John Milton, 'A Masque Presented at Ludlow Castle, 1634', in John Carey (ed.), *Complete Shorter Poems* (London: Longman, 1971).

66. John Selden, *Table Talk*, ed. Frederick Pollock (London: Selden Society, 1927), p. 24.

67. James Duport's instructions for students, as recorded in Trinity College, Cambridge, MS O.10A.33, p. 13. Cf. Cambridge University Library, MS Add. 6986, fol. 11v.

68. Selden, *Table Talk*, p. 24.

69. R. W. Serjeantson, 'Testimony and Proof in Early-Modern England', *Studies in History and Philosophy of Science* 30 (1999), 195–236.

70. B. J. Shapiro, *A Culture of Fact: England, 1550–1720* (Ithaca: Cornell University Press, 2000). Steven Shapin, *A Social History of Truth: Civility and Science in Seventeenth-Century England* (Chicago: University of Chicago Press, 1994).

71. R. W. Serjeantson, 'Proof and Persuasion', in Katharine Park and Lorraine Daston (eds.), *The Cambridge History of Early Modern Science* (Cambridge: Cambridge University Press, 2006), pp. 132–75.

72. Hobbes, *Leviathan*, ed. Richard Tuck, rev. edn (Cambridge: Cambridge University Press, 1996), p. 490.

73. Hugo Grotius, *De jure belli ac pacis libri tres* (Paris, 1625), sig. ĩ1v. Hobbes alludes critically to Grotius's argumentative procedures in this regard in *De cive* (1642): see Perez Zagorin, 'Hobbes without Grotius', *History of Political Thought*, 21 (2000), 16–40 (27).

74. Alexander Pope, ΠΕΡΙ ΒΑΘΟΥΣ: *or, Martinus Scriblerus his Treatise of the Art of Sinking in Poetry* [1728], in Rosemary Cowler (ed.), *The Prose Works*, vol. II: *The Major Works, 1725–1744* (Oxford: Basil Blackwell, 1986), pp. 171–276 (p. 225). See further R. A. Lanham, *A Handlist of Rhetorical Terms*, 2nd edn (Berkeley: University of California Press, 1991), pp. 169–70.

75. Trinity College, Cambridge, MS O.10A.33, p. 10; James Duport, *Homeri poetarum omnium saeculorum facile princeps gnomologia* (Cambridge, 1660); Rosemary O'Day, 'Duport, James (1606–79)', in H. C. G. Matthew and Brian Harrison (eds.), *Oxford Dictionary of National Biography*, 60 vols. (Oxford: Oxford University Press, 2004), vol. XXIV, pp. 951–4.

76. Michael Hunter, *John Aubrey and the Realm of Learning* (New York: Science History Publications, 1975), p. 41.

77. William Wotton, *Reflections upon Ancient and Modern Learning*, 2nd edn (1697), p. 416. See further Mordechai Feingold, 'The Humanities', in Nicholas Tyacke (ed.), *The History of the University of Oxford*, vol. IV: *Seventeenth-Century Oxford* (Oxford: Clarendon Press, 1997), pp. 211–357 (pp. 241–2).

11 HYPERBOLE: EXCEEDING SIMILITUDE

For invaluable assistance with this chapter I would like to thank Gavin Alexander, David Colclough and Janel Mueller.

1. Throughout this chapter, the term 'figure' will be used in its general sense. In technical discussions of the rhetorical devices, hyperbole is more commonly referred to as a trope.
2. Henry Peacham, *The Garden of Eloquence* (1593), sig. F4r.
3. Richard A. Lanham, *A Handlist of Rhetorical Terms*, 2nd edn (Berkeley and Los Angeles: University of California Press, 1991), p. 86.
4. Henry George Liddell, Robert Scott, *et al.* (eds.), *Greek-English Lexicon* (Oxford: Clarendon Press, 1996), *hyperbole*, 1.1 [from *hyper*, 'over' and *bollein*, 'to throw']. Other meanings include 'an overshooting' (1.2), 'excess' (1.3), 'perfection' (1.5), and 'a crossing over' (II.1).
5. See Charlton Thomas Lewis, Charles Short, and E. A. Andrews (eds.), *A Latin Dictionary* (Oxford: Clarendon Press, 1969), *superlatio*, a; *superiectio*.
6. On the vices of style, see William Poole's chapter in this volume.
7. John Prideaux, *Sacred Eloquence: Or, the Art of Rhetorick, As it is layd down in Scripture* (1659), sig. A3v.
8. Demetrius, *On Style*, 114.
9. *Ibid.*
10. Demetrius's treatise was made available to Renaissance readers through Aldus Manutius' collection *Rhetores Graeci* (1508–9) and Petrus Victorius's Latin translation and commentary (1562).
11. Seneca, *Epistles*, 114.13.
12. On this point, see Introduction, pp. 9–11.
13. George Puttenham, *The Arte of English Poesie* (1589), sig. Y2r-v. The square brackets around the terms are Puttenham's.
14. The classic account of epideictic in the early-modern period is O. B. Hardison, *The Enduring Monument: A Study of the Idea of Praise in Renaissance Literary Theory and Practice* (Chapel Hill: University of North Carolina Press, 1962).
15. Castiglione's treatise was published in Venice in 1528, and translated into English by Thomas Hoby in 1561.
16. Puttenham, *Arte*, sig. Y2v. Puttenham suspends his strictures for love poetry; hyperbolic praise is one of the best ways to a lady's heart. The most significant account of hyperbole to date, Brian Vickers's 'The "Songs and Sonnets" and the Rhetoric of Hyperbole', presents a brilliantly suggestive discussion of rhetorical exaggeration in Donne's poetry. Vickers's essay can be found in A. J. Smith (ed.), *John Donne: Essays in Celebration* (London: Methuen, 1972), pp. 132–74.
17. Hyperbole lends itself especially well to dramatic characterisation because some rhetorical theorists (notably Aristotle and Puttenham) tend to associate its use with particular kinds of human behaviour (usually unflattering ones).
18. *1 Henry IV*, 1.3.274, in G. Blakemore Evans (ed.), *The Riverside Shakespeare* (Boston: Houghton Mifflin, 1974). All quotations from Shakespeare's plays are taken from this edition.
19. Aristotle, *Rhetoric*, 3.11.16.
20. On hyperbole in Shakespeare's plays see Madeleine Doran, '"High Events as These": The Language of Hyperbole in *Antony and Cleopatra*', *Queen's*

Quarterly, 72 (1965), 26–51; and, more recently, Michael Harrawood, 'Overreachers: Hyperbole, the "circle in the water," and Force in *1 Henry 6*', *English Literary Renaissance*, 33 (2003), 309–27. The seminal discussion of hyperbole in Marlovian drama is Harry Levin, *The Overreacher* (London: Faber and Faber, 1954), esp. pp. 41–2. See also Goran Stanivukovic, 'Hyperbole at the Rose Theatre', *The Canadian Journal of Rhetorical Studies*, 5 (1995), 95–108.

21. Demetrius, *On Style*, 125.
22. Quintilian, *Institutio oratoria*, 8.6.76. Vickers suggests that hyperbole 'goes beyond normal speech . . . in order to express a supra-normal idea or experience' ('The "Songs and Sonnets" and the Rhetoric of Hyperbole', p. 143).
23. Quintilian does not give a specific account of the things that may lie beyond 'the ordinary limits of nature'. However, most of his examples are taken from the *Aeneid*, and this may suggest that hyperbole is most at home in the epic scenery of imperial wars and divine interventions. Quintilian also provides some grounds for reconsidering hyperbole's position in the wider stylistic taxonomy: if it helps create the elevated rhetoric of epic, as Quintilian's examples imply, hyperbole might legitimately claim to be a part of the grand style (rather than of its distorted reflection, frigidity).
24. Longinus analyses the five principal sources of sublimity in rhetoric. Hyperbole features in the third of these categories, 'the proper construction of figures' (*On the Sublime*, 1.1).
25. *Ibid.*, 7.1.
26. *Ibid.*, 35.3.
27. *Ibid.*, 1.4.
28. *Ibid.*, 1.4. It should be noted that Quintilian's and Longinus's comments on hyperbole are qualified by an acute awareness of its risks. The rules of decorum and the problems of overt artifice still feature prominently in their accounts.
29. A fuller discussion would examine the neo-Latin manuals of rhetoric to consider hyperbole's place in the Christian grand style, a vital element of early-modern rhetorical thought that has been persuasively delineated by Debora K. Shuger. See her *Sacred Rhetoric: The Christian Grand Style in English Renaissance* (Princeton: Princeton University Press, 1988).
30. *Peri hypsous, or Dionysius Longinus of the height of eloquence. Rendred out of the originall. By J[oseph].H[all]. Esq.* (1652).
31. Prideaux, *Sacred Eloquence*, sig. A2r.
32. *Ibid.*, sig. A4v.
33. *Ibid.*, sig. A2v. Grace Dillon suggests that hyperbole can become an instrument of religious prophecy. See 'Mocking Imperialism: A Lively Hyperbolical Amplification in Spenser's *Faerie Queene*', *Renaissance Papers* (1998), 19–28 (Prideaux's wording echoes 2 Corinthians, 10:5).
34. H. M. Margoliouth (ed.), *Thomas Traherne: Centuries, Poems and Thanksgivings*, 2 vols. (Oxford, 1972), Century II, § 52.
35. 'Upon Mr. *Staninough's* Death', in L. C. Martin (ed.), *The Poems, English, Latin, and Greek of Richard Crashaw*, 2nd edn (Oxford: Clarendon Press, 1957), lines 7–16 [1646 version].

36. See Liddell and Scott, *hyperbole*, 1.7. Its Latin synonym *superlatio* also signifies 'the raising of an adjective, etc. to the superlative degree' (see Lewis, Short, and Andrews, *superlatio*, b).
37. Hyperbole, as Peacham reminds us, can be used for 'the cause of... diminishing' as well as 'increasing' (sig. F4r).
38. *Rhetorica ad Herennium*, 4.53.67. The importance of soliciting the audience's active contribution is noted by Vickers ('The "Songs and Sonnets" and the Rhetoric of Hyperbole', p. 143).
39. Thomas Wilson, *The Arte of Rhetorique* (1553), sig. 2B1v.
40. Thomas Wilson, *The Rule of Reason Conteinyng the Arte of Logique* (1551), sig. R8v.
41. Philip Sidney, *The Defence of Poesy*, in Gavin Alexander (ed.), *Sidney's 'The Defence of Poesy' and Selected Renaissance Literary Criticism* (London: Penguin, 2004), pp. 1–54 (pp. 9–10). For a more extensive account of hyperbole in Sidney (and elsewhere), see Christopher Johnson, 'Exemplary Excess in Early Modern English and Spanish Poetry and its Origins in Classical Rhetoric and Epic' (unpublished PhD dissertation, New York University, 2001).
42. *Ibid.*, p. 34
43. *Ibid.*, pp. 34–5.
44. *Ibid.*, p. 9.
45. Hyperbole enables these processes partly by crossing the boundaries to other figures. Paradox facilitates the interplay of humility and ecstasy that characterises many versions of the Christian sublime. Sidney's golden worlds draw on the rhetoric of exemplarity.

12 METALEPSIS: THE BOUNDARIES OF METAPHOR

1. William Shakespeare, *Macbeth*, 5.5.19–23; text from the first folio of 1623. All further quotations are from this text, unless otherwise indicated, with line references to Charlton Hinman (ed.), *The First Folio of Shakespeare: The Norton Facsimile*, 2nd edn (New York: W. W. Norton, 1996); here lines 2340–4.
2. This reading of 'creepes' is suggested in Nicholas Brooke (ed.), *The Tragedy of Macbeth* (Oxford: Oxford University Press, 1990), p. 205 (5.5.20).
3. *OED*, pace, 2.a and fig. ('a road or passage through dangerous territory'); it is possible that 3. ('In a church: a passage between the pews or seats') may be relevant, as applying to a burial site within a church.
4. Brooke (ed.), *Macbeth*, p. 205 (5.5.21).
5. Alastair Fowler, *Conceitful Thought* (Edinburgh: University of Edinburgh Press, 1975), pp. 87–113.
6. George Puttenham, *The Arte of English Poesie*, ed. Gladys Doidge Willcock and Alice Walker (Cambridge: Cambridge University Press, 1936), p. 183.
7. Richard Volkmann, *Die Rhetorik der Griechen und Römer in systematischer Übersicht* (Berlin: H. Ebeling and C. Plahn, 1872), p. 364.

8. Paul de Man, 'Shelley Disfigured' (originally published in *Deconstruction and Criticism* (1979)), cited here from *The Rhetoric of Romanticism* (New York: Columbia University Press, 1984), pp. 114–15.

9. Harold Bloom, *A Map of Misreading* (New York: Oxford University Press, 1975), p. 102.

10. John Hollander, *The Figure of Echo: A Mode of Allusion in Milton and After* (Berkeley: University of California Press, 1981), ch. 5 (pp. 113–32) and Appendix (pp. 133–49).

11. Gérard Genette, *Métalepse: de la figure à la fiction* (Paris: Éditions du Seuil, 2004).

12. Cited here from an edition of *De copia* with a preface by Sebastian Murrho (Strasbourg: Matthias Schurer, 1513), sig. B4v. On catachresis see William Poole's chapter in this volume.

13. All further references from Erasmus, *Opera omnia*, ed. J. Le Clerc, 10 vols. (Leiden: Pieter van der Aa, 1703–6), vol. 1 [henceforth LB], pp. 19–20; or as revised in *Opera omnia*, 10 vols. in 35 (Amsterdam: North-Holland, 1969–2005), vol. 1/VI, ed. Betty I. Knott (1988) [henceforth ASD], p. 68; translation from Erasmus, *Literary and Educational Writings 2: De Copia and De Ratione Studii*, ed. Craig R. Thompson, Collected Works of Erasmus, 24 (Toronto: University of Toronto Press, 1978) [henceforth *CWE*], p. 339.

14. Virgil, *Aeneid*, 1.60.

15. Tryphon defines *metalēpsis* in *Peri Tropōn*, in Leonard Spengel (ed.), *Rhetores Graeci*, 3 vols. (Leipzig: Teubner, 1853–6), vol. III, p. 195.

16. Quintilian, *Institutio oratoria*, 8.6.39.

17. Tryphon, *Peri Tropōn*, p. 195.

18. On puns see Sophie Read's chapter in this volume.

19. E.g. Richard A. Lanham, *A Handlist of Rhetorical Terms*, 2nd edn (Berkeley and Los Angeles: University of California Press, 1991), pp. 99–100.

20. Cited here from Melanchthon's last revision of the *Rhetorices elementa* (Lyon, 1539), lib. ii, p. 71. In his earlier work, Book III of *De rhetorica* (Wittenberg, 1519), where it is called *transumptio*, it is placed sixth (sig. IIv); it is placed seventh in the *Institutiones rhetoricae* (Hagenau, 1521), sig. C3v.

21. Homer, *Odyssey*, 15.299; Virgil, *Aeneid*, 1.60; Virgil, *Eclogues*, 1.69. A full list of examples of metalepsis in rhetorical handbooks is given in A. Burckhardt's article on the figure in Gert Ueding (ed.), *Historisches Wörterbuch der Rhetorik*, 6 vols. (Tübingen: Max Niemeyer, 1992–2003), vol. V (2001), pp. 1084–99.

22. Joseph Xavier Brennan (ed.), 'The *Epitome troporum ac schematum* of Johannes Susenbrotus: Text, Translation and Commentary' (unpublished doctoral thesis, University of Illinois, 1953), p. 11.

23. Quintilian, *Institutio oratoria*, 8.6.1.

24. Philipp Melanchthon, *Elementa rhetorices: Grundbegriffe der Rhetorik*, ed. Volkhard Wels (Berlin: Weidler, 2001), p. 184.

25. *Ibid.*, p. 184.

26. Heinrich Lausberg, *Handbuch der literarischen Rhetorik*, 3rd edn (Stuttgart: Steiner, 1990), p. 573. Melanchthon's definition is also followed in English

by Richard Sherry, *A Treatise of the Figures of Grammer and Rhetorike* (1555), fol. 22r.

27. *De copia*, 1.19, ASD, p. 66; *CWE*, p. 336.
28. *Hamlet*, 3.2.385, in William Shakespeare, *The Complete Works*, ed. Stanley Wells and Gary Taylor (Oxford: Oxford University Press, 1986); Rosemary Cowler (ed.), *The Prose Works of Alexander Pope*, vol. 2 (Oxford: Blackwell, 1986), p. 206.
29. Cyprianus Soarez, *De arte rhetorica* (Coimbra, 1562), 'De metalepsi', Lib. III, cap. 16, fol. 55r. See Jean Dietz Moss and William A. Wallace (eds.), *Rhetoric and Dialectic in the Time of Galileo* (Washington, D.C.: Catholic University of America Press, 2003), p. 166.
30. Puttenham, *The Arte of English Poesie*, p. 183.
31. Quintilian, *Institutio oratoria*, 8.6.37. Quintilian makes one other reference to metalepsis at 6.3.52 to explain the effect of a joke.
32. Paul de Man, *Blindness and Insight: Essays in the Rhetoric of Contemporary Criticism*, 2nd edn (London: Methuen, 1983), p. 274.
33. *CWE*, p. 333.
34. Quintilian, *Institutio oratoria*, 8.6.4.
35. John Locke, *An Essay Concerning Human Understanding*, ed. Peter H. Nidditch (Oxford: Clarendon Press, 1975), p. 508.
36. Quintilian, *Institutio oratoria*, 8.6.5.
37. *Ibid.*, 8.6.7.
38. *Ibid.*, 8.6.6.
39. See the textual apparatus in Quintilian, *Institution oratoire*, ed. Jean Cousin, 7 vols. (Paris: Les Belles Lettres, 1975–80), vol. V, p. 114.
40. Aristotle, *Rhetoric*, 3, 1406b; Quintilian, *Institutio oratoria*, 8.6.9.
41. Quintilian, *Institutio oratoria*, 8.6.38.
42. Terence Cave, *The Cornucopian Text: Problems of Writing in the French Renaissance* (Oxford: Clarendon Press, 1979), ch. 1, 'Copia'.
43. Cicero, *De oratore*, 3.21.125.
44. Cave, *The Cornucopian Text*, p. 19.
45. Erasmus, *De copia*, 1.7; ASD, p. 32; *CWE*, p. 301.
46. Cave, *The Cornucopian Text*, p. 21.
47. On Erasmus's theory of synonymia see further Sylvia Adamson's chapter in this volume.
48. Aristotle, *Categoriae*, 1a1–6.
49. ASD, p. 39; *CWE*, p. 307.
50. Erasmus, *De copia*, 1.xiii, ASD, p. 54; *CWE*, p. 321.
51. Erasmus, *De copia*, 1.viii, ASD, p. 32; *CWE*, p. 302.
52. Jacques Chomarat, *Grammaire et rhétorique chez Érasme*, 2 vols. (Paris: Les Belles Lettres, 1981), vol. II, p. 725.
53. Horace, *Odes*, 1.4.13; Melanchthon, *Elementa rhetorices: Grundbegriffe der Rhetorik*, p. 184.
54. Erasmus, *De copia*, 1.23, *CWE*, p. 341.

55. Bloom, *A Map of Misreading*, p. 102, cribbing from Quintilian in the modern text which restores the word *tropo* (see above).
56. LB, p. 3; ASD, p. 26.
57. Shakespeare, *Macbeth*, 1.3.97.
58. *Macbeth*, 1.3.137–42 (Folio 248–53).
59. *Macbeth*, 1.7.1–7 (Folio 475–81).
60. I would like to thank Jon Haarberg of the University of Oslo for inviting me to present a version of this essay in April 2006 at the Institutt for litteratur, områdestudier og europeiske språk, and Terence Cave (who graciously acted as respondent) for his typically dazzling commentary.

13 THE VICES OF STYLE

1. George Puttenham, *The Arte of English Poesie* (1589), p. 128.
2. *Ibid.*, pp. 135–217.
3. *Ibid.*, p. 140 (hyperbaton), p. 150 (catachresis).
4. John Hoskyns, 'Direccions For Speech and Style', in Louise Brown Osborn, *The Life, Letters, and Writings of John Hoskyns 1566–1638* (New Haven: Yale University Press, 1937), p. 129: 'let Discrecion bee the greatest and generall figure of figures'.
5. The *figurae* of rhetoric may have developed from the *topoi* of logic (on which see R. W. Serjeantson's essay in this volume): James J. Murphy, '*Topos* and *Figura*: Historical Cause and Effect?', in G. L. Bursill-Hall, Sten Ebbesen and Konrad Koerner (eds.), *De Ortu Grammaticae: Studies in Medieval Grammar and Linguistic Theory in Memory of Jan Pinborg* (Amsterdam and Philadephia: John Benjamins, 1990), pp. 239–53.
6. E.g. Puttenham, *Arte of English Poesie*, p. 210: 'every poore scholler knowes the fault [*solecismus*], and cals it the breaking of *Priscians* head, for he was among the Latines a principall Grammarian'. For an excellent summary of grammar school education as it pertains to literary application, see Colin Burrow, 'Shakespeare and Humanistic Culture', in Charles Martindale and A. B. Taylor, eds., *Shakespeare and the Classics* (Cambridge: Cambridge University Press, 2004), pp. 9–27.
7. *Rhetorica ad Herennium*, 4.14.21, 4.19.26, 4.21.29; Quintilian, *Institutio oratoria*, 9.3.69–70, 9.3.98 (for traductio, tricolon, and adnominatio).
8. Quintilian, *Institutio oratoria*, 9.3.99.
9. *Ibid.*, 8.6.24–5, 61, 67.
10. Quintilian, *Institutio oratoria*, 8.3.41f. is his list of vices; metalepsis is discussed at 8.6.37–9, and hyperbole at 8.6.67. But see also the *Rhetorica ad Herennium*, 4.12.18. On metalepsis and hyperbole see the essays in this volume by Brian Cummings and Katrin Ettenhuber respectively.
11. Two good introductions to, respectively, the classical and early-modern traditions are George A. Kennedy, *A New History of Classical Rhetoric* (Princeton:

Princeton University Press, 1994) and Wilbur Samuel Howell, *Logic and Rhetoric in England, 1500–1700* (Princeton: Princeton University Press, 1956).

12. Henry Peacham, *The Garden of Eloquence* (1577), sig. E3r.

13. *Ibid.*, sig. E3v.

14. Peter Mack, *Elizabethan Rhetoric: Theory and Practice* (Cambridge: Cambridge University Press, 2002), pp. 97–9.

15. Peacham, *The Garden of Eloquence*, sig. E3r.

16. *Ibid.*, sig. A4r (for 'cacosintheton', 'polysindeton', and 'polyptoton').

17. Mosellanus was the cognomen for the Leipzig professor of Greek Peter Schade, who died in 1524.

18. T. W. Baldwin, *Shakspere's Small Latine and Lesse Greeke*, 2 vols. (Urbana: University of Illinois Press, 1944), vol. I, p. 157.

19. Sherry, *A Treatise of Schemes and Tropes* (1550), sigs. B8v–C2v. All the following vices lie between these pages. I have used the Greek terms, which Sherry places in his margins. He supplies Latin equivalents in his text, as well as the occasional English gloss. Sherry's relation to his sources is analysed by Baldwin, *Small Latine*, vol. II, pp. 35–9.

20. All the Shakespearean examples have been taken from Sister Miriam Joseph, *Shakespeare's Use of the Arts of Language* (New York: Columbia University Press, 1947), pp. 64–78. The text used here, though, is G. Blakemore Evans (ed.), *The Riverside Shakespeare* (Boston: Houghton Mifflin, 1974).

21. *Much Ado About Nothing*, 4.2.56–7.

22. *Romeo and Juliet*, 3.2.52.

23. *Antony and Cleopatra*, 2.7.42–3.

24. *2 Henry IV*, 3.2.96–7.

25. *A Midsummer Night's Dream*, 5.1.108–17.

26. *Troilus and Cressida*, 1.2.249.

27. *Hamlet*, 5.2.112–14.

28. *Love's Labour's Lost*, 4.2.81.

29. *Ibid.*, 5.1.152.

30. *The Merry Wives of Windsor*, 1.1.144–5.

31. *Ibid.*, 2.2.83–90.

32. Quintilian, *Institutio oratoria*, 8.3.58.

33. *Ibid.*, 8.3.42.

34. Desiderius Erasmus, *Literary and Educational Writings 2*: *De Copia and De Ratione Studii*, ed. Craig R. Thompson, Collected Works of Erasmus, 24 (Toronto: University of Toronto Press, 1978), p. 295; Henry Peacham, *The Garden of Eloquence* (1593). See William G. Crane, *Wit and Rhetoric in the Renaissance* (New York, 1937), pp. 104–6, for a discussion of the relation between Peacham's first and second editions.

35. Puttenham, *Arte of English Poesie*, p. 208. Puttenham does attempt an absolute ban on 'barbarousnesse, incongruitie, ill disposition, fond affectation, rusticitie, and all extreme darknesse' (p. 207), but is otherwise no enemy of the vices, insisting that moderate use is licit, and that poets and especially women writers (lest they become shrewish in marriage) are to be excused such behaviour.

36. On another connection between rhetoric and the Aristotelian model of the relation of virtue to vice see Quentin Skinner's essay on paradiastole in this volume.

37. Hoskyns, 'Direccions', pp. 152–3.

38. Johannes Susenbrotus, *Epitome troporum ac schematum et grammaticorum et rhetorum* (Zurich, [1540?]). London editions of 1562, 1570, 1572, 1574, 1576, 1586, 1608, 1612, 1616, 1621, 1627, and 1635 are extant.

39. Peacham, *The Garden of Eloquence* (1577), sig. E3v. All the following material falls between sigs. E3v and H4v.

40. John Donne, *Poems* (1633), p. 38.

41. Josuah Sylvester, *Bartas, his Devine Weeks and Works Translated* (1605), p. 135.

42. For this play and this allusion, see *The Times Literary Supplement* (25 November 2005), 12–13.

43. *Merry Wives*, 1.1.148–50; Baldwin, *Small Latine*, pp. 213–16.

44. *Hamlet*, 2.2.92.

45. Nicholas Udall, *Ralph Roister Doister* (1566?), sigs. C2v–C3r, cited from Thomas Wilson, *The Rule of Reason* (1553), fols. 67r–68r. For a related effect, in which the sense is Protestant if the verse is read continuously, and Roman Catholic if the half-lines are read vertically, suddenly resolving into two 'hidden' independent texts, see 'The Catholique' in Bodleian MS Malone 21, fol. 28r.

46. *2 Henry VI*, 1.4.59–62 ('I tell you that you, a descendant of Aeneas, can conquer the Romans', or '. . . the Romans can conquer you, a descendant of Aeneas').

47. Mosellanus, *Tabulæ de Schematibus et Tropis* (1577), sig. A8r.

48. Christopher Marlowe, *The Troublesome Raigne and Lamentable Death of Edward the Second* (1594), sig. L1r.

49. Noel Malcolm, *The Origins of English Nonsense* (London: Harper Collins, 1997), pp. 30–51, 78–124.

50. Oxford, Bodleian Library, Rawlinson MS D 399, fol. 184r (part of Hearne's Collections). The letter shows that Paracelsian vocabulary was also a target here.

51. Sherry, *Treatise*, sig. A4v.

52. R. L. Colie, *Paradoxia Epidemica: The Renaissance Tradition of Paradox* (Princeton: Princeton University Press, 1966); Ian Maclean, 'Foucault's Renaissance Episteme Reassessed: An Aristotelian Counterblast', *Journal of the History of Ideas* 59 (1998), 149–66, esp. 163–4.

53. Quintilian, *Institutio oratoria*, 8.2.12–21.

54. Erasmus, *De copia*, p. 336.

55. Peacham, *Garden of Eloquence*, sig. D2r-v.

56. Angel Day, *A Declaration of . . . Tropes, Figures or Schemes* (1592), p. 85.

57. Johannes Susenbrotus, *Epitome troporum ac schematum* (1562), p. 14.

58. See notably the edition of Thomas Swynnerton, *A Reformation Rhetoric: Thomas Swynnerton's 'The Tropes and Figures of Scripture'*, ed. Richard Rex (Cambridge: RTM, 1999).

59. Joachim Camerarius, *Notatio figurarum orationis et mutatae simplicis elocutionis in apostolicis scriptis* (Leipzig, 1572), p. 347.

60. Joachim Camerarius, *Notatio figurarum sermonis in libris quatuor evangeliorum* (Leipzig, 1572), pp. 56–7. See more generally Frank Kermode, *The Genesis of Secrecy* (Cambridge, MA: Harvard University Press, 1979), pp. 23–47.

61. 1 Cor. 13:12; Augustine, *De trinitate*, 15.9.15. See Eleanor Cook, 'The Figure of Enigma: Rhetoric, History, Poetry', *Rhetorica* 19 (2001), 349–78. Aenigma was also schematised around the 3rd century AD as one of the seven types of allegory (Cook, 'Enigma', 359–60).

62. John Hales, *Golden Remains* (1659), p. 22. On hysteron proteron see the essay by Patricia Parker in this volume.

63. See above, p. 5.

Suggestions for further reading

The following list includes standard reference works, selected general treatments of Renaissance rhetoric in its historical context and works that look in more detail at its literary applications. Many contain advice for further reading on specific authors or topics. The field of rhetorical studies is far busier now than it was thirty years ago. The journal *Rhetorica*, founded in 1983, provides a forum for debate as well as publishing and reviewing new research in the field.

REFERENCE WORKS

Burton, Gideon, 'The Forest of Rhetoric', http://humanities.byu.edu/rhetoric/
Lanham, Richard A., *A Handlist of Rhetorical Terms*, 2nd edn (Berkeley and Los Angeles: University of California Press, 1991)
Lausberg, Heinrich, *Handbook of Literary Rhetoric: A Foundation for Literary Study* (Leiden: Brill, 1998)
Murphy, James J. and Lawrence D. Green, *Renaissance Rhetoric Short-Title Catalogue 1460–1700* (Aldershot: Ashgate, 2006)
Plett, Heinrich F., *English Renaissance Rhetoric and Poetics: A Systematic Bibliography of Primary and Secondary Sources* (Leiden and New York: E. J. Brill, 1995)
Preminger, Alex and T. V. F. Brogan (eds.), *The New Princeton Encyclopedia of Poetry and Poetics* (Princeton: Princeton University Press, 1993)
Sloane, Thomas O., (ed.), *Encyclopedia of Rhetoric* (New York: Oxford University Press, 2001)
Sonnino, Lee A., *A Handbook to Sixteenth-Century Rhetoric* (London: Routledge and Kegan Paul, 1968)

SELECTED STUDIES

Adamson, Sylvia, 'Literary Language', in Roger Lass (ed.), *The Cambridge History of the English Language, Volume III, 1476–1776* (Cambridge: Cambridge University Press, 1999), pp. 539–653
Baldwin, T. W., *William Shakespere's Small Latine and Lesse Greeke*, 2 vols. (Urbana: University of Illinois Press, 1944)
Cave, Terence, *The Cornucopian Text: Problems of Writing in the French Renaissance* (Oxford: Clarendon Press, 1979)

Howell, Wilbur Samuel, *Logic and Rhetoric in England, 1500–1700* (Princeton: Princeton University Press, 1956)

Joseph, Sister Miriam, *Shakespeare's Use of the Arts of Language* (New York: Columbia University Press, 1947; repr. Philadelphia: Paul Dry Books, 2005)

Jost, Walter and Wendy Olmsted (eds.), *A Companion to Rhetoric and Rhetorical Criticism* (Oxford: Blackwell, 2003)

Kennedy, George A., *Classical Rhetoric and Its Christian and Secular Tradition from Ancient to Modern Times* (Chapel Hill: University of North Carolina Press, 1999)

Lanham, Richard A., *The Motives of Eloquence: Literary Rhetoric in the Renaissance* (New Haven: Yale University Press, 1976)

Mack, Peter, *Elizabethan Rhetoric: Theory and Practice* (Cambridge: Cambridge University Press, 2002)

——(ed.), *Renaissance Rhetoric* (Basingstoke: Macmillan, 1994)

Mueller, Janel, *The Native Tongue and the Word: Developments in English Prose Style, 1380–1580* (Chicago: University of Chicago Press, 1984)

Murphy, James J. (ed.), *Renaissance Eloquence: Studies in the Theory and Practice of Renaissance Rhetoric* (Berkeley and London: University of California Press, 1983)

Plett, Heinrich F. (ed.), *Renaissance Rhetoric* (Berlin: de Gruyter, 1993)

Rebhorn, Wayne A., *The Emperor of Men's Minds: Literature and the Renaissance Discourse of Rhetoric* (Ithaca: Cornell University Press, 1995)

Rhodes, Neil, *The Power of Eloquence and English Renaissance Literature* (London: Harvester Wheatsheaf, 1992)

Ronberg, Gert, *A Way with Words: The Language of English Renaissance Literature* (London: E. Arnold, 1992)

Shuger, Debora K., *Sacred Rhetoric: The Christian Grand Style in the English Renaissance* (Princeton: Princeton University Press, 1988)

Skinner, Quentin, *Reason and Rhetoric in the Philosophy of Hobbes* (Cambridge: Cambridge University Press, 1996)

Vickers, Brian, *Classical Rhetoric in English Poetry* (London: Macmillan, 1970; repr. with a new preface and annotated bibliography, Carbondale: Southern Illinois University Press, 1999)

——*In Defence of Rhetoric* (Oxford: Clarendon Press, 1988)

PRIMARY TEXTS: CLASSICAL

The Loeb Classical Library includes parallel text editions of most of the key ancient Greek and Latin treatises on rhetoric and poetics. The following volumes contain texts of particular importance, and are referred to frequently in the chapters in this volume:

Aristotle, *The Art of Rhetoric*, trans. J. H. Freese (Cambridge, MA: Harvard University Press, 1926)

Aristotle, *Poetics*; Longinus, *On the Sublime*; Demetrius, *On Style*, trans. Doreen
    C. Innes (Cambridge, MA: Harvard University Press, 1995)
Rhetorica ad Herennium ['Rhetoric to Herennius'], trans. Harry Caplan (Cam-
    bridge, MA: Harvard University Press, 1954)
Cicero, *De oratore* ['On the Orator'], trans. E. W. Sutton and H. Rackham, 2 vols.
    (Cambridge, MA: Harvard University Press, 1942); *Brutus; Orator*, trans. G. L.
    Hendrickson and H. M. Hubbell (Cambridge, MA: Harvard University Press,
    1939)
Quintilian, *Institutio oratoria* ['Education of an Orator'], trans. Donald A. Russell,
    5 vols. (Cambridge, MA: Harvard University Press, 2001)

The following anthology includes excellent translations of the major classical texts
on poetics:

Russell, D. A. and M. Winterbottom(eds.), *Ancient Literary Criticism: The Principal
    Texts in New Translations* (Oxford: Clarendon Press, 1972)

PRIMARY TEXTS: RENAISSANCE

References to many of the key Renaissance books on rhetoric are included in
the chapters in this volume. Here we provide a chronological list of the major
English treatises that focus particularly on the figures. The only Latin work
included is Erasmus's *De Copia*, a seminal work in shaping rhetorical culture in
England.

Erasmus, Desiderius, *De Copia* (1512); translation in Erasmus, *Literary and Edu-
    cational Writings 2: De Copia and De Ratione Studii*, ed. Craig R. Thomp-
    son, Collected Works of Erasmus, 24 (Toronto: University of Toronto Press,
    1978)
Swynnerton, Thomas, *The Tropes and Figures of Scripture* [*c.* 1535], ed. Richard Rex
    (Cambridge: RTM, 1999)
Sherry, Richard, *A Treatise of Schemes and Tropes* (1550)
Wilson, Thomas, *The Arte of Rhetorique* (1553)
Peacham, Henry, *The Garden of Eloquence* (1577; rev. 1593)
Fraunce, Abraham, *The Arcadian Rhetorike* (1588), ed. Ethel Seaton (Oxford: Black-
    well, 1950)
Puttenham, George, *The Arte of English Poesie* (1589), ed. Gladys Doidge Willcock
    and Alice Walker (Cambridge: Cambridge University Press, 1936); substantial
    selections in the anthologies edited by Alexander and Vickers (below)
Day, Angel, *A Declaration of . . . Tropes, Figures or Schemes*, in *The English Secretorie*
    (1592)
Hoskins, John, *Directions for Speech and Style* (*c.* 1599), ed. Hoyt H. Hudson
    (Princeton: Princeton University Press, 1935); also published in Louise Brown
    Osborn (ed.), *The Life, Letters, and Writings of John Hoskyns, 1566–1638* (New
    Haven: Yale University Press, 1937)
Hobbes, Thomas, *A Brief of the Art of Rhetorique* (1637)
Smith, John, *The Mysterie of Rhetorique Unvail'd* (1657)

Two recent anthologies of Renaissance literary criticism bring rhetoric to the fore:

Vickers, Brian (ed.), *English Renaissance Literary Criticism* (Oxford: Clarendon Press, 1999)

Alexander, Gavin (ed.), *Sidney's 'The Defence of Poesy' and Selected Renaissance Literary Criticism* (London: Penguin, 2004)

Index

Abraham, *see* Bible, Genesis
abuse, abuser, *see* catachresis
abusio, *see* catachresis
Accius, 176
actio, *see* rhetoric, five parts of
acyrologia, 240
  (*see also* vices of style)
Adamson, Sylvia, 12, 86, 94, 259n.14
Addison, Joseph, 81, 82, 85, 86, 90, 94
Ad Herennium, see Rhetorica ad Herennium
adnominatio, 287n.7
Aeneid, see Virgil
aenigma, enigma, 237, 247, 249–51, 290n.61
  (*see also* vices of style)
Aeschylus, 176
aischrologia, 241
  (*see also* vices of style)
Aldine Press, *see* Manutius, Aldus
Alexander, 259n.13
Alexander, Gavin, 12–13
allegory, allegoria, 5, 127, 129, 201, 225, 249,
  269n.43, 290n.61
alliteration, 32, 33, 34, 40, 44, 46, 57
amphibologia, 167, 241, 244, 247
  (*see also* vices of style)
Anacreon, 175
anaphora, 46–7, 265n.47
anapodoton, 244
anastrophe, 244
  (*see also* hysteron proteron and anastrophe)
Andrewes, Lancelot, 12, 81–2, 84, 85, 87, 91, 92,
  93, 94, 262n.22
  eighteenth-century criticism of, 81, 85, 86, 93
antanaclasis, 81, 82, 83, 84, 86, 87–8, 89, 90, 91,
  92, 94, 262n.20
  definition of, 80, 83–4
  (*see also* puns)
antimetabole, 6, 47, 265n.47
antirrhesis, *see* testimony and antirrhesis
antistoecon, 239
antistrophe, 265n.47

antithesis, 23, 29, 30, 40, 46, 49, 72, 75
antitheton, 45
antonomasia, 221
Aphthonius, 2, 115, 275n.3
apodixis (experientia, evidens probatio), *see*
  testimony and apodixis
apomnemonysis (dicti commemoratio), *see*
  testimony and apomnemonysis
aporia, 232
aposiopesis, 5, 7–8, 10, 244, 253n.25
apostrophe, 8, 18
  (*see also* prosopopoeia and apostrophe)
Ariosto, Ludovico, 3
Aristotle and Aristotelianism, 2, 70, 175, 193,
  259n.13
  on analogy, 69
  on ethos, 99–100
  on hyperbole, 202, 204, 282n.17
  on logic, 69, 182
  on the mean, 155–6, 242
  on metaphor, 226
  on paradiastole, 152–3, 154, 155, 156
  on periodos, 61–2, 64, 77, 258n.3, 259n.13,
    260n.27
  and Plato, 154
  on poetics and rhetoric, 3
  silence on puns, 81
  on representation, 102, 115
  on syncrisis, 274n.1
  on synonyms and homonyms, 228
  on testimony, 184, 188
  on tragedy, 85
Ascham, Roger, 48–50, 55–6, 57, 66
  criticism of, 48, 257n.30
aschematiston, 241, 242
  (*see also* vices of style)
assonance, 44, 46
asteismus, 261n.4
  (*see also* puns)
asyndeton, asindeton, 32, 245
Aubrey, John, 194